EUROPEAN CUSTOMS AND MANNERS

How to make friends and do business in Europe

by Nancy L. Braganti and Elizabeth Devine

 Meadowbrook Press
Distributed by Simon & Schuster
New York

Library of Congress Cataloging-in-Publication Data

Braganti, Nancy L., 1941–
    European customs and manners : how to make friends and do business in
    Europe / by Nancy L. Braganti and Elizabeth Devine.
        p.   cm.
    Rev. ed. of : The travelers' guide to European customs & manners /
    Nancy L. Braganti and Elizabeth Devine. ©1984.
    ISBN 0-88166-190-2
    1. Europe—Description and travel—1971–   —Guide–books.
    2. Europe—Social life and customs.   I. Devine, Elizabeth, 1938–
    II. Braganti, Nancy L., 1941–   Travelers' guide to European
    customs & manners. III. Title.
    D909.B722   1992
    914.04'559—dc20   91-42042
                                                          CIP

Simon & Schuster Ordering #: 0-671-76030-0

Published by Meadowbrook Press, 18318 Minnetonka Boulevard, Deephaven, MN
55391.

BOOK TRADE DISTRIBUTION by Simon & Schuster, a division of Simon and
Schuster, Inc., 1230 Avenue of the Americas, New York, NY 10020.

Manuscript Editor: Katherine Stevenson
Senior Editor: Kerstin Gorham
Book Development Manager: Jay E. Johnson
Production Manager: Lynne Cromwell
Production Assistant: Matthew E. Thurber
Typography: Jon C. Wright
Cover illustration: Harold Henriksen
Interior art: Thomas Boll

97 96 95 94 93 92   6 5 4 3 2 1

Printed in the United States of America

To Fausto, who cooks lots of pasta and offers his support and encouragement; to Tanya, who lends her enthusiasm to all my projects; to Susan Indresano, who enriches my life with her caring and laughter; and to ТАТЬЯНА ГАССЕЛЬ (Tatyana Gassel), who has opened up the world of my forefathers, for her warmth and Russian soul.

N.L.B.

To La, Patrick, Caitlin, and Tim, who give me more joy than they will ever know, and to Miss Dorothea Federgren, who showed me the riches in the world of books.

E.D.

ACKNOWLEDGMENTS

We wish to thank the following people for their assistance in this project: Luis Abiega, Beatia Ahmad, Birgitta Amsler, Helle Andersen, Angela Anderson, Sandra Anitua, Carol Antonsson, Belma and Sam Baskett, Dorothy W. Bennett, Eleanor and Nancy Benson, James Berry, Evan Bogan, Miljana Boran, Fatima Brazâo, Jan Buechting, Pamela Cabell-Whiting, Joseph Callewaert, Joan Campagne, Maria Grazia Caporali, Maureen and Michael Carey, Hans Cedarblad, Tanya Chebotarev, Jonathan and Beverly Cohen, Elizabeth Colliard, Roberta Cores, Benjamin Crocker, Monique, Brigitte, and Arsen Darnay, Riet DeKleermaeker, Mari Delagran, Francis P. Devlin, Eeve de Felice, Natalio Diaz, Sila Dikici, Vesco Dimitrov, Ivan Dimov, John and Georgiana Dolejsi, David DuBusc, Nicola Dyde, Victor Eugene Dyer III, Barbara Eachus, Aline Egger, Jared Eigerman, Milagros Emmart, Mary Farrell, Kevin Featherstone, Magdaléna and Martin Feldek, Nancy Ferguson, Bernardo and Christine Fernandes, Martha and Richard Forsyth, Loreto and Trudi Forti, Graham Frear, Slawomir Fryska, Jana Furda, Tatyana Gassel, Üstün Germen, Jennifer Guernṣey, Kari Hamre, Jon Hancke, Theodore Hecht, Socrates Heracleous, Gail Pike Hercher, Patricia Howes, David Hughes, Andreas Iacovides, Kimberly Indresano, Vladimir Janovsky, Lars Johannessen, Anne-Marie Jouglarisse, Thomas Kelsey, Alison Kimber, Patricia Klecanda, Josef Klima, Peter Knight, Dr. Judith I. Knorst, Kirsti Kosonen-Brown, Jane Lakatos, Bistra Lankova, Jean Leathers, Cybèle Léger, Kelley Leveque, Hanibal Lopez-Molne, Liv Lyons, Patricia McGurdy, Elizabeth MacLean-Musso, Shelley Madson, Paivi Manner, Margaret Mariani, Hanna Matousek, Lillian Maury, Lois and Ole Meerwald, Kimberly Menard, Elaine Metzler, Margrith Mistry, Genevieve Moloney, Eileen Morgan, Antonio Musso, Marie Nappi, Costantino and Johanne Negulescu, Robert Newman, Lennart Nielsen, Ira Alexandra Nopola, Thomas O'Donnell, Christine Oprecht, Katalin Palotay, Alexandra Papazoglou, Patricia Parker, Bert and Anne-Lise Paulsen, Veerle Persoons, Seija Peterson, Simona Petrova, Ray Phillips, Mary Pierce, Hervé Pierre, Marie Jose Pierrot, Bojan Pomorišac, Jill Potter, Anna and Piotrunio Przytula, Alex, Beatriz, and Marcel Quiroga, Michael Radovanovic, Susan Raskin, Mark and Ghyslaine Renn, Dr. Diana Reynolds, Mojca Rijavec, Barbro Roehrdanz, Victoria Vargas Rosello, Irving Rubin, Nikolai Sakharov, Anelise Sawkins, Thomas Schlück, Rosemary Schneider, Karen Bachant Sellars, Jan Smith, Marie Luise Smith, Karin Solstad, Jose Sousa, Krzysztof Sliwa, Catherine Spirer-Sliwa, Gerd Steckel, Henry Steiner, Jürgen Steiner, Eva Ström, Mark Szajner, Helen Szakacs, Jane Taubman, Argie Tiliakos, Janos Tisovsky, Monica Tucker, Dincer and Priscilla Ulutaş, Mijke VanOtterloo, Rose-Marie VanOtterloo, Liudmila Voitsekhovskaya, Anna Vojtech, Dragoş Vrânceanu, Peter Wanka, Laura Warren, Thomas Webb, Trautel Wiechman, Elsa Wiersma, Birthe Winer, Peter Wishnock, Karen Wylie, Jane Wyman, Margaret Young, Katerina Zencuch.

And, finally, a special note of thanks to Kerstin Gorham and Kathy Stevenson for their careful, astute, and meticulous editing.

PREFACE

The more we've traveled for our *Customs and Manners* series, the more we've enjoyed experiencing new cultures and reacquainting ourselves with cultures we've visited before. The research for this book involved making new friends in Russia, Hungary, Czechoslovakia, and Germany and dropping in on old friends in such places as Italy, France, and Ireland. Between the two of us, we have lived in or visited 20 of the countries covered in this book.

In addition to footwork, we have conducted hours of interviews with people from each country and with Americans who have lived there. Our sources came from all walks of life—from secretaries to screenwriters, engineers to poets, bankers to homemakers. We also spent countless hours on the phone with travel agents and embassy and consulate employees.

One of our favorite phone interviews was with an American woman who worked at a Polish consulate. We explained our project to her and asked if she knew the Polish word for eels, since they are so commonly eaten in Poland. The woman protested, "I've just come from living in Poland for six months and never heard of eels being served." We persisted, and the woman finally looked up the word in her Polish dictionary. When she came back with the answer, she wailed, "Do you mean that's what I was eating all that time?" (If she'd read this book, she would have known.)

We hope this book will help you do as the Romans do in Rome, as the Parisians do in Paris, as the Czechs do in Prague. . . . Bon voyage.

Nancy L. Braganti
Elizabeth Devine

Contents

Introduction

We've all heard the advice: when in Rome, do as the Romans do. Why is that so important? Because part of the joy of traveling is fitting in with other cultures. Throughout Europe, you'll find people are highly sensitive to good manners. Not knowing a country's customs can lead to inadvertent rudeness, resulting in red faces for you and your European acquaintances and sometimes even the loss of valuable business.

Potential gaffes range from minor to offensive, and they're all too easy to make. You might think you're just being friendly calling new French acquaintances by their first names, but they might think you're being quite rude. And plunging right into a business discussion in Spain, bypassing the customary getting-to-know-you chat, could blow a potential deal.

Lots of books tell you where to go, stay, and dine in Europe and what to see and do there. But travelers looking for advice on how to make a good impression abroad, and on what to expect from the people who live there, found little to help them until *European Customs and Manners* came out in 1984.

Because Europe—particularly Eastern Europe—has changed so dramatically since 1989, we decided to revise the 1984 edition so we could provide the most up-to-date advice available. We've updated the information on each European country, including expanding the business sections and adding a chapter

on the Russian Republic—a destination more and more travelers choose. We suggest appropriate behavior for a variety of settings—from restaurants to private homes to business meetings—to help you make a good impression and avoid embarrassment.

For easy reference, we've divided each chapter into sections, each of which deals with a major concern of travelers:

Greetings

First impressions are crucial, so each chapter begins with how to greet people—when and how to say hello, what forms of address to use, and, when the practice differs from ours, when and how to shake hands.

Conversation

In the past, one had to converse carefully in Eastern Europe; almost no subject was safe. Now, however, people are eager to discuss the revolutions that have brought democracy to their countries. Still, it's easy to make a faux pas in any foreign country when you strike up a conversation without knowing the pitfalls.

We'll tell you which topics to discuss and which to avoid, and which conversational styles people are comfortable with—whether casual or formal, personal or reserved. In France, for example, beginning a chat with the classic American opener, "What do you do for a living?" invites an icy response. The French regard questions about their work as highly personal.

We'll also provide tips on appropriate behavior while conversing, from nodding your head to putting your hands in your pockets.

Money

Here we'll explain the country's unit of currency, both notes and coins.

We haven't provided rates of exchange because they tend to fluctuate frequently.

When we refer to some currencies as "hard currencies," we mean that the currency is convertible: you can buy the currency when you enter the country, and you can sell it when you leave the country.

A nonconvertible currency can be bought, but it can't be sold outside the country. The currencies of the Russian Republic and of many Eastern European countries that were once Soviet satellites are not yet convertible.

Telephones

Most European countries have modernized their phone systems in the last several years—good news for travelers, who rely heavily on public phones. We'll tell you how to use the phones in each country and whether they take coins or phone cards (convenient for frequent or long-distance callers). We also provide each country's emergency numbers (the equivalent of the United States' "911").

In Public

This section explains the customs that govern behavior in public places, so you won't embarrass yourself in a crowd. Imagine the titters in a crowd of Hungarians if you ask for a "bus" (a word that's obscene in Hungarian). In Switzerland, on the other hand, tossing a gum wrapper on the street will prompt strangers to reproach you as rude and inconsiderate.

We also mention restrictions and taboos governing photography. Eastern European countries have relaxed such restrictions, but some countries still forbid photographing military installations or nuclear power plants.

We'll also tell you where to find public bathrooms—and what to expect when you find one.

Dress

It's hard to offend by dressing con- servatively, but, nevertheless, every country has its unofficial dress code. You'll upset 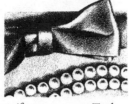 people, for instance, if you enter a Turk- ish mosque in shoes or show up at an Austrian dinner party in casual dress.

In this section, we describe what to wear to a variety of different places and func- tions, both formal and informal.

Meals

One of the joys of traveling is being able to sample some of the world's finest cuisines on their  home ground. We describe the customary times and foods for each meal, so you'll know what to expect. If you're invited to dinner in Spain, for example, the meal will begin no earlier than 9:00 P.M.

We also cover table manners, so you won't unintentionally offend. Americans, for instance, often put one hand in their lap while eating, an action that may invite giggles in Europe. And in some countries, such as Poland, you'd better take small first portions, because you'll be pressured to have seconds or even thirds, and refusing them says you didn't like the food. Oddly enough, you'll face the greatest pressure to overeat in coun- tries where food isn't abundant—and where your hosts might go to incredible trouble putting together a sumptuous meal to show you warmth and hospitality.

The last two parts of this section are devoted to eating out—what types of eating and drinking places you'll find— and the country's culinary specialities.

Hotels

Since most hotels in Western Eur- ope are similar to those in the U.S., most of our advice here is on Eastern Euro-  pean and Russian hotels—which can be quite different. Many, for example, don't provide soap or washcloths.

In many European countries, you'll find *pensions,* a type of accommodation rarely found in North America. Pensions are small hotels or inns (usually family run) that offer full or half board.

If you choose another popular type of lodging—"Bed & Breakfasts"—follow the advice for manners when staying in pri- vate homes (except that you don't offer to help with the dishes or bring your hosts a gift).

Tipping

Tipping etiquette has probably bothered trav- elers for centu- ries. We'll tell you whom to tip— and how much.  Most European restaurants and bars in- clude a 10–15 percent service charge in the check, but customs vary on whether you should leave more.

We'll also tell you how much to tip porters, hotel maids, taxis, ushers, cloakroom attendants, and washroom attendants. We do not list them if no tip is required.

Private Homes

This section discusses how to behave when you're paying a call or staying with a family, so you don't acci-

dentally offend. In a Greek home, innocently filling the tub to take a bath might seem rude to your hosts; most Greek homes have tiny hot-water tanks and you'd be depriving others of hot water.

We also discuss good—and poor— choices of gifts for your hosts (including flowers, which have a host of taboos associated with them).

Business

We've greatly expanded the business sections in this edition of the book. First we give typical

hours for businesses, government offices, banks, and stores. Next comes a detailed discussion of business practices, including how to initiate contacts and set up meetings; what to expect during meetings and negotiations; how to present proposals and negotiate effectively; what language, gender, or technology barriers to expect; and how to entertain and give gifts.

Holidays & Celebrations

Some travelers like to plan a trip to coincide with a special holiday so they can see or participate in a

country's festivals. Business travelers, on the other hand, often want to avoid holiday periods. We list each country's holidays so you can aim for them or avoid them, as you wish. We also describe some special holiday customs.

Transportation

Unless you're on a tour, you need to know how to get around within cities, within countries, and

from one country to another. We give advice on using buses, subways, taxis, and trains (which in Europe are a joy).

On many long-distance trains, you'll find *couchettes*. These are compartments for six people. During the day, people sit on two upholstered benches; at night, they sleep in six bunk beds, usually with a pillow and blanket on each. Both sexes share couchettes. If you sleep in one, keep your valuables under your pillow.

Get used to using the 24-hour system Americans call "military time," which is used on all European transportation schedules; 1:00 P.M. is 13:00, and 6:00 P.M. is 18:00.

We also tell you what to do (and what not to do) if you decide to drive. Most European countries have strict laws on seat belts (they're mandatory) and drunk-driving (in Ireland, failing a Breathalyzer test can bring a £500 fine [roughly $1,000 U.S.] and/or six months in jail).

Speed limits for continental Europe are given in kilometers per hour (kph). A kilometer is six-tenths of a mile, so multiply the distance in kilometers by .60, and you'll have the mileage. For example, 300 kilometers equals 180 miles. The United Kingdom (England, Northern Ireland, Scotland, and Wales) still gives speed limits in miles per hour (mph).

Legal Matters & Safety

Laws and regulations in each country can be complex and can change frequently. We cover some of the important legal issues, such as the legal drinking age and when you need to register with the police. But you should always check with the Citizens' Emergency Center of the State Department at (202) 647-5225 for changes and details before you travel. They are open from 8:15 A.M. to 5:00 P.M., Monday through Friday, and from 9:00 A.M. to 3:00 P.M. on Saturday (Eastern Standard Time). We also discuss crime and safety, a particular concern for women travelers.

Key Phrases

We end each chapter with a few useful phrases and their phonetic pronunciations. If you take the time to learn a few phrases in the country's language, your effort will be richly repaid. Even the simple words "Please" and "Thank you"

work magic.

Note: As you read, you might detect what seems like sexism in our advice or in the behavior ascribed to men and women. It's simply a reflection of reality for the country we're describing. Much as we might hope for men and women to be treated equally, they aren't—especially in the more traditional European countries. We've avoided as much bias as we could; whatever remains is a product of each country's customs.

We've based all of our advice on the most conservative acceptable behavior and the most traditional behavior you're likely to encounter. You can't err by being too polite, but you certainly can by being too informal. If you notice that people in any situation are more casual than we've suggested, take your cue from them.

General Guidelines for European Travel

Here are a few guidelines to help you get along with people throughout Europe:

◆ *Don't judge.* Enjoy each country on its own terms, rather than drawing comparisons to the U.S.—especially when you're speaking to natives of the country. And don't consider American customs the standard against which all others must be measured. How many times have you heard Americans ask "How much is that in 'real' money?" or say that the British drive on the "wrong" side of the road?

◆ *Do your homework before you go.* Read about the countries you plan to visit. Check your local library for histories of various countries. The Michelin Green Guides, the Companion Guides, and the Insight Guides all provide good background information. Pay special attention

ground information. Pay special attention to the news from Europe before you leave. You'll be surprised—perhaps embarrassed—by how much Europeans know about American history and politics, and how little Americans know about other countries.

◆ *Ask questions and listen.* Try interviewing people, without being pushy or intrusive. When you bring up one of the topics we suggest, show genuine interest, and use questions to draw your new acquaintance out—then listen to the answers. Most people love to give advice on local sights to see or good restaurants to try. A sure way to charm people is to be a good audience.

◆ *Be sincere.* Don't flatter people or their country so obsequiously that you come across as insincere. If you like something, say so, but be low key and understated. People in some European countries feel awkward rather than pleased when they receive outright compliments.

◆ *Familiarize yourself with the language.* Learn a few words and phrases in the language of each country you plan to visit, but don't fret over the language barrier; it's not as formidable as many people think. If you're going as a tourist or on a short business trip, you can probably get along with a phrase book and a slight flair for drama. Sign language can be amazingly effective; one traveler finally got hard-boiled eggs in Greece by clucking like a chicken, flexing a solid arm muscle, and shaping an egg with her fingers. Another strategy is pointing—either to words in a pocket dictionary or to items you want in a restaurant or shop.

If your stay will be a long one, you'd be well advised to study the language. Every American community has adult-education language courses. You can also buy—or borrow from your library—language records or tapes that teach basic phrases and vocabulary. (Keep in mind, however, that native speakers talk much more rapidly than the people on the recordings.) If you like gadgets, you can also get pocket-sized electronic translators, some of which also serve as currency converters and calculators.

◆ *Keep your sense of humor.* Humor is probably a traveler's most important asset. If you're in a situation that seems increasingly irksome, try viewing it from the outside; chances are it will be a funny moment to treasure and tell your friends about when you return home. A few years ago, a traveler wrote in the *New York Times* about being hospitalized for appendicitis in Greece. Her doctor left on vacation during her recuperation, and when she went to check out, the staff handed her a baby—and nothing she said could convince them it wasn't hers. When she said, "I'm not even married," a nurse consoled her: "Don't worry. Your family will help you." Finally the staff tracked down her doctor, and he assured them the baby wasn't hers. Despite her frustration at the time, she ended up with a very funny memory to savor for the rest of her days.

Additional Tips

Certain customs and manners apply throughout Europe. Here are some of the most important to remember, along with some helpful hints for making the most of your travels:

◆ Europeans shake hands more often than Americans do. For example, they shake hands with the bank teller when they go to cash a check and with the grocer when they come to choose vegetables. Don't be the first to extend your hand, but be prepared to shake hands often.

◆ Many European countries use professional titles more often than in the U.S. For example, architects, engineers, or lawyers may be addressed by their professional title. If speaking English, only use professional titles when addressing those who would have titles in the U.S. (i.e., doctors, dentists, and professors). If speaking in a foreign language, find out how different professionals should be addressed in that language.

◆ When European dates are given in numbers, the day precedes the month. Thus 12/8/91 is August 12, 1991, *not* December 8, as it would be in the U.S.

◆ The European numbers 7 and *1* look different from their American counterparts. The European 7 has a slash through the middle of it (7), and the European *1* has a long flag and is sometimes mistaken for an American 7.

◆ In Europe, a period instead of a comma is used with numbers above 999, while a comma instead of a period sets off decimal fractions. For example, the American number 14,538.25 would be written in Europe as 14.538, 25.

◆ If you want to make a long-distance call and have an AT&T credit card, get the company's book listing the numbers to use in each country so you can charge calls to the card and avoid hotel surcharges.

◆ If you have an expensive camera, cover the brand name with black electrical tape to make the camera less attractive to thieves.

◆ When bargaining in Europe, begin by offering 50 to 75 percent of the asking price and bargain from there. If you can't reach an agreed upon price, try walking away—sometimes the vendor will call you back.

◆ The toilet is usually in a room separate from the tub or shower; a request for a "bathroom" may get you a room with just a bath. If you're not aware of this, you may think with alarm that no toilet is available.

◆ Public toilets are often unisex. Be prepared to see a person of the opposite sex at the sink when you enter or leave the bathroom.

◆ Women should never throw tampons into the toilet.

◆ Finding laundry facilities with dryers is difficult in Europe.

◆ When dining in Europe, if you wish to eat European-style, hold your fork (tines down) in your left hand and your knife in your right. Do not switch your fork to your right hand after cutting. Use the knife to push food onto the back of the fork. Hold on to your knife even when you're not using it. Foods such as salads require only a fork, kept in the right hand. Keep your wrists on the table, and never put your hands in your lap during a meal.

◆ In many countries, the dessert fork and spoon are placed above the plate.

◆ If fish is to be served, you might be given a special fish knife and fork. The fish knife looks like a butter knife, and the fish fork like a salad fork. (If you aren't given special utensils, cut the fish with your dinner fork, not your knife.)

◆ If assembling a picnic for lunch or dinner (a wonderful opportunity to sample one of a country's major activities— shopping for food), be sure to bring a bag with you, or you'll have to buy a plastic bag from the market.

◆ Europeans consider drinking ice water unhealthy. If you want ice, you'll have to request it, and then you may be given only one ice cube. Some homes may not have ice at all.

◆ Avoid ordering specialty cocktails such as whiskey sours or piña coladas. Europeans are in general not familiar with them, and bars and restaurants will probably not have the right ingredients to make them properly.

◆ In some countries, hotels keep your passport when you register, either for a short time or overnight. In these countries, hotel guests must be registered with the local police.

◆ In all countries, you would be well advised to keep your valuables in a hotel's safe deposit box.

◆ In Europe, the voltage for electrical outlets is 220. If you need a hair dryer, buy a travel hair dryer that can use either 110 or 220 volts, or buy a voltage converter before you go abroad.

◆ A wonderful gift for Europeans who read English would be a subscription to a magazine that covers a topic of special interest to them.

◆ If considering videotapes as gifts, note that only blank tapes work on European VCRs. American movie videos can be made to work, but it's extraordinarily expensive. Likewise, European movie videos don't work on U.S. VCRs.

◆ Many European businesspeople feel they need to know and trust people before doing business with them. Don't feel confused by or frustrated with the personal conversation that often precedes business transactions.

◆ Use caution in entering the new markets created by changes in Eastern Europe and the former Soviet Union. Many American businesspeople have unrealistic expectations of both the markets and the ability of countries to adapt quickly to a free-market economy. For example, many businesspeople don't know how to read a profit-and-loss statement or develop a realistic schedule for the delivery of products or services. (For information on the implications of the European Community for business, see "The European Community," below.)

◆ If you plan to drive in Eastern Europe, note that not all car rental companies allow you to rent a car in Western Europe and drive it into Eastern Europe. When you book a car, you must notify the company of your planned itinerary. Be sure to find out whether the car requires unleaded gas, which is scarce in many Eastern European countries.

◆ Never pick up hitchhikers. In recent years, this custom has become a way for terrorists to "use" naive tourists.

◆ If you are taking any prescription medication, bring more than you will need with you. Brand names and dosages are different in Europe, and sometimes a country will not have the drug you're taking. Be sure to pack your medication in a carry-on bag and keep it with you on the airplane.

◆ If you wear prescription eyeglasses, take an extra pair or your prescription with you to Europe.

◆ In Eastern Europe, the following items may be difficult to obtain, so you may want to bring them with you:

- antacids
- antibiotic ointments
- bandages
- cough medicines
- decongestants
- headache or fever remedies such as aspirin and acetaminophen
- insect-bite ointments
- insect repellents
- laxatives
- menstrual discomfort medications
- motion sickness medications
- muscle pain medications
- sunburn lotions
- sunscreen
- tampons and/or sanitary pads
- a thermometer
- vaginal yeast infection medications

◆ Bring a flashlight with batteries. Some European hotels have hall lights that switch off automatically, and in Eastern Europe, the electricity sometimes shuts down.

◆ International travelers often unknowingly harbor bombs and smuggle goods. No matter how pleasant or kindly someone appears to be, *never* agree to watch someone's parcel or luggage in an airport lounge, train waiting room, or anywhere else, or to take a package on a bus, train, or anywhere else for a stranger.

◆ Always pack your own luggage and know exactly what's in it—*never* let anyone else pack for you.

◆ Be patient when stopped and asked questions at customs. These precautions are being taken for your safety.

◆ European streets are usually much safer at night than those in American cities. In London, for example, it's usually safe to go home on the subway after the theater. However, it's still wise—especially for women—to exercise caution. Before venturing into an area you don't know well—particularly in a large city—ask at your hotel or ask your hosts whether it's safe.

◆ When you leave the country, remove the film from your camera. If you put all your film in clear plastic bags, you can show them to customs officials and the film won't have to go through the X-ray machine. It simplifies going through security, because the officials can see exactly what you have without digging through boxes and other bags.

The European Community

In 1991, 12 countries in Europe—Belgium, Denmark, France, Germany, Greece, Ireland, Italy, Luxembourg, the Netherlands, Portugal, Spain, and the United Kingdom—embarked on the first step of a journey toward what some visionaries hope will be a United States of Europe. By joining to form the European Community (EC), they hope to create a single business market, the largest in the world.

What does the formation of the EC mean to travelers? Pleasure travelers will probably notice only the convenience of having to go through passport control only once—when they enter Europe.

The EC will have a more profound effect on businesspeople—it creates a single market as big as the U.S. and Japan combined. A Europe-wide unit of currency (the European Currency Unit, or ECU) may be used for some business transactions, though it won't be in general circulation for many years, if ever. Overall, changes caused by the EC will not be so profound as some businesspeople have feared. In some respects, the EC should simplify business by instituting a single set of standards for measurements and for health, safety, and environmental requirements. Europeans hope these uniform standards will lower costs.

One way to break into the EC business market is to have a booth at one of the big international fairs (such as those in Geneva, Budapest, or Leipzig). The booths are expensive, so you might want to share one, preferably with a European businessperson whose contacts would be helpful to you. Other sources of contacts are Chambers of Commerce—either your local one or the one in the place where you propose to do business.

After you've established good business relationships within the EC market, you might want to establish a joint venture with someone there. Don't go in planning to make a quick profit and get out; instead, think of the venture as a long-term commitment.

For more information on the EC and what it means to your business, contact the Delegation of the Commission of the European Communities at one of three locations:

♦ 2100 M Street NW, Suite 707, Washington, DC 20037; (202) 862-9500 or fax (202) 429-1766. (This is the main office.)

♦ 3 Dag Hammarskjöld Plaza, 305 E. 47th Street, New York, NY 10017; (212) 371-3804 or fax (212) 758-2718.

♦ 44 Montgomery Street, Suite 2715, San Francisco, CA 94104; (415) 391-3476 or fax (415) 391-3641.

Austria

For Austrians, the good life is filled with comfort and the pleasures of food and friends. They enjoy spending hours in a cafe having coffee and pastries and visiting.

Austrians also value good manners and have made graciousness a way of life. When Austrians enter a shop, for example, they greet each person there. To Americans this might seem unnecessary and almost silly. To Austrians, however, it's only common courtesy to acknowledge that the people aren't part of the shop scenery.

This graciousness might make Austrians seem more formal than Americans, but they are rarely rigid or stiff.

Greetings

♦ Shake hands when you're introduced, when you greet someone, and when you leave. Austrian men often kiss women's hands when they meet them, but American men may simply shake hands with Austrian women.

♦ A man should wait for a woman to extend her hand before offering his.

♦ Don't introduce yourself to people in a group. Wait for your host to introduce you.

♦ If speaking German, address men as *Herr* (Mr.) and married women as *Frau* (Mrs.), with their last names. Address single women over 20 as *Frau;* under 20, as *Fräulein* (Miss). (See Key Phrases for Germany.)

♦ Use first names only with very close friends. Austrians are quite formal in this respect—many business colleagues address each other by last names throughout their careers.

Conversation

♦ English is spoken in larger cities and in tourist/resort areas.

♦ Good topics of conversation: what you like about Austria, American technology (Austrians are interested in and impressed by it), professions, families, cars, music (Austrians know a lot about classical music), hiking, or skiing (people will be impressed if you know something about Austrian skiing champions).

♦ Topics to avoid: money, religion, divorce, or separation.

♦ Never call an Austrian a German. Although they speak the same language, Austrians and Germans have different customs, values, and histories.

♦ Don't tease anyone playfully. Austrians won't understand what you're doing and might be offended.

♦ Don't offer casual compliments such as "I like your dress" or "That's an attractive hairstyle." An Austrian will likely demur and might be embarrassed.

♦ Be cautious about making promises of any kind; Austrians take them seriously.

Money

♦ The unit of currency is the Austrian schilling (plural schillinge, abbreviated AS), made up of 100 groschen.

♦ Coins come in denominations of 1, 2, 5, 10, and 50 groschen; and 1, 5, 10, 25, and 50 schillinge.

♦ Notes come in denominations of 20, 50, 100, 500, and 1,000 schillinge.

♦ If you're planning to use a credit card at one of the more traditional hotels or restaurants in the countryside, check first to make sure they accept them. Many don't.

Telephones

♦ You'll find coin-operated telephones everywhere; from them you can dial anywhere within Austria and to most countries abroad.

♦ Deposit 1 schilling for a local call or 9 schillinge for a long-distance call within Austria. When your party answers, push the button to complete the connection. At the end of three minutes you'll hear a tone, after which you have 20 seconds to deposit more money.

♦ If you'll be using public telephones often and don't want to carry a lot of change, buy a telephone card (called *Telefonwertkarte*) at a post office, bank, or tobacconist shop. The cards come in denominations of 50 and 100 schillinge. Each pay phone has a slot into which you can insert the card to find

out how much time is left on it.

♦ For long-distance international calls, go to the main post office or telephone center, or use your phone card or AT&T number. You can also use coins, but the amount might be cumbersome.

♦ Long-distance international operators speak English.

♦ Two types of beeps you might hear on Austrian phones are similar to those used in the U.S.—evenly spaced beeps for a dial tone and long beeps for ringing. The third type, however, might be unfamiliar: beeps with three ascending tones indicate a malfunction.

♦ When answering the phone, say "hah-LO" or "yah."

♦ Emergency numbers are as follows:

Police	133
Fire	122
Ambulance	144
Automobile breakdown	120 or 123

In Public

♦ Men should stand when a woman enters a room and when talking to a woman who is standing.

♦ To attract someone's attention, hold up your hand with the index finger extended.

♦ When you enter a shop, always greet the salespeople.

♦ Look for public toilets on streets and in hotels and restaurants. The men's room is labeled *Herren;* the women's room, *Damen.*

Dress

◆ For casual wear, men usually wear pants and shirts; women wear pants, skirts, or dresses. Jeans are acceptable, but don't wear shorts in towns or cities.

◆ For business, men should always wear dark, conservative suits and ties, though in summer lighter colors are acceptable. Women should wear suits or dresses.

◆ To elegant restaurants, men should wear jackets and ties and women should wear skirts or dresses. To other restaurants, men don't have to wear jackets, and women can wear pants.

◆ For dinner parties, men should wear suits; women, dresses.

◆ For theater openings, dress formally: tuxedos for men and cocktail dresses for women. At other theater events, men should wear suits, and women should wear dresses.

◆ If you go to the theater, don't try to wear or take your coat into the auditorium with you. Check it at the cloakroom (in fact, an usher will probably prevent you from entering until you do).

◆ On special occasions you might see Austrians in native dress—men in loden jackets (loden is a thick wool that comes in olive green, gray, or black) and women in dirndls (dresses with full, gathered skirts).

Meals

Hours and Foods

Breakfast (Früh-stück): 8:00 A.M. The morning meal usually includes rolls with butter and jam, cheese and some-times cold cuts, a soft-boiled egg, and *melange* (coffee with hot milk).

Lunch (Mittagessen): Between noon and 2:00 P.M. The meal starts with soup, often a beef broth with dumplings or noodles. A meat dish such as roast pork or broiled chicken follows, along with vegetables and potatoes, rice, or noodles. A salad is often served with the meal, and fruit, cheese, or dessert with black coffee follows. Drinks are beer, wine, or mineral water.

Dinner (Abendessen): Between 6:00 and 9:00 P.M., except in late-hour restaurants. The Austrian dinner is a substantial hot meal, much like lunch. At a dinner party, wine or beer might be served before the meal, with an appetizer such as smoked salmon or caviar on bread. The meal itself will be much like the noon meal. Expect to be served an after-dinner brandy: *Kirschwasser* (cherry), *Himbeergiest* (rasp-berry), or *Slivovitz* (plum).

Breaks: Many Austrians have *Jause* (a cof-fee break) at 4:00 P.M. Sandwiches and pas-tries accompany the coffee.

Table Manners

◆ Be punctual when invited to a meal.

◆ The male guest of honor sits next to the hostess, and the female guest of honor sits next to the host.

◆ Don't begin eating until your hostess does.

◆ If platters of food are passed around the table, serve yourself. In some homes you might be handed a plate with food already on it.

◆ Keep both hands on the table while eating.

◆ Don't cut fish or potatoes with a knife; it implies they aren't tender enough.

◆ Never bite into a whole roll. Break it apart with your fingers first.

◆ When you finish eating, put your utensils side by side on the plate.

◆ Smoking between courses is acceptable.

◆ Don't feel obliged to drink alcoholic beverages. People will not press you to, especially if you are driving, since the laws prohibiting drunk driving are strict.

◆ At a dinner party, be sure to leave by 11:00 P.M., especially if it's the first time you've been to your hosts' house for a meal.

Eating Out

◆ Try the following alternatives to standard restaurants:

• A *Beise* is similar to a British pub. Guests can eat, drink, and play chess or cards.

• A *Heuriger* offers wine and food.

• A *Kaffeehaus* is a cafe that offers several different types of coffee. You can also order wine, although it's not what most people drink there. If you go to a cafe, don't feel as though you must leave or reorder after one cup; Austrians often spend a long time in cafes chatting, reading newspapers (often available in English), and playing cards.

• A *Keller* is a restaurant with a lively, noisy, convivial atmosphere. Many

have live entertainment.

• A *Kellerlokal,* a cellar restaurant, offers inexpensive meals.

• A *Konditorei* serves pastries, coffee, tea, and cold drinks. Some also offer soufflés and sandwiches.

• A *Stube* serves wine and appetizers and offers a lively, friendly atmosphere. Many have live music.

◆ Austrian restaurants don't post menus in their windows, but the exteriors often indicate how fancy the decor—and prices—will be.

◆ At the entrance to a restaurant, look for a shield with a *G* on it, signifying that government inspectors have checked the quality of the food and service.

◆ Lunch is served between noon and 2:00 P.M. Dinner is served between 6:00 and 9:00 P.M.

◆ Most large restaurants serve meals until midnight.

◆ To call a waiter, say "hair O-behr." To call a waitress, say "FROY-line."

◆ Don't expect waiters to bring bills. Instead, when you're ready to pay, tell them what you've ordered, and they'll calculate what you owe on the spot.

Specialties

◆ Austria is famous for its elaborate cream-filled pastries. Also try *Serbische Bohnensuppe* (Serbian bean soup); *Goulasch* (stew); *Tafelspitz* (boiled beef with horseradish or chive sauce); *Schnitzel Cordon Bleu* (veal, ham, and cheese dipped in batter and deep-fried); *Spanferkel* (roast suckling pig); *Bauernschmaus* (ham, salt pork, sausage, sauerkraut, and dumplings); *Rehrüken* (venison); *Rotkraut* (sweet-and-sour red cabbage with caraway seeds);

Knödel (a dumpling, more popular than potatoes or rice, used in soups, as a side dish with meat, or with jam as a dessert).

♦ For dessert, try *Palatschinken* (pancakes filled with jam); *Salzburger Nockerl* (oven pancake); *Sachertorte* (chocolate cake); and *Strudel* (pastry filled with apples, cherries, or cheese).

Hotels

♦ The summer months are considered "high season," as are other periods in different regions: in ski areas, Christmas

through the first week in January, and February 1 through Easter; in Vienna, December 27–31; in Salzburg, December 20 to January 9, January 26 to February 5, and Easter week. Book *far* ahead of time for the Christmas and New Year's period.

♦ Most four-star hotels have swimming pools, and some have indoor and outdoor saunas. Even moderately priced hotels in smaller cities and towns offer high-quality food, service, and cleanliness.

♦ The sign *Zimmer Frei* outside a private home means that rooms are available there.

♦ If you want a room with a bath and a toilet, ask for a bath *and* a *W.C.* The two don't necessarily go together.

♦ If you are told a room is *"garni,"* it means that breakfast is included.

♦ In hotels, as in other buildings, what Austrians call the "first floor" is the American second floor.

Tipping

♦ *Restaurants:* Service is included, but leave an additional 5 percent.

♦ *Porters:* Tip 10 schillinge per bag.

♦ *Hotel maids:* Tip 10 schillinge per day.

♦ *Taxis:* Give 10 percent of the fare.

♦ *Cloakroom attendants:* Give 7–15 schillinge.

♦ *Washroom attendants:* Tip 5 schillinge.

Private Homes

♦ Plan to visit around 3:00 P.M., the customary visiting hour. Always call in advance; don't simply drop in. When you visit, expect to be served coffee and cake.

♦ If you make a phone call from a private home, offer to pay for it.

♦ If you're staying for a few days or more, offer to help with the cleaning up. Your hosts will probably welcome your offer.

♦ Feel free to take a daily bath or shower. Most homes have no shortage of hot water.

Gifts: If you're invited to someone's home for a meal, bring flowers and unwrap them before you present them. Don't give red roses, a symbol of romantic love, or carnations, which are usually reserved for cemeteries (red carnations are reserved for May Day). Always give an odd number of flowers. Another welcome gift is a bottle of wine.

♦ If you're staying with a family, bring gifts from the U.S., such as records, calculators, portable cassette players with headphones, and flannel shirts for men to wear while hiking. If you'll be giving the gift shortly after you get off the plane, consider bringing lobsters or steak; have them packed securely in dry ice and check them through as baggage so they'll be in the coldest part of the plane.

Business

Hours

Businesses: 8:00 A.M. to 12:30 P.M. and 1:30 to 5:30 P.M., Monday through Friday.

Government offices: 8:00 A.M. to 4:00 P.M., Monday through Friday.

Banks: 8:00 A.M. to 12:30 P.M. and 1:30 to 3:30 P.M., Monday through Friday (on Thursday, until 5:30 P.M.).

Stores: 8:00 A.M. to 6:00 P.M., Monday through Friday, and 8:00 A.M. to noon on Saturday. Many stores, however, close for two hours around lunchtime.

Business Practices

Consult the Austrian Trade Commission in New York to find business contacts in Austria.

♦ Most businesspeople speak English. To get a step ahead of your competition, however, have any written materials translated into German.

♦ Most offices have fax machines.

♦ Foreign businesswomen will be treated with great respect in Austria.

Meetings and negotiations: Make appointments with high-level people—whether in government or private business—two months in advance. For other businesspeople, one month in advance is enough.

♦ Suggest appointment times between 8:00 A.M. and noon or 2:00 and 5:00 P.M.

♦ Don't try to schedule appointments for the Austrian vacation periods: August, the Christmas–New Year period, and Easter.

♦ Be on time for business meetings.

♦ When you arrive, shake hands with each person. If you know the "pecking order," begin with the most important person and work down.

♦ Bring business cards—if possible, with a German translation on one side. Be sure your cards have the German translation of your title. Give your card to secretaries and receptionists as well as the businesspeople with whom you meet.

♦ If an Austrian gives you a business card with several titles, ask which one you should use.

♦ Use charts and visuals only if they are essential to your presentation, not just to appear impressive.

♦ Prepare for some small talk before the business discussion. Expect to discuss general topics, such as the weather and what you have liked about Austria. Bone up on skiing and classical music (Austria being the home of Mozart, Strauss, and the Salzburg music festival), so you can converse intelligently on these subjects.

♦ Austrians conduct business much more slowly than do Americans. Be patient; each detail of a business deal will be scrutinized carefully.

Entertainment: Business lunches are more common than business dinners. Viennese often take business guests to a wine garden.

♦ Business dinners are usually reserved to celebrate the completion of a deal. Austrians value their private lives, and dinners take time away from private life.

♦ If Austrians have hosted you at lunch or dinner, be sure to reciprocate before you leave the country. Never take people to a higher-priced restaurant than the one to which they took you.

♦ Invite Austrian spouses to business dinners, if you wish. If present, your spouse should not take a leading role in the conversation.

Gifts: Give electronic calculator watches or a bottle of an unusual brand of bourbon. If you know the person's family, give the children hand-held electronic games.

♦ If you are invited to the home of a married businessman, be sure to bring flowers. Don't bring red roses (appropriate for girl-friends) or carnations (for cemeteries). Always give an odd number of flowers.

Holidays & Celebrations

Holidays:
New Year's Day (January 1); Epiphany (January 6); Easter Monday; Labor Day (May 1);

Ascension (five weeks after Easter); Whit Monday (eight weeks after Easter); Corpus Christi (approximately eight weeks after Easter); Assumption Day (August 15); National Day (October 26); All Saints' Day (November 1); Immaculate Conception (December 8); Christmas (December 25);

and St. Stephen's Day (December 26).

♦ If you want to follow Austrian tradition on National Day (October 26), go mountain climbing. For the less agile, there are parades everywhere.

Transportation

Public Transport

Mass transit:
When you ride on a streetcar or bus, buy your

ticket from a kiosk or pay on the vehicle. In Vienna, you need exact change. In other cities you do not. If you have a ticket, stamp it in a machine when you board.

♦ In Vienna, save money on bus and streetcar tickets by buying them in strips of four at tobacconist shops (*Tabak Trafik*) or kiosks. With one ticket you can change forms of transportation if you're continuing in the same direction without interruption.

♦ Streetcars stop operating sometime between 11:00 P.M. and midnight. At each stop you'll find a sign telling which cars stop there, where they go, and at what times they make their first and last trips.

♦ Vienna subways cost 20 schillinge. Buy your ticket at the booth near the entrance. You don't need exact change.

♦ Trains offer first, second, and third class, the major difference being the extra space in first class. For long trips within Austria, you can take a first- or second-class sleeper or couchette.

♦ Seat reservations are required for some trains. On most others, you can reserve seats for a small extra charge up to a few hours before departure.

Taxis: Don't try to hail a taxi on the street. Instead, go to a taxi stand or ask the desk clerk at your hotel to call a taxi for you.

◆ Taxi drivers charge extra for luggage.

Driving

◆ An American driver's license is acceptable, but it's better to bring an International Driver's License in case you're involved in an accident.

◆ Seat belts are required for all occupants of a car.

◆ The speed limit in built-up areas is 50 kph; outside built-up areas, 100 kph; and on main highways, 130 kph.

◆ Drive defensively, as Austrians are aggressive drivers.

◆ At an intersection, give priority to cars coming from the right. Always give way to streetcars.

◆ Be sure to obey parking laws. Parking zones, which are clearly marked, are patrolled constantly by police.

◆ Don't have even one drink if you expect to drive. The penalties are severe and are strictly enforced, especially on Friday and Saturday nights.

Legal Matters & Safety

◆ If you buy a valuable art object, ask where you can get the export license you'll need to take it out of the country.

◆ The drinking age in bars and restaurants is 16 (14 if accompanied by a parent). There are no age restrictions on buying liquor in stores.

◆ You can feel safe in Austria; women can take public transportation after dark.

Key Phrases

See Germany.

Belgium & Luxembourg

In Belgium, you won't find one language but three, with legal borders between them. A majority of the people are Flemings, who speak a dialect similar to Dutch, while a sizeable minority, the Waloons, speak a dialect of French. There is also a German-speaking population of less than 100,000. All public signs are in the language of the region, except in Brussels, where signs are in both Flemish and French.

Brussels is the center for branches of the European Community (see Introduction, p. 9) and is highly international. It's also a bit "pricey," as is the country as a whole, since Belgium has one of the highest standards of living in Europe.

The small country of Luxembourg is very similar to Belgium in customs and manners, so we've included it here, noting only those times when Luxembourgeois customs differ from the Belgian.

Greetings

◆ When first introduced to someone, shake hands quickly, with a light pressure, and repeat your name. Also shake hands when greeting or leaving someone.

◆ Members of the opposite sex and women who are good friends kiss on the cheek three times in greeting. Men shake hands with each other.

◆ When you arrive at an office or a business meeting, shake hands with everyone there, including the secretaries. Do the same when you leave.

◆ If you haven't met someone in a group, introduce yourself and shake hands.

◆ At a large party, rely on your hosts to introduce you to the entire group. It's not necessary to shake hands with each person.

◆ Never use a person's first name unless invited to do so.

◆ Children usually kiss adult hosts or the parents of friends when saying "thank you" or "good-bye."

Conversation

◆ The official languages are Flemish (a Dutch dialect), French, and German. Many people speak some English.

◆ To please people in the Flemish region, learn a few words of Dutch (see Key Phrases for the Netherlands).

◆ If you don't speak Dutch, you might want to speak English rather than French in Flemish Belgium. Also remember that Belgian cities often have different names in Flemish and French.

◆ People are reserved and formal, especially at first meeting. They value tact and diplomacy and see blunt honesty as rudeness.

◆ Good topics of conversation: sports, such as soccer and bicycle racing; recent and popular books; political events (but don't take sides on political issues); the town you're visiting; or Belgian cultural heritage.

◆ If you wish to make a favorable impression, read about the area you're visiting. Belgians will be pleased if you know something of and ask questions about the history and attractions of their area.

◆ Topics to avoid: language differences in Belgium, highly controversial political issues, or religion.

◆ Don't ask personal questions (e.g., questions regarding a person's occupation or family) when first meeting someone.

◆ The French/Flemish situation can be uncomfortable. You can inquire about the two regions, but it's rude to make fun of one area while in the other or to praise one group extravagantly to the other.

◆ Never snap your fingers or put your hands in your pockets while talking to someone.

In Luxembourg:

◆ Don't worry about language problems. English is widely spoken and understood. The everyday spoken language is Luxembourgish, a German dialect, but almost everyone speaks both French and German. People will be impressed and grateful if you take the trouble to learn a few phrases in the local dialect.

Money

◆ In Belgium the unit of currency is the Belgian franc (abbreviated BF), made up of 100 centimes.

◆ Coins come in denominations of 50 centimes and 1, 5, and 20 BF.

◆ Notes come in denominations of 50, 100, 500, 1,000, and 5,000 BF.

◆ Belguim and Luxembourg accept one another's currency; however, some Belgian shopkeepers do not want to accept Luxembourgeois banknotes.

In Luxembourg:

◆ In Luxembourg the unit of currency is the franc (abbreviated Fr or F), made up of 100 centimes.

◆ Coins come in denominations of 25 centimes and 1, 5, 10, 20, and 50 francs.

◆ Notes come in denominations of 100, 500, 1,000, and 5,000 francs.

Telephones

◆ You'll find public telephones on the streets. You can make regular and collect calls from them.

◆ When calling from a public telephone, insert two 5-BF coins. The cost of each call is determined by zone. If you're telephoning within a single zone, you'll get three to four minutes for the basic rate. When your time is up, you'll hear a beep. Deposit more money or you'll be cut off.

◆ Most public telephones that use coins are being replaced with those that use telephone cards. Buy the cards, which are sold in 10-BF units, at kiosks, post offices, and train stations.

◆ You can make international calls from public phones that display symbols of different countries; just buy a phone card with lots of units. Instructions are displayed in several languages. You can also make international calls at the post office.

◆ When answering the phone, people in French Belgium and Luxembourg say "ah-LO." In Flemish Belgium, just say your last name. Some people in Flemish Belgium say "hah-LO."

◆ The Emergency Number to summon the police, the fire department, or an ambulance is **100.**

In Luxembourg:

◆ There are no telephone cards.

◆ The Emergency Number is **012.**

In Public

◆ Belgians greatly respect personal privacy. Even neighbors who live close to one another are formal and reserved.

◆ Backslapping and being loud are considered especially rude.

◆ You'll find public toilets in bars, cafes, restaurants, and hotels. The sign may be *W. C.* or *OO, Dames* or *Damen* for women, *Messieurs* or *Herren* for men.

Dress

◆ In general, people dress stylishly. Men and women can wear pants and jeans but should wear shorts only in the countryside or at beach areas.

◆ For a business meeting, men generally wear suits and well-polished shoes. Women typically wear dresses or skirts and blouses.

◆ To informal restaurants, both men and women can wear pants or clean, neatly pressed jeans. To formal restaurants, men should wear a jacket and tie, and women should wear skirts or dresses.

◆ For dining in a home, men should wear a sport jacket or blazer and tie. Women should wear a dress, skirt, or dressy pants.

◆ If an invitation to a meal or other social gathering calls for formal dress, men should wear tuxedos or dark suits; women, cocktail dresses.

◆ To theaters and concerts, men should wear dark suits and ties, and women should wear cocktail dresses—unless the invitation is to an opening and specifies formal wear.

◆ In rural areas, Sunday is a "dress up" day. People wear their best finery to go walking or visiting relatives.

Meals

Hours and Foods

Breakfast (French, *petit déjeuner;* Flemish, *het ont bijt*):

7:30 A.M. In French Belgium, you'll have croissants, bread, butter, jam, and coffee with milk. In Flemish Belgium, you'll be served bread and rolls, a variety of cheeses (sometimes eggs), butter, jam, and coffee.

Lunch (French, *déjeuner;* Flemish, *de lunch*): About 1:00 P.M. In the countryside, it's the main meal of the day, consisting of soup followed by meat, potatoes, and vegetables, then dessert. In cities, lunch is a light meal of either cold cuts with rolls and bread or sandwiches (always made with butter, never mayonnaise), followed by fruit and a dessert of cake, pudding, or ice cream. Beer sometimes accompanies lunch.

Dinner (French, *dîner;* Flemish, *het avondeten*): About 8:00 or 8:30 P.M. At a typical dinner or small dinner party, there will be an appetizer and sometimes a soup, then meat or fish with side dishes, dessert, and coffee.

◆ At a formal dinner party, the meal begins with soup, followed by a fish dish, such as stuffed flounder or *croquettes* (deep-fried fish balls). A light sherbet might be served to cleanse the palate, followed by meat, potatoes, and vegetables. If a salad is served, it will follow the main course. Dessert might be cake, fruit, or pudding.

◆ Typical appetizers at a formal dinner are smoked salmon served with capers, chopped onion, and parsley; in season, asparagus with melted butter and sieved egg yolk sprinkled on top; a half melon with port; shrimp or fish *croquettes;* or cold cuts. If the appetizer is smoked salmon, vodka will probably accompany it.

◆ Wine is served throughout the dinner. If you would prefer a nonalcoholic drink, ask for water. Mineral water is usually available at both lunch and dinner.

◆ In Flemish Belgium, bread isn't served if there are potatoes. In French Belgium, there will be bread but not butter.

◆ Coffee (very dark and strong) is usually served with cookies or chocolates.

◆ After-dinner drinks will be served at the table after an informal meal, or in the living room after a formal dinner. Men usually drink whiskey after dinner, while women have Grand Marnier or Cointreau.

Breaks: People usually stop for a coffee break about 10:00 A.M.

Table Manners

◆ Be punctual when invited to a dinner party.

◆ If your hosts offer a before-dinner drink, wait for them to name a selection of drinks and don't ask for anything not offered. They'll probably offer aperitifs, such as vermouth or Cinzano, rather than mixed drinks. Nuts, chips, or hot cheese *croquettes* often accompany before-dinner drinks.

◆ At a dinner party, the hosts will seat everyone. Husbands and wives are never seated together. The host and hostess sit at either end of the table, with the male guest of honor to the right of the hostess and the female guest of honor to the right of the host.

◆ At a large dinner party, groups might be seated at separate tables in more than one room. Most Belgian dining rooms are small.

◆ You might be given three glasses: one for water, one for red wine (if there is a meat course), and one for white wine (if there is a fish course).

◆ Sometimes settings include bread-and-butter plates. If there aren't any, place the bread on the rim of your plate.

◆ If dishes are passed around the table, serve yourself.

◆ Even if your white wine isn't as chilled as you would like, never put ice in it.

◆ Don't smoke during dinner unless you see an ashtray on the table.

◆ To show you've finished, place your fork and knife horizontally across the top of the plate, with the tines of the fork and the point of the knife facing left. It's impolite to cross the knife and fork.

♦ Plates are not cleared, either in a home or in a restaurant, until everyone has finished.

♦ After dinner in a home, you'll often be invited to the living room for liqueurs and cigars. Stay until the cigars are finished—about 30 minutes to an hour after the meal. If you move to leave and your hosts press you to stay, you may stay another half hour.

Eating Out

♦ For variety, try these types of eating places:

- *Bistros* are small restaurants that offer hot meals and alcoholic beverages. Many feature live music in the evenings.

- *Cafés* serve beer, wine, and other alcoholic drinks; coffee; and some snacks, such as *croque monsieur* (a grilled ham and cheese sandwich made with Belgian bread) or *croque madam* (a grilled ham, cheese, and tomato sandwich).

- *Cafetarias* are attached to supermarkets or located on highways in big cities. They offer hot dishes, cold cuts, sandwiches, and beer and wine.

- *Pâtisseries* serve coffee, tea, pastries, and ice cream.

♦ In downtown areas, you'll find stands on the streets selling french fries and sausages. It's okay to eat these snacks as you're walking on the street.

♦ Many restaurants are very expensive. If you're a guest, either ask your hosts to recommend some choices and order in that price range, or select one of the fixed-price meals, usually less expensive than ordering à la carte.

♦ To get scotch whiskey, ask for "whiskey." "Scotch" is a brand of beer.

♦ Never order tea or coffee with a meal. Wait until you've finished eating.

♦ Note that Belgian beer has a much higher alcohol content than American beer.

♦ To call the waiter, use the French or Dutch word for "Sir" or "Miss" (see Key Phrases for France and the Netherlands).

In Luxembourg:

♦ Expensive restaurants offer international cuisine, but most restaurants have German-style cooking.

♦ Most menus are written in both French and German.

Specialties

In cases where a dish has more than one name, we've given the French name first and the Flemish second.

♦ Try these Belgian specialties: *anguilles* (eels); *anguilles au vert* or *puiltng in 't groen* (eels in a thick parsley sauce); *hochepot* or *hutsepot* (a stew of pork and mutton); *carbonnades flamandes* (beef cooked in beer); *civet de lièvre à la flamandes* (rabbit or hare cooked in wine with carrots, mushrooms, and onions); *waterzooi* (stewed chicken, leeks, and celery in a broth thickened with eggs and cream); and *chicon* (endive, a delicate-tasting vegetable that looks like a small, elongated lettuce).

♦ Be sure not to miss mussels when you're in Belgium. Some restaurants serve nothing else, and on Fridays most restaurants feature *moules marinière* (mussels steamed in white wine, garlic, and parsley) served with french fries.

In Luxembourg:

♦ Don't miss these special foods when you're in Luxembourg: *quenelles* (dumplings of calves' liver served with sauerkraut and potatoes); *civet de lièvre* (rabbit or hare stew); *liewerkniddellen* (meat and suet dumplings); *tartes aux quetsches* (plum tarts); and *gebeck* (a soup of pork and veal lungs with plums).

Hotels

♦ Hotel clerks might ask to keep your passport while they fill out forms. It will usually be returned promptly if you need it right away.

♦ Never go out of a hotel without leaving your key at the desk.

♦ In some hotels, you can leave your shoes outside your room to be shined. Other hotels have rooms with double doors, both of which lock; you can leave shoes to be shined and clothes to be pressed in the space between the doors.

♦ Campsites are clean and well organized.

Tipping

♦ *Restaurants:* If a restaurant service charge is not included, leave 15 percent of the check. If the service is especially

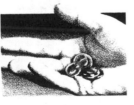

good, leave another 3–5 percent on the table. In an elegant restaurant tip the *sommelier* (wine steward) 10 percent of the wine bill if he helps you select the wine.

♦ *Porters:* Tip hotel porters 50 BF per bag. Railway station porters charge a fixed fee of 20–25 BF per bag.

♦ *Hotel maids:* If service isn't included in the hotel bill, leave 30 BF per day. If it is included and the service is especially good, leave 8–10 BF per day.

♦ *Taxis:* Don't tip in Belgium; a tip is included in the fare. In Luxembourg, tip 10–20 percent.

♦ *Ushers:* Tip 10 BF for each person in your party.

♦ *Cloakroom attendants:* Tip 20–50 BF per article. In Luxembourg, there's usually an obligatory 20-franc charge; don't tip extra.

♦ *Washroom attendants:* Tip 7 BF.

♦ If you're invited to stay with a family for a few days and they have a maid, ask your hostess how much to tip.

Private Homes

♦ Always phone before visiting; never drop in. Belgians don't even drop in on family members.

♦ Always be on time for any prearranged visit.

♦ Don't make telephone calls from a private home if at all possible, since they are extremely expensive. If you must use the phone, find out how much the call costs and pay for it.

♦ Don't call people before 10:00 A.M. or after 10:00 P.M.

♦ When staying with a family, offer to help prepare the food, set the table, and do the dishes.

Gifts: If you're invited to dinner at a home, bring flowers (but not chrysanthemums or carnations) or fancy chocolates. If there are children, bring them candy or cookies as well.

♦ If you're staying with a family, bring a book about your home town or area, or bring phonograph records, which are very expensive in Belgium.

♦ Wine or other alcoholic beverages are appropriate gifts only for close friends.

♦ If you receive a gift, open it immediately or you'll disappoint the person who gave it to you.

Business

Hours

Businesses and government offices: In Brussels, 8:30 A.M. to noon and 2:00 to 6:00 P.M., Monday through Friday. In Antwerp, 9:00 A.M. to noon and either 1:00 to 5:00 or 5:30 P.M., or 2:00 to 6:00 P.M., Monday through Friday.

Banks: 10:00 A.M. to 6:00 P.M., Monday through Friday.

Stores: Between 9:00 and 10:00 A.M. to 6:00 or 7:00 P.M., Monday through Friday, and 10:00 A.M. to 6:00 P.M. on Saturday.

♦ The Belgian work day usually lasts from 8:30 A.M. to 6:00 P.M., with a lunch break of one and one-half to two hours at noon. Embassies and consulates, however, close at 4:00 P.M.

In Luxembourg:

Businesses: Same as Brussels.

Government offices: 9:00 A.M. to noon and 2:00 to 5:00 P.M., Monday through Friday.

Banks: 8:30 A.M. to noon and 1:30 to 4:30 or 5:00 P.M., Monday through Friday.

Stores: 8:00 A.M. to noon and 2:00 to 6:00 P.M., Monday through Saturday.

Business Practices

♦ Don't use the same person as a business contact in both French and Flemish Belgium.

♦ Avoid business trips during July and August, Holy Week, and the Christmas–New Year period.

♦ If you are using mailings or sales brochures, have them written in both French and Dutch. You don't need a separate copy for each language; instead, have a single copy with the two languages side by side under each section. Note, however, that many Belgian companies use English for internal memos, a practice that both avoids the touchy French/Flemish issue and saves the expense of making two copies of everything.

♦ You'll find fax machines everywhere. Some hotels have faxes but no telexes.

♦ Bring business cards; they are widely used. They should be printed in English on one side and in French or Dutch on the other, depending on where you're doing business.

Meetings and negotiations: Before calling on business or government offices, make an appointment. When you write or phone to make the arrangements, the Belgian firm will usually select the time. If they make the appointment for 11:30 A.M., assume you'll be invited to lunch.

♦ Don't try to schedule an appointment on a Saturday, even though some companies might be open. The day is reserved for sales meetings and conferences.

♦ It's sometimes difficult to get appointments on Bourse Days, which are Mondays in Antwerp and Wednesdays in Brussels. These are the days when businesspeople meet professional colleagues for lunch.

♦ When you arrive at an office or a business meeting, shake hands with everyone there, including the secretaries. Do the same when you leave.

♦ The first meeting with Belgian businesspeople is for getting acquainted. You should exchange business cards and answer questions about yourself. Belgians must trust you before they will have confidence in your company. Don't try to do business immediately, or you'll seem pushy.

♦ Proceed cautiously until you have developed a sense for the company you're dealing with. Don't be overly aggressive in presenting an opinion or a solution to a problem.

Entertainment: Belgian businesspeople prefer to spend evenings with their families. (Business colleagues don't become good friends, and they rarely socialize.) To entertain a Belgian businessperson, it's best to arrange a lunch date. The typical business lunch lasts from 1:00 to 3:00 P.M., with one drink before lunch and wine during the meal. If you do invite a businessperson to dinner, however, be sure to include the spouse in the invitation.

♦ Don't expect your French-Belgian business colleague to invite you home to dinner. Business entertaining at home has increased in popularity as Belgians have traveled to the U.S. and enjoyed invitations to eat with American families. Still, a spouse who does not speak English might prefer that the entertaining be done in a restaurant. Flemish-Belgian businesspeople are more likely to invite you home. If you're invited to a meal in a home, don't discuss business.

♦ When American businesswomen entertain Belgian businessmen, they should either make payment arrangements in advance or indicate that their company is paying. Belgian businessmen won't allow a woman to pay under any other conditions.

Gifts: If you want to give a business gift, choose a recent book related to the type of business you're in.

In Luxembourg:

Meetings and negotiations: Don't try to schedule afternoon meetings before 2:30 P.M. Many businesspeople go home for lunch.

Entertainment: If you entertain business colleagues at a restaurant, they will appreciate a French wine.

Holidays & Celebrations

Holidays:
New Year's Day (January 1); Easter Monday; Ascension Day (five weeks after Easter); Whit Mon-day (eight weeks after Easter); Labor Day (May 1); National Day (July 21); the Assumption (August 15); All Saints' Day (November 1); Armistice Day (November 11); Christmas (December 25); and December 26.

♦ If one of the above holidays falls on a Sunday, it is celebrated on the following Monday.

♦ On All Saints' Day and All Souls' Day (November 2), people go to church, visit cemeteries, and stay at home. Don't invite people to dinner or a party during that time.

In Luxembourg:

♦ Holidays are the same as in Belgium, with the addition of Shrove Tuesday (the day before Ash Wednesday), National Day (June 23, the birthday of His Royal Highness, the Grand Duke), and All Souls' Day. (July 21 and November 11 are not public holidays in Luxembourg.)

♦ *Schobermess*, the Luxembourg Fair, is held annually in the spring and fall and is also a public holiday.

♦ If you have a chance, go see the "Jumping Procession" in Echternach on the Tuesday after Whit Sunday. Thousands of people form rows and weave their way around the cathedral with a jumping, kicking step. The procession is a tradition dating back to the early sixteenth century, when local people danced and prayed to get rid of the plague.

Transportation

Public Transport

Mass transit: You can buy bus or streetcar tickets when you board. The fare depends on the number of zones through which you travel.

♦ For the Metro (subway), pay at the ticket window. The Metro has first- and second-class fares. Keep your ticket; it will be checked when you exit, and you'll pay a fine if you don't have it.

♦ To save money, buy a 5- or 10-ride card for the bus, streetcar, or Metro; they're available at Metro stations.

♦ On all public transportation, men should let women precede them when boarding, and should stand until the women present are seated.

♦ Trains are a very practical form of transportation; you can get to even the tiniest village. First class has velvet seats and is quieter than second class—especially during rush hours. Second class is also comfortable; it's just more crowded during rush hours.

♦ Trains have smoking and nonsmoking cars. On suburban trains, downstairs is for nonsmoking and upstairs is for smoking.

♦ You're supposed to buy your train ticket before you board. If you don't have time, tell a conductor as soon as you get on the train that you don't have a ticket and would like to buy one. Otherwise, if the conductor finds you without a ticket, you'll pay a steep fine.

♦ Special, cheaper weekend train tickets are available if you travel from Thursday night through Monday night.

Taxis: You can't hail a taxi on the street; instead, either go to a taxi stand or telephone for one.

♦ Taxis are very expensive.

In Luxembourg:

Mass transit: Buy 10-ride passes for city buses at banks and bus stations. You can also get 5-day, unlimited-ride passes for buses and trains throughout the country; buy them at main stations in Luxembourg City.

Driving

♦ You don't need an International Driver's License to drive in Belgium or Luxembourg.

♦ Seat belts are mandatory for all occupants of a car.

◆ Children under 12 must sit in the back seat.

◆ Belgian highways were renumbered in 1986, so make sure you have an up-to-date map.

◆ The speed limit in Brussels and urban districts is 60 kph; outside towns, it is 90 kph. On motorways, the minimum speed is 70 kph, and the maximum speed is 120 kph.

◆ Traffic coming from the right has the right of way, even if it's coming from a tiny side street. Streetcars have priority at all times.

◆ In both countries, time-limited parking areas are designated *les zones bleues/ blauwe zone*. At a kiosk or tourist office buy a small card called *disque bleu/blauweschijf,* which allows you to park in all designated areas. Leave the card so that it's visible in the car's front window.

◆ Drivers tend to be undisciplined and insist on being accorded priority, which can lead to dangerous situations.

◆ Be cautious on hilly countryside roads in both countries.

◆ Check place names, because signs may be in Flemish or French.

◆ In case of emergency, use the special telephones located along highways.

◆ Many highways are patrolled by expert mechanics called *Touring Secours/Wegen-hulp;* if you break down, look for their yellow vehicles.

◆ The police enforce traffic laws strictly, even with foreigners. Never argue with the police, even if you believe you've done nothing wrong.

◆ Don't drink and drive. The police conduct spot checks and Breathalyzer tests. If you test positive, you'll be taken to a police station for further tests. As a noncitizen, you'll be fined and put in jail, and your license will be taken away if you're found guilty.

In Luxembourg:

◆ Don't honk your horn, except to warn another driver of imminent danger.

◆ For traffic violations, police can issue on-the-spot fines of up to 600 francs. You are supposed to carry this amount with you at all times when you drive.

◆ Parking in Luxembourg City, despite the many lots, is difficult. Try to arrive before 8:00 A.M. or park at the train station and take a bus into the center.

Legal Matters & Safety

◆ The drinking age is 18.

◆ Women should take taxis after dark.

◆ In Belgium, it's illegal to operate a noisy machine (such as a lawn mower) on Sunday. You may, of course, drive your car.

Key Phrases

See France and the Netherlands.

Bulgaria

Until fairly recently, permission to travel to Bulgaria was difficult to obtain, and Bulgarians rely received permission to travel to the West. Although Bulgarians now receive permission or travel, they are still hampered by currency conversion problems.

s a traveler in Bulgaria, you'll be the object of great curiosity. For years the only sources of formation about the West came from the official press (which stressed the negative aspects f Western life) and from movies. In fact, your Bulgarian acquaintances' impressions of the .S. might be formed by you and Gary Cooper!

Greetings

Always shake nds when you're troduced.

If you haven't et someone in a oup, introduce urself and shake hands.

At a party, wait for your hosts to introduce ou. You need not shake hands with each rson in the room; simply nod to the entire oup.

Use first names only after your Bulgarian ends do so; that form of address is gener- ly reserved for close friends.

Conversation

While Bulgarian the official lan- age, Russian is sily understood, t Bulgarians n't like to speak German and French are the next most miliar languages. Young people may eak some English.

Good topics of conversation: family and me life, or your profession.

♦ Expect people throughout Bulgaria to be curious about American life. Bring photos of your family and home, and photos or post-cards of your town. Try not to suggest that life in America is better than that in Bulgaria.

♦ Bulgarians discuss and criticize their gov-ernment openly. The Parliament is now composed of different political parties. Ask people what the objectives of the main par-ties are; they'll enjoy telling you, and you'll understand the government better.

♦ Be careful about discussing the Turkish problem in eastern Bulgaria.

♦ Don't be surprised if people ask how much money you earn. If you prefer not to answer, a tactful response is "Our life-style is so different, it doesn't make sense to com-pare."

♦ The Bulgarian gestures for "yes" and "no" are the opposite of those in the U.S. To indi-cate "yes," shake your head horizontally; signal "no" with a vertical nod. Watch for these expressions carefully, because Bulgar-ians make them subtly.

Money

◆ The unit of currency is the lev (plural leva; abbreviated Lv), which is composed of 100 stotinki (singular stotinka).

◆ Coins come in denominations of 1, 2, 5, 10, 20, and 50 stotinki and 1, 2, and 5 leva.

◆ Notes come in denominations of 1, 2, 5, 10, 20, and 50 leva.

◆ Don't accept 100-lev notes. They are worthless old currency.

◆ Don't agree to change money with people you meet on the street. Not only is it illegal, but you might be tricked into receiving old, worthless currency.

Telephones

◆ Make local phone calls from public telephone booths or from larger restaurants and cafes. Deposit a 5-stotinka coin before you pick up the receiver. Local calls have no time limit.

◆ Private homes have direct dialing to other European countries, but not to the U.S. To reach the U.S., call the operator, place the call, and prepare to wait about 30 minutes. You can also make international calls from the post office. Long distance operators speak English.

◆ Bulgaria doesn't yet have telephone cards.

◆ When you answer the phone, say "ah-LO."

◆ Emergency numbers are as follows:

Police	166
Fire	160
Ambulance	151

In Public

◆ A common American gesture has political connotations in Bulgaria: The V gesture, made with the index and middle fingers, is a sign of the opposition party the Union of Democratic Forces, to which most people in larger cities and almost all young people belong.

◆ Before taking photographs of people, or in a cathedral or a monastery, ask permission.

◆ Don't photograph military zones or facilities.

◆ Look for public toilets on main streets an in most restaurants, hotel lobbies, airports, train stations, municipal parks, and central squares. They are almost always clearly marked: either *M* or *H* (for *hommes*) for men and either *Ж* or *D* (for *dames*) for women.

◆ To use a toilet, you must pay an attendar 20 stotinki. Attendants sometimes ask foreigners for more but generally won't insist you refuse.

◆ Public toilets are often unclean. Most are Turkish style—simply a hole in the floor with places on each side for your feet. Brin toilet paper or tissues with you; it is seldon available.

Daress

◆ For casual wear, men should wear pants and shirts, adding jackets or sweaters in winter. Women should wear sundresses, skirts, or pants.

◆ For a business meeting, dress elegantly—men in suit and tie, and women in suit or dress.

◆ When invited to someone's home for dinner, men should wear shirts and pants, and women should wear dresses, skirts, or pants.

◆ To elegant restaurants, men should wear suits, and women should wear dresses. At other restaurants, casual dress is fine.

◆ Formal dress for official parties, the theater (especially on weekends), theater openings, and weddings consists of dark suits for men and short cocktail dresses for women. You won't need a tuxedo or long gown.

◆ When visiting churches, women may wear sundresses but should not wear shorts. They don't have to cover their heads.

Meals

Hours and Foods

Breakfast (zakuska): About 7:00 A.M. (most people begin work

at 8:00 or 9:00 A.M.). A typical breakfast is bread and butter, sometimes with either cheese, fruit, or yogurt. Coffee is the most popular beverage.

Lunch (obet): 12:00 to 1:00 P.M. Expect salad or soup, then a meat or fish dish with a vegetable, and then fruit and yogurt or a pastry. Soft drinks usually accompany the meal. In winter, when few fresh vegetables are available, pickled vegetables (peppers, green tomatoes, and cucumbers) are common.

Dinner (vecherya): 7:00 to 8:00 P.M. Enjoy a light, hot meal of soup, bread, and pickled vegetables. At a dinner party, the meal will be similar to *obet*, described above. Before the meal you'll be offered *slivova*, a plum or grape brandy usually served in shotglasses. Bulgarians sip *slivova* instead of drinking it in one gulp, and always eat something with it.

◆ *Slivova* is potent, so be cautious when you drink it. If your hosts press you to drink, be firm (even to the point of being unpleasant) if you don't want to drink a great deal.

Table Manners

◆ Try to arrive at a dinner party a little late—15 minutes is acceptable.

◆ If you're the guest of honor, you'll sit at the middle of the table so everyone can converse with you easily.

◆ Never put your elbows on the table.

◆ Drink wine and/or mineral water with the meal.

◆ Take very small first portions and be prepared to have several helpings. Bulgarians often show hospitality to foreign guests by serving much more than they normally would. If you're on a diet, say so; people are becoming more health conscious and won't be offended.

◆ Take as much bread as you wish. Bulgarians eat bread with every meal and might consume as much as an entire loaf each day.

◆ Sop up gravy with bread if you wish. Just break the bread into pieces, put them on your plate, and use your fork to pull the bread through the gravy.

◆ Don't try to converse during the meal. Enjoy the food as the Bulgarians do and reserve serious discussions for dessert or later.

◆ Smoking between courses is acceptable.

◆ After the meal, you might be offered either European-style instant coffee or espresso. Bulgarians serve coffee black. Your host might provide sugar but probably won't offer milk or cream.

◆ At the end of the evening, don't expect your hosts to signal when it's time for you to leave. If you try to leave, they'll insist you stay longer. If you're using public transportation, however, leave by 11:00 P.M., since mass transit closes down at midnight.

Eating Out

◆ Look for the following types of eating places:

● *Mehahnah* are taverns much like British pubs. You can order both drinks and meals.

● A *restorahnt* is a full-service restaurant.

● A *skahra beera* offers quick meals. The specialties are grilled meats, sausages, cheese, and bread. You'll find these eating places only in small towns and villages, not in cities.

● A s*latkarneetsa* serves ice cream, pastries, sandwiches, coffee, and tea; many also offer beer.

◆ Sofia restaurants offer a variety of cuisines, including French, Italian, Korean, and Japanese.

◆ Self-service restaurants are of two types. In one kind, you tell the cashier what you want and pay for it before you receive the food. In the other, you choose your own food as you go through a cafeteria line and pay at the end.

◆ For Saturday or Sunday dinners at fine restaurants, make reservations more than a few days in advance. These restaurants are completely booked with wedding parties on those days.

◆ In most restaurants, you must seat yourself. If there are no empty tables, join other diners. As a courtesy, ask if you may sit down, but don't feel uncomfortable—it's a common thing to do.

◆ Not all restaurants have menus; in some places the waiter tells you what the choices are. In better restaurants, everything on the menu will be available, but that might not be the case in small restaurants.

Specialties

◆ Bulgarian food features Balkan specialties such as lamb, mutton, cheese, and yogurt.

◆ Try these special foods: *tarator* (a cold soup of sour milk, chopped cucumbers, walnuts, dill, and olive oil); *panagyurishte* (poached eggs with whipped yogurt, butter, and paprika); *gjuvéch* (a stew of onion, eggplant, beans, peas, and peppers); *soupa* (a meat and vegetable stew); *sarmi* (cabbage or grape leaves filled with rice, ground pork, and veal); *meshana skara* (mixed grill); *shishcheta* (pork roasted on a spit); *shopska salata* (a salad of tomatoes, peppers, cucumbers, onions, and white goat's cheese [feta]); *imam bavaldá* (cold eggplant stuffed with onions, carrots, tomatoes, and celery); *haidushki kebab* (lamb grilled with onion); *bánitsa* (flaky pastry filled with cheese); and *kebaches* (chopped meat rolls made of spicy veal and pork and grilled on skewers).

◆ For dessert, try *kisselo mlekó* (a thick, creamy yogurt that also appears in many dishes) and *garash* (sponge cake).

Hotels

◆ The best hotels usually require hard currency—even for drinks.

◆ If the clerk asks for your passport, be prepared to leave it overnight.

◆ When you go out, leave your key at the desk.

◆ Don't expect round-the-clock hot and cold water. Look for a notice with times when water will be available.

◆ Bring along a plug for the sink; many sinks don't have them.

Tipping

◆ *Restaurants:* A service charge is included in the check. If you wish, leave an additional 2–5 leva on the table.

◆ *Porters:* Pay a fee of 1–3 leva per bag.

◆ *Hotel maids:* A tip isn't required or even expected, but if the service has been especially good, leave the equivalent of 50 stotinki per day.

◆ *Taxis:* Give 50 stotinki or 1 lev. The driver, aware that you're a foreigner, might ask for more money, but you don't need to give it.

◆ *Washroom attendants:* Give them 20 stotinki for toilet paper.

Private Homes

◆ Always call before visiting someone. Only very good friends are welcome to drop in.

◆ When visiting, anticipate refreshments—probably preserved fruits, nuts, or cake served with coffee, tea, beer, wine, or *slivova* (plum or grape brandy).

◆ If you're staying with a family, give them your passport so they can register you with the police. If they don't register you immediately, they might get into trouble.

◆ Feel free to go sightseeing on your own. In fact, it's unlikely that a family member will have time to go with you, since most people work during the day. If you would like to have someone show you around, however, ask your hosts; they might be able to find someone to accompany you.

◆ Before you take a bath, ask. The water might have to be heated, or the hot-water system might be turned off for repairs.

◆ Offer to help clean up if you wish, but expect your offer to be refused. As a guest you'll hold a special place of honor.

Gifts: If you're invited to a meal, bring flowers, candy, or wine. The flowers should be wrapped. Don't bring gladioli or calla lilies; they're reserved for solemn events such as weddings and funerals.

◆ If you're staying with a family, bring marking pens in unusual colors (such as silver or copper), coffee beans, blue jeans, cassettes of American music, cigarettes, American liquor, and Parker or Bic ballpoint pens. For a woman you know very well, bring lingerie or stockings.

Business

Hours

Businesses and government offices: 8:00 or 9:00 A.M. to 5:00 or 6:00 P.M., Monday through Friday. Lunch breaks start at noon and last until 1:00 or 2:00 P.M.

Banks: 8:00 to 11:45 A.M., Monday through Friday, and 8:00 to 11:00 A.M. on Saturday.

Stores: 8:30 or 10:00 A.M. to 7:00 or 8:00 P.M., Monday through Saturday.

Business Practices

◆ Cultivate business contacts in Bulgaria. The closer Bulgaria comes to a free-market economy, the more important those contacts will become. More and more people are eager to become entrepreneurs by opening and running privately owned companies.

◆ To find reliable partners, ask your embassy in Sofia for information on the Union of Private Producers. Another source of information is the Bulgarian National Bank/ Bulgarian Foreign Trade Bank, #2 Sofiiska Komuna Street, Sofia, 1000. Phone: 8551.

◆ Another source of contacts: Eastern Europe Business Information Center, Room 7412, U.S. Department of Commerce, Washington, DC 20230. Phone: (202) 377-2645.

◆ Foreign businesswomen will have no difficulty doing business in Bulgaria. However, you will not find Bulgarian businesswomen in high positions.

◆ If you're dealing with older people (those over 50), make an impression by staying in the best hotel and eating in the best restaurants. Young people are less impressed by such status symbols.

◆ English is the most common second language for business. If you're preparing literature or proposals, you need to translate only instructions for complex equipment that will be used by unskilled workers.

◆ To find an interpreter, inquire at your hotel. You'll find many interpreters' bureaus in Sofia and throughout the country.

◆ Bring business cards in English.

◆ Have many copies of proposals and distribute them widely. The more copies you distribute, the better your chances of meeting the right people. You needn't bring the copies from abroad; photocopying facilities are easy to find and inexpensive.

◆ Fax machines are not yet common, but you can find them at some businesses and at main post offices.

Meetings and negotiations: Make appointments with official state businesses by telephone, at least two weeks in advance. Private businesses are much more flexible, so you can wait a little longer with them. People don't take telephone requests seriously, so confirm your appointment with another phone call just before you leave for Bulgaria.

◆ Schedule appointments around 10:00 or 11:00 A.M., or around 2:00 or 3:00 P.M. You might also suggest a business lunch or dinner.

◆ On Saturday, no official state business is done, but private businesspeople might be willing to meet with you.

◆ Be on time for appointments—though Bulgarians might not be.

You'll be offered an aperitif: *slivova* (plum brandy) or vodka. Accept this display of hospitality unless you don't or can't drink.

When you're negotiating with older Bulgarians, be careful how you phrase questions, since they'll say what they think you want to hear. For example, if you say "Can this be delivered by June 15?" they might reply "Yes" even if delivery by that date is impossible. Better phrasing would be "When can this product be delivered?" Younger people, in contrast, are likely to be more frank.

• Time estimates for completion of activities are usually inaccurate.

Expect the pace of business to be *very* slow. One Bulgarian said, "It may be that your grandchildren will have to finish your undertaking in the late twenty-first century."

• Written contracts are common; you should have no difficulty getting one.

Entertainment: Business dinners are more common than business lunches. For casual evenings, people prefer native ethnic restaurants or taverns of the *mehahnah* type (see Eating Out). For official dinners, expensive hotel restaurants are the usual favorite. Restaurant food is extremely expensive for Bulgarians; be understanding if they don't initiate an invitation or if they don't accept your invitation because they would have to reciprocate.

Include your business colleagues' spouses in a dinner invitation if you wish, but don't feel obliged to do so. Invite them only if the meal will be a social occasion, however, not a "working dinner."

Gifts: Give whiskey, American-made cigarettes, high-quality pens, toilet water for men, or perfume for women.

Holidays & Celebrations

Holidays:
New Year's Day (January 1); Day of Liberation (March 3); Women's Day (March 8); Easter Sunday; Day of Bulgarian Culture (May 24); Christmas (December 25).

◆ An invitation to celebrate Christmas means Christmas Eve.

◆ Expect lively festivities on New Year's Eve and New Year's Day. At that time people have Christmas trees and exchange gifts. At 8:00 or 9:00 P.M. on New Year's Eve, families feast on roast suckling pig or turkey. At midnight, everyone drinks wine or champagne and exchanges kisses.

◆ On March 1, people give each other good luck charms as a springtime ritual. The red-and-white string or silk charms are sold at kiosks and on the streets.

Transportation

Public Transport
Mass transit:
In Sofia, buy interchangeable tickets for

buses, streetcars, and trolleys. They cost 6 stotinki and are sold at kiosks near the stops. The kiosks also sell passes good for a month and packets of 10 or 20 tickets.

◆ When you get on the vehicle, cancel your ticket in the machine. Keep your ticket; there are frequent inspections.

◆ Long-distance buses are uncomfortable and don't match Western standards: the buses lack air-conditioning, run on unreliable schedules, are crowded, and lack spare parts, which means you may be stuck for hours if there's a breakdown. Renting a car is much better than taking a bus.

◆ If you decide to take a bus, buy a ticket 1 to 10 days in advance at the bus station or at a travel bureau. Since seats are reserved, it's important to reserve early during holiday periods.

◆ For a train journey, avoid a long line on the day of your trip by buying a ticket in advance at a railway ticket office. You'll find one in each major city. All medium- and long-distance trains offer first and second class, as well as limited food service. Overnight trains have first- and second-class sleeping cars.

Taxis: To get a taxi, phone for one, hail one on the street, or go to a taxi stand.

Driving

◆ Get an International Driver's License before driving in Bulgaria, and carry it with you when you're driving.

◆ Seat belts are required for front-seat occupants. Children under twelve must sit in the back seat.

◆ Study the Cyrillic alphabet, in which Bulgarian is written, so you'll be able to read street signs.

◆ Speed limits are 60 kph in built-up areas and 80 kph elsewhere, except on highways, where the limit in 120 kph.

◆ Don't sound your horn after dark and avoid using it at all in towns.

◆ Most highways are good, but be cautious when driving at night. Many unlit farm vehicles use the roads.

◆ Gas stations are fairly common on main roads but are scarce elsewhere. Free maps showing gas stations are available from Balkantourist (the state tourist office).

◆ If you're stopped for a traffic violation, expect to pay a heavy fine.

◆ Don't drive if you've had even one drink. You'll be charged with drunk driving if you have *any* alcohol in your blood. The law is strictly enforced.

Legal Matters & Safety

◆ When you arrive in Bulgaria, you'll fill out a yellow card with information about yourself and the  purpose of your trip. Keep this card; you must produce it when you leave or face a major delay in your departure.

◆ If you bring in costly objects, such as a camera or a tape recorder, a note will be made on your passport. Have these items with you when leaving the country, or you'll have to pay duty on them.

◆ It's illegal to take out items of significant folkloric value, such as costumes or old musical instruments.

◆ Bulgaria has no legal age limit on drinking, nor are there any restrictions on when you can drink. However, Bulgarians frown on young people drinking, and many shops will refuse to sell or serve alcohol to minors.

◆ Crime has increased since Bulgaria's liberation. Women should not go out alone at night.

Key Phrases

Below we give each word in English and its pronunciation—but not its spelling—in Bulgarian. Since the Bulgarian language uses the Cyrillic alphabet, a Bulgarian wouldn't recognize the word printed in the Roman alphabet (and you probably wouldn't recognize it printed in the Cyrillic alphabet).

English	Pronunciation of Bulgarian
Good morning	DO-bro oo-tro
Good day	Do-bur dehn
Good evening	DO-bur VEH-cher
Please	MOL-yah
Thank you	mehr-SEE*
You're welcome	MOL-yah
Yes	dah
No	neh
Mr., Sir (talking about someone)	gos-po-DIN
Mr., Sir (talking directly to someone)	gos-po-DI-NEH
Mrs., Madam (talking about someone)	go-spo-ZHA
Mrs., Madam (talking directly to someone)	go-spo-ZHO
Miss	go-spo-ZHI-tza
Excuse me	eez-vee-NAY-tay
Good-bye	Dough-VEEZH-dah-nay
I don't understand.	nay rahz-bee-RAHM
I don't speak Bulgarian.	nay go-VOR-yah boo-GAHR-skee
Does anyone speak English?	go-VO-ree lee NYAH-koi ahn-GLEE-skee

*Bulgarians use the French word *merci*.

Czechoslovakia

Shakespeare, who often took liberties with historical fact, once set a scene on "the seacoast of Bohemia," Bohemia being the old name for the Czech part of Czechoslovakia. A traveler in search of that seacoast is in for a disappointment, because Bohemia—indeed the whole of Czechoslovakia—has no seacoast. It does, however, have abundant, beautiful mountains and a countryside awash with fruit trees. It also has, in Prague, one of the most beautifully preserved medieval cities in Europe. To visit Prague Castle or Old Town Square is to pay a visit to the fourteenth century.

Travelers to Czechoslovakia might not realize initially that the country consists of two republics, the Czech Republic and the Slovak Republic, joined together in a federation, each with its own state government and language. Although the customs and language are similar, it's best to speak Czech in the Czech Republic and Slovak in the Slovak Republic.

Greetings

♦ When you arrive at or leave any meeting—formal or informal, social or business— shake hands with everyone.

♦ Women extend their hands first when greeting men, and older people extend their hands first to young people.

♦ At formal parties, don't talk to someone unless you've been introduced. At informal parties, go ahead and introduce yourself if your hosts seem busy.

♦ Never use a Czech's first name until he or she has used yours. Younger people tend to use first names more readily than older people.

♦ Among the older generation, German is the most widely spoken second language. People in tourist areas usually speak English. Almost everyone under 55 knows Russian, but they don't like to speak it.

Conversation

♦ Good topics of conversation: sports, especially soccer and ice hockey; politics; traveling; music (including the Czech composers Dvořák and Smetana); or your impressions of Czechoslovakia.

♦ Don't ask people if they were dissidents under the Communist regime; let them bring up the subject.

♦ Don't joke with people unless you know them very well.

♦ Feel free to ask questions about job or family, even if you've just met a person.

♦ Czechs might ask you very personal questions when they first meet you—even how much you make. You can evade this question tactfully by saying something like "Just enough for my family's needs."

♦ Don't worry about feeling like an outsider. Czechs are not clannish and, in fact, will court you; they're tremendously interested in talking with foreigners and are somewhat in awe of them.

♦ Don't compliment people effusively or they'll think you're insincere.

♦ People leave others much less "personal space" than they do in the U.S. It's insulting to back away when someone stands very close to you while conversing.

Money

♦ The unit of currency is the koruna (plural koruny, abbreviated Kčs), made up of 100 halers.

In English, a koruna is called a crown.

♦ Coins come in denominations of 5, 10, 20, and 50 halers and 1, 2, 5, and 10 koruny.

♦ Notes come in denominations of 10, 20, 50, 100, 500, and 1,000 koruny.

♦ People will approach you constantly on the street with offers to change money. *Don't do it.* You might receive counterfeit, old, or Yugoslav currency, all of which are worthless. Changing money on the black market is not worth the risk (a six-month jail sentence or a penalty), since the rate of exchange is no better than at officially sanctioned exchanges.

♦ Save your proofs of exchange. When you leave the country, you'll need these receipts to change your Czech koruny into dollars. If you don't have them, your only option is to open a "bank account" in Czechoslovakia, where the money will be held for three years. (This system is intended to prevent people from changing money on the black market.)

Telephones

♦ Look for public telephones in train and Metro subway stations and on streets everywhere.

(Many people use public telephones because the waiting list for private phones is so long. However, most of the public telephones don't work.)

♦ There are two types of public phones: one is for local calls only; the other, larger type is for both local and international calls. You'll need lots of change for an international call.

♦ Public phones take 1- and 5-koruna coins.

♦ The most common type of phone has a coin holder on the outside. Place the coin in the holder, but hold it with your finger while you dial the number. When your party answers, or when you hear the word "MIN-tse," push the coin in immediately. If you want to speak for more than three minutes, deposit another coin in the slot as soon as your party answers.

♦ Other phones have a digital screen that registers the amount of money deposited. Insert one coin and dial; when you are connected, the coin will drop and, after a short gap, you can start to talk. (This system sounds simple enough but doesn't always work in practice.) If you hear "MIN-tse," you must deposit a coin to extend your call. If the coin box is full, you'll be cut off.

♦ To make an international call, you can use a public phone (see above), go to the post office (where you book the call, pay a deposit in advance, and wait for the operator to call you to a booth), or place the call from your hotel, which may be more expensive but is more convenient if you don't speak Czech.

◆ The easiest and best way to make both local and international phone calls is from the post office.

◆ People answer the phone by saying "PRO-scem."

◆ Emergency numbers are as follows:

Police	158
Fire	150
Medical emergency	155

In Public

◆ Be patient in lines. Don't ask salespeople to hurry or you'll seem aggressive and rude.

◆ Don't be loud or boisterous in restaurants or in other public places.

◆ Be discreet with your money. Don't flash it around. What might be a small amount to you—500 koruny, for example, worth about $20 U.S.—might be a fortune to a Czech.

◆ If people seem cold initially, don't be put off. They've lived for years constantly afraid to trust anyone.

◆ Bargain only with street vendors. Don't try to bargain in shops, stores, or markets, where prices are fixed.

◆ The practice in many shops is to make a selection, go to the cashier and pay, and then bring your receipt back to the original salesperson.

◆ When paying a cashier in a shop, put your money on the counter. Wait for the cashier to put your change on the counter, don't extend your hand for it.

◆ A common phrase in Czech translates as "Everything is negotiable." That sentiment permeates Czech society—nothing is written in stone. For example, if a waiter says "We don't serve wine after 10:00 P.M.," be polite but persistent and you might get served anyway.

◆ If you go to a concert in a church, don't be the first to applaud. In some churches, people don't applaud at concerts.

◆ Don't take photographs in museums or art galleries. Also avoid taking pictures of policemen, military installations, airports, and railroad stations.

◆ Public toilets are scarce, but can be found in large hotels, restaurants, railroad stations, and in separate buildings in the center of town.

◆ Many public toilets have signs that say *W.C.* Some men's rooms are labeled *Muži;* women's rooms, *Ženy.*

◆ Most public toilets are dirty. Bring tissues with you, because in most of them you'll encounter an attendant who will offer two tiny, flimsy pieces of toilet paper for 1–2 korunas. (You'll have to pay the koruna even if you bring your own, though, since it's the "price" of using the toilet.) Few toilets have towels on which to dry your hands.

Dress

◆ For casual dress, jeans and shorts are acceptable even in cities.

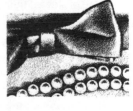

◆ For business, men should wear suits and ties, and women should wear suits or dresses—even though Czechs sometimes wear blue jeans.

◆ For dining at a home or in a small restaurant, men should wear pants, shirts, and sweaters, and women should wear dresses, skirts and blouses, or dressy pants. In better restaurants, men should wear suits and ties.

◆ For an opening at the National Theater, men should wear jackets, shirts, and ties, and women should wear skirts or dresses. For an ordinary performance, anything from pants to suits is appropriate.

◆ For a formal ball or the opening of a play, opera, or ballet, men should wear tuxedos or dark suits, and women should wear long dresses.

Meals

Hours and Foods

Breakfast (snídaně): 6:00 A.M. (since many people begin work at 7:00 A.M.). Rolls, butter, jam, and tea or coffee are standard fare. Sometimes eggs or sausage are served.

Lunch (oběd): 11:30 A.M. to 2:00 P.M. Usually the main meal of the day, lunch begins with soup, followed by meat, potatoes or dumplings, a vegetable (in winter, usually canned; fresh green vegetables are rare and expensive), and dessert, usually cakes or a compote of stewed fruits.

Dinner (večeře): 6:00 to 7:00 P.M. At a dinner party, slivovitz (plum brandy), becherovka (herb brandy), or borovička (juniper brandy) might be served before the meal. The meal itself features a main course such as roast pork, sauerkraut, and dumplings. Dessert might be apple strudel,

fruit, cake, or cookies. Regular, Turkish, or espresso coffee follows the meal. If lunch was a full meal, however, supper will be lighter—cheese or meat sandwiches and milk. A family dinner is typically the lighter meal.

Breaks: People break at 10:00 A.M. for sandwiches or hot sausages and yogurt. At 4:00 P.M., Czechs eat sandwiches and have regular, Turkish, or espresso coffee.

Table Manners

◆ Try to be on time when invited to a meal, though Czechs might be late.

◆ Don't pick up your glass until everyone has been served a drink. If the dinner is a special occasion, toasts will probably be proposed; feel free to offer one yourself. To toast, say "nah ZDRAH-vee," which means "To your health."

◆ Guests are usually served first, but sometimes the oldest woman at the table is served first.

◆ Food is usually served in the kitchen, so your plate will probably appear with food already on it. Often the person who prepared the meal does not eat with the guests.

◆ Expect a hot meal, even in hot weather. Czechs aren't fond of cold meals such as salads.

◆ Before you eat, say "DO-broo choot" ("ch" is pronounced like a gutteral "k," as in the Scottish word "loch"), which means "Have a good appetite."

◆ Czechs are very hospitable and will press you to eat more. The first time you are offered a second helping, say "No, thank you" to be polite. Your hostess will then say "Please do," and you are expected to accept.

◆ Czechs smoke continuously during a meal.

◆ To show you're finished, place your utensils together at one side on the plate. To signal that you're just taking a break, cross your knife and fork on the plate.

◆ If you drink coffee at someone's house, it may already be heavily sweetened. Let your hosts know if you would prefer it unsweetened. Watch out for the thick grounds at the bottom of the cup. In restaurants, you'll need to add your own sugar. Stir in the sugar, then wait for the grounds to settle before drinking.

Eating Out

◆ Try different types of eating places for a variety of foods and atmospheres:

- A *bufet* serves fast meals and snacks and usually has no place to sit.

- A *cukrárna* offers pastries, ice cream, and coffee.

- A *hospoda* is primarily for drinking, but most also offer good meals.

- A *kavárna* offers alcoholic drinks, coffee, sandwiches, and pastries, but no warm meals.

- A *koliba* is an ethnic restaurant that serves regional specialties, such as Slovak, Moravian, Hungarian, and Polish.

- A *pivnice* (beer hall—the beer is not particularly potent) tends to be "clubby." You have to visit one a few times before people become friendly. Wait for a free table; don't join others unless they invite you to do so. Beer halls serve steamed or grilled sausages with bread or eggs. Most are associated with old breweries, and meals are secondary to drinking.

- A *restaurace* is a regular restaurant that serves full meals.

- A *vinárna* is a wine cellar, where you'll be served a glass of wine from a barrel. You can get either snacks or full meals there. They usually open in the late afternoon.

- A *zahradní restaurace* is a garden restaurant that offers beer or wine with your meal.

◆ If you are on business at a factory and are invited to eat lunch there, accept—the food is usually both good and inexpensive.

◆ Hotels and pubs sell bottled liquor and soft drinks to take out.

◆ Before you make your meal plans, check to make sure the restaurant you want to go to is open. Some close for all or part of the weekend, and nontourist restaurants often close by 8:00 P.M.

◆ Make reservations ahead of time; there is a notorious shortage of places to eat.

◆ The rating of each restaurant is written in Roman numerals on the menu posted near the entrance. The best restaurants are rated one; the lowest, four. At fourth-class restaurants, expect to stand while you eat.

◆ When you enter a restaurant, be sure to check your coat. The charge is 1 koruna. If you leave your coat on a chair, the waiter will tell you to check it.

◆ If a restaurant is crowded, look for an empty seat at an occupied table, ask whether it is free, and sit down. No one will be surprised or upset; in fact, they might strike up a conversation with you.

◆ Service has improved considerably in recent years, but you still may find it poor or have a long wait. Complaining or demanding will only make the situation worse.

♦ To summon the waiter, say "PAH-neh vrch-NEE" ("ch" is pronounced like a gutteral "k," as in the Scottish word "loch").

♦ When you order, the check will be left at the table. To pay, notify your waiter and a cashier will come to the table.

♦ Some restaurants do not permit smoking at lunch or dinner times. Other restaurants, however, permit smoking and don't separate smokers from nonsmokers. Smoking is not permitted in a *bufet* or a *cukrárna*.

Specialties

♦ *Vepřová* (roast pork and dumplings) are very popular in Czechoslovakia (in fact, roast pork is the national dish of the Czech Republic). Also try *slaneček* (salty herring); *sardinky* (sardines); *zavináč* (stuffed rolled herring); *husa* (roast goose); *svíčková na smetaně* (filet of beef with sour cream); *párky* (long, thin sausages eaten in pairs); *jelita* (sausages made of blood, rice, and liver); *kapustnica* (sauerkraut soup); *zemiakové placky* (potato pancakes); *bryndzové halušky* (sheep's milk cheese dumplings); and *houskové knedlíky* (bread dumplings served with almost every dish— soups, stews, and even dessert).

♦ For dessert, try *koláč* (turnovers filled with jam, poppy seeds, nuts, or cottage cheese); *palačinky* (crepe-like pancakes with jam or chocolate on top); and *pischinger torte* (a cake made of wafers, chocolate meringue, and chocolate frosting).

Hotels

♦ Make reservations several months in advance, if possible, especially for visits during festivals or congresses. Hotel rooms are in short supply, and tourism has surged since the 1989 "Velvet Revolution." You can't just land in a city and expect to find a room.

♦ If no hotel rooms are available, contact Čedok, the national travel agency, which might be able to find you a room in a private home. If you arrive in Czechoslovakia without a room, go to Čedok's main office in central Prague.

♦ Several private companies can arrange accommodations in private homes at a fraction of the cost of a hotel room. These companies have offices at the main railroad station (Hlavní Nádraží) and near Main Square (Václavské Náměsti), the center of town.

♦ Hotels are ranked from *A* to *C*. *A* denotes a luxury hotel with such amenities as minibars and satellite TV. Hotels rated *C* are strictly no-frills—you might find just one small bar of soap.

♦ If you're feeling adventurous, try one of the three *botels*, riverboats converted into hotels and moored in the Vltava River.

♦ When you check in to a hotel, leave your passport at the desk. You'll probably get it back within a couple of hours.

♦ When you go out, be sure to leave your key at the desk.

Tipping

♦ *Restaurants:* In all restaurants and pubs, leave 10–15 percent. Give the tip to the cashier who collects the money. Don't leave it on the table.

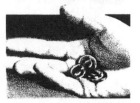

♦ *Porters:* Give 5–10 koruny.

♦ *Hotel maids:* Leave soap, tea, coffee, lipstick, or pantyhose for maids. They'll appreciate it more than money.

♦ *Taxis:* Tip 10–15 percent of the fare.

♦ *Cloakroom attendants:* It's customary to leave some small change in addition to the cloakroom charge.

♦ *Washroom attendants:* You must give the attendants a 1-koruna fee.

♦ People appreciate tips in hard currency (especially dollars or marks).

Private Homes

♦ Set aside Sunday as the day for visiting. Feel free to drop in at any time of day except near mealtimes; 2:00 to 5:00 P.M. is good.

♦ Before you enter someone's home, remove your shoes. Usually your hosts will provide you with slippers.

♦ During a visit you'll be offered homemade cakes, sweets, and Turkish coffee.

♦ If you stay at someone's home for several days, offer to do some of the food shopping. Since most men and women work, they must shop in the evening, and they'll be grateful for your help with this chore.

♦ Water might be turned off in apartments at any time. Sometimes there might be cold water but not hot.

Gifts: If you're invited to dinner in a home, bring flowers (if you can obtain them) or a bottle of wine, whiskey, or cognac.

♦ Czechs will go out of their way to welcome you. They might insist that you take their beds (while they sleep on the floor) or might prepare special foods too expensive for everyday meals. Be sure to reciprocate by taking your hosts to a nice restaurant or giving them a special gift. Food is most welcome—particularly fruit or chocolates—but any scarce item will do.

♦ If you stay with a family, bring toys of any kind for children and blue jeans for teenagers. Bring cosmetics or clothing for women you know well. Other welcome gifts: ballpoint pens, cigarette lighters, American cigarettes, pocket calculators, anything electronic, portable cassette players, tapes for cassette players (anyone under 40 will appreciate rock-and-roll cassettes of groups such as the Beatles or the Rolling Stones), rechargeable battery kits, fancy tea, cocoa, chewing gum, and T-shirts.

Business

Hours

Businesses and government offices: 8:30 A.M. to 5:15 P.M., Monday through Fri-

day. Business is conducted from 9:00 A.M. to 5:00 P.M., with a lunch break from noon until 2:00 P.M. Most businesses and shops shut down during lunchtime. Sometimes businesses will close for no apparent reason.

Banks: Bank hours vary. They may open at 8:00 or 9:00 A.M. and close anywhere from 2:00 to 6:00 P.M. Many close from 11:30 A.M. to 1:30 P.M. for lunch. Those that do usually reopen in the afternoon. On Saturday, banks open from 8:00 A.M. to noon.

Stores: 9:00 A.M. to 6:00 P.M., Monday through Friday. On Saturday some shops are open until noon; others are closed all day. On weekdays some small shops close between noon and 2:00 P.M. for lunch, and some shops in Prague close between noon and 4:00 P.M.

Business Practices

◆ Seek contacts through your country's embassy in Prague, Czech government organizations (such as the Ministries of Finance, Education, and International Affairs), or academic institutions.

◆ If you're interested in a long-term business relationship, be prepared to make several trips.

◆ Avoid business trips to Czechoslovakia from mid-July to mid-August, when most people vacation.

◆ A business letter to a company should be addressed to the firm, not to an individual there, so it will be opened immediately, even if the individual is away.

◆ Czech organizations usually provide interpreters. If you don't trust their interpreters' reliability, bring your own. German is the most common second language among businesspeople. Among younger people, English is the most common second language, but it is not spoken well. You will need translated versions of your presentations.

◆ Business cards are essential. You'll make a better impression if your cards are in English on one side and in Czech or Slovak on the other, depending on where you're doing business.

◆ Czechoslovakian women aren't at all liberated; however, foreign women can be successful in business because they're regarded as a novelty. For best results, businesswomen should be very feminine and not aggressive.

◆ Staying at the best hotels doesn't impress people. (However, you might not be comfortable in any but a first- or second-class hotel.)

◆ Fax machines are common, but the telephone system is so poor that telexes are safer.

◆ The frequent problems with the telephone system mean you can't be sure of communicating with someone at a precise time, as you would in Western Europe. (Don't say, for example, "I'll call you at 2:00 P.M.," because you might not be able to get through until the next day).

◆ Photocopying shops are available but often have very long lines. Make copies only for people with whom you will be dealing directly.

Meetings and negotiations: How far in advance you need to plan a visit depends on your level of contacts. If you're meeting with someone in your embassy to arrange contacts, plan three to four weeks ahead. If you already have a contact in the country, you can usually arrange meetings in a day or two. Once you're in the country, meetings can be impromptu.

◆ If you're making appointments yourself from the U.S., allow one month by letter and two weeks by telex.

◆ You may not want to suggest an appointment before 9:00 A.M. or try to arrange a business breakfast; such early meetings are uncommon in Czechoslovakia.

♦ Be punctual. Czechs may not be, but you should be.

♦ The country's current hectic business and political climate means that people sometimes miss business appointments. You might arrive for a meeting to find a message asking you to wait an hour or more. Don't schedule several appointments close together on the same day, in case you have to wait.

♦ Men who are meeting a businesswoman for the first time should present flowers.

♦ At business meetings, your hosts will offer you drinks and coffee. Accept something and if a toast is offered, return it.

♦ Keep your presentation simple. People are only beginning to understand a market-driven economy. Don't bring complicated visuals. Most Czechs are still working with manual typewriters, so clear typewritten material is fine.

♦ Take proposals from Czechs with a grain of salt. They might say they can do something that is actually only a possibility. And they might say "Of course, we can do that—no problem" when they aren't able to do it.

♦ Decisions are made by a few people at the top. You might meet with people at various levels, however, before you meet with the company's director.

♦ The speed of business depends on how badly the Czechs want what you are offering. If they are really desperate for your product or service, negotiations will move rapidly.

♦ If Czech businesspeople seem overly cautious, it's because they must be absolutely certain they aren't violating any of their country's laws.

♦ Czechs aren't enthusiastic about written contracts, but try to get them anyway. If there are changes later, they are usually by mutual agreement. The Czechs will apologize about the changes and will try to involve you in making them.

♦ Offices have been swamped since the Revolution. People intend to be reliable but might miss deadlines because of the sheer volume of work. Follow up with phone calls or telexes.

Entertainment: Czech business associates have little contact outside the office. Having a meeting in a restaurant or hotel often takes advance preparation, so don't expect or offer any spontaneous invitations (such as "Let's have dinner tonight").

♦ Entertain only the people with whom you are negotiating.

♦ Make sure you have restaurant reservations *before* you extend invitations, because of the restaurant shortage.

♦ Treat people to restaurants that specialize in Czech food. People are proud of their local cuisine. If you issue the invitation, ask your Czech guests for suggestions about restaurants.

♦ Spouses—both foreign and Czech—are seldom invited to business lunches but may be invited to evening social events.

♦ If you're a businesswoman entertaining Czech businessmen, and the headwaiter speaks English, arrange in advance to pay for the meal without a check coming to the table. Another option is to excuse yourself toward the end of the meal and pay then.

Gifts: Businesspeople appreciate electronic items such as pocket radios and solar calculators. They also enjoy high-quality chocolates and candies.

Holidays & Celebrations

Holidays:
New Year's
Day (January 1);
Easter Monday;
Labor Day (May
1); National Day
(May 9); the Feast

of Sts. Cyril and Methodius (July 5); the
Death of Jan Hus (in the Czech Republic
only, July 6); Anniversary of the Founding
of Czechoslovakia (October 28); Christmas
(December 25); and St. Stephen's Day
(December 26).

♦ People celebrate the feast of their name
saint with parties and dancing. If you know
someone who is celebrating a name-saint's
day, bring a small gift. (All the saints' days
are listed on calendars.)

Transportation

**Public
Transport**

Mass transit:
Public trans-
portation is
excellent and
widely used.

♦ Buy tickets (called *jizdenky*) for the bus,
streetcar, or Metro at kiosks. If you exit the
Metro line or change your mode of transportation, you must buy another ticket.

♦ If you stay inside the Metro you can travel
on several lines with the same ticket for a
limited time.

♦ A 4-koruna ticket gives you a full ride on
any bus, Metro, or streecar in Prague. In
other cities, a ticket usually costs 2–3
korunas. Keep a supply of small change if
you're riding the Metro, since some ticket
halls have automated machines and provide
no facilities for making change.

♦ In Metro stations, keep to the right when
descending or ascending stairs or escalators.
You'll anger people if you don't observe this
custom.

♦ On the Metro, after purchasing your
ticket, insert it with the number grid facing
down in a slot in the orange machine at the
entrance. The machine prints the time and
station.

♦ Either on the Metro platform or on trains,
Metro police (in plain clothes) may ask to
see your ticket. They will flash an orange
and white porcelain badge. If you don't
have a ticket, the fine is 100 koruny,
payable on the spot. The Metro police
speak only Czech.

♦ Buses and streetcars have a little machine
mounted on a pole inside the door. Put
your ticket in, with the number grid facing
you, and pull the little collar toward you.
The machine will punch holes in the number grid.

♦ On buses or streetcars, signal that you
want to get off by pressing the button above
the exit door just before the vehicle reaches
your station—drivers do not automatically
stop at stations.

Taxis: Taxis are hard to find. Have your
hotel call one for you, especially at night.

♦ When you get into a taxi, establish the
price. Often taxi drivers try to charge foreigners double or quadruple the correct
fare. If you ask for a receipt, they will
charge the legitimate fare. Some taxi drivers
use meters.

Driving

♦ Have an International Driver's License as
well as your U.S. license on you at all times.

♦ Seat belts are mandatory for all occupants
of a car.

◆ Some traffic signs are unusual, so if you plan to drive, request a list of traffic signs at a gas station or when entering the country.

◆ The speed limit in built-up areas is 60 kph, on other roads is 90 kph, and on motorways is 110 kph.

◆ In Prague, blowing your horn is illegal unless you are warning another driver of impending danger.

◆ The roads between major cities are long stretches of good, straight two-lane highway.

◆ Gas stations are scarce, especially inside cities. Fill up whenever you can.

◆ Never leave valuables in your car.

◆ Parking is limited to one side of the street on certain days and at certain hours.

◆ If you're stopped for a traffic violation, pay your fine immediately. The fine could range from 20 to 500 koruny, depending on the infraction and the leniency of the police. If you don't have enough money with you at the time, you must pay the fine before leaving the country.

◆ Don't have even one drink if you're going to drive. Drunk-driving laws are strictly enforced.

Legal Matters & Safety

◆ When you enter the country, bringing food, clothing, or electronic equipment for gifts won't cause problems at customs.

◆ If you're staying in Czechoslovakia for more than 30 days, register with the police. If you're staying at a hotel, the staff will take care of this.

◆ To buy art works or antiques to take home with you, visit one of the many branches of the Tuzex Shops or Artia Publishing House. Keep your sales slip to show at customs when you leave.

◆ Crime has increased since the Revolution. Nevertheless, the streets are relatively safe by American standards. Physical violence is rare. Guard against pickpockets, however; they work in groups, jostling you, and they often use children as distractions.

◆ Some cafes are centers for prostitution and criminal activity. Get advice on safe places to dine.

◆ Women should not smile at strange men or make eye contact if they aren't interested in pursuing a relationship.

◆ Women are generally not safe walking alone after dark.

Key Phrases

English	Czech	Pronunciation
Good morning	Dobré ráno	DO-breh RAH-no
Good day	Dobrý den	DO-bree DEN
Good evening	Dobrý večer	DO-bree VEH-cher
Please	Prosím	PRO-seem
Thank you	Děkuji	deh-KU-yee
You're welcome	Rádo se stalo	RAH-do say STAH-lo
Yes	Ano	AH-no
No	Ne	neh
Mr., Sir	Pane	PAH-neh
Mrs., Madam	Paní	PAH-nee
Miss	Slečna	SLEHCH-nah
Excuse me	Promiňte	pro-MEEN-tay
Good-bye	Nashledanou	nahsh-lay DAH-noo
I don't understand.	Nerozumím.	ne-ro-zum-EEM
I don't speak Czech.	Nemluvím česky.	nem-LOO-veem CHES-kee
Does anyone here speak English?	Mluvíte někdo anglicky?	MLOO-vee-teh NEK-doe ahn-GLIT-skee

English	Slovak	Pronunciation
Good morning	Dobré rano	DO-brah RAH-no
Good day	Dobrý deň	DO-bree DYEN
Good evening	Dobry večer	DO-bree VYEH-cher
Please	Prosím	PRO-seem
Thank you	Ďakuyem	dyah-koo-YEM
You're welcome	Nech sa páči	nyech* sah PAH-chee
Yes	Áno	AH-no
No	Nie	nyeh
Mr., Sir	Pán	pahn
Mrs., Madam	Pani	PAH-nee
Miss	Slečna	SLECH-nah
Excuse me	Prepáčte	preh-PAHCH-tyeh
Good-bye	Do videnia	do vee-DEN-yah
I don't understand.	Nerozumiem.	nyeh-ro-zoo-MYEM
I don't speak Slovak.	Nehovorím po slovensky.	neh-ho-vo-reem po slo-VEN-ski
Does anyone speak English?	Hovori niekto po anglicky?	ho-vo-REE NYEG-toe po ahn-GLEET-ski

*"ch" is pronounced like a gutteral "k," as in the Scottish word "loch."

Denmark

If any people have mastered the art of living in simple comfort and beauty, it's the Danes. Consider Danish furniture and porcelain: their beauty derives from their very simplicity.

Danes have also mastered the art of being efficient without being cold and being good managers without seeming hurried.

Since the country relies on imported goods more than the other Scandinavian countries do, you'll probably find it more cosmopolitan than Sweden or Norway.

Greetings

◆ When you are introduced to someone in either a business or a social setting, rise and shake hands. Looking at the other person, nod and say "hello" (in English) or "Good day" (see Key Phrases).

◆ When you meet or leave someone you know, shake hands heartily.

◆ Feel free to introduce yourself.

◆ If your Danish acquaintance uses first names, feel free to do the same.

Conversation

◆ Most people speak English. In hotels, restaurants, bars, museums, and tourist offices, English is almost as common as Danish.

◆ Good topics of conversation: food, what you like about the city you're staying in, your own home town or area, or current issues in the news.

◆ Topics to avoid: income, religion, or any other personal subject, such as a divorce.

◆ Don't comment on someone's clothes, even with a compliment; such personal remarks are considered odd.

Money

◆ The unit of Danish currency is the krone (plural kroner; abbreviated DKr), made up of 100 øre.

◆ Coins come in denominations of 25 øre (with a hole in the middle), 50 øre, and 1, 5, 10, and 20 kroner. Recent additions are a silver 5-krone coin and a gold 20-krone coin.

◆ Notes come in denominations of 50, 100, 500, and 1,000 kroner.

Telephones

◆ Look for public telephones in restaurants, hotels, train stations, and post offices. You will also find a few telephone booths on the streets.

◆ To use a public phone, lift the receiver

and insert a 1-krone piece for a 2-minute local call.

◆ When you hear a beep from a public phone, your money has run out. Deposit more to continue the call.

◆ You can make collect calls from public phones.

◆ Telephone cards are just being introduced in Denmark.

◆ To make a long-distance call, go to the post office.

◆ When you use a telephone directory, note that the following letters are at the end of the alphabet: Å, AE, and Ø.

◆ Danes answer the phone by stating their name or their phone number.

◆ The Emergency Number to summon the police, the fire department, or an ambulance is **000.** (You don't need coins to call 000 from a public phone.)

In Public

◆ If you want to meet members of the opposite sex, go to a restaurant that features dancing. (This applies to women as well as men.)

◆ Danes commonly go to public baths. If you decide to try one, you can enjoy a sauna before your bath and a massage after it, if you like. When you enter the building, buy tickets for the facilities you want to use. You can get towels and soap too. The baths are in rows of private compartments, and the saunas are communal by sex.

◆ Look for public toilets on streets. The sign

on men's rooms says *Maend* and on women's, *Kvinder.*

◆ Be sure to ask people's permission before photographing them.

Dress

◆ Even in the summer, prepare for a cool, rainy climate. Bring a lined raincoat.

◆ For casual occasions, men should wear slacks and sport shirts; women, slacks and shirts or sweaters.

◆ For business, men should wear sport jackets or suits and ties, with neatly pressed pants and polished shoes. Women should wear suits or dresses, and heels.

◆ Businessmen should consider bringing a tuxedo and businesswomen a cocktail dress, because Danish senior businesspeople host more black-tie dinners than those in any other country.

◆ If you're invited to a casual dinner, or go to a casual restaurant, feel free to wear clean jeans.

◆ At a more formal dinner party, or at elegant restaurants, men wear jackets and ties, and women wear dresses or blouses with skirts or dressy pants.

◆ To theater events and openings, men should wear a dark suit, and women should wear a cocktail dress.

◆ On beaches, people change into their bathing suits using a towel as a cover. At many beaches and pools, you'll find women topless, and sometimes both men and women will be completely nude. Danes accept this nudity as normal.

Meals

Hours and Foods

Breakfast (morgenmad): 8:00 A.M. Typical fare is cereal, *ymer* (a type of yogurt), bread or hard rolls, cheese, soft-boiled eggs, butter, marmalade, and tea, coffee, or milk.

Lunch (frokost): 12:00 to 2:00 P.M. Open-faced sandwiches on thin rye bread with a variety of toppings (cheese, herring) are standard fare at lunch. The usual drinks are beer, soft drinks, or milk, followed by coffee after the meal.

Dinner (middag): 6:00 to 8:00 P.M. A formal meal begins with soup, followed by a fish dish, then meat, potatoes (usually boiled), and cooked vegetables. Wine is served with the meal. If a salad is served, it usually comes with the meat course. The dinner ends with cheese and fruit, then dessert, then coffee and sometimes brandy and cognac. After that, hosts might offer after-dinner drinks such as scotch and soda or gin and tonic.

♦ A less formal dinner might start with sandwiches and beer or consist only of a main course and dessert. Sometimes the sandwiches are served with *akvavit,* an alcohol made from potatoes and served ice cold with a beer chaser.

Breaks: Danes take a coffee break at 9:00 or 10:00 A.M., a tea break at 3:00 P.M. and, often, an evening snack of pastries or fruit at 10:00 P.M.

Table Manners

♦ If you're invited to dinner in a home, be *punctual*—not even five minutes late. There will probably be no before-dinner cocktail hour; you will be seated in the dining room immediately.

♦ The host and hostess will sit at either end of the table, with the guest of honor seated next to the host.

♦ Don't taste the wine (or any other alcohol) until the host makes the first toast.

♦ Before you take the first sip of wine, lift your glass and look around at everyone. After you've tasted the wine, look around at everyone again.

♦ Guests can propose subsequent toasts. If you're the guest of honor, propose a toast by tapping your glass with a spoon. Say "Thank you for having the dinner in my honor."

♦ Serve yourself from platters of food as they go around the table. It's important to try everything, but take small portions the first time around. The platters will be passed around more than once, and it's an insult not to take seconds of at least some dishes.

♦ Smoking during the meal is acceptable.

♦ Don't leave food on your plate. If you didn't care for a particular dish, however, you need not take seconds of it.

♦ During dessert, the man seated to the left of the hostess should propose a toast to her.

♦ To show you've finished eating, place the knife and fork (tines down) side by side, vertically, on the plate.

♦ Expect a long, slow dinner with lots of conversation. The Danes will also stay at the table talking long after they have finished the meal.

♦ Don't get up from the table until your hosts do. Before leaving the table, thank them for the meal.

♦ Move to the living room for after-dinner cocktails.

◆ Guests often stay as late as 1:00 A.M. after a dinner party. Your hosts might serve coffee, soup, or sandwiches between 11:00 P.M. and 1:00 A.M.

Eating Out

◆ Look for these types of eating places:

• *Bars* serve drinks only.

• *Basement cafes* (they have no special name in Danish) are restaurants that have retained their nostalgic, cozy charm and serve moderately priced Danish food.

• *Cafes* offer snacks with drinks.

• *Cafeterias* serve American-style meals.

• *Grills* are just for fast food such as fried chicken, hamburgers, or saté (Indonesian marinated meat or chicken on a stick). They serve beer and wine but not hard liquor. Most grills are run by Asians and are open longer than are other eating places.

• *Pølsevogne* are trucks on the streets that sell long, skinny pork sausages, beer, and soda.

• *Restaurants* range from gourmet to family style.

• *Smørrebrødsforretning* offer open-faced sandwiches to take out.

◆ You will usually find menus, often translated into English, posted in restaurant windows.

◆ At a place serving coffee and snacks, feel free to join others at a table.

◆ If you're invited to a *koldt bord* (cold buffet) or a *højt smørrebrød* (sandwich buffet), begin with the herring course, which might include 6 to 15 different kinds of pickled herring in various sauces, and sometimes salmon, tuna, or shrimp. Drink *akvavit* and beer with the herring. Follow the herring with a hot fish course, such as a fried fish fillet, then choose from the different warm and cold lunch meats and pâtés. Finish with cheese, fruit, and *akvavit*. Don't be surprised if this meal lasts four or five hours.

◆ In Copenhagen, expect to find a wide variety of foreign restaurants, including French, Italian, Greek, Turkish, Israeli, Indian, Pakistani, and Japanese.

◆ Most restaurants serve lunch between noon and 2:00 P.M. and dinner between 6:00 and 9:00 P.M., though some places are open later.

◆ In many restaurants, you'll save money if you order the daily special *(dagens ret)*, which consists of two courses.

◆ Women can feel comfortable going into a bar alone and even initiating a conversation there.

◆ To summon a waiter, raise your hand or make eye contact.

Specialties

◆ Try these Danish specialties: *bøf tartare* (raw ground sirloin on white bread with a raw onion ring and raw egg yolk on top); *flaeskesteg* (roast pork, usually served with red cabbage); *frikadeller* (meatballs); *øllebrød* (rye bread mixed with black beer, sugar, and lemon and cooked to a souplike texture); *rødspaetter* (sole); and *sild* (herring).

◆ For dessert, try *lagkage* (sponge cake layered with custard, strawberries, and whipped cream) and *rødgrød* (fruit compote).

Hotels

◆ For a stay during the summer months, book well in advance.

◆ When booking a room, be sure to ask whether there is a bathroom *in* the room and whether breakfast is included in the room rate.

◆ Many moderately priced hotels are closed during the Christmas–New Year's holiday.

Tipping

◆ *Restaurants:* A service charge is included in your check. If you dine in a fine restaurant and the service is excellent, leave an additional 5–10 percent.

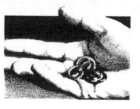

◆ *Porters:* Give 5–10 kroner.

◆ *Hotel maids:* No tip is expected, but if the service is especially good, you might want to leave 5 kroner per day.

◆ *Washroom attendants:* Give 2–3 kroner.

Private Homes

◆ Don't ever drop in unexpectedly.

◆ If you're invited to a Danish home for the evening, don't assume dinner is included unless your host makes that clear. A family meal might be over as early as 7:00 P.M.

◆ Don't jump up after a meal to do the dishes; the Danes prefer to sit and chat. You can offer to help with the dishes later, but your hosts will probably refuse.

◆ If you make a telephone call from a private home, ask the operator to find out the cost of the call. Even local calls cost money. If the operator does not speak English, he or she will connect you with someone who does. Have the correct amount ready and give it to your hosts.

◆ If you're spending a week or so with a family, offer to cook one entire meal. Your hosts will probably accept with pleasure.

◆ If there is no maid, clean your room and make your bed.

◆ If you have special interests, let your hosts know, and they'll try to cater to them. Don't, however, expect to be entertained constantly. Be independent enough to go off on your own part of the time.

◆ If you're staying in a Danish home, don't use the family bath facilities every day, because your hosts must supply towels, soap, and hot water. If you want a daily bath, go to a *badeanstalt,* a public bath (see In Public).

Gifts: If you're invited to dinner in a home, bring liquor or wrapped flowers. (Liquor is appreciated because taxes on it are very high.) Good flower choices are tiny roses, anemones, or seasonal flowers.

◆ If you know a Danish family well, bring them gifts from the U.S.: blue jeans, T-shirts, records, towels, or even cosmetics, which are very expensive in Denmark. Other good gifts from abroad: CDs (many people have CD players) or cassettes featuring popular American groups or classical music.

Business

Hours

Businesses and government offices: 8:00 or 9:00 A.M. to 4:00 or 5:00 P.M., Monday through Friday.

Banks: 9:30 A.M. to 4:00 P.M., Monday through Friday (until 6:00 P.M. on Thursday).

Stores: 9:00 A.M. to 5:30 P.M. during the week. Some close at 1:00 P.M. on Saturday, and some stay open until 7:00 P.M. on Friday. On the first Saturday of the month, shops are open until 7:00 P.M.

Business Practices

♦ Business in Denmark has become increasingly fast-paced since the mid-1980s.

♦ If you're going to be involved in a major deal, you'll probably need to make several trips.

♦ Seek contacts in Denmark through the Chamber of Commerce *(Handelskammer)* in Copenhagen.

♦ Avoid business trips to Denmark from June 20 to August 15 (the July Industrial Vacation) and around national holidays. Most nonretail businesses are closed between Christmas and New Year's Day, and many businesspeople vacation around Easter.

♦ If you represent an old firm, be sure to mention it. Danes respect tradition.

♦ Expect the Danes to be straightforward and honest. If they seem abrupt, it's probably because, though they speak English, they aren't aware of some of its subtleties.

♦ Foreign businesswomen won't encounter barriers in Denmark.

♦ If you're involved in an important deal, you might want to enhance your image by staying at one of the best hotels. For an ordinary deal, one of the middle-range hotels is fine.

♦ Don't feel obliged to have business cards or other materials translated into Danish.

♦ You'll find fax machines everywhere.

Meetings and negotiations: Make appointments at least two weeks in advance. Fax messages are acceptable.

♦ Suggest appointments between 10:00 and 11:00 A.M. or 2:00 and 3:00 P.M.

♦ Though the normal working day is either 8:00 A.M. to 4:00 P.M. or 9:00 A.M. to 5:00 P.M., people usually stay later during the winter. On Fridays, people tend to leave about 3:00 P.M.

♦ Don't suggest a business meeting on the weekend. Danes spend weekends with their families.

♦ Be punctual. It's very important.

♦ Don't expect a lengthy, personal initial conversation. People will want to discuss business right away. It wouldn't hurt, however, to read up on Denmark's history, possibly paying special attention to the heroism of the Danish people during World War II.

♦ Use charts and visuals if they are pertinent, but not simply to impress.

♦ Decisions will be made by a few people at the top.

♦ Once Danes have reached an agreement, they'll stick to it. Their estimated times of production and delivery will be reliable.

Entertainment: Business entertaining is done at lunch, not at dinner.

♦ If you are entertaining Danes, consider going to one of the basement cafes, which erve traditional Danish fare and are popular with businesspeople. An alternative is to ask your guests which restaurant they would prefer.

Gifts: Bring liquor, a product typical of your hometown, or a book about your area preferably with abundant photographs). Don't give American cigarettes; most Danes don't like them.

Holidays & Celebrations

Holidays:
New Year's
Day (January 1);
Maundy Thurs-
day; Good Friday;
Easter Sunday and
Monday; Whit

Monday (eight weeks after Easter); Constitution Day (June 5); St. Hans' Eve (June 23); Christmas Eve and Day (December 24 and 25); and December 26.

On St. Hans' Eve, Danes get together with friends and family; they sing, play musical instruments, and drink *akvavit* and beer. People clean out their houses and make a big pile outdoors of things they want to get rid of (the pile can also be made of driftwood). A witch, made out of straw and old clothes and filled with firecrackers, is placed on top of the pile. (In the past few years, pressure has decreed that the witch be sexless, rather than a woman.) At night the pile is burned, and everyone stands around and sings. The witch is supposed to take sorrows on its broom to Bloksberg, Germany.

St. Martin's Eve (November 10) is also celebrated, although businesses and schools don't close. Goose or duck is traditionally eaten on this day.

Transportation

Public Transport

Mass transit:
When taking a
bus, buy your
ticket—either a

single or a 10-trip card—from the driver. Have the card stamped in the machine you'll find on the bus. The time will be printed on your ticket, which is then good for 90 minutes on both buses and subways. You can transfer during that period.

♦ Before you get on the subway *(S-Bane),* buy your ticket with exact change. Subways work on the honor system, so don't expect a conductor to collect the ticket. Do, however, expect spot checks by inspectors.

♦ You'll find an excellent network of buses all over the country; in fact, bus travel is the only form of transportation in some remote areas. Buy tickets at bus stations.

♦ High-velocity, quiet trains called IC3 (Intercity 3) travel throughout Denmark. They have only one class, which costs the same as first class on a regular train. IC3 trains have dining cars, carpets, attendants, and fax machines. Buy tickets at train stations or travel agencies.

♦ When traveling by regular train, about 90 percent of Scandinavians use second class. It's very comfortable, though first class offers more space.

♦ If you'll be traveling by train on a Friday night, reserve a seat in advance, since trains are usually crowded.

♦ Trains that make long journeys have restaurant cars offering beer and wine; for shorter distances, trains have snack bars with sandwiches, beer, and coffee.

◆ In Copenhagen, consider buying the Copenhagen Card, which you can purchase at major train stations, travel agencies, hotels, and tourist information offices. It provides unlimited travel by bus or train in the metropolitan area, reductions on fares for crossings to Sweden, and free admission to 40 museums. You can purchase cards for one, two, or three days.

Taxis: Hail taxis on the street. When the green light is on, the cab is available.

Driving

◆ By law, drivers and front-seat passengers must wear seat belts.

◆ To rent a car, you must be at least 20 years old. Some firms won't rent to anyone under 25.

◆ The speed limit within towns is usually 50 kph, outside towns, 80 kph, and on motorways, 100 kph.

◆ Road signs are excellent, and even back roads are asphalt. Don't hesitate to venture off the main highways.

◆ For any ferry crossing, reserve a space well in advance. Otherwise, you'll have to wait for hours. (At holiday times you might wait for days.)

◆ If possible, avoid driving in cities such as Copenhagen that have narrow streets and little parking.

◆ Copenhagen has parking meters.

◆ In every town with time-limited parking restrictions, you must use a parking disk unless you're parked at a meter. Buy disks at banks, police stations, tourist offices, FDMs (Danish motoring organizations), and at some shops. Show the disk in the front window of your car with the pointer placed on the time of arrival. Don't exceed the time limit, or your car may be towed.

◆ If you are stopped for a traffic violation, pay the fine immediately or your car will be confiscated until you can pay.

◆ Don't drink and drive. If you are found to have excessive alcohol in your blood, you'll lose your license, pay a heavy fine, or go to jail—or all three! .

◆ If you're going to a party where there will be drinking, go by taxi or in a carpool with a driver who plans not to drink.

Legal Matters & Safety

◆ Don't plan to stay in Denmark for more than three months. If you must prolong  your stay, visit the passport police and offer an excellent reason. They will then decide whether you can remain.

◆ Work permits are extremely difficult to obtain. Even people who marry Danish citizens are not guaranteed work permits.

◆ The drinking age is 18. Bars and restaurants serve liquor 24 hours a day, unlike those in other Scandinavian countries.

◆ Women are safe walking alone at night (except behind the railroad station in Copenhagen) and riding alone at night on the subway.

Key Phrases

English	Danish	Pronunciation
Good morning	Godmorgen	go-MOHRN
Good day	Goddag	go-DAY
Good evening	Godaften	go-AHF-tehn
Please	Vaer så venlig at	VAHR so ven-lee aht
Thank you	Tak	tahk
You're welcome	Velbekomme	VEL-beh-kom-meh
Yes	Ja	yah
No	Nej	nigh
Mr., Sir	Hr.	hair
Mrs., Madam	Fru	froo
Miss	Frøken	FRUH-ken
Excuse me	Undskyld mig	OON-shkewl my
Good-bye	Farvel	far-VELL
I don't speak Danish.	Jeg kan ikke tale Dansk.	yay ken EE-keh TEH-leh dansk
I don't understand.	Jeg forstår ikke.	yay fohr-STOHR EE-keh
Does anyone here speak English?	Hvem kan tale engelsk her?	VEHM kan TEH-leh EHN-gelsk HAIR

Finland

The Finns, oddly enough, share an outlook on the world with the Irish. Both peoples have lived for centuries in the shadow of great powers (Finland was long an outpost of the Russian Empire). Like the Irish, the Finns have developed both a wry sense of humor and a cheerful fatalism.

When it comes to conversation, however, the two peoples are vastly different: the Finns are as quiet as the Irish are talkative. Sometimes it seems as though the Finns express themselves most in the language of color and form, as seen in the bold designs of their fabrics and ceramics. Be sure to look for these when you visit Finland.

You'll also want to experience that venerable Finnish tradition, the sauna. And if you really want to earn the respect of your Finnish hosts, plunge through a hole in the ice afterwards!

Greetings

◆ Shake hands when introduced, when greeting someone you know, and when leaving. Even children should shake hands.

◆ At a small party, which is the typical way Finns entertain, let your hosts introduce you to the others. At a large party, introduce yourself.

◆ Do not use first names until your Finnish acquaintance starts using them.

Conversation

◆ Although the official languages are Finnish and Swedish, English is spoken widely. (Signs, however, are only in Finnish and Swedish.)

◆ Good topics of conversation: sports such as soccer, hockey, skiing, and skating; or the history, sights, and architecture of the city in Finland you are visiting.

◆ Don't ask questions regarding someone's personal life, such as family or job.

◆ When you speak to people, look them directly in the eye.

◆ Don't criticize Swedes. Finland has a large Swedish population, and you might be insulting someone's family.

Money

◆ The unit of currency is the mark (abbreviated Fmk), made up of 100 pennies.

◆ Coins come in denominations of 5, 10, 20, and 50 pennies and 1 mark.

◆ Notes come in denominations of 10, 50, 100, 500, and 1,000 marks.

Telephones

♦ Look for public telephones in phone booths and at restaurants and cafes. For local calls, deposit a 1-mark coin. If you want to talk for a long time, deposit a 5-mark coin. When your money runs out, an operator will tell you to deposit more money.

♦ For international calls, a few telephones accept credit cards. Other options are to go to the post office or to call collect.

♦ There are no telephone cards.

♦ When you use a telephone directory, note that the letters Ä and Ö are at the end of the alphabet.

♦ Finns answer the phone by stating their name.

♦ The Emergency Number to summon police, the fire department, or an ambulance is **000.** (You don't need coins to dial 000 from a public telephone.)

In Public

♦ Finns don't show emotion in public the way Americans sometimes do. Finns kiss and hug only close relatives and friends they haven't seen for a long time.

♦ Be punctual for both business and social occasions.

♦ If you see someone you know at a distance, wave.

♦ Traditionally, men remove their hats when greeting or talking to someone and when entering a house, church, or elevator.

♦ Don't fold your arms. It's considered a sign of arrogance.

♦ Smoking is forbidden in some official buildings and cafes.

♦ If you want to meet members of the opposite sex, go to one of the many restaurants that feature dancing.

♦ Look for public toilets in restaurants, bars, and department stores. You can recognize them by the picture of a man or a woman on the door.

Saunas: Saunas—pronounced sow-nah ("sow" rhymes with "cow")—are central to Finnish life and are regulated by an unwritten code. The sauna itself is usually a small wooden house with a small changing room and a main room where bathers sit or lie on wooden shelves. Heat comes from rocks on top of a small stove. From time to time, water is splashed on the rocks to produce more steam. People often hit one another with birch leaves to improve blood circulation. At the end of the session, people take a shower or a swim in a lake or pool. Some even jump into a frozen lake or roll in the snow.

♦ If you're invited to a sauna, consider it a great compliment.

♦ When you first enter the sauna, drink a few glasses of water so you won't get dehydrated. The temperature is usually 200 to 250° F.

♦ There are no set rules for how long one stays in a sauna. Get out when you feel uncomfortable, whether that is after 5 minutes or 30. No one will think less of you if you leave. Since heat rises, you can stay in longer if you stay low. You can also take a bucket of water in with you and pour it over your head to cool off.

◆ Saunas are usually segregated by sex, although close friends of opposite sexes sometimes share a sauna. Traditionally, the women in a party have their sauna first so they'll be free to prepare the postsauna refreshments.

◆ Finns take saunas naked; however, they won't be uncomfortable if you do otherwise. In hotels you'll receive a terry cloth wrap you can wear. You can also wrap a towel around you. When people have saunas at summer homes on a lake, many wear bathing suits because they swim after the sauna.

◆ After most saunas, a massage will be available, usually given by an older woman.

◆ People generally have a sauna once a week for three hours in the winter, and twice a week for three hours at their summer homes.

◆ Be subdued in a sauna. Act as you would in a place of worship.

◆ Expect snacks after a sauna. Popular after-sauna snacks are sausages or salty fish with rye bread and butter. The salty fish is eaten to replace the salt lost by the body in the extreme heat. The beverage might be vodka, beer, or *Kalja,* which is similar to beer but nonalcoholic.

Dress

◆ Finns dress rather formally and follow Paris fashions closely. All men, even teenagers, wear ties when they dress up.

◆ For casual dress, men and women can wear slacks, jeans, and even shorts (both in the city and the countryside).

◆ For business, women wear dresses or suits, while men wear suits and ties. In the summer, men can remove their jackets if their Finnish colleagues do.

◆ Better restaurants require men to wear jackets and ties.

◆ For a dinner in someone's home, whether in the city or the country, women should wear dresses, and men should wear suits and ties.

◆ For openings at theaters and concert halls, wear formal dress: short cocktail dresses for women and tuxedos for men. For other theater or concert events, women should wear dresses, and men should wear suits and ties.

Meals

Hours and Foods

Breakfast (*aami-ainen*): 7:30 to 9:00 A.M. People eat hot cereal, *pulla* (yeast bread), and either open-faced sandwiches of meat or cheese, or yogurt and fruit. The breakfast drink is coffee.

Lunch (*lounas*): Noon to 1:00 P.M. This is a light meal consisting of soup, sandwiches, salad, and milk or buttermilk.

Dinner (*illallinen*): 5:00 or 6:00 P.M.; 7:00 P.M. for a dinner party. A family dinner consists of meat, fish, potatoes, vegetables or salad, and pudding. Milk accompanies the meal.

◆ At a dinner party, drinks usually precede the meal. Finns commonly drink beer, straight vodka, or whiskey, although they also drink American martinis, or gin and tonic. The meal begins with soup, sometimes followed by a fish dish, such as smoked or salted salmon or herring salad (herring mixed with sour cream, apples, and onions).

◆ The main course is meat, often a roast or stew, with potatoes and vegetables. Bread (usually a heavy, dark rye) and butter accompany the meal. Beer or sometimes wine is generally served with the meal, but you can request mineral water or fruit juice instead. Cheese and a sweet dessert end the meal. Coffee is served later in the evening, not immediately after dinner.

Breaks: Finns normally take coffee breaks at 10:00 A.M. and 2:00 P.M.

Table Manners

◆ Be punctual when invited to a meal.

◆ One of the Finns' favorite ways of entertaining is to invite people to a "coffee table" in the afternoon or evening. Cookies and cake—sometimes just one kind of each and sometimes an elaborate variety—and coffee are served.

◆ At a dinner party, expect the host to sit at one end of the table, the hostess at the other. Guests sit on the sides, often women on one side and men on the other. Children are usually included at meals with guests.

◆ Don't start eating or leave the table before your hosts do.

◆ At mealtime, don't drink until the host has offered a toast. The host and hostess never receive toasts from others.

◆ At large parties, food is usually served buffet style. At a sandwich table, begin with smoked and salted fish, such as herring, then take a fresh plate for the cold meats, which are roasted or smoked. Use another plate for the hot dishes. End the meal with fresh or stewed fruits, and cheeses. Coffee is served later, sometimes with cookies.

◆ If the meal is not a buffet, wait to see if the hostess intends to serve the guests. Otherwise, help yourself from the plates and bowls of food as they are passed around.

◆ It's rude to leave food on your plate, so take small first portions.

◆ If you are served something that tastes strange to you, don't make a negative comment.

◆ Finns tend to press guests to eat more food; it's their way of showing friendliness. If you simply can't eat seconds, however, politely say, "No, thank you."

◆ Don't eat anything, even fruit, with your fingers. (For fruit, stick your fork into the fruit and peel and slice the fruit with your knife.)

◆ Don't joke about the food.

◆ People tend to smoke between courses, but it's polite to ask permission first.

◆ When you finish eating, you can leave your silverware in any position on your plate.

◆ When the meal ends, go to your hostess and thank her. This gesture does not signal the end of the evening.

◆ Stay about one and a half to two hours after dinner.

Eating Out

◆ Look for these types of eating places:

• A *baari* is usually a milk bar—sometimes cafeteria style—where you can get soup, sandwiches, doughnuts, and coffee.

• A *kahvili* is a cafe or shop that has pastries, coffee, tea, and milk.

• A *ravintola* is a restaurant.

♦ Finns are more likely to entertain foreign visitors in restaurants than in their homes.

♦ If you invite someone to join you for a meal in a restaurant, pick up the bill. Finns never split restaurant bills

♦ Only restaurants and bars with licenses are allowed to serve liquor. Restaurants serve beer from 9:00 A.M. on and spirits from 11:00 A.M. on. They stop serving alcoholic drinks 30 minutes before closing.

♦ Women should feel free to go into restaurants or bars alone.

♦ In cafeterias and small lunch restaurants, you might share a table with strangers, although this practice doesn't carry over to regular restaurants. In regular restaurants, wait to be seated.

♦ Avoid loud talking or noise in restaurants.

Specialties

♦ Try these special Finnish foods: *vorsmack* (beef, mutton, and salt herring); *merimies-pihvi* (beef chunks baked with onions, potatoes, and beer); *kalakukko* (fish-and-pork pie); *rapuja* (crayfish, a great delicacy eaten between July 21 and October 31); and *kiisseli* (a thick fruit pudding).

♦ Try a Finnish favorite with your meals—berry liqueurs, which are often served ice cold. Two popular choices are *mesimarja,* made of Arctic bramble, and *lakka,* made from cloudberries.

Tipping

♦ *Restaurants:* A service charge of 14 percent is added to your bill (16 percent on Sundays and holidays). If the service was good, leave a small additional amount on the table. Tip the restaurant doorman 5 marks.

♦ *Porters:* Give 5 marks per bag.

♦ *Taxis:* Just round the fare up to the nearest mark.

♦ *Cloakroom attendants:* Give 5 marks.

♦ *Saunas:* Tip people who help you in the sauna 2–3 marks.

Hotels

♦ Almost all hotels have saunas; many have swimming pools, shops, restaurants, and bars.

♦ Hotel prices include breakfast.

Private Homes

♦ When you visit or dine at a home, don't be surprised if you're invited to take a sauna.

♦ If you stay with a family, ask if you can help with the dishes. You'll probably be refused, but it's polite to offer.

♦ Be sensitive to people who don't want smoking in their homes. If you want to smoke, ask if you should go outside.

Gifts: If you're invited to dinner, bring or send cut flowers, which Finns prefer to potted plants. Don't choose a large bouquet, which would be considered ostentatious. You could also give a bottle of wine or a box of chocolates.

◆ If you stay with a family, bring liquor, perfume, or historical dolls from the U.S.

Hours

Businesses and government offices: 8:00 or 8:30 A.M. to 4:00 or 4:30 P.M., Monday through Friday.

Banks: 9:30 A.M. to 4:00 P.M., Monday through Friday.

Stores: 9:00 A.M. to 8:00 P.M. on Monday and Friday; 9:00 A.M. to 5:00 P.M., Tuesday through Thursday; and 9:00 A.M. to 2:00 P.M. on Saturday.

Business Practices

◆ In recent years, Finns have picked up a new international nickname. Finland is sometimes called "the Japan of Scandinavia," because of its citizens' business acumen.

◆ For initial contacts, get in touch with the Finnish Foreign Trade Association, the Ministry of Foreign Affairs, or Finnfacts Institute—all located in Helsinki.

◆ Before you plan a business trip to Finland, make sure your timing doesn't conflict with that of a trade fair in another country. If it does, all the Finnish businesspeople will be out of the country, attending the fair.

◆ Personal relationships are very important. You'll have a much greater chance of success if the Finns find you sincere.

◆ Finland is a small country, so don't expect to go there and make huge purchases. People are cautious and deliberate and prefer that you start slowly, by ordering small amounts.

◆ When dealing with the government, expect delays and complications caused by the many layers of bureaucracy.

◆ Foreign businesswomen will be accepted.

◆ To generate a positive image, stay in a very good—though not necessarily the best—hotel.

◆ English is spoken widely, so you don't need to have materials translated or arrange for an interpreter.

◆ Faxes and telexes are readily available.

◆ Have a business card that's a little larger in size than the typical American card; it will make you stand out from other Americans.

Meetings and negotiations: Make appointments well in advance. Try to arrange to meet with the firm's managing director, who will make the decisions.

◆ When scheduling appointments, remember that most businesses close at 1:00 P.M. on any workday preceding a holiday.

◆ Punctuality is extremely important.

Entertainment: An invitation to a sauna is the equivalent of an invitation to a corporate golf course in the U.S. At a sauna, games of one-upmanship and ego are put aside, and people can start negotiating if they haven't already done so. The sauna is a good place to reflect and recap; eventually everyone will reach an accord. (An invitation to a sauna is unlikely if you are a businesswoman dealing with businessmen.)

◆ The conclusion of a business deal is usually celebrated with a long lunch.

◆ Spouses are not usually included in business dinners.

Gifts: Good business gifts for companies are ornamental objects, such as glass vases;

or a company manager, sporting equipment; from an organization to a customer, a flag with the organization's logo.

Holidays & Celebrations

Holidays:

New Year's Day (January 1); Good Friday; Easter Monday; Labor Day (May 1); Midsummer Day celebrations start on the afternoon of the Friday closest to June 24 and continue through Saturday); All Saints' Day (the Saturday nearest to the end of October); Independence Day (December 6); Christmas (December 25); and December 26.

◆ May 1 is Labor Day, but since the 1920s many students and professors have used the day to protest against communism. On the evening of April 30, there are parties at which people drink *sima* (fermented lemonade) and eat *tippaleipä* (doughnuts). Students often parade in the streets. If you're invited to a Labor Day party, bring champagne.

◆ December 6 is Independence Day. In the evening, everyone turns out the lights and puts candles in the windows. People walk through the streets to admire the effect, then have parties.

Transportation

Public Transport

◆ No matter how far you travel, you pay one fare.

◆ Buy tickets for buses, streetcars, and the Metro (subway) on the vehicle itself, or else purchase a 10-trip ticket at City Transport offices or R-kiosks (the logo has a white *R* on a blue background). A 10-trip ticket is valid for a year.

◆ When you enter a bus, streetcar, or the Metro, put your ticket into the validating "slot machine." If you have a 10-trip ticket, the machine will click off a piece of the ticket to indicate that you've used a unit.

◆ You can transfer on a single or a multi-trip ticket within one hour of the time stamped on the validated ticket.

◆ When people speak of ferries, they mean the overnight ferries from Helsinki to Leningrad, which are cruise ships with mediocre facilities and accommodations.

◆ The bus network is extensive and provides good connections with trains. In the north and parts of the east, buses are the only form of transportation.

◆ Most trains have first and second classes, but a few have only second class. First class is less crowded, has wider seats, and offers more leg room, but second class is also very comfortable.

◆ Trains on some long-distance routes have special playroom cars for children.

◆ Consider buying a Finnrail Pass, available at railroad stations, which offers unlimited travel on trains for either 8, 15, or 22 days.

Taxis: Taxis are common. Look for taxi stands, which are listed in the telephone book under *Taksiasemat*.

Driving

◆ By law, all occupants of a car must wear seat belts.

◆ Speed limits are 60, 80, 100, or 120 kph. The limit, indicated by signs, depends on the road's classification. If you don't see a sign, the basic rules are to drive 50 kph in built-up areas, 80 kph in the countryside, and 120 kph on highways.

◆ Traffic coming from the right has the right of way.

◆ Outside urban areas, drive with your headlights on, both day and night.

◆ Blow the horn only in cases of danger.

◆ During the spring thaw—from April until early June—some roads are impassible. Look for the sign *Kelirikko;* it warns of bad road conditions.

◆ If you see signs with pictures of elk or reindeer, be cautious. These animals tend to appear at dusk.

◆ Drinking and driving laws are strict. Exceeding a blood alcohol content of .5 milligrams can lead to imprisonment or a heavy fine.

Legal Matters & Safety

◆ The drinking age is 18.

◆ To stay in Finland longer than three months, request permission from the passport police.

◆ Women should take taxis after dark in any unfamiliar areas.

Key Phrases

English	Finnish	Pronunciation
Good morning	Hyvää huomenta	WHO-vah WHO-o-men-teh
Good day	Hyvää päivää	WHO-vah PAH-vah
Good evening	Hyvää iltaa	WHO-vah ILL-tah
Please	Ole hyvä	OH-le WHO-vah
Thank you	Kiitos	KEY-eat-ohs
You're welcome	Ole hyvä	OH-leh WHO-vah
Yes	Kyllä	COOL-lah
No	Ei	ay
Mr., Sir	Herra	HAIR-rah
Mrs., Madam	Rouva	ROH-vah
Miss	Neiti	NAY-tee
Excuse me	Anteeksi	awn-TEK-see
Good-bye	Näkemiin	KNACK-eh-me-ccn
I don't understand.	En ymmärrä.	en EUH-mer-reh
I don't speak Finnish.	En puhu suomea.	en POO-hoo SWO-may
Does anyone here speak English?	Onko englantia puhuvaa?	ON-ko EN-glahn-tya POO-hoo-vay

France

No people have a more undeserved reputation than the French. Many travelers decide not to visit France because they fear the alleged scorn and rudeness of its inhabitants.

The French are *not* generally arrogant or rude. It's true that in Paris— as in any large city— there are some rude and unpleasant people. And if you're looking for or expecting rudeness, you just might provoke it.

Most French people are as kind as you could wish. You'll find warmth and acceptance, especially in the countryside. One traveler who took a trip to Normandy stopped in a shop in Bayeux, a town not far from the D-Day beaches, to buy a bottle of mineral water. When the shop attendant realized the traveler was American, she took the woman's hand and said, "Thank you." "For what?" the traveler asked, surprised that a 30-cent bottle of mineral water could produce such gratitude. "For saving us," the attendant replied.

Greetings

◆ When greeting someone or saying good-bye, always shake hands. Don't use a firm, pumping handshake; shake hands with a quick, slight pressure. Children should shake hands too.

◆ When you enter a room, greet everyone in it.

◆ If speaking French, when greeting a man, say "Good day, sir." Address a married woman or an older woman whose marital status you don't know with "Good day, madame." To a single young woman, say "Good day, miss." (See Key Phrases.) *Don't* use the last name in greeting ("Good day, Mr. Dupont"); it's considered too familiar.

◆ Don't call people by their first names unless you're close friends. (Students and young people might relax this rule; take your cue from the French.) Children should not call any adults except relatives by their first names.

◆ If you meet a person you know very well, use his or her first name and kiss both cheeks. Men, however, seldom kiss each other unless they're relatives. The French never embrace upon meeting.

◆ When leaving a group, shake hands and say "Good-bye, madame" (or miss or sir). (See Key Phrases.)

Conversation

◆ English is the most widely spoken second language.

◆ Early in your acquaintance with someone, stick to general topics such as music, sports (especially soccer), books, and the theater. Don't discuss French politics until you know someone well. The French, however, will want to hear about your country's political situation and foreign policy.

◆ Topics to avoid: the prices of items or where they were bought; or a person's work, income, or age.

◆ Also avoid questions about personal and family life, which is considered very private. Even a question such as "Do you have brothers and sisters?" is too personal.

◆ When you praise someone, don't be surprised if he or she makes a self-deprecating comment instead of saying "Thank you." The French are customarily modest about receiving compliments.

◆ The French are well informed about the history, culture, and politics of other countries. To gain their respect, read up on the history and politics of France.

◆ When speaking with someone, don't keep your hands in your pockets.

◆ When listening to someone, nod and respond with little comments throughout.

Money

◆ The unit of currency is the franc (abbreviated Fr), which is made up of 100 centimes.

◆ Coins come in denominations of 5, 10, 20, and 50 centimes and 1, 2, 5, and 10 francs.

◆ Notes come in denominations of 20, 50, 100, 200, and 500 francs.

◆ In the provinces, some older people still think in terms of old francs: instead of saying "10 francs," they'll say "1,000 francs." If a price seems absurdly high, drop off two zeros.

Telephones

◆ There are three kinds of public phones: those that take cards; those that take coins; and some very old ones, found principally in bars, that take tokens *(jetons)*.

◆ Both the phones that take cards and the cards themselves are called *TéléCarte*. Buy the cards, available in different denominations, at post offices or tobacconist shops. Before dialing, put the card into a slot on the phone and close the hood. When the card's remaining franc value is displayed, dial your call.

◆ On coin phones you'll find slots for 1-, 5-, and 10-franc coins. When you hear a tone, deposit more money if you wish to continue the call. You'll often find coin telephones next to phones that take cards; frequently, the coin phones are broken or damaged.

◆ If you wish to use one of the old phones (called *taxiphones*) in a bar or cafe, buy *jetons* from the cashier.

◆ Don't try to make a collect call within France. That service doesn't exist.

◆ You can make international calls from any phone booth or from the post office.

◆ When answering the phone, say "ah-LO."

◆ The Emergency Number to summon police, the fire department, or an ambulance is **17.**

In Public

♦ Avoid speaking or laughing loudly in public. Americans tend to talk more loudly than the French, so lower your voice if you don't want to be conspicuous.

♦ Don't chew gum in public.

♦ Don't walk and smoke or walk and drink at the same time—the French consider doing so extremely bad taste.

♦ As you enter and leave a shop, say "Good day" to the salesclerk (see Key Phrases).

♦ In markets or small stores, don't select your own fruits and vegetables; instead, let the vendor serve you. If you pick up produce, the vendor is likely to tell you off in no uncertain terms.

♦ Public toilets are called either *Toilettes* or *W.C.* Men's rooms say *Messieurs* on the door, and women's rooms say *Dames.* If you see *OO* on the door, that means it's unisex.

♦ Look for public toilets in Metro (subway) stations, train stations, underground garages, and the street. You may also ask to use the lavatory in a cafe, even if you don't buy anything. Some toilets are the squat type (with just a hole in the floor). Bring a package of tissues, since many public toilets don't have toilet paper.

♦ Women might have to pass a row of urinating men to reach a bathroom stall with a door.

♦ In French washrooms, *C* marks the hot water faucet, and *F* identifies the cold. Sometimes they are marked with colors, red signifying hot and blue indicating cold.

Dress

♦ French dress, even casual dress, is more formal than American dress. Students and young people commonly wear jeans, but middle-class people wear attractive, expensive clothing.

♦ Women shouldn't wear shorts. You might see foreign women in shorts, but many French people don't like it.

♦ For business, men should wear conservative business suits with colored, striped, or white shirts, and ties. Women should wear conservative suits or dresses, but dress in a feminine style, softening their ensemble with a scarf or jewelry.

♦ For the theater, men should wear dark suits, and women, dresses. Openings call for tuxedos and long dresses.

♦ For visiting a church, men should wear jackets.

♦ At the beach, you may change into your bathing suit right on the sand. Just hold a towel around yourself and change under it.

♦ Don't be surprised if you see topless women at public beaches and swimming pools.

Meals

Hours and Foods

Breakfast *(petit déjeuner):* 7:00 to 8:00 A.M. A typical breakfast consists of *café au lait* (coffee with milk) or *chocolat chaud* (hot chocolate), bread, butter, jam, and sometimes croissants. Breakfast is the only meal at which butter is served with bread.

Lunch (déjeuner): Noon to 2:30 P.M. Traditionally the main meal of the day, *déjeuner* consists of hors d'oeuvres, a fish course (at a formal meal), a meat course with vegetables, a salad, cheeses, fruit, pastries (on special occasions) and *un exprès* (espresso). Wine accompanies the meal.

Dinner (dîner): 7:00 to 9:00 P.M. Usually much simpler than the noon meal, *dîner* might include soup, a casserole, and bread.

◆ If dinner is a social occasion, however, it will be like *déjeuner*. On these occasions your host will likely offer you pernod, kir, vermouth, or even champagne before the meal. If you ask for a drink such as scotch before the meal, you might offend some French who believe it will numb your palate, interfering with your ability to enjoy their exquisite cuisine. It's best to have an aperitif rather than a mixed drink. Drinks are usually taken in the living room. Some hosts serve an appetizer such as pâté or smoked fish. Others serve only nuts or small crackers to avoid spoiling the appetite.

◆ The usual after-dinner drinks are cognac and fine champagne. Many people make their own liqueurs from raspberries, blackberries, and cherries and are very proud of them.

Cocktail parties: These events usually begin between 7:00 and 8:00 P.M. and last for two hours or more.

Table Manners

◆ It's acceptable to be late for cocktail parties, but arrive on time for dinner parties.

◆ If you are offered a drink before dinner, rise from your seat to accept it.

◆ At a formal dinner, wait for your hosts to tell you where to sit at the table. The host and hostess usually sit at the center of the table opposite each other. Guests are seated in positions of descending importance to their right and left.

◆ Tables are set with the forks and spoons turned downward. Use the spoon and fork placed above the dinner plate for dessert.

◆ If there is a little rack or glass block next to your plate, it's a knife rest.

◆ Keep both hands on the table.

◆ Wine is served with lunch and dinner. The French consider it a digestive aid and appetite stimulant.

◆ Before you drink, wait until your host has served wine to everyone and proposed a toast. Everyone will then say "sahn-TAY" ("To your health").

◆ The host will continue to pour wine throughout the meal. If you do not care to drink much, take small sips, leaving your glass almost full.

◆ If you pour wine for someone, fill the glass only about three-quarters full.

◆ You may drink mineral water, either sparkling or flat, in addition to or instead of wine.

◆ Don't add sparkling water to wine or you'll insult your host by implying that the wine is of poor quality.

◆ When dining in a home, don't add salt or pepper to your food. It's insulting to your hosts. The French take great pride in the proper seasoning of foods.

◆ Finish everything on your plate, because leaving food is considered impolite and wasteful. You should also taste everything. (If you must follow a special diet, explain this briefly and quietly to your hosts.)

◆ Feel free to accept or turn down a second helping.

◆ Put your portions of bread on the table next to the dinner plate (there won't be any bread-and-butter plates). Break the bread with your fingers. Never cut it.

◆ At family-style dinners, bread is often used to soak up gravy or to push food on the fork, but don't do this in more formal company or in restaurants.

◆ When you cut a piece of cheese from a wedge, don't cut off the point. Instead, slice the wedge vertically so each person will have an equal share of the whole thing.

◆ To show you've finished, place your knife and fork on your plate side by side, with the handles pointing to the right and the fork tines up.

◆ If you have fruit for dessert, peel and slice it before eating it.

◆ Don't smoke between courses in either a home or a restaurant.

◆ Dinnertime conversation is important to the French, who will sit for hours in lively discussion at the table. The French enjoy controversy and might get into a rousing debate over such topics as the merits of French wine versus California wine.

Eating Out

◆ Look to see what an eating place is called to find out what kind of food it serves:

  • An *auberge* is an inn, often in the country, that serves full meals and drinks.

  • A *bistro* is a bar, much like an English pub.

  • *Brasseries* are really restaurants, though some keep longer hours and

some offer snacks as well as meals. Many *brasseries* specialize in Alsatian food and beer.

• A *buffet exprès* is a cafeteria where customers sometimes eat standing up (but they're not as fast as American fast-food restaurants).

• *Cafés* usually limit their food choices to croissants and sandwiches. Most close by midnight, but some are open 24 hours.

• *Libre-service* describes a self-service cafe; they are usually found on the outskirts of towns.

• A *relais de campagne* is a country inn, which typically serves foods ranging from snacks to several-course meals and drinks.

• *Restaurants* are, as the name suggests, regular restaurants. Their hours are usually noon to 2:30 P.M. and 7:00 or 7:30 to 9:30 P.M. In Paris, most restaurants don't start serving until 7:30 and stay open later than 9:30 P.M. Many restaurants are closed on Sunday. In the provinces, restaurants serve dinner between 7:00 and 8:30 P.M.

• A *routier* is a roadside diner. Their food is simple but often good.

• A *salon de thé* is a tea room, where people have tea, coffee, cakes, or ice cream.

◆ When you make a reservation, use the European method of stating time (see Introduction, page 4).

◆ Once you've made a reservation, don't add another person without calling in advance. Never just appear and say "We have one more with us." Often, the restaurant won't have room to squeeze another person in.

◆ If you have a reservation, be on time! Your table might be given to someone else if you're only 15 or 20 minutes late.

◆ If you don't have a reservation, you might be told that the restaurant is full—even though you see many empty tables. The empty tables are reserved.

◆ If you're unfamiliar with a restaurant, check the menu posted outside. All restaurants are required to post menus, so you can check both the food and the prices. The shorter the menu, the more likely that the food is prepared personally by the chef.

◆ Every restaurant offers both *un menu* (a set menu at a fixed price) and *une carte* (an a la carte menu). Usually you get better food and value by choosing the set menu. Most menus have at least four courses: hors d'oeuvres; entrée; salad or cheese; and dessert. Coffee is never included in the menu price, but wine sometimes is.

◆ You can order wine in several quantities: *un verre* (a glass); *un quart* ($\frac{1}{4}$ liter); *une demi* ($\frac{1}{2}$ liter); or *une carafe* (a liter).

◆ To call a waiter, say "gahr-SON"; to call a waitress, say "mahd-mwah-ZEHL." Never whistle or snap your fingers to attract the waiter's attention.

◆ In some restaurants, you're expected to use the same fork and knife for the entire meal. Use the knife rest by your plate, if there is one.

◆ If you go with a group to a *café,* take turns buying rounds of drinks rather than splitting the bill each time.

Specialties

◆ A highlight of any trip to France is the opportunity to sample the special foods of the country's diverse regions. Try the pastries, bread, cheese (more than 400 varieties), and wine everywhere.

◆ In Alsace and Lorraine try *choucroute garnie* (sauerkraut with sausage and pork), *pâté de foie gras* (goose liver paste), and *quiche Lorraine* (pastry filled with bacon, cheese, eggs, and cream).

◆ Bordeaux's specialties are *confit d'oie* (potted preserved duck), and *lamproie à la bordelaise* (eels cooked in red wine).

◆ In Brittany, sample *crêpes* (especially those with jam or Grand Marnier and sugar poured over them), seafood, and *agneau pré-salé* (lamb reared on salt-marsh grasses).

◆ Burgundy is known for *boeuf bourguignon* (the classic beef stew with wine, carrots, onions, and mushrooms), *escargots à la bourguignonne* (snails served in shells with garlic butter—usually six or twelve for a first course), *quenelles de brochet* (pike dumplings), and goat's or cow's milk cheese.

◆ In Normandy, sample *sole Normande* (poached sole served with a butter, egg, and cream sauce), *tripes à la mode de Caen* (a stew of tripe, cider, and vegetables), and *calvados* (the region's very strong apple brandy).

◆ Provence offers *bouillabaisse* (a seafood soup made with saffron, herbs, garlic, tomatoes, and olive oil), and *ratatouille* (a mixture of eggplant, tomatoes, onion, zucchini, and peppers, cooked in olive oil).

France ───────────────────────── 77

Hotels

◆ Don't expect air conditioning except in large, modern hotels, mainly in the south of France. Swimming pools are also rare in Paris but are relatively common in the south.

◆ Don't expect a toilet and bath in your room unless you specifically ask for them (and pay a higher rate).

◆ Most hotels offer a continental breakfast of coffee, croissants, and rolls at an extra charge (often considerably more than you'd pay at a cafe 50 yards from the hotel). A traditional breakfast of bacon, eggs, and toast is usually available, but at a hefty charge. Some hotels require that you pay for a breakfast; at others it's optional. If breakfast is included in the price of your room, your room rate will state *petit déjeuner compris* (breakfast included); a notice to that effect will also be posted at the reception desk.

◆ If you're hoping to find secretarial services or a translator at your hotel, note that only the most luxurious hotels in Paris and on the Côte d'Azur offer such services.

◆ In hotels and public buildings, *première étage* (first floor) refers to what Americans call the second floor. *Rez-de-chaussée (R.C.)* is what the French call the ground floor.

◆ The bed will probably have a hard-as-a-rock bolster where you would expect pillows. You can usually find a regular pillow in a closet or armoire.

Tipping

◆ *Restaurants:* A 10–15 percent service charge is added to checks (indicated by the words *service compris*—service included—on the menu). If the service was really good, leave the waiter an additional 10–20 francs.

◆ *Porters:* Give airport or hotel porters 5 francs per bag.

◆ *Hotel maids:* The maid is covered by the hotel's service charge, but leave something if you found her service outstanding.

◆ *Taxis:* Tip drivers 10 percent of the fare.

◆ *Ushers:* In movie theaters, give ushers 2 francs; in theater or concert halls, 3 francs.

◆ *Cloakroom attendants:* Tip 2 francs.

◆ *Washroom attendants:* Leave 1 franc.

Private Homes

◆ Never drop in on someone in France, no matter how well you know them.

◆ When you are invited to a French home, don't expect a house tour. Guests are usually received in the living room, with the doors to other rooms closed. Don't wander around, either outside or inside the house.

◆ When staying with a family, avoid making loud noises or bathing late at night. The French are very concerned about what neighbors think (even though they rarely know them).

♦ In old buildings it's customary to take the elevator up but walk down. Many elevators are tiny, and people going up take precedence.

♦ Always ask before using the TV, phone, or stereo components.

♦ If you stay with a family for several days, you may keep the same cloth napkin for each meal. Each person will have an individual napkin ring to hold it between meals.

♦ No matter how short your visit with a family, offer to help with the dishes or even prepare a meal.

♦ In most French homes, the toilet is in a room separate from the bathroom. When leaving either room, close the door.

♦ When you want to take a bath or shower, inform your hostess well in advance, because often the water must be heated for an hour or two beforehand.

♦ The electricity used to heat the water in most French homes is expensive, and many people don't take daily baths or showers. Try to do as the family does, and when you do take a shower, make it a short one.

♦ When staying with a family, shake hands with each person as you say "Good night."

♦ Don't be surprised if the French people you're visiting have absolutely no relationship with their neighbors—no matter whether they live in an apartment building or a house. Living in close proximity is not regarded as sufficient reason to develop a relationship.

Gifts: If you're invited to a French home for dinner, bring a box of candy or cookies or an odd number of flowers. Don't choose chrysanthemums, which are used only for funerals, or red roses, which express intimate affection and are also identified with the Socialist Party. Bring wine only to good friends (and it should be an excellent, expensive wine or a bottle of champagne).

♦ If you're staying for a few days, bring a gift from the U.S.: towels (which are much thicker and fluffier than the European variety), drip-dry sheets (flat if you don't know the bed size), books with photographs of your town or area, a typical product of your region (such as maple syrup or special textiles), or good California wines. Give teenagers cassettes or records of popular music, or T-shirts with American sayings on them.

Business

Hours

Businesses and government offices: Generally 8:00 or 9:00 A.M. to noon, and 2:00 to 5:00 or 6:00 P.M., Monday to Friday. Many businesses open Monday at 2:00 P.M. and are open Saturday from 9:00 A.M. to noon or 1:00 P.M. It is not common for business people to go home for lunch, as they used to.

Banks: 9:00 A.M. to 4:00 or 5:00 P.M., Monday through Friday. In towns with a Saturday market, banks sometimes stay open on Saturday and close on Monday.

Stores: 9:00 A.M. to noon and 2:00 to 6:30 or 7:00 P.M., Tuesday through Saturday. Most small shops and department stores are closed on Sunday and Monday. Stores close at lunchtime, so buy food beforehand if you're planning a picnic lunch.

♦ In Paris, executives might arrive at work at 8:30 or 9:00 A.M. and stay until 7:00 or 8:00 P.M. It's a status symbol for workers to stay late because it suggests they're doing important work. In the south, senior staff seldom work late, especially in the summer.

Business Practices

♦ During the 1980s, entrepreneurship and privatization emerged in France and the French business world experienced "culture shock." The state, for example, no longer has a monopoly on radio and TV stations, and there are now many privately owned outlets for both media. This change augurs well for U.S. business relationships with France.

♦ To find business contacts in France, get in touch with the American commercial counselor at the American Embassy in Paris, or with the Office of the European Community, French Desk, Room 3042, U.S. Department of Commerce, Washington, DC 20230. Phone: (202) 944-6300.

♦ To open a branch or office of your business in France, contact the Invest in France Agency, 401 North Michigan Avenue, Chicago, IL 60611. Phone: (312) 661-1640.

♦ Don't plan to do business in France during the two weeks before and after Christmas or Easter. Also avoid August, when stores, restaurants, theaters, and businesses close for the annual vacation. (August is vacation month for 80 percent of the French.)

♦ Send letters written in perfect French. Even though the person to whom you're writing might understand English, the letter might be passed on to people who don't.

♦ Decisions will be made by the *président-directeur général (P-DG)*, the head of the company who functions as chairman, C.E.O., and managing director. All employees below the P-DG are part of a rigid chain of command, with the junior staff always

handing over problems to a superior. There is really no such thing as teamwork. As a foreign businessperson, contact the P-DG initially. Send the most senior official from your company.

♦ Some newer and larger businesses have been reorganized by American management consultants. They tend to be more flexible and have less centralized decision making than the older, family-owned, hierarchical businesses.

♦ Business begins with establishing a personal relationship. The French really want to know about you. Before going to France, bone up on its history, culture, politics, and economics. If you don't show interest in the country, you won't impress the French.

♦ Expect to encounter an elitist "old boy network." Being from one of the "right" families and going to one of the "right" schools leads to a position in management. Don't get angry if a French businessperson seems arrogant; just take it in stride.

♦ Women hold many senior positions in advertising, retail, and media. In industry—especially in the south—there still exists some prejudice against women. French men generally treat businesswomen flirtatiously but not condescendingly.

Meetings and negotiations: To schedule appointments from abroad, contact executives several weeks in advance. Keep in mind, however, that some French executives believe their prestige will be enhanced if they don't confirm an appointment until the last minute.

♦ Don't expect secretaries to be able to make appointments for their employers. Many French secretaries don't have access to their bosses' mail or diaries. If the person to whom you've written is away, your letter might not be acknowledged. In general, don't expect a great deal of help from secretaries, except those in media and government, who have more power.

♦ Try to schedule appointments for about 11:00 A.M. or 3:30 P.M. In Paris, lunch usually begins at 1:00 P.M., and in the provinces at noon or 12:30 P.M.

♦ Even if your time in France is limited, don't suggest a weekend meeting. Weekends and holidays are usually reserved for family.

♦ Be punctual. People in Paris and the north are very punctual, although Paris traffic might make punctuality difficult, and people won't be upset if you're 10 or 15 minutes late. In the south, people are more relaxed about schedules.

♦ When you arrive, give your business card to the receptionist or secretary.

♦ Expect your initial contact to be in an office. Unlike in many countries, you probably won't be offered refreshments.

♦ When you want to enter someone's office, knock and wait for an answer; don't just knock and walk in. When you leave an office, be sure to close the door behind you.

♦ The person sitting in the middle is usually the most influential, sitting in a central spot to control things on all sides.

♦ At a business meeting or dinner, don't be the first person to remove your jacket. Wait until a French person suggests taking off jackets.

♦ Don't be surprised if the French initially react negatively to new ideas. The French consider themselves philosophers and enjoy arguing and debating. They can be won over by rational arguments supported with facts and figures.

♦ The French are inquisitive and want to understand *why* they should accept a proposal. They want to know the risks involved and possible alternative strategies. The process gets more attention than the goal. Let people question and discuss all aspects of your proposal without putting any pressure on them.

♦ In the past there was less need to rush and compete than in the U.S. Many French people have been with the same company for years (40-year pins are common). When they are negotiating a deal, they know they'll be with the company for a long time to come and don't feel pressured to clinch a deal quickly.

♦ Avoid direct confrontations. The French dislike them. They dislike losing and prefer to work around problems.

♦ During any meeting, take careful notes. Being precise is important to the French.

♦ Though the French will insist that a contract be written in precise, legal detail, it will really be a point of reference—the French might not stick to it.

Entertainment: You might be invited to a business breakfast, either in a company's dining room or in a hotel. Business breakfasts—usually buffets—have become popular recently.

♦ The French keep their business and private lives separate. Expect to be entertained in a restaurant rather than in a home, though outside Paris you might be invited home to a meal.

♦ Business lunches are more common than business dinners. Lengthy, lavish lunches are usually reserved for a first meeting or for celebrating the conclusion of a deal.

♦ If you're a guest at a business meal, take

your cue on ordering from your host. You might want to ask your host to recommend a choice, especially if he or she has the only menu that shows prices.

◆ At a business meal, don't initiate the business discussion. The French person might either discuss business right away or wait until the after-meal coffee has been served.

◆ When you invite people to a meal, be sure to take them to an elegant restaurant. Ask the concierge at your hotel for a recommendation, or check the red Michelin restaurant guide.

◆ Entertain business colleagues at dinner rather than lunch. At either meal, don't try to demonstrate how much you know about French food and wine. The French have spent their lives learning about those subjects. Ask your guests for suggestions on the food, and let them or the *sommelier* (wine steward) choose the wine.

◆ French executives who host a dinner might bring their spouses. If you are the host, don't invite the French spouses unless you've already met them.

◆ If a businessperson invites you to a country house for the weekend, be sure to accept. The gesture is a real sign that the person thinks of you as a friend.

Gifts: Give items with aesthetic appeal—books, records, cassettes, or art work—rather than something with your company's logo.

Holidays & Celebrations

Holidays:
New Year's Day (January 1); Easter Monday; Labor Day (May 1); Victory Day (May 8, the end of

World War II); Ascension Day (five weeks after Easter); Whit Monday (eight weeks after Easter); Bastille Day (the national holiday, July 14); the Assumption (August 15); All Saints' Day (November 1); Armistice Day (November 11); and Christmas Day (December 25).

◆ New Year's Eve is a festive occasion. Families have a large meal featuring raw oysters as a first course, often followed by turkey. On New Year's Day relatives give children money. If you visit friends, bring a small gift.

◆ On Mardi Gras (the Tuesday before Ash Wednesday), the French celebrate with costume parties and street processions. *Crêpes* are generally eaten on this day (traditionally, to use up butter before Lent!).

◆ On Labor Day (May 1), people visit friends and neighbors and give each of them a sprig of lily of the valley for good luck and happiness. You might also see union demonstrations in the cities.

◆ If a holiday falls on a Tuesday or a Thursday, people often take off that Monday or Friday as well.

◆ Many French treat August as a month-long holiday. You'll find the seashore packed with vacationers and many businesses, restaurants, and museums closed.

Transportation

Public Transport

Mass transit:
The Métro (subway), which you'll find in Paris, Marseilles, Lyon, and Lille, operates from 5:30 A.M. to 1:00 A.M. Keep your ticket in case an inspector asks to check it.

♦ To save money, buy a 10-ticket book for the Métro. You can also buy a tourist ticket, called the Paris-Sésame card, that permits two, four, or seven consecutive days of unlimited travel on the Métro and on intercity buses. You can buy the cards at Métro stations or any train station, if you present your passport.

♦ On buses and subways, do not sit in certain seats specially marked for senior citizens and veterans. As a common courtesy, give up any seat to a senior citizen.

♦ If you know your itinerary, consider making train reservations through your travel agent at home. (SNCF, the French national railroad system, has offices in many cities abroad.) In France, you can phone or go to the train station for reservations.

♦ You must have reservations to ride the TGV *(train à grande vitesse),* the high-speed trains that connect 36 European cities. You can make reservations until ten minutes before departure. The TGVs are smooth and comfortable, even in second class. (We have found them to be among the world's most pleasant forms of transportation.)

♦ At the entrance to any train station platform, validate your ticket in the orange-colored machine or you'll pay an extra charge.

♦ Smoking is banned on most commuter trains except for on special smoking cars, in the corridors of nonsmoking cars, and on platforms reserved for nonsmokers on long-distance trains. On the RER commuter trains, downstairs is for nonsmoking and upstairs is for smoking.

♦ If you want to get acquainted with someone on a train, you'll usually have to make the first move. The French tend to be reserved and discreet.

♦ If someone bothers you on a train, don't hesitate to tell them to stop. If the person is persistent, speak to the conductor. Be assertive but try not to make a scene.

♦ Bring bottled water on trains, even on a short trip, because there's no drinking water in the cars or lavatories. You might also want to bring food on long-distance trains because the dining cars are sometimes removed with no advance notice.

♦ Though the efficiency and speed of French trains make them the most popular form of travel, buses are good for connections in rural areas. Some are designed to complete SNCF service and others to provide transportation for market days.

♦ Look for bus stations near the railroad station in most communities.

Taxis: Either hail a taxi on the street or line up at one of the taxi stands (to which taxis come frequently) you'll see on the main streets of towns, at train stations, or at airports. You can also call a taxi from a restaurant or a hotel.

♦ Be sure to take an "official" taxi—one with a sign on the roof (illuminated if the taxi is free) and a meter. Avoid taxis without meters; their drivers charge whatever they wish.

♦ Taxi rates are higher at night and on Sunday. There is an extra charge for each piece of luggage.

♦ Taxi drivers are strict about how many passengers they will take. They usually take only three people—sometimes four if one sits in front. As likely as not, however, the front seat will already be occupied by a dog.

Driving

♦ You do not need an International Driver's License.

♦ By law, everyone in a car must wear seat belts, and children must sit in the back seat.

♦ The speed limit in towns is 50 kph; on rural roads, 90 kph; on major highways, 110 kph; and on expressways, 130 kph.

♦ Watch out for very fast drivers who pass constantly, even on narrow roads.

♦ Don't blow your horn in cities; it's illegal.

♦ At an intersection, the vehicle on the right has the right of way.

♦ Don't turn right on a red light.

♦ Most towns have parking meters and expensive underground garages. (A few hotels in Paris have garages.) Towing illegally parked cars has become more common.

♦ In Paris, check parking regulations carefully. On-street parking is severely restricted in most of the areas travelers are likely to visit. Violators might be towed and will have to pay a hefty fine.

♦ If you see a sign *Éteignez vos phares* (most common at autoroute tollbooths), dim your lights, don't turn them off (even though *éteignez* means to "put out" or "blow out").

♦ On the autoroute, trucks must stay in the right lane except to pass.

♦ There are hefty on-the-spot fines for traffic violations.

♦ Women stopped for a traffic violation often face an easier time than men do. If you're a woman, apologize profusely and you might avoid a fine.

♦ Laws against drinking and driving are strict. The police administer Breathalyzer tests and may impose fines of $90 to $1,400 U.S. and/or a prison term.

♦ On autoroutes, you'll find free emergency telephones every 2 kilometers.

♦ Many autoroute gas stations are open 24 hours; others are open from 8:00 A.M. to 6:00 P.M., except on Sundays and public holidays.

♦ Never leave valuables in your car, as break-ins are common.

Legal Matters & Safety

♦ Be cautious in the Paris Métro at rush hours, at airports, in train stations (especially during  holiday times), and at department store sales. There are many pickpockets, as well as bands of children who have perfected the art of purse snatching.

♦ Muggings of tourists are extremely rare in Paris; still, don't walk alone at night in the areas of Pigalle, les Halles, Montmartre, and St. Germain-des-Prés. In other cities, ask at your hotel about unsafe areas.

♦ Women should avoid using the Métro after 10:00 P.M. The corridors are not safe.

♦ The drinking age is 18. Drinking hours are unrestricted—you can drink 24 hours a day if you can find an open bar.

Key Phrases

English	French	Pronunciation
Good day	Bonjour	bawn-ZHOOR
Good evening	Bonsoir	bawn-SWAHR
Please	S'il vous plaît	seel-voo-PLEH
Thank you	Merci	mehr-SEE
You're welcome	De rien	de ree-en
Yes	Oui	wee
No	Non	nawn
Mr., Sir	Monsieur	meh-SYEU
Mrs., Madame	Madame	mah-DAHM
Miss	Mademoiselle	mahd-mwah-ZEHL
Excuse me	Excusez-moi	ex-kyou-zay MWAH
Good-bye	Au revoir	o reh-VWAHR
I don't understand.	Je ne comprends pas.	zhe ne kawn-prahn PAH
I don't speak French.	Je ne parle pas français.	zhe ne pahrl pah frawn-SEH
Do you speak English?	Parlez-vous anglais?	pahr-lay voo ahn-GLEH

Germany

Will anyone forget November 9, 1989, when the Berlin Wall came down? The champagne toasts mingling with tears as East and West Berliners embraced one another? Who that visited the city soon after the wall came down will forget the youthful entrepreneurs who sprang up—one ten-year-old chipping away at the wall and his partner selling the pieces for souvenirs?

Some economists predict that the economic fallout from reunification will be felt into the next century. Meanwhile, foreign businesspeople have unfettered access to the world-famous Leipzig Fair, and tourists have access to the treasures of such formerly off-limits cities as Dresden.

Be tolerant, especially in former East Germany. It will probably take years for the two Germanys to achieve the same standards in accommodations, restaurants, transportation, and business.

Greetings

♦ The general rule is to shake hands at meetings and departures, although customs vary from region to region. If you're unsure about the local custom, watch the people around you.

♦ If you see people you know at a distance, wait until you are within close range before greeting them. You'll probably see and hear young people yelling at one another across the street, but never shout greetings yourself.

♦ If you meet someone you know on the street, you don't need to shake hands unless you are stopping to talk.

♦ When you shake hands, don't keep your other hand in your pocket.

♦ If four people shake hands simultaneously, they don't shake hands crosswise (making an X). That's considered bad luck.

♦ At a party or business meeting, it's acceptable to introduce yourself to people, but it's better to be introduced by a third party.

♦ If you are introducing two people in a formal situation, such as a business meeting, a reception, or a formal dinner party, give the name of the younger or lower-ranking person first.

♦ When a woman enters the room, men should rise. Traditionally, men stand when speaking to a woman who is standing; however, a man who is much older or of a higher social standing may sit down. Women need not rise when someone enters the room.

♦ If speaking German, address men as "hair," married women and single women over 20 as "frow," and single women under 20 as "FROY-line."

♦ Use last names until you are invited to use first names. It's customary for people who have become good friends to share a ritual drink. If a German friend makes this suggestion, intertwine right arms, drinks in hand, and say "BROO-lehr-shahft" ("To brotherhood"). Following this ritual, use first names and the informal form of "you" *(Du)* in conversation.

◆ For business and social occasions, people use last names even when they know one another fairly well.

Conversation

◆ English is the most widely spoken foreign language; however, people in southwestern Germany often speak French.

◆ Good topics of conversation: the German countryside, travel abroad, international politics, hobbies, or sports such as soccer. (Germans take soccer very seriously, so *never* say anything negative about the sport or the local team.) Don't expect Germans to know anything about American baseball or football.

◆ Topics to avoid: World War II—especially questions regarding what people were doing during the war—or questions about personal life, such as "Are you married?" or "Do you have children?"

◆ Germans have strong opinions on political issues, both domestic and international. They will also want to know your opinions on international events, especially German-American issues.

◆ If Germans seem cool and reserved at first, it's because they believe it's inappropriate to be casual and overly friendly with strangers. If you're going to be in Germany for a long time, you might feel isolated at first, since it takes a long time for friendships to develop.

◆ Don't expect to receive compliments even when you've done something well—and don't offer compliments too freely yourself. Most Germans are embarrassed, rather than pleased, by compliments.

◆ Germans are quite outspoken. For example, an American would think it tactless to tell a friend that her outfit was unbecoming, but a German would merely think it honest.

◆ In what was formerly East Germany, don't make derogatory remarks about the non-functioning telephones; the poor condition of cities, hotels, and bathrooms; or the unmotivated salespeople. Be sensitive to the fact that the residents put up with those conditions for 45 years.

◆ Don't keep your hands in your pockets while speaking. Germans consider it a sign of disrespect.

Money

◆ The unit of currency is the Deutschmark (abbreviated DM), made up of 100 pfennige.

◆ Coins come in denominations of 1, 2, 5, 10, and 50 pfennige and DM 1, 2, and 5.

◆ Notes come in denominations of DM 10, 20, 50, 100, 200, 500, and 1,000. Notes are of different colors and sizes, so they're easy to tell apart.

Telephones

◆ Regular public telephones are yellow and are marked *Telefon* or *Fernsprecher*. You can make

international calls from phones in booths with a green sign marked *Inlands und Auslandsgesprache*. At some booths, mainly at train stations, you can also receive calls; these phones are called *Anrufbares Telefon* and have a sign showing a red bell.

◆ Phones for local calls only have slots for 10-pfennig coins. An eight-minute local call costs 30 pfennige. Phones from which you can make both local and long-distance calls have slots for 10-pfennig, DM 1, and DM 5 coins.

◆ Many telephones take telephone cards *(Telefonkarte)*, which you can buy at post offices or kiosks.

◆ Make long-distance calls either with a telephone card or from the post office. Don't call from your hotel room, where you'd probably pay a large surcharge, or from a coin-operated telephone, where you'd have to deposit coin after coin to keep the connection.

◆ At the post office, the operator will place your long-distance call and direct you to a booth. You might have to pay a deposit when you place your call. Be patient if you call from former East Germany, because many phones don't work, and if you find one that does you might have a long wait before your call goes through.

◆ Answer the phone by saying your last name.

◆ The Emergency Number to summon police, the fire department, or an ambulance is **110**.

In Public

◆ When entering and leaving a shop, always say "Good day" and "Good-bye" to the salesclerk. (See Key Phrases.)

◆ If you buy food in a local market, you're supposed to provide your own bag. If you don't have one, you can buy one for 10 pfennige.

◆ To attract someone's attention, raise your hand with the index finger extended.

◆ Germans attach great importance to privacy. No matter whether you're in a home or an office, if the door to a room is closed, don't enter without first knocking—and waiting for an answer.

◆ Don't congratulate anyone ahead of an important event such as a birthday or a wedding. It's considered bad luck.

◆ During a theater performance, don't whisper or cough or you might be reprimanded by the Germans around you. Germans are extremely quiet during a performance and try to sit very still.

◆ Men should allow older women or people of higher status to enter a room or a house first. However, they should walk in front of women into a restaurant.

◆ When walking down the street with a woman, a man should walk on the curb side. A woman walking with two men walks between them, as should a man walking with two women. A young girl walking with an older woman should be on the curb side.

◆ If a man compliments a German woman, it's not customary for her to thank him.

◆ Don't take photographs near a military

installation, or inside a church while a service is in progress.

◆ Museums and galleries that forbid photography post signs to that effect.

◆ If you wish to take a close-up photo of a person, ask permission first.

◆ Look for public toilets in bars, cafes, and restaurants. Those for women are marked *F* (for *Frauen*), and those for men are marked *H* (for *Herren*).

Dress

◆ Teenagers can feel comfortable wearing the same casual clothes they would in America, but anyone older might want to dress a little less casually. Smart pants, shirts, and sweaters are German standards. Jeans are fine if they're not worn-out or dirty.

◆ For business, wear conservative clothes in dark colors. Both men and women should wear suits, and men should wear ties. (In warm weather, you can take off your jacket if your German colleagues do so first.) In summer, women should wear suits or short-sleeved dresses, but nothing sleeveless.

◆ When invited to dinner, women should wear dresses or skirts and blouses, not pants. Men should wear jackets and ties.

◆ To elegant restaurants, men should wear a jacktet and tie, and women should wear a dress or skirt.

◆ When dining in casual restaurants, men don't have to wear jackets, and women can wear pants.

◆ For theater events, men should wear dark suits and ties, and women should wear fancy short dresses. For an opening night, men should wear dark suits; women, long dresses. When buying your tickets, ask if it's an opening night.

◆ If you are going to the theater and tend to get chilly, bring a sweater, since you must check your coat; you can't wear or carry it into the auditorium.

◆ If you're in former East Germany, dress simply. Don't wear flashy jewelry and clothing to show off; you'll only make people feel inferior and make a bad impression.

◆ In southern Germany, even in large cities, you'll see people wearing traditional costumes such as *Lederhosen* (leather shorts), dirndls (dresses with full, gathered skirts), jackets, and alpine hats.

◆ If you go to a beach, don't be surprised to see nude people of all ages.

Meals

Hours and Foods

Breakfast (*Früh-stück*): 7:00 to 8:30 A.M. The meal usually consists of rye bread, rolls, butter, jam, coffee with milk, and sometimes sausage and cheese.

Lunch (*Mittagessen*): 1:00 P.M. People who go home for the midday meal usually eat a large one. It begins with soup, followed by meat, potatoes, vegetables, and salad. Rye bread (but no butter) and beer often accompany the meal. Germans seldom have dessert and coffee after the meal; instead, they have a coffee and pastry break at 4:00 P.M.

Dinner *(Abendessen):* 6:00 to 7:30 P.M. The evening meal is usually lighter than the midday meal, consisting of cold meat, eggs, salad, cheese, or open-faced sandwiches.

♦ A dinner party in a home will usually be a special occasion, such as the celebration of an engagement. At such a party, drinks such as sherry, vermouth, or wine will be served before dinner in the living room. Only rarely are appetizers served with the drinks. The meal will feature the same courses as a typical noontime meal. Wine will accompany the meal, and after-dinner drinks will be served with coffee. Often you'll be offered one of three strong brandies: *Kirschwasser* (cherry), *Himbeergeist* (raspberry), or *Pflaumenwasser* (prune).

Breaks: Germans take a coffee break between 9:00 and 10:30 A.M., and a coffee and pastry break at 4:00 P.M.

Table Manners

♦ If you're invited to dinner, be on time. Germans seldom have long cocktail hours before sitting down to dinner.

♦ The male guest of honor will sit to the right of the hostess, and the female guest of honor to the right of the host.

♦ Meals begin with the greeting "Goo-ten ah-pay-TEET," the equivalent of *"Bon appétit."*

♦ In some regions you might see both knives and forks to the right of the plate. Spoons are usually placed above the plate.

♦ At a dinner party, don't drink until the host has toasted everyone and taken the first drink.

♦ Clink glasses only when a toast is offered for a special occasion, such as someone's birthday. If you are toasted, return the favor later in the meal, if you like. Traditionally, a man toasts a woman, never the opposite.

♦ At informal dinners, you might receive a plate with the food already on it. At more formal dinners, serve yourself from the platters passed around.

♦ When passing food or a beverage to another person, say "BIT-teh," which in this case means "You're welcome."

♦ Don't use your knife to cut potatoes, pancakes, or dumplings or you'll imply that the food isn't tender enough.

♦ Never eat with your fingers. Use a knife and fork to eat sandwiches and, usually, even fruit. (In some homes people eat fruit with their hands; take your cue from your hosts.)

♦ You're supposed to eat everything on your plate—even in restaurants. If you can't finish, make up a good excuse.

♦ When you finish eating, lay your knife and fork vertically, side by side, on your plate.

♦ Smoke between courses only if you see others doing so. Smoking usually begins after coffee is served. Always ask permission before smoking.

♦ Plan to leave shortly after dinner is over. If you've come at 7:00 P.M., leave no later than 11:00 P.M.—earlier on a weeknight. Guests are expected to make the first move to leave, but if your host doesn't refill your glass, consider that a signal that it's time to go. It's always better to leave too early than too late.

Eating Out

♦ Look for the following eating places:

• A *Bierkeller* offers beer and food such as sausages, pork cutlets, and spare ribs, all accompanied by sauerkraut.

• A *Café* serves drinks and snacks.

• A *Gasthof* or *Wursthaus* is a regular restaurant. Don't go there if you just want a drink.

• A *Konditorei* serves pastries, coffee, and tea.

• A *Schnellimbiss* is a snack bar that serves sausages, bread, soft drinks, and beer. Usually you eat standing at a small table or counter.

• A *Weinstube* offers wine and a limited selection of snacks such as bread sticks, pretzels, and *Harzer*—a cheese mixed with wine, onions, and caraway seeds that you spread on rye bread.

♦ Opening and closing hours for places that serve alcohol differ by region, since they're regulated locally.

♦ Make reservations in advance, especially if your group has more than four people or if you're at one of the trade fairs, when restaurants are very busy.

♦ If you're concerned about a restaurant's prices, check the front window before entering. A menu with prices should be displayed there.

♦ By custom, German men precede women when they enter a restaurant. The man holds the door for the woman, and she then lets him lead the way to the table.

♦ Unless you're at one of the best restaurants, seat yourself. If there's no vacant table, look for an empty seat at a table with other people, but ask permission before you sit down. Don't be surprised if the other people at the table strike up a conversation with you.

♦ Address a waiter as "hair O-behr" and a waitress as "FROY-line."

♦ Don't ask for coffee with a meal; it's drunk afterward. If you ask for cream, you might get condensed milk.

♦ Shops close at 6:30 P.M., but if you want to buy beer, you can go to a restaurant or shops in bus or train stations and buy several cans or bottles (you'll pay double, however).

Specialties

♦ Germany is famous for its beers, white wine, *Wienerschnitzel,* and sausages.

♦ Try the following sausages: *Bratwurst* (pork sausage); *Leberwurst* (liver sausage); *Thuringer Rostbratel* (grilled sausages); *Weisswurst* (a white sausage made of veal and pork); and *Würstchen* (a sausage much like an American hot dog).

♦ Other main courses to sample: *Falscher Hase* (mock hare, meatloaf); *Hasenpfeffer* (rabbit stew); *Hoppel-Poppel mit Salat* (hash with lettuce and sour cream); *Kalbsvögel* (rolled veal stuffed with spinach, egg, and bacon); *Kartoffelpuffer* (potato pancakes); *Kasseler Rippenchen* (smoked pork chops); *Leber im Grünen* (sauteed liver with herbs and wine); *Plinsen* (pancakes made of wheat, buckwheat, and lemon); *Sauerbraten* (beef marinated for several days in vinegar, sugar, raisins, and crumbled gingersnaps, then prepared like a pot roast); *Spätzle* (noodle dumplings).

♦ For dessert, try *Bienenstich* (pastry with honey and nuts); *Berliner Pfannkuchen* (jelly doughnuts); and *Schwarzwälder Kirschtorte* (Black Forest chocolate-and-cherry cake).

♦ Depending on your feelings about slightly unusual food, you might want to try—or avoid—*Eisbein* (pig's knuckle) and *Schavelfleish* (raw hamburger).

Hotels

◆ Usually the price of your room includes breakfast (coffee or tea, rolls, bread, butter, and jam and/or honey). Some hotels offer their patrons breakfast buffets.

◆ You might be charged extra for heat in your room.

◆ Many hotel registration forms are rather complicated.

◆ If the down comforter on your bed is too warm, ask for a sheet and blanket.

◆ In many hotels, beds are made every day, but linens are changed only once a week.

◆ If your room doesn't have a bath, get the key to the bathroom from the desk clerk. You might pay an extra charge for a bath.

◆ If you're traveling in what was East Germany, you'll encounter a shortage of hotel rooms. Book *at least* a month (preferably more) in advance. You can book rooms in private homes at the Tourist Information Office in each town. Be sure to ask whether there is a private bath; many private homes share a bathroom in the hall with people in other apartments, or else have a bathtub in the apartment and share a toilet in the hall.

Tipping

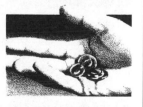

◆ *Restaurants:* A 10–15 percent service charge is usually added to the check as a tip (don't confuse this with the 14 percent value-added tax). You don't need to leave an additional tip, but most people round the amount of the check up to the nearest DM. Let servers know the change is theirs; don't just leave it on the table.

◆ *Porters:* Give DM 1 or DM 2 per bag.

◆ *Hotel maids:* Give DM 2 per day.

◆ *Taxis:* Give a 10–15 percent tip.

◆ *Cloakroom attendants:* Tip 50 pfennige.

◆ *Washroom attendants:* If you see a plate in a public toilet, leave 20–50 pfennige for the cleaning woman.

◆ *Gas station attendants:* If they perform some extra service, tip DM 1.

Private Homes

◆ Call ahead before visiting people; don't just drop in.

◆ If you need to make a telephone call from a private home, ask permission first and offer to pay for the call. People are charged for each call.

◆ Three rules if you're staying with a family:

- Always close inside doors, such as those to the bedroom, bathroom, or living room, behind you.

- If you're the last to leave a room, turn off all the lights. Even small children are trained to do this to conserve energy.

- Be especially quiet from 10:00 P.M. to 7:00 A.M. and 1:00 to 3:00 P.M.—times when people sleep.

◆ In Dusseldorf and Cologne the water contains a great deal of lime, which leaves a thin white film on dishes, cups, and glasses.

Don't think people are giving you dirty dishes.

Gifts: If you're invited to dinner, bring flowers. Be sure to unwrap them before presenting them to your hostess. Bring a small bouquet—large ones are considered ostentatious—that contains an uneven number of flowers (but never 13). Don't give roses, which are an expression of romantic love, or calla lilies, which are used for funerals.

♦ Don't bring wine (unless it's a special California wine) as a dinner gift; your hosts might think you consider their wine cellar inadequate.

♦ If you attend a large party, send flowers either ahead or with a thank-you note the day after.

♦ If you stay with a family, bring American college sweatshirts for the children and teenagers. For your hosts, bring drip-dry tablecloths, bourbon whiskey, small pocket calculators, and classical or rock records. Avoid giving perfume, soap, or clothing (other than scarves); such gifts are considered too personal.

Business

Hours

Businesses and government offices: 8:00 or 9:00 A.M. to 4:00 or 5:00 P.M., Monday through Friday.

Banks: 8:30 A.M. to 1:00 P.M. and 2:00 to 4:00 P.M., Monday through Friday; Thursday until 5:30 P.M. (Times might vary in different regions.)

Stores: 8:00 or 8:30 A.M. to 6:00 or 6:30 P.M., Monday through Friday, and 8:00 A.M. to

2:00 P.M. on Saturday. (Times vary considerably from town to town.)

♦ By law, all shops must close at 6:30 P.M. If you are in a major city and need groceries, a snack, an international newspaper, or a drink after that hour, go to the train station.

Business Practices

♦ In your own country, look for contacts in Germany through the U.S. Department of Commerce, the Commercial Section of the German Embassy, banks, trade associations, and the German Chamber of Commerce and Industry (the equivalent of the Chamber of Commerce in U.S. cities), which has offices in New York, Los Angeles, and London.

♦ In Germany, good sources of contacts are the Commercial Section of your embassy and commercial attachés at the embassy or consulates. Another good source is the German Foreign Trade Information Office in Cologne; it produces publications and forwards import and export requests to appropriate organizations and companies.

♦ The Federal Statistical Office in Wiesbaden publishes data on exports, imports, the economy, and production, all of which can be invaluable for market research.

♦ In business, Germans look for steady growth and minimal risks. They want to receive high-quality goods over a period of time and aren't interested in one-time purchases. If you aren't interested in long-term business arrangments, find another country for your product or service.

♦ Trade fairs are important places for foreign businesspeople to make contacts. Obtain a catalogue ahead of time, and arrange meetings with companies in which you're interested.

♦ Address a business letter to the firm rather than to an individual executive. Begin your letter, "Dear ladies and gentlemen." If you address a letter to a specific executive who happens to be away, the response will be greatly delayed.

♦ Avoid making business trips to Germany in July, August, and December, which are vacation times.

♦ Don't expect to find women in top positions in German firms. Foreign businesswomen must make a very good impression to be taken seriously. Some German clients might expect a woman to consult her male boss before making a decision.

♦ English is widely used, especially among senior businesspeople. In southwestern Germany, people also speak some French. To make a good impression, learn a few words of German.

♦ Most offices have fax service. Many post offices have a fax service called *Telebrief* for documents up to A4 size.

♦ Bring a large supply of business cards, printed in English on one side and German on the other. If you'll be doing business in small towns, be sure your title is featured prominently on the card. People in smaller communities are more conscious of titles than are people in cities.

♦ If you plan to distribute any materials, have them translated into German.

♦ Germans seldom take work home and rarely receive business calls at home. If you must call someone at home regarding business, be sure to apologize.

Meetings and negotiations: If you're trying to make an appointment from abroad with a director at a large firm, contact him or her a month in advance. The arrangements will take longer than if you're dealing with a medium-sized or small firm, which

you should contact two to three weeks in advance.

♦ Public agencies and government offices have individual schedules for seeing people. Write or call for an appointment well in advance.

♦ Good times for business appointments are either between 9:00 A.M. and noon or 1:30 and 4:00 P.M. Don't plan Friday afternoon appointments, since many offices close about 2:00 P.M. Appointments at 8:30 A.M. aren't uncommon; however, bankers won't usually see people before 9:00 A.M. Some high-level managers work until 7:00 P.M., but most Germans are not inclined to work long overtime hours.

♦ Don't be surprised if a company director passes you on to a junior executive.

♦ Be punctual. It's very important.

♦ You'll probably meet in a company office with a group consisting of the chief executive and several subordinates.

♦ Germans have a strong sense of privacy and always keep their office doors closed. That isn't a signal that a person doesn't want to be disturbed; instead, it's meant to keep protective boundaries between people who feel "exposed" and unbusinesslike with doors open.

♦ Keep this sense of privacy in mind when you are offered a chair in an office. Don't try to move your chair closer to the Germans' or you'll make them uncomfortable.

♦ The atmosphere at German business meetings is serious and formal. Don't try to "lighten things up" by telling what you think are humorous stories.

♦ Expect to be offered coffee, a drink, or both.

◆ There might be a bit of preliminary conversation—but not much. A German might inquire about your flight or your accommodations but will get down to business quickly, even at the first meeting.

◆ To impress people, use visuals and advertising materials and show them samples of your product.

◆ German businesspeople operate more slowly than Americans do. They believe that doing a good job requires time, so they proceed very deliberately. They generally distrust the quality of businesses specializing in fast service.

◆ Don't force the pace of meetings. Let the Germans take the lead. If things are going well, a meeting might continue for several hours. If the Germans aren't interested, it probably won't last more than an hour.

◆ Germans are slow and conservative in making decisions, but are also thorough and efficient.

◆ Plan to present agreements in writing. Germans want concrete, precise offers.

Entertainment: Business meals tend to be social occasions rather than business discussions.

◆ Expect a business lunch to begin at noon (occasionally 1:00 P.M.) and last no more than $1\frac{1}{2}$ hours. You might be entertained at the company canteen.

◆ If you wish to invite someone to a business dinner, set the time for 6:30 P.M. Again, the meal should last no more than $1\frac{1}{2}$ hours, since many German executives live a long distance from work. If you want the meal to be a social occasion, include the German's spouse and set the time for 8:00 P.M.

◆ Ask the concierge at your hotel to recommend a restaurant if you plan to entertain.

Gifts: Give something small and simple, such as a pen. Germans will consider an expensive present tasteless.

Holidays & Celebrations

Holidays:
New Year's Day (January 1); Good Friday; Easter Monday; Labor Day (May 1); Ascension Day (five weeks after Easter); Whit Monday (eight weeks after Easter); National Holiday (October 3); Prayer and Repentence Day (mid-November); and Christmas (December 25 and 26).

◆ *Fasching* (Carnival) is a three-day celebration that ends on Shrove Tuesday (the day before Ash Wednesday). There are parades, costumes, parties, and revelry not seen at any other time of year. Normal business stops and "anything goes."

Transportation

Public Transport

Mass transit: Buy tickets for buses, streetcars, or subways at kiosks or from machines before you board. You can also buy strips of 6 to 12 tickets. Your ticket must be cancelled in a machine you'll find near the entrance—sometimes in the area where you wait to board, and sometimes inside the entrance.

◆ When you take the subway, be sure to have change, since many stations have only ticket machines.

◆ Germany has several types of trains:

Nahverkehrszuge, which make frequent stops; *Eilzuge,* semi-fast and advisable for trips up to 50 kilometers; *D-Zuge,* faster and with fewer stops than *Eilzuge,* but a bit more expensive; and *Intercity Express* (ICE), which leave every hour between 7:00 A.M. and 11:00 P.M. and link cities throughout Germany. In the first-class sections of ICE trains, conductors serve drinks and snacks at your seat.

♦ Buy train tickets at a travel agency or the train station. Choose either first or second class. Some cars are for smokers, some are for nonsmokers, and some are half and half.

♦ Two cautions regarding trains: (1) When getting on a train, be sure you get on a car with your destination on it. Some cars are disconnected at certain stops. (2) Not all trains have dining cars. If you're not sure, bring your own food.

♦ When you enter a train compartment, greet everyone in it and ask if the seat is occupied or reserved.

♦ Trains do not have drinking water, so bring bottled water along.

♦ On long-distance trains, you can get either a couchette with a blanket and pillow (on cars called *Liegewagen*), or the more luxurious accommodations of a sleeping car (*Schlafwagen*). To get a sleeping car during a holiday season, book well ahead.

♦ Many services in Germany's excellent bus network are integrated with the train services. Buses often offer adjustable seats, lavatories, nonsmoking areas, radio loudspeakers, public-address systems, and large windows.

♦ In most cities, look for bus stations next to railroad stations.

Taxis: Either find a taxi at a taxi stand or phone for one. You can hail taxis on the street that have their yellow dome lights on, but they're less common than in the U.S.

♦ Taxi rates vary depending on the number of passengers, the time of day, and the amount of luggage. Drivers often carry little change, so carry currency in small denominations.

Driving

♦ You must carry an International Driver's License.

♦ Seat belts are mandatory for all occupants of a car.

♦ Children under 12 must sit in the back seat.

♦ At zebra crosswalks, pedestrians have the right of way.

♦ When driving through intersections, be careful. Legally, when the red light at a stoplight changes to yellow, you are supposed to wait until it changes to green before you move. Many Germans, however, shoot ahead as soon as it turns yellow.

♦ On-street parking is limited in city centers, and garages are expensive.

♦ There are severe penalties for drunken driving, and police can stop cars for spot checks if they suspect that a driver has been drinking.

♦ German filling stations are very competitive, so you can shop around. Self-service stations are the least expensive. You won't find competitive prices among gas stations on the *Autobahn.*

♦ The speed limit in built-up areas is 50 kph and on all other roads except the *Autobahn* is 100 kph. The *Autobahn* has no official limit, but the recommended limit is 130 kph; however, most cars will exceed this limit, sometimes traveling up to 210 kph.

◆ On the *Autobahn,* right-hand lanes are for slow-moving traffic. Slow-moving cars must change lanes to allow faster-moving cars to pass them—cars that wish to pass will flash their lights.

◆ If you have a breakdown or accident on the *Autobahn,* look for arrows near the tops of white posts on the side of the road. They mark emergency call boxes, never more than one kilometer apart. Lift the cover of the microphone completely. An operator, who probably speaks English, will ask you your problem and location. The location of the box is printed under the speaker at the bottom.

◆ Any two-wheeled vehicle must have its headlights on night and day.

◆ In what was East Germany, the roads are in poor condition. In the countryside, drive slowly, because tractors or animals often cross the road and train crossings are not always clearly marked.

◆ In former East Germany, street and town names are being changed. Use the most up-to-date map you can find.

Legal Matters & Safety

◆ Drinking hours differ from community to community. Most bars and restaurants stop serving liquor at 1:00 A.M. on weekdays and 2:00 A.M. on Saturdays. Some nightclubs serve liquor later. Berlin has no fixed closing hours. Throughout Germany, you can buy liquor in any supermarket or delicatessen.

◆ Prostitution is legal in Germany and is tightly supervised by the government. Many cities have one street where the prostitutes sit in shop windows. Other women are not allowed on those streets.

◆ In cities, wide red lines down the middle of sidewalks mark bicycle paths. Be careful not to walk on one, since bicyclists usually ride like mad and give little warning that they are behind you.

◆ Jaywalking is illegal. If you jaywalk in small towns, older people will shout at you and report you to the police.

◆ Pedestrians are conscientious about waiting for their green light before crossing, even if there is no traffic. If you don't want people to shout at you, wait for the green.

◆ Women can feel safe going almost anywhere in Germany, without worrying about verbal or physical harassment. In larger cities, however, women are safer taking taxis after dark. In small towns, it's safe to walk alone if the streets are well lit. Avoid train stations at night.

◆ It's unsafe for women to hitchhike alone. It's illegal for anyone to bike, hike, or hitchhike along the *Autobahn.* Fines are severe.

◆ In West Berlin, beware of pickpockets in department stores and subway and train stations.

◆ In any town along the Rhine, don't drink the tap water or even brush your teeth with it. It's loaded with dangerous chemicals. Drink bottled water instead.

◆ Don't drink tap water in former East Germany until the process of replacing all pipes has been completed.

Key Phrases

English	German	Pronunciation
Good morning	Guten Morgen	GOO-tun MOHR-gun
Good day	Guten Tag	GOO-tun TAHK
Good evening	Guten Abend	GOO-tun AH-bent
Please	Bitte	BIT-teh
Thank you	Danke	DUNK-uh
You're welcome	Bitte	BIT-teh
Yes	Ja	ya
No	Nein	nine
Mr., Sir	Herr	hair
Mrs., Madame	Frau	frow (rhymes with "how")
Miss	Fräulein	FROY-line
Excuse me	Verzeihung	fare-TSY-oong
Good-bye	Auf Wiedersehen	owf VEE-der-zeyn
I don't understand.	Ich verstehe nicht.	Eech* fehr-SHTAY neecht*
I don't speak German.	Ich spreche nicht Deutsch.	Eech SPREH-cheh NEECHT* DOYTSCH
Does anyone here speak English?	Spricht hier jemand Englisch?	SPREECHT* here YAY-mahnd EHN-gleesh

*"ch" is pronounced like a gutteral "k," as in the Scottish word "loch."

Great Britain

Most travelers imagine they'll find the British stuffy and starched. And that is indeed one side of the coin: the gentleman going to work in "the City," wearing pinstripes and derby, and the oh-so-proper lady shopping at Harrods. But turn the coin and you'll find purple-haired "punks" and eccentrics of all types.

All British have at least one thing in common—a respect for privacy so strong that they sometimes seem aloof. Yet if you ask people for help, most will give it cheerfully.

We've included Scotland and Wales in this chapter because their customs are generally the same as those in England. We've indicated only where they differ. But be sure to note these differences—and whatever you do, don't call Welsh or Scottish people English! (Great Britain includes England, Scotland, and Wales; the United Kingdom includes all these countries plus Northern Ireland.)

Greetings

◆ When greeting someone, shake hands and say "How do you do?" The person will respond with "How do you do?" No one will expect an answer to the question.

◆ When a man is introduced to a woman, he should wait for her to extend her hand. Men should also remove their gloves when shaking hands with women. Women may keep their gloves on.

◆ When leaving a group, shake hands with each person.

◆ Address surgeons and dentists as "Mr.," not "Dr."

◆ Address a knight as "Sir" with his first name (Sir Alec Guinness is "Sir Alec"). If you'll be meeting royalty or members of the nobility or the upper clergy, check for polite forms of address in *Debrett's Correct Form.*

◆ In both business and social settings, you may use first names after a short acquaintance. (Take your cue from the British.)

◆ If you want to avoid obvious Americanisms, say "Hello," not "Hi."

◆ Another Americanism to avoid: When leaving someone, don't say "Have a nice day." The British think it's funny and dislike the tone of command.

◆ Begin formal letters with "Dear Sir" or "Dear Madam" and end with "Yours faithfully." A less formal letter can begin "Dear Mr. (Mrs., Miss) Jones," and close with "Very truly yours" or "Yours sincerely."

Conversation

◆ During a discussion, maintain eye contact. The English are taught that one must listen carefully to be polite and that good eye contact is a sign of attention.

◆ Good topics of conversation: the city you're visiting; history; architecture; gardening; or the positive aspects of the British role

in world affairs, past and present.

◆ Topics to avoid: politics (especially socialism), money and prices, England's decline as a world power, religion, the Falklands War, Scottish-English history and relations, dissolution of the union between England and Scotland, or Northern Ireland. If your host asks your views on Northern Ireland, be noncommittal. Say, for example, "It is so difficult for us to judge."

◆ Don't ask about a person's profession.

◆ Avoid discussing race and class.

◆ British people often end a definite statement with a question—for example, "The sun rises in the morning, doesn't it?" No one expects you to answer the question.

◆ The British are somewhat more subtle and less straightforward in conversation than are Americans. They are reluctant to be direct for fear of offending someone.

◆ English humor is of two varieties. On the one hand, there's the dry, satirical humor we associate with such writers as Noel Coward. On the other, there's the broadest slapstick, replete with the bathroom jokes common in TV shows and stage comedies.

◆ One Britishism that tends to puzzle foreigners: if a person says, for example, "He wasn't half angry," it means he was mad as hell. "He isn't half handsome" means he makes a good-looking man look ordinary.

◆ If a conversation turns to an argument, keep cool and be ultrapolite. In arguments, the British become cooler and cooler, rather than overtly angry.

In Scotland and Wales:

◆ While Scottish people might drink scotch, they don't want to be called Scotch and Scotchmen. Scot or Scotsman are the correct terms.

◆ It's in poor taste to joke about what men wear (or don't wear) under their kilts, or about the heritage of kilts or bagpipes.

Money

◆ The unit of currency is the pound (abbreviated £), made up of 100 pence (abbreviated p).

◆ Coins come in denominations of 1, 2, 5, 10, 20, and 50p and £1. You may still find shillings (equal to 5p) in circulation; they are left over from the old currency system.

◆ Notes come in denominations of £5, 10, 20, and 50.

◆ Shops sometimes don't accept £20 or £50 notes, either because they fear forgeries or because they don't have change.

Telephones

◆ The British "ring up" people instead of "calling" them on the phone. "Calling" means going to someone's home.

◆ Ask for a "call box" or "telephone kiosk," not a telephone booth. Dial the number, listen for a beeping sound, and put in 10p to be connected. Every time you hear beeps, put in more money. If you overpay, the money won't be refunded from the phone, but will be sent to you if you call and give the operator your name and address.

◆ To avoid carrying large numbers of coins (which are heavy), buy a telephone card, available in denominations of 20, 50, and

100 units. You can buy these green British Telecom cards at post offices, kiosks, and anywhere else you see the British Telecom logo (a green *T*). The rival card service is Mercury, which some people say is a better value for calling very long distances.

♦ To use a telephone card, you must find a phone that accepts them. Put the card into the slot and dial the number. The phone will show how many units you have left; the number will keep going down as you talk.

♦ Try to find a phone directory before you call Inquiries (Directory Assistance), which costs the equivalent of $1.00 U.S. per use.

♦ You can't make a person-to-person call unless you are phoning outside the United Kingdom.

♦ To make a collect call, ask the operator to "reverse charges."

♦ Many people answer the phone by giving the last four digits of their phone number.

♦ The Emergency Number to summon police, the fire department, or an ambulance is **999.**

In Public

♦ Avoid demonstrative gestures, such as slapping a person on the back or putting your arm around someone's shoulder. It's unusual to display affection to anyone but family members and close friends.

♦ To avoid appearing rude, say "please" and "thank you" whenever appropriate. The British use these words much more than Americans do.

♦ Never stare at people or bother them in public. (Many celebrities say they enjoy being in Great Britain because people leave them alone.)

♦ Never shout in public.

♦ If you're a woman, don't feel insulted when porters, newspaper vendors, and bus or train conductors call you "Love," "Duck," "Dearie," or even "Darling." These are common expressions. Female vendors also call men "Love."

♦ Go to the end of the "queue" (line) and wait your turn for buses, taxis, and trains and in cinemas, theaters, and shops. The British will get angry if you "jump the queue"—attempt to push ahead.

♦ In markets, don't handle the fruits and vegetables. Vendors will be displeased if you do.

♦ You'll hear the national anthem—"God Save the Queen"—at the end of some movies and plays. Stand while it is playing.

♦ At a cricket match, keep quiet and clap whenever someone makes a good play—regardless of which team they're on. The rules are complicated, so you might want to go with someone who can explain the game to you. Casual dress is appropriate.

♦ One of the most civilized aspects of Britain is the presence of public toilets everywhere. They are called "W.C.s," "lavatories (lavs)," "toilets," or "cloakrooms." You'll find them in parks, garages, gas stations, bus and train stations, and department stores, and on the streets. They are usually clean. Most are free, but some require a 2p or 5p coin.

Dress

◆ In cities, you can wear shorts and jeans, as long as they're clean and neat.

◆ For casual occasions, if you really want to fit in, wear tweedy clothes: slacks with sweaters and sporty jackets, for both men and women.

◆ For business meetings, men should wear a dark suit and tie, a white or neutral shirt, dark socks, and black shoes. Women should wear dressy suits.

◆ For dining in a home, men should wear a jacket and tie; women may wear pants or a dress.

◆ For dining in restaurants, get dressed up. Men should wear jackets; some restaurants also require ties, so it's a good idea to bring one along. Women should wear dresses or skirts and blouses.

◆ To theater events, you can wear almost anything from clean jeans to dressy outfits. Dress at these events has become increasingly informal.

◆ For theater openings, men should wear suits, and women should wear dresses.

◆ If an invitation says "formal," it could mean anything from a morning coat to tails. Take your invitation to one of the many formalwear rental shops; they'll tell you what to wear and can outfit you if necessary.

Meals

Hours and Foods

Breakfast: 7:30 to 8:00 A.M. on weekdays; 8:30 to 9:00 A.M. on weekends. A light breakfast is cereal, toast, and coffee or tea. An "English" breakfast is a feast: juice and/or cereal; bacon and/or sausages; eggs; toast, sometimes fried in bacon fat; and sometimes kippers (smoked herring served hot), kidneys, fried mushrooms, and fried tomatoes.

Lunch: Noon to 2:00 P.M. The usual fare is sandwiches, salads, fruit or dessert, and coffee (served after, not with, dessert). Accompanying beverages might be beer, soft drinks, lemonade, or orange "squash" (concentrated orange syrup diluted with water). On Sunday, however, the main meal is at noon and almost always features a roast, called "the Sunday joint."

◆ **Tea:** 3:30 to 4:30 P.M. Tea can be either a light snack or a full meal ("high tea"). Savories (small sandwiches of cucumber, egg, and watercress) come first, followed by sweets: biscuits (cookies), pastries, and gateaux (cakes). Tea accompanies the entire meal. High tea features at least one hot dish, such as meat pie, and is usually eaten a little later, in place of dinner.

Dinner: 7:00 P.M.; 8:00 P.M. for a dinner party. At a dinner party, the meal begins with an aperitif (gin and tonic, whiskey, or sherry) and small appetizers, such as nuts or crisps (potato chips). The starter (first course) is often soup or a prawn cocktail and is followed by meat or fish with potatoes and vegetables. Salad may accompany the meal. Wine may be served. Dinner ends with cheese and crackers, dessert, and coffee and liqueurs (port, cognac, or Grand Marnier). A family meal may include only the main course—with or without salad—and dessert.

Breaks: At most businesses, workers take a midmorning coffee break and a midafternoon tea break.

In Scotland and Wales:

Breakfast: In Scotland, a traditional breakfast includes porridge, toast with marmalade and butter, and tea with milk. Bacon and eggs are usually reserved for Sunday.

◆ In Wales, the meal consists of porridge followed by bacon and eggs and fried bread.

Lunch: In Scotland, lunch was once the main meal of the day, but it is becoming a lighter meal now that many women work outside the home. Nowadays people typically eat broth (homemade soup) and a sandwich, followed by fruit or cheese and biscuits (crackers).

◆ In Wales, the traditional meal is fish or meat with two vegetables. Dessert might be steamed pudding or canned fruit with cream. Beer or tea might accompany the meal.

Dinner: Scottish dinners begin with soup, followed by a main course of meat with two vegetables. Bread or rolls and butter are always served, but salad is uncommon. Dessert ends the meal.

◆ Scottish people who eat a main meal at noon have tea around 5:30 P.M. instead of dinner. Common dishes at this meal are boiled eggs and toast, Welsh rarebit, macaroni and cheese, or fish and salad. Bread and jam, scones, and cakes or biscuits follow.

◆ The Welsh eat a light evening meal (such as cold meat and pickles with bread and butter, or sausages and beans) at 5:00 or 6:00 P.M. Tea accompanies the meal.

Table Manners

◆ Be prompt when invited to dine in someone's home.

◆ Before-dinner drinks such as sherry, gin and tonic, scotch, or wine are popular.

◆ You will usually help yourself from platters of food on the table.

◆ When you finish eating, place your knife and fork side by side on your plate.

◆ Some people don't object to others smoking between courses, but be sure to ask permission before lighting up.

◆ At a formal dinner, don't smoke until after the toast to the Queen at the end of the meal.

◆ After lunch or dinner, coffee is usually served, not tea.

◆ If you are dining with people of the upper class, expect the women to follow traditional practice and withdraw to another room to converse after dinner, leaving the men alone for port and cigars.

◆ At a dinner party, plan on leaving between 11:30 P.M. and midnight. The meal itself will probably end about 11:00 P.M.

◆ If you eat something with garlic, be sure to use a breath mint afterwards. Having garlic on your breath is a social offense.

Eating Out

◆ In any eating place, expect to get smaller portions than you would in the U.S. at every meal except breakfast.

◆ If you order a sandwich, expect to get only one paper-thin slice of meat or cheese on the bread.

♦ If you go to an inexpensive restaurant and must share a table, don't make eye contact and don't initiate a conversation. Behave as though you're alone at the table.

♦ A single woman eating in a restaurant can signal that she wants to be left alone by bringing a book or magazine to read.

♦ Many top restaurants require that you make reservations several days in advance and often ask for a telephone number at which to contact you.

♦ If you've made a reservation and find that you're going to be even 10 or 20 minutes late, call the restaurant or you might lose your table.

♦ To attract a waiter's attention, make eye contact. Don't wave.

♦ The waiter or waitress will say "Thank you" every time he or she brings something to the table.

♦ Try a popular British eating place: a fish-and-chips shop. You'll find genuine fish-and-chips shops primarily in English country towns. You'll get fried fish and chips (french fries) wrapped in paper. Try adding malt vinegar to both the fish and the fries, as the English do.

♦ For interesting, inexpensive meals, try Indian restaurants.

Pubs: For a taste of the local social life, go to the neighborhood pub. All pubs serve drinks, and most serve lunches and light meals.

♦ Some pubs in England and Wales stay open nonstop from 11:00 A.M. to 11:00 P.M., Monday through Saturday. However, other pubs in England, Wales, and Scotland observe the traditional hours: 11:30 A.M. to 3:00 P.M. and 5:30 to 11:00 P.M., Monday through Saturday. Sunday licensing hours in

England have remained the same: noon to 3:00 P.M. and 7:00 to 10:30 P.M.

♦ Women visiting a pub alone might prefer its saloon bar section over its public bar. A woman can go to a pub alone without signaling that she wants to be picked up.

♦ Children are not allowed in pubs unless there is a garden where they can eat and play.

♦ Order beer by the pint or half-pint. Also specify the kind you want—ale, stout (Guinness is the strongest), lager (the English equivalent of American-style beer), or bitter. You might, for example, order "a half of bitter" or a "pint of stout."

♦ Women should note that ordering a pint is considered unladylike; a half-pint is better. A typical "woman's drink" is lager and lime.

♦ You might want to try gin and tonic, or sherry, both popular drinks with the British.

♦ For an American-style martini, ask for either gin and French or an American martini. If you simply order a "martini," you'll get vermouth.

♦ Beer is served at room temperature, and other drinks are served without ice. (Some pubs have an ice bucket on the counter.)

♦ If you're in a pub with a group, it's customary to "buy rounds," with each person taking a turn paying for the group.

♦ An alternative to pubs are wine bars, which serve a large variety of wines by the glass or by the bottle. (Wine is the only alcoholic beverage they serve.) Most wine bars also offer food—pâtés, salads, cheeses, and sometimes hot dishes.

In Scotland and Wales:

♦ Pub hours in Scotland and Wales might vary slightly from those in England. In Scotland, Sunday pub hours vary from region to region; in Wales, pubs are closed on Sundays.

♦ In Scotland, try ordering whisky (spelled without the *e*), the national drink. Order a malt whisky rather than a cheaper blended variety and drink it neat or add water, never ice.

♦ In Scotland, most restaurants outside of major cities close around 8:30 P.M.

♦ In Wales, check to see whether a restaurant serves dinner. Many serve only a main meal at noon, then close.

Specialties

♦ Try these English specialties: crumpets (similar to English muffins, served at breakfast and teatime); Cornish pasties (turnovers filled with meat or vegetables and potatoes); Scotch eggs (hardboiled eggs covered with sausage meat and breadcrumbs and then deep-fried); bangers and mash (sausages and mashed potatoes); steak-and-kidney pie; and toad-in-the-hole (sausages baked in batter).

♦ For dessert, try clotted cream (a thick cream of butterlike consistency, served with scones and jam); gooseberry fool (pureed gooseberries mixed with custard); and trifle (sponge cake soaked in sherry or whiskey and topped with custard, fruit, and cream).

In Scotland and Wales:

♦ In Scotland, try cock-a-leekie soup (chicken and leek soup); cullen skink (fish soup); partan bree (crab with rice and cream); haggis (sheep's stomach stuffed with sheep's innards, spices, oatmeal, and suet, eaten on New Year's Eve and Robert Burns's night, January 25); bannocks (flat cakes of oats, barley, or rye, baked on a griddle in the oven); crowdie (a kind of cottage cheese with double cream and salt added, served with oatcakes and butter at teatime); Dundee cake (a rich fruit cake); black bun (fruit cake in a pastry crust, traditionally served on New Year's Eve); Aberdeen Angus beef; herring; salmon; and trout.

♦ In Wales, try chicken-and-leek pie; sewin (sea trout); Glamorgan sausages (bread crumbs, grated cheddar cheese, and egg yolk, shaped like sausages and deep fried); and faggots (meatballs made of pig's liver, bread crumbs, oatmeal, onions, and spices, baked and served either hot or cold).

Hotels

♦ Hotel clerks might ask whether you would like "early morning tea"— tea delivered to the door of your room as soon as you wake up.

♦ Breakfast is usually included in the price of a hotel or "Bed & Breakfast" room. However, many hotels—especially the larger ones—have recently taken one of two courses: (1) including a continental breakfast (rolls and coffee or tea) in the price of the room, and providing an English breakfast at an extra (often hefty) charge; or (2) not including breakfast in the room price, but providing both continental and English breakfasts at an extra (again often hefty) charge.

♦ If you're staying near the center of a city, you can save money by seeking out a cafe, where you can usually have breakfast for less than half the price your hotel will charge.

♦ At Bed & Breakfasts (B&Bs), don't expect to have breakfast late in the morning, as you might in a hotel. Most B&Bs serve breakfast during a one-hour period, usually 7:30 to 8:30 A.M. Rarely, except on weekends, can you have breakfast after that hour. The menu for breakfast will be fixed and will usually offer some form of eggs with sausage and/or bacon. Don't ask for any variations unless your hosts offer them.

♦ At some B&Bs you'll be charged for a bath. Most operate on a tight profit margin, and hot water is expensive.

♦ Business-type hotels often say they'll provide photocopying and secretarial service, but in practice those services might be difficult to obtain.

In Scotland and Wales:

♦ In Scotland, hotel rooms can be very cold, even in summer. When you book a room, ask whether there is central heating or a room heater. Take rooms with central heating if possible.

♦ Many Scottish hotels and B&Bs, especially during the winter, serve bacon and eggs for breakfast, rather than the traditional porridge.

Tipping

♦ *Restaurants:* If the service charge isn't included, leave 10–15 percent.

♦ *Porters:* Tip 20p a bag, except in luxury hotels, where a minimum of £1 is expected.

♦ *Hotel maids:* Leave £1 per day.

♦ *Taxis:* Tip about 10–15 percent. If the trip has been through central London—a low-fare but high-aggravation route for the driver—you might wish to be a bit more generous.

♦ *Cloakroom attendants:* Give 20–50p.

♦ *Washroom attendants:* Leave a 20p coin.

♦ *Housemaids:* If you're lucky enough to spend a weekend with a family that has a maid, leave her £5 at the end of your stay.

Private Homes

♦ Always phone ahead before visiting. Don't just drop in.

♦ If you're visiting for an evening, don't expect your hosts to show you around the house, and don't wander through the house or garden on your own.

♦ Smokers are now in the minority in Great Britain. Be sure to ask first whether you may smoke.

♦ If you are staying with a family, be sure to make your bed and tidy your room every day. You might also offer to clear the table after meals and help with the dishes. Unlike hosts in some other countries, the British are not reluctant to accept help from guests.

♦ If you make a local phone call from someone's home, try to keep it brief—and be sure to offer to pay for the call. The United Kingdom has the most expensive rates for local calls in the world, and there is a charge for each call. In addition, the British believe the phone is for business and emergencies, and regard frequent social calls as intrusions.

♦ If you call long-distance from the phone in a private home, find out from the operator how much it will cost. Don't plan to settle when the phone bill arrives; only out-of-town calls are itemized.

◆ If you use an appliance such as an electric kettle or a TV, you must turn on the outlet as well as the appliance. Look for a rectangular switch next to the outlet. When you push it in and the top shows a red line, the outlet is on.

◆ Don't be offended if people send out "Do Not Disturb" signals, even if you're sitting in the same room. They might continue to read or knit and not respond to your questions. They aren't trying to be rude; they merely want privacy.

◆ Ask your hosts when it would be convenient for you to take a bath, since sometimes the water must be heated first. The British are frugal with hot water.

Gifts: If you're invited to dinner, bring flowers or —even better—send them in advance. Other good gifts are wine, champagne, or a box of chocolates.

◆ If you stay with a family, bring adults foods from your area (e.g., live lobsters, canned clam chowder, maple syrup, blue corn tortilla chips, pralines, etc.), a book of photos of your area, thick American towels, unusual wall calendars, a current book (if you know the person's taste), or a bottle of duty-free gin, cognac, or California wine. Bring children T-shirts.

Business

Hours

Businesses and government offices: 9:00 A.M. to 5:00 P.M., Monday through Friday. A few businesses are open from 9:00 A.M. until noon on Saturday.

Banks: 9:30 A.M. to 3:30 or 4:30 P.M., Monday through Friday. Some are open Saturday morning. In some small towns, banks are open only two or three days a week.

Stores: 9:00 A.M. to 5:30 P.M., Monday through Saturday. Some stay open until 7:30 P.M. on Wednesday or Thursday, and some close on Saturday afternoon. In small towns, shops observe "early closing" one day during the week, shutting at 1:00 P.M.

◆ In London and southern England, work hours are usually between 9:30 A.M. and 5:30 P.M., while in northern England, Scotland, and Wales, people usually begin work earlier.

In Scotland:

◆ Hours are generally the same, except that banks are open from 9:30 A.M. to 12:30 P.M. and 1:30 to 3:30 P.M., Monday through Thursday. On Thursday, they also reopen from 4:30 to 6:00 P.M. On Friday, banks are open from 9:30 to 3:30 P.M. They are closed Saturdays and Sundays.

In Wales:

Businesses and government offices: 9:00 A.M. to 5:00 P.M., Monday through Friday. Other hours are the same as England's.

Business Practices

◆ A good source of business contacts for the U.K. is the Invest in Britain Bureau (I.B.B.), which has its main American office in New York (11th Floor, 845 3rd Ave., New York, NY 10022; telephone [212] 745-0495; fax [212] 745-0456). You can also reach the I.B.B. through the British consulates in Boston, Chicago, Cleveland, Dallas, Houston, Los Angeles, San Francisco, and Seattle, and through the British Embassy in Washington, D.C.

◆ An I.B.B. contact can help you find premises, decide what type of venture will be best, and file any necessary documents.

(Realize, however, that you're not required to have an agent). Ask for a copy of *Invest in the U.K.,* a valuable guide to investment opportunities and protocol.

♦ Avoid making business trips to Great Britain in June, July, or August, which are vacation months. You'll also see little business done during the week between Christmas and New Year's.

♦ Temporary-office rental companies will help you rent an office with a telephone and a fax number for as long as you want. The Commercial Section of your embassy can supply a list of their names.

♦ Don't make yourself conspicuous by staying at *the* most expensive hotel. The British might think "Why should we buy this product from you when you're obviously running up overheads?" Choose your hotel for its convenience.

♦ In most companies, people—senior and junior executives—will be on a first-name basis. People will probably start to use your first name soon, your cue to use first names with them. The general custom is to use first names in person and last names on the telephone. Use whatever form of address your British counterpart does.

♦ You won't find many women at high echelons of companies. Foreign businesswomen might find their male British counterparts condescending; attitudes vary with the age of the businessman and the type of business.

♦ It's acceptable to telephone business contacts at home until 9:30 or 10:00 P.M.

Meetings and negotiations: Make business appointments well in advance—as much as six weeks is advisable. The British arrange their calendars months ahead of time. Write a letter explaining when you'll be in the country and what you would like to discuss, and giving several optional dates. If time is short, fax your message, but a letter is preferable.

♦ Don't ask the U.S. Embassy to help you make appointments until you've arrived in the country.

♦ A letter of introduction from a colleague will facilitate getting an appointment.

♦ A business meeting will probably be an informal meeting in an office and will begin and end with social conversation. Despite the informal atmosphere, don't engage in familiar gestures such as backslapping.

♦ Your British counterpart might be less prepared for your meeting than you had hoped. After the meeting, send a written confirmation of what you discussed and what you agreed on.

♦ Visual aids are a useful adjunct to your presentation if they are well done; however, they aren't as important as they are in the U.S.

♦ If you're asked to speak to a group of English businesspeople, leave time for questions.

♦ British business dealings move more slowly than they do in the U.S.

♦ Final decisions are usually made by a firm's managing director.

♦ The British are honest and forthright in business dealings. Delays occur only when something unforeseen happens. If you're dealing with tradespeople, however, "pretty soon" might mean a week or two.

♦ If someone suggests that a verbal agreement is sufficient (from the old days of "a man's word is his bond"), say "I have a solicitor [the English word for attorney] back in my home office who insists on a written contract. It's not me, it's the solicitor's requirement."

◆ While Americans say "agreed on terms," the British say "agreed terms."

Entertainment: Don't suggest a business breakfast; few British businesspeople are familiar with that custom. Business lunches are popular. If you're dealing with people in the private sector, you might be invited to dinner—for example, after you've visited a facility.

◆ For a business meal, anticipate going to a French or Italian restaurant, which are usually the most elegant.

◆ Wait for the British businessperson to issue the first invitation. When you reciprocate, ask either the businessperson or the concierge at your hotel to suggest a restaurant.

◆ Business lunches begin about 12:45 or 1:00 P.M. and last until 2:30 P.M. People usually drink aperitifs and wine, but mineral water will be available if you don't want to drink.

◆ A British businessperson who suggests lunch in a pub isn't trying to avoid paying for a restaurant meal. Many British people take Americans to pubs because they know of the American fascination with pubs. The usual drinks at a pub lunch are beer, lager, or shandy (beer and lemonade).

◆ Business lunches are usually half social. Business might not be discussed until coffee is served. The person who issues the invitation pays, but sometimes the British will want to pay. Insist on paying anyway.

◆ If you cannot accept a dinner invitation, it's all right to decline. If someone invites you to a major event that required getting tickets, however (such as a tennis match at Wimbledon), accept if at all possible.

◆ Feel free to bring up business at dinner, but don't expect an in-depth discussion.

◆ You might be invited to a meal at a British businessperson's home. Such invitations are more common than in other European countries. They're also gestures of friendship.

◆ For an evening function or a large party, expect spouses to be included.

◆ You might encounter the "old boy network" on social occasions. It won't show during business dealings, but you might feel left out of dinner conversations when the "old boys" discuss their shared pasts and make inside social jokes.

Gifts: Giving gifts is not a normal part of business, perhaps because the British make such a clear distinction between business and personal life. Don't offer a gift until one is given to you.

In Scotland:

Entertainment: A dinner invitation is likely to be in a businessperson's home; home entertaining for business is more popular in Scotland than in England. You might want to reciprocate by inviting your hosts (and their spouses) to dinner in a restaurant.

Holidays & Celebrations

Holidays:
New Year's Day (January 1); Good Friday; Easter Monday; May Day (the first Monday in May); Spring Bank Holiday (the last Monday in May); Summer Bank Holiday (the last Monday in August); Christmas Day (December 25); and Boxing Day (December 26).

◆ Guy Fawkes Day (November 5) commemorates the capture of Guy Fawkes, who plotted to destroy the Houses of Parliament in 1605. The English celebrate with fireworks, bonfires, and burning effigies of Guy Fawkes. (This is not a public holiday, however.)

◆ Boxing Day is traditionally a servants' holiday to compensate for work on Christmas. On that day their employers would give them Christmas boxes—often leftover food—hence the name.

In Scotland and Wales:

◆ In Scotland, public holidays are the same as those in England, except that January 2 is added, and the Summer Bank Holiday is on the first Monday in August instead of the last.

◆ In Wales, an additional holiday is St. David's Day (March 1), the anniversary of the death of the patron saint of Wales.

◆ In Scotland on Hogmanay (December 31), many people have parties that last until 7:00 A.M. the next day. On the morning of the new year there is what is called "First Footing." To ensure good luck in the coming year, the first person who enters a home should be a tall, dark male carrying a piece of coal, a black bun, and a bottle of whisky, from which he gives the host a drink. In the afternoon, friends, neighbors, and relatives gather at one house to wish each other a happy new year. Each guest brings a small gift to be used by everyone in the house, such as a calendar. Everyone partakes of a buffet, usually with ham, bread, black buns, and shortbread.

Transportation

Public Transport

Mass transit: When people refer to the "tube" or the "Underground," they mean the subway.

◆ Most Underground ticket sales are automated; you buy your ticket from a machine. Fares are based on distance by zones. Keep your ticket, because you'll need it to operate the turnstile when you leave.

◆ On some buses you pay as you enter; on others, you choose a seat and wait for the conductor to come and collect your fare (take your cue from the other passengers). Fares are based on distance.

◆ Smoking is forbidden on any London Transport property—stations, trains, or buses.

◆ Buses that aren't the traditional "London red" cover privatized routes. The fare base is the same as for public buses, and bus passes are accepted.

◆ In London, you can buy a transportation pass for any period from a day up to a year, with all sorts of variations in between. You can get a pass for one zone, two zones, or all five. If you want a pass for more than a week, you'll need a photocard; bring some passport photos with you. You can also get a pass for both the bus and the Underground or just for the bus. The passes are available at all Underground ticket offices.

◆ All intercity trains have first- and second-class seats. The wider first-class seats are arranged so two seats face two other seats across a table. On older trains, first and second class are separated by compartments.

First class costs 50 percent more than second class, which is more crowded but still comfortable. Round-trip tickets (called "return") for both classes cost twice as much as one-way (called "single") except for long-distance trips at certain times of the day. Special rates exist for off-peak hours and weekends.

♦ Most intercity trains have a restaurant car or a buffet (pronounced "BUF-fee" in England) car for snacks. Reserve seats in the dining car with the steward before boarding or soon after boarding.

♦ Sleeping cars are available to Scotland, north and west England, and Wales. In first class, you have a single compartment; in second class, there are two bunk beds.

♦ You can reserve seats in both classes on intercity trains in advance, either before leaving home or in Great Britain.

♦ You can buy rail passes for unlimited travel within a set period of time.

Taxis: You can hail taxis on the street and order taxis or minicabs (a regular small car, less expensive than the usual large London taxicabs) by telephone.

♦ When you hail a taxi on the street, give the driver your destination before you get in. The driver will lower the passenger-side window so you can say where you're going.

♦ At the end of a taxi ride, get out of the cab before you pay. The driver will again lower the passenger-side window so you can pay.

♦ At night, if you see an empty taxi without its "for hire" light on, try hailing it anyway.

Driving

♦ You do not need an International Driver's License.

♦ Seat belts are compulsory for drivers and front-seat passengers.

♦ Distances are measured in miles, not kilometers.

♦ The speed limit in built-up areas is 30 mph, on other roads is 50 mph, on two-lane highways is 60 mph, and on motorways is 70 mph (even if the limit isn't posted).

♦ If you're driving on the left side of the road for the first time, be cautious—especially if you come to a roundabout (rotary or traffic circle), which you must enter clockwise.

♦ A "Halt" sign is a stop sign; a "Diversion" is a detour; and a "Zebra crossing" is a pedestrian crossing.

♦ If you want to drive slowly on a motorway, stay in the left lane. Other drivers might get annoyed if you're driving too slowly.

♦ Don't turn left at a red light.

♦ Acknowledge the courtesy of other drivers by raising your hand to thank them.

♦ Street signs in British cities are usually plaques on the sides of buildings; they are difficult to read while driving.

♦ In cities, park at meters and in parking garages. London has complex parking rules—it's easier to use public transportation or taxis.

♦ When traveling in rural areas, fill your gas tank whenever you can; gas stations may be scarce.

♦ Drinking and driving laws are strict. British police routinely administer sobriety tests and enforce strict fines.

In Scotland:

♦ In Scotland, many service garages are closed on Sundays. Garages are scarce in northern Scotland.

Legal Matters & Safety

◆ For help with directions or any other traveling problems, ask the British police. They're friendly, helpful, and usually tolerant of travelers' minor mistakes.

◆ The legal drinking age is 18.

◆ Great Britain is reasonably safe, even in urban areas, but an unaccompanied woman in an unfamiliar area might be wise to take a taxi.

◆ Be careful when crossing streets! It's the biggest danger for foreigners because they're not used to cars driving on the left side of the road. Some streets have signs warning "Look Right." Take extra care at intersections.

Key Phrases

Below, we provide American words or terms and their English and Scottish counterparts.

American/English	**American/Scottish**
apartment/flat	dust and dirt/stour
attorney/solicitor	know/ken
candy/sweets	lake/loch
dessert/pudding	mess/guddle
doctor's office/surgery or consulting room	oh! (an exclamation)/ach!
drug store/chemist	serious/dour
elevator/lift	small/wee
flashlight/torch	small river or stream/burn
french fries/chips	valley/glen
gasoline/petrol	
hood of car/bonnet	
to phone/to ring up	
potato chips/crisps	
raincoat/mac	
soccer/football	
subway/tube	
toilet/loo (informal)	
trunk of car/boot	

Greece

Like Zorba the Greek, Greek people tend to be free-spirited and to love life. Sitting in a *taverna*, you'll see both men and women spontaneously leap to their feet and dance. Dancing is as central to Greek life as television is to American. Greek people also tend to be warm and demonstrative. Travelers in Greece will find this warmth and acceptance a real boon.

Do a little homework before you visit Greece; learn to read the Greek alphabet so you can sound out the names of restaurants, towns, and other destinations for taxi drivers and bus drivers.

Greetings

◆ Shake hands firmly when introduced to someone and when greeting or leaving someone you already know.

◆ Close friends of the same sex kiss and embrace when they meet. Men might do this only after a long absence.

◆ Don't use people's first names until they use yours, especially when doing business. People working at the same office for 20 or 30 years might still call each other by last names.

Conversation

◆ English is the second major language in tourist areas and among businesspeople.

◆ Good topics of conversation: international politics, music, sports such as soccer, your host's family or job, or the favorite conversation opener—the weather.

◆ Topics to avoid: the lengthy dispute between Greeks and Turks over Cyprus, American involvement in Greek affairs, or any pro-Turkish feelings you might have. And don't downplay Greece's role in World War II.

◆ Greeks might ask you personal questions, such as how much you earn. Don't be offended; it's their way of getting to know you. If you prefer not to answer, try to be tactful.

◆ If you compliment Greeks, don't be surprised if they puff a breath through their pursed lips to ward off the jealousy of the evil eye.

◆ Greeks sometimes indicate no by tipping their heads back slightly and raising their eyebrows (or sometimes by just raising their eyebrows), without saying a word.

Money

◆ The unit of currency is the drachma (abbreviated Dr).

◆ Coins come in denominations of 1, 2, 5, 10, 20, and 50 drachmas.

◆ Bills come in denominations of 50, 100, 500, 1,000, and 5,000 drachmas.

Telephones

◆ Look for pay phones at kiosks, in booths on the street, and attached to newer kiosks (at an older kiosk you can pay the vendor to use the telephone).

◆ In Athens, silver-and-blue telephones are for local calls within the city; silver-and-orange phones are for calls outside Athens.

◆ In towns outside Athens, telephones are located at kiosks. To make calls within Greece, pay the kiosk attendant, who will tell you how much it costs.

◆ To make international calls in Athens, go to the telephone office (O.T.E.).

◆ To make long distance calls in towns outside Athens, go to the post office or, if available, telephone office.

◆ You can make both local and long-distance calls at the O.T.E. You can either dial local and long-distance calls directly or book them through an operator. You can also make collect calls to the U.S., but you'll have to wait about an hour to get through.

◆ Greece has no telephone cards.

◆ Emergency numbers are as follows:

Police	100
(in Athens suburbs)	109
Fire department	199
Ambulance	166
Automobile breakdown	104

In Public

◆ Greeks are demonstrative and physically affectionate. Feel free to be the same.

◆ Don't wave American-style (showing your palm with your fingers extended). It's an insult. Instead, raise your index finger while keeping your palm closed.

◆ Many men finger worry beads constantly. It's considered calming and has no religious significance.

◆ Don't expect orderly lines at bus stops or banks. People simply elbow ahead in such situations. Do as the Greeks do, or you'll be left waiting.

◆ Never joke about or show disrespect toward the Greek flag or national emblem.

◆ Punctuality is not important in Greece, so keep a flexible schedule. It's perfectly acceptable to arrive 30 minutes late (except for a business appointment).

◆ If you go to a shop or market, try to bargain by asking, "Is this the final price?" Vendors will make it clear if they don't want to bargain. If they are willing to bargain, start by offering half the asking price.

◆ Guard against being overcharged at shops. Places catering to tourists must post prices in a prominent place, so be sure to check them.

◆ Greeks smoke constantly, even while eating. Be prepared for a great deal of "passive" smoking.

◆ In a Greek Orthodox church, women shouldn't go behind the altar.

◆ Look for public toilets in hotels, restaurants, museums, and parks. Always bring tissues, because there might not be toilet paper. If there is a bin, put the tissue in it; don't put it in the toilet, or the toilet will flood.

◆ The sign for public toilets is *W.C.,* or sometimes "Toilet" in English or "Toilettes" in French. Men's rooms will say ΑΝΔΡΩΝ. or ΚΥΡΙΟΙ; women's rooms will say ΓΥΝΑΙΚΩΝ or ΚΥΡΙΕΣ.

Dress

◆ For casual wear, you can wear jeans in cities, but don't wear shorts except in resort areas.

◆ When invited to dinner at someone's home, women should wear dresses or dressy pants. Men should wear jackets and ties in the winter, but shirts and trousers are fine for summer.

◆ To theater events, men should wear a jacket and tie, and women should wear a dress, skirt, or dressy pants. To theater openings, men should wear a dark suit, and women should wear a dress or skirt.

◆ Men and women can wear jeans or pants to most restaurants. To formal restaurants, men should wear jacket and tie, and women should wear dresses or skirts.

◆ For business, women should wear shirt-dresses or suits, with heels. Men should wear suits and ties in the winter. In the summer, Greek businessmen dress more casually, but you'll make a better impression if you start with a suit and tie.

◆ To theater events, men should wear a jacket and tie, and women should wear a dress, skirt, or dressy pants. To theater

openings, men should wear a dark suit, and women should wear a dress or skirt.

◆ If an invitation says "formal dress," women should wear long dresses; men, tuxedos.

◆ Women visiting churches or monasteries should have their arms covered and should wear skirts, never pants.

Meals

Hours and Food

Breakfast *(toh proeeno):* 7:00 A.M. Expect a roll or bread, butter, jam or honey, and coffee (either Turkish or instant).

Lunch *(toh gevma):* 1:30 to 2:00 P.M. Some people have a light meal: a sandwich or salad, cheese, and yogurt. Others have a main meal: appetizers, meat or fish with salad, fruit or yogurt with honey, and Turkish coffee. People drink water and either beer or wine with the meal.

Dinner *(toh theepno):* 8:30 to 9:30 P.M. A family dinner consists of the same courses as the main meal described at lunch, except that a dessert follows the fruit course.

◆ A dinner party begins with appetizers such as meatballs, or cheese or spinach pies, served with *ouzo,* an aniseed liquor usually served with water, or *retsina,* a wine with resin added. (Greece also produces good unresinated wines.) The main course might be roast lamb or a dish such as *moussaka* (a casserole of eggplant, ground lamb, and cheese) served with potatoes or rice pilaf and a salad. Wine will be served throughout the meal. The meal will end with fruit, Turkish coffee, or brandy and scotch.

Table Manners

◆ Greeks enjoy meals primarily for the company of friends; eating is secondary.

◆ If you're invited to dinner, arrive about 30 minutes late. People don't expect you to be on time.

◆ When appetizers are served before lunch or dinner—often on one plate in the middle of the table—use your fingers to help yourself.

◆ Your hosts will pressure you to drink, especially if you're a man. Don't use the excuse that you have work to do; they'll simply tell you to take it easy for the day. If you really don't want to drink, take very small sips, leaving your glass almost full. If you can't drink, explain that you can't drink for health reasons.

◆ If you're the male guest of honor, sit to the right of the hostess. If you're the female guest of honor, sit to the right of the host.

◆ Traditionally, women do all the serving while men stay with the guests. The oldest guest is served first.

◆ Some foods can be eaten with the fingers. Take your cue from your host.

◆ Enjoy the relaxed atmosphere at meals. Close friends or relatives often share foods and eat from one another's plates.

◆ Keep your wrists on the table. In informal company, you may even put your elbows on the table.

◆ Bread accompanies every meal, but don't expect a bread-and-butter plate. Put your bread on the table.

◆ To avoid offending your hosts, plan to eat a great deal. If there's one dish you don't care for, say you really loved one of the other dishes and eat a bit more of that.

◆ To show you're finished, either cross your utensils, with the knife under the fork and the fork tines down, or remove your napkin from your lap and put it next to your plate.

◆ Coffee is served Turkish-style, unless you ask for Nescafé. Turkish coffee is served in small cups and is very strong. You can ask for it bitter, medium, or sweet. Do not drink it all or you will end up with muddy grounds in your mouth.

◆ If you're invited to dinner, stay until about 11:00 P.M. If the conversation is animated, though, feel free to stay until it starts dying down.

Eating Out

◆ For variety, try the following types of eating places:

● A *galaktoplia* is a milk shop. You can order yogurt, rice pudding, custard, and sticky, sweet desserts.

● A *kafenion* is a coffeehouse or cafe, with the emphasis on conversation. In cities, both men and women frequent *kafenions,* but in the country only men go.

● A *zakharoplastio* is a pastry shop, which serves soup, homemade yogurt, puddings, coffee, alcohol, and soft drinks. Women often frequent these shops instead of cafes. Also, since Athens nightclubs now must close at 2:00 A.M., many people go to pastry shops late at night. If you're out late, stop in one to watch the people.

● Stands on the street and at beaches serve snacks such as *souvlakia, giro, tyropitta,* and *spanakopitta* (see Specialties).

◆ In most restaurants you seat yourself.

♦ If you are a woman traveling alone, choose a fairly elegant restaurant for your evening meal to avoid being harassed by men.

♦ Don't ask the price of a meal before you order; it's considered rude. As a rule of thumb, meat is usually inexpensive and fish expensive.

♦ Except in the most deluxe restaurants, you may walk into the kitchen and choose the food you'd like (an especially useful custom in places with menus written only in Greek).

♦ Most frying is done in heavy olive oil. You might want to stick to nonfried foods (if you don't, for example, relish an egg fried in olive oil).

♦ To attract a server's attention, say "pah-rah-kah-LOW" ("please"). Some people bang on a glass with a spoon, but that's considered impolite.

♦ You must be assertive with waiters to attract their attention and to get what you want, when you want it.

Specialties

♦ Be sure to sample some of these Greek specialties: *dolmades* (grape leaves stuffed with rice); *keftedes* (meatballs); *barbounia* (red mullet fish, usually grilled); *kalamarakia* (squid); *souvlakia* (lamb and vegetables grilled on a skewer); *moussaka* (a casserole of eggplant, ground lamb, and cheese); *spanakopitta* (spinach pie); *tyropitta* (cheese pie); *giro* (pressed lamb and herbs cooked on a vertical spit, with slices carved off and served on pita bread with salad); or *taramousalata* (a dip made of salted roe of gray mullet).

♦ For dessert, try *baklava* (a pastry with thin layers of flaky dough, nuts, and cinnamon in a honey syrup).

♦ If you're not interested in exotic foods, avoid *miala* (brains) and *kokoretsi* (intestines stuffed with sweetbreads, liver, and spices).

Hotels

♦ In towns, hotels are open all year round, but most in beach resorts close from November through April 15. For a summer stay, book a hotel room several months in advance.

♦ When you check in, the hotel clerk will usually ask you to leave your passport overnight.

♦ Even in a luxury hotel, don't expect the same amenities you would find in luxury hotels in other European countries (such as TVs, little packages of soap, or refrigerators).

♦ In Athens, try to avoid taking a room facing the street because you'll probably find the street noise bothersome.

Tipping

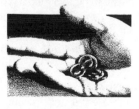

♦ *Restaurants:* Even though the tip is usually included in the bill, leave an extra 50 drachmas per person on the table (not on the plate with the check).

♦ *Hotel maids:* Tip 855–1,710 drachmas per week, depending on how much you've asked of her.

♦ *Porters:* Give 50 drachmas per bag.

◆ *Taxis:* Tip 5–10 percent, the higher amount if the driver performed some special service such as carrying your bags or obtaining information.

◆ *Ushers:* Tip 20–40 drachmas.

◆ *Cloakroom attendants:* Tip 70 drachmas.

Private Homes

◆ Visiting time usually begins about 5:30 P.M., but telephone ahead to ask whether it's convenient for you to come. You'll be offered cold water and preserved fruits (take a spoonful of fruit and then drink some water), *ouzo,* pastries, and Turkish coffee.

◆ If you arrive at 5:30, leave by about 7:30 (earlier if you hear dinner preparations), or your hosts will feel obliged to invite you to dinner. If they do invite you, don't stay unless they really insist.

◆ Don't compliment your hosts on a specific object, such as a knicknack or a vase, or they'll probably insist on giving it to you.

◆ If you stay with a family, your hosts will want to be included in your plans for the day. Even if you would prefer to be alone, find a polite way of including them, such as meeting for lunch or in the late afternoon.

◆ If you spend several days with a family, help with small chores such as setting the table. Offer to help with the dishes, though your hosts will probably refuse.

◆ If you've been wearing sandals, wash your feet before going to bed.

◆ As a courtesy, ask before you take a bath. Hot-water tanks in Greece are very small, so use very little water in case someone else wants a bath.

◆ Don't expect to find a shower curtain. The shower itself is a hand-held sprayer that looks like a telephone receiver. Be careful when using it, because its flexible hose can twist unexpectedly, sending water all over the bathroom floor.

Gifts: If you're invited to dinner, bring a flower arrangement or a potted plant. (Cut flowers are so inexpensive in Greece that they aren't a suitable gift.) Be sure the plant or arrangement is wrapped when you present it to your hosts. If possible, send it in advance. Other good gifts are wine, brandy, or pastries.

◆ If you're staying with a family, bring gifts from the U.S.: whiskey, towels, sheets (queen-size, because most Greek beds are large), or pocket calculators.

◆ If a family has children, they expect visitors to bring gifts for them, even for a casual visit. If you're invited to drinks or dinner, bring the children candy. If you're staying with a family, bring the children toys.

Business

Hours
Businesses and government offices: 8:00 A.M. to 1:30 P.M. and 4:30 to 7:30 P.M.,

Monday through Friday; 8:00 A.M. to 1:30 P.M. on Saturday. Many businesses are closed on Wednesday afternoons.

Banks: 8:00 A.M. to 1:30 or 2:30 P.M., Monday through Saturday. Many are also open from 5:30 to 8:30 P.M. on Tuesday, Thursday, and Friday.

Stores: 9:00 A.M. to 2:30 P.M., Monday, Wednesday, and Saturday; 9:00 A.M. to 1:30 P.M. and 5:30 to 8:30 P.M., Tuesday, Thursday, and Friday. This schedule is experimental and may change. When you arrive, ask for current hours at your hotel.

Business Practices

♦ Avoid business trips to Greece during June, July, and August and during the week before and after both Christmas and Greek Orthodox Easter (see Holidays & Celebrations).

♦ Greek businesspeople are quite hospitable. Your business contacts might pick you up at the airport, even if you arrive very early in the morning, and might take you out to every meal.

♦ Personal contact is important to Greeks, and they go out of their way to take care of business guests. Don't, however, be overly familiar yourself. For example, don't slap people on the back when you've known them only a few days and say "Let's have a drink tonight."

♦ Study Greek history before your trip. The Greeks are proud of their history, and ignorance of the subject will undermine your chance of success.

♦ You'll find many women actively involved in business—but not in top management echelons. Greek men tend to be chauvinists. They enjoy seeing women in business but believe that at some point women should think about having families instead.

♦ Foreign businesswomen will be taken seriously but need to remain very professional, as Greek men will be flirtatious.

♦ Doing business in Greece requires navigating many layers of bureaucracy to obtain permits, approvals, and signatures. Your counterpart will obtain the necessary docu-

ments, but it will take time.

♦ Most Greek businesspeople are highly educated and speak at least two foreign languages—English and French or German.

♦ Bring business cards printed in English, and give one to everyone you meet on business. The cards will ensure that your name is spelled correctly.

♦ If you need to describe items to be sold to the general public, bring literature in Greek. For business and industrial literature, however, English is fine.

♦ Fax machines are widely available.

♦ Greeks tend to complain a great deal; don't be put off by it. If you ask people "How's business?" they might answer, "Things are terrible." To find out the truth, ask them where they spent their vacation and check how they're dressed. Don't judge them by their words alone.

Meetings and negotiations: Many businesses close on Wednesday afternoon, so you might find it difficult to make appointments then.

♦ Be sure to make appointments in advance with both private and government businesspeople.

♦ Be on time. Punctuality is expected of foreigners, although it probably won't be reciprocated.

♦ You'll probably be escorted to a conference room in which seven or eight people will be waiting, perhaps with the owner sitting in the back. The owner or the person with controlling interest will make the decisions.

♦ Don't expect to get right to business. Morning discussions might begin with a review of the previous day's economic news or what happened in Parliament. Politics is a national pastime, so keep up on world affairs.

♦ You'll be offered Greek coffee and ice water, or perhaps *ouzo* or whiskey.

♦ Expect to hear many strong opinions. Greeks are the champions of free expression; many have an opinion about everything and tend to think theirs is the *only* opinion.

♦ In any negotiations, be prepared for formidable adversaries. Greeks have a long history of bargaining.

♦ Expect a great deal of bargaining. If you're not prepared to bargain, you won't be taken seriously. Avoid saying "That's the price; take it or leave it."

♦ Most businesses are family owned, and Greeks are highly protective of family honor. Don't do or say anything that might reflect badly on a family member.

♦ Don't try to impose a deadline on a meeting ("We have to work this out by 6:00 P.M."). Greeks work out all the details of any business arrangement with those involved, and a meeting lasts as long as is necessary.

Entertainment: Greeks are bon vivants for whom enjoying life is a primary goal. They want to make money so they can have fun, and they want to have fun making money. This quality can lead to some evening marathons. Business discussions might go from 6:00 to 10:00 P.M., followed by dinner from 11:00 P.M. to 2:00 A.M. Greeks think nothing of going to bed at 2:00 or 2:30 A.M. and being at work at 9:00 A.M.

♦ Business lunches generally begin at 2:00 or 3:00 P.M. Discussions might cover many topics—except business. Don't put a contract on the table and start discussing it.

Gifts: Give your business colleagues pens,

pocket calculators, or leather desk accessories.

Holidays & Celebrations

Holidays:
New Year's Day (January 1); Epiphany (January 6); Independence Day (March 25); Shrove Monday; Good Friday; Easter Monday; Labor Day (May 1); Pentecost; Feast of the Virgin Mary (August 15); National Day (October 28); Christmas (December 25); and December 26.

♦ Before you go to Greece, check the date of Greek Orthodox Easter, which changes every year. It is held on the first Sunday after the first full moon after the first day of spring after the Mosaic Passover.

♦ Don't invite Greeks to dinner or other entertainment on Good Friday. Religious people consider it a day of mourning.

♦ Visitors are welcome at Easter celebrations. Church services begin at midnight on Saturday, with people lighting one another's candles outside the church. After the church services there are parties and meals of lamb roasted outdoors, followed by dancing and games.

♦ Greeks celebrate their patron saint's day rather than their own birthday. (For example, everyone named George receives visits from friends and relatives on St. George's Day.) If you know someone celebrating a name day, take a small gift to the house, where you'll be offered light refreshments.

Transportation

Public Transport

Mass transit: Athens has 40 bus and trolley routes that operate from 5:00 A.M. to midnight or 12:30 A.M. The fare is 30 drachmas for any distance, provided you don't transfer. The Athens subway costs 30 drachmas and runs between 5:30 A.M. and midnight.

◆ Posted bus schedules are often inaccurate. A good source of local bus information is vendors at kiosks. Be sure you can pronounce your destination so that you'll get the correct bus. Sit next to the driver, so that he can tell you where to get off. The ticket collector on board will take your fare after the bus departs.

◆ A network of bus services extends to even the smallest villages. Athens has two main bus terminals—one for western and northern Greece and one for central and eastern Greece.

◆ For most trains within Greece, tickets are available at the train station up to 30 minutes before departure.

◆ Train service is both infrequent and slow. Second class is crowded in the summer; a first-class ticket is well worth the price.

Taxis: Look for taxis at main squares, hotels, and train stations, or on the street. Finding one on the street is difficult during rush hours: 7 to 9:00 A.M., 2 to 3:00 P.M., 5 to 6:00 P.M., and 8 to 10:00 P.M.

◆ Taxis are supposed to display fares prominently, but guard against being overcharged by asking at your hotel what the fare should be. There is an extra charge for luggage.

◆ Although sharing taxis is common, each person pays full fare.

Driving

◆ Consider carefully whether you want to drive in Greece, which has an extremely high accident rate. If you do decide to drive, car rentals are available in Athens and in resort areas.

◆ If you plan to drive in Greece, get an International Driver's License before you arrive and carry it with you at all times.

◆ By law, seat belts are required for all occupants of the car.

◆ Be cautious when driving, because Greek drivers tend to ignore traffic laws, pedestrian signs, and traffic lights. They also weave in and out of traffic and pass on both the right and the left.

◆ Speed limits in built-up areas are 30–50 kph per hour. On other roads, the speed limit is 100 kph, unless lower limits are posted.

◆ At intersections, vehicles approaching from the right have the legal right of way, but in practice the right of way goes to whoever gets there first.

◆ Don't use your horn in cities (it's illegal), but do use it in the country, especially on mountain roads, to signal that you're coming around a curve.

◆ The police can stop you for a traffic violation and demand immediate payment of a fine. Most speak a few words of English or will find someone who does.

◆ Police can impose on-the-spot fines for drunk driving, but rarely do so.

◆ Always park on the right side of the street. Illegal sidewalk parking is common, but there's a fine even foreigners will have to pay.

◆ Don't start a journey after dark. Few oncoming drivers dim their lights. If you break down in a remote area at night, you'll likely be stranded.

Legal Matters & Safety

◆ To find an English-speaking police officer, look for tourist police headquarters with signs in English.

◆ To take any archeological items out of the country, you must get an export license.

◆ Women should take a taxi at night unless they know an area well. Verbal harassment from men is common. Women alone should also avoid the Plaka area in Athens after dark.

◆ Feel free to go to gambling casinos, but any Greeks accompanying you must bring their income tax returns to prove they can afford to gamble.

Key Phrases

Below we give each word in English and its pronunciation—but not its spelling—in Greek. Since the Greek language uses the Greek alphabet, a Greek wouldn't recognize the word printed in the Roman alphabet (and you probably wouldn't recognize it printed in the Greek alphabet). You may want to learn to read the Greek alphabet, so that you can at least read signs.

English	**Pronunciation of Greek**
Good morning	kah-lee-MEH-rah
Good afternoon (evening)	kah-lee-SPEH-rah
Please	pah-rah-kah-LOW
Thank you	ef-kah-ree-STO
You're welcome	TEE-po-tah
Yes	neh
No	O-chi*
Mr., Sir	KEE-ree-yay
Mrs., Madam	KEE-ree-yah
Miss	theh-speen-EES
Excuse me	may seen-CHO-ree-tay*
Good-bye	CHEH-reh-teh*
I don't understand.	then kah-tah-lah-VEH-noo
I don't speak Greek.	then mee-LO ell-een-ee-KA
Does anyone here speak English?	mee-LAH KAH-nees ahn-glee-KAH

* "ch" is pronounced like a gutteral "k," as in the Scottish word "loch," only softer.

Hungary

Hungarians have a strong sense of both personal and national pride, a pride that until recently made men of the upper classes scorn any job that could be regarded as money-making. The only three occupations suitable for gentlemen were public affairs, land ownership, or the military.

The key to Hungarian character is the ability to survive and adapt. The country's history has been one long series of invasions: Genghis Khan, the Turks, the Hapsburgs, the Nazis, and the Russians. Through it all, Hungarians learned to adjust to what they could not change. And, perhaps because they are acutely conscious that one never knows what the future holds, they have developed a reputation for living beyond their means.

Since their liberation in 1989, Hungarians have rushed to erase all traces of Soviet domination. One of their first moves was to reinstate pre-Soviet place names—a change that can be confusing to a traveler. If you're in Budapest, ideally you'd be best off with maps from both the 1930s and the 1980s.

Greetings

♦ Shake hands when you're introduced, greeting someone, or departing.

♦ When two good male friends meet after a long separation, they shake hands and embrace, making cheek-to-cheek contact: first the left cheek, then the right. Close female friends embrace but don't shake hands.

♦ If speaking Hungarian, address people by their last name followed by "Mr." (úr), "Mrs." (né), or "Miss" (kisasszony). For example: Bean úr (Mr. Bean), Beanné (Mrs. Bean), or Bean kisasszony (Miss Bean). (See Key Phrases.)

♦ Use last names until Hungarian acquaintances suggest you use first names.

♦ At formal parties, wait to be introduced. At informal gatherings, introduce yourself.

♦ Hungarians tend to say "hello" (in English) both when greeting and when leaving people.

Conversation

♦ Many Hungarians have conveniently forgotten the Russian they were required to learn under communist rule. German is more widely spoken than English, especially among older people, but a new trend is toward learning English.

♦ Good topics of conversation: food, wine, or what you like about Hungary. If people have children, they enjoy talking about them, since children are central to Hungarian life.

♦ Topics to avoid: religion or income.

♦ If you compliment Hungarians about anything, expect them to belittle their achievements rather than simply saying "Thank you."

◆ Hungarians bend over backwards for Americans because they admire American products and services. They also, however, have a warped impression of how Americans live—they think all Americans live like millionaires.

◆ Hungarians value personal relationships and will be curious about your life in the United States. Downplay what you have. If you say you have a three-bedroom, two-bathroom house, people will think you have a mansion.

Money

◆ The unit of currency is the forint (abbreviated Ft), made up of 100 filler. Filler are practically useless, although you will find them in circulation.

◆ Coins come in denominations of 1, 2, 5, 10, and 20 forints.

◆ Notes come in denominations of 10, 20, 50, 100, 500, and 1,000 forints.

◆ Never accept an offer from anyone on the street to change money at an exceptionally favorable rate. It's too risky. The discount is only about 33 percent, and you're in danger of getting counterfeit forints or useless foreign currency. The practice is illegal; if you're caught, you could lose your money or end up in jail.

Telephones

◆ To call from a public phone, deposit a 2-forint coin. (Wait for the dial tone; it might be slow in coming.)  You'll get a three-minute local call (six minutes after 6:00 P.M.). If you want more time, insert more money before the time is up or you'll be cut off.

◆ For calls within Hungary, use 2-forint and 10-forint coins.

◆ In tourist areas, you'll find telephones with instructions in English as well as easy-to-follow visual instructions.

◆ Hungary has no telephone cards.

◆ On any call, you might not get through on the first few attempts. Many Hungarians say it's more unusual to be connected to the correct party than to get no answer or a wrong number.

◆ Make long-distance calls from the post office or private phones.

◆ Budapest and some towns have red telephone booths from which you can make international calls, using 10-forint and 20-forint coins.

◆ Two Budapest post offices are open 24 hours for international calls: The Western Railroad Station at 1062 Lenin Körút 105 and the Eastern Railroad Station at 1087 Baross tér 11/c.

◆ To make an international call, you can dial direct from a private phone or a red telephone booth. Wait for a dial tone, dial 00, pause and wait for a long tone, then dial the country code (which you will find in the Hungarian phone book), the area code, and the number you wish to call.

◆ When answering the phone, say "HEL-lo." Many Hungarians end phone conversations with close friends or relatives by saying the Hungarian word for "kisses," which sounds like "pussy" in English.

◆ Phone calls might be monitored.

◆ The Emergency Number to summon police, the fire department, or an ambulance is **07**.

In Public

◆ A man should always walk to the left of a woman or an honored guest of either sex.

◆ One can bargain in markets, especially in provincial towns.

◆ Don't throw money around as though it has no meaning. Show that you value money; otherwise, people will try to manipulate you to obtain what they *think* you have.

◆ To buy Western products, go to one of the "dollar stores," called *Intertourist*, found in shopping areas and international hotels. Prices are comparable to those at duty-free shops. Show your passport and pay in Western currency.

◆ Public toilets are located in cafes, bars, and restaurants. Men's rooms will say *Fer-fiak*; women's, *Nök*.

Dress

◆ For casual dress, jeans are acceptable. Wear shorts only on country outings or at the beach.

◆ For business, men should wear suits, white shirts, and ties. Women should wear suits or dresses.

◆ For dinner in a home, men should wear a shirt and tie, and women should wear a dress or skirt.

◆ For elegant restaurants, women should wear dresses and skirts, and men should wear jackets and ties.

◆ For theater events, both men and women should wear business attire.

Meals

Hours and Foods

Breakfast (reggeli): 7:00 to 9:00 A.M. The usual meal is bread, butter, and jam. Eggs are seldom served; when they are, they are soft boiled. Espresso is served with hot milk.

Lunch (ebéd): Noon or 12:30 P.M. to 2:00 P.M. On weekends and when entertaining, this is the main meal of the day. It usually begins with soup—often a thick meat soup or, in the summer, a cold fruit soup. Next comes the main course, often a pork stew with paprika, or *wienerschnitzel* and pickled vegetables. Dessert follows, then espresso.

◆ When people entertain, they serve *schnapps* (brandy) or wine before the meal, and wine with the meal. Dessert is elaborate, perhaps a *dobos torta* (a 12-layer cake with chocolate filling), or pancakes with cream cheese filling and wine sauce. Drinks served after the meal might include Tokay, a sweet dessert wine, or Pear William, a strong pear-flavored brandy.

Dinner *(vacsora):* 7:00 to 8:00 P.M. This is usually a light meal consisting of open-faced sandwiches or salad and cold cuts, with tea. Dessert is not served. During the work week or at a dinner party, the meal will be much like lunch.

Breaks: At 5:00 P.M. many people meet friends for cake and coffee.

Table Manners

◆ Arrive on time when invited to a meal.

◆ The host and hostess sit at opposite ends of the table, with the guest of honor at the hostess's right.

◆ If wine is served, the guest of honor should propose a toast before drinking, saying "eh-gay-SHEH-ged-reh" ("To your health").

◆ Before you start to eat, wish everyone a good appetite by saying "yo ATE-vahd-yaht."

◆ As each course is served, don't begin eating until your hostess does.

◆ Start with small portions of various dishes. Many Hungarian foods are rich, and you're expected to eat everything on your plate. If you can't finish something, apologize to your hosts.

◆ Taste food before adding salt, pepper, or paprika, or you'll insult your hosts.

◆ If you ask for tea with lemon, you might get tea with a pitcher of bottled lemon juice.

◆ To show you've finished eating, place your knife and fork side by side in the middle of your plate.

◆ When complimenting your hosts on the meal, expect them to make light of their efforts.

◆ Hungarians tend to talk and entertain long after the meal is over.

Eating Out

◆ Note the variety of Hungarian eating places:

● A *bisztró* or *étel-bar* is a snack bar.

● *Borozó* serve nothing but alcoholic drinks and are frequented mainly by men.

● *Cukrászda* are pastry or tea shops; their specialties are *dobos torta* (many-layered cakes), marzipan balls dipped in chocolate, and glacéed chestnuts.

● An *eszpresszó* is a coffee bar.

● *Étterem* are large, elaborate restaurants.

● *Önkiszogáló étterem* are self-service restaurants.

● *Söröső* (taverns) offer snacks, which are eaten with draft beer or apricot or plum brandy.

● *Vendéglő* or *maszek* are usually simple, family-run restaurants that follow ethnic and country traditions.

◆ Restaurants are officially divided into four classes. Most hotel restaurants are "above class," or better than all the ranked restaurants. Of the ranked restaurants, the highest class is I, and the lowest is IV. Look for the classification on the menu displayed near the entrance.

◆ Leave your hat and coat in the cloakroom before entering a restaurant.

◆ Fixed price meals called *menü* are found

at the bottom of menus in Hungarian or German.

♦ Better restaurants and cafes have menus in English or German.

♦ Prices in many restaurants are higher in the evening because they have live music.

♦ To attract the waiter's attention, say "KAY-rem" ("Please").

Specialties

♦ Many Hungarian foods are rich and spicy. Try the following specialties: *balászlé* (a paprika-flavored fish soup made from carp, onions, and potatoes or pasta); *pörkölt* (a paprika-flavored pork stew served with sour cream and dumplings); *töltött paprika* (green peppers stuffed with ground meat in a tomato sauce); *töltött káposzta* (stuffed cabbage); *fatányéros* (a mixed grill of veal, pork, beef, and sausages served on a wooden platter with red cabbage, pickles, and potato salad); *idei sült liba* (roast goose served with cucumber salad); and *rétes* (strudel).

♦ Try also *palacsinta,* crepe-like pancakes used in almost every course. Two varieties are *pörkölt palacsinta* (crepes filled with chicken, paprika, and sour cream), and *palacsinta* (dessert crepes filled with cheese, raisins, jam, or chocolate).

♦ For dessert, try *somola* (a custard and bread pudding).

Hotels

♦ To get a hotel room between mid-June and mid-September, book well in advance. Rooms are also often booked—up

to a year in advance—during the big trade fairs, held during the last week of May and September and during the Budapest Spring Festival, held in March.

♦ Allow hotels to record the information they need from your passport, but do not leave your passport with them overnight—it might be copied for illegal purposes.

♦ If hotels are booked up, ask a travel agent to find accommodations for you in a private home. You might even prefer this to a hotel, since you'll get a chance to meet some Hungarian people.

♦ Hungary also has good pensions that offer many of the services that hotels do, including booking theater tickets.

♦ Another less expensive alternative to a hotel is renting a room or apartment through IBUSZ (the state travel agency). If you're renting sight-unseen, try to have a Hungarian associate check out the accommodations to make sure you get hot water, a refrigerator, and an elevator. Ask for your own key, so you won't have to depend on the superintendent or manager.

♦ If you expect language to be a major problem, stick to large hotels and IBUSZ-organized tourist activities.

♦ Don't expect air-conditioning in any but luxury-class hotels.

♦ Find the fire escape route from your room. Many hotels have no smoke detectors.

♦ Bring your own soap and washcloths; they are not always provided.

♦ Some hotel bathrooms have an object that looks a bit like a vacuum for a car. It's a hair dryer, activated simply by pulling the nozzle out of its mounting.

♦ In large hotels, the desk clerk can help you make restaurant reservations or get theater tickets (hotels get most of the best seats for theaters, concerts, and operas). Most desk clerks speak English.

Tipping

♦ *Restaurants:* Leave the waiter 10–15 percent. If gypsy musicians play at your table, give the leader 100–300 forints. Give it subtly, without making a big production.

♦ *Porters:* Give 25–30 forints per bag.

♦ *Hotel maids:* Leave 50 forints for each night of your stay.

♦ *Taxis:* Tip 10–15 percent of the fare.

♦ *Cloakroom attendants:* Give 20 forints per coat.

♦ *Washroom attendants:* Have some small change handy. The usual charge is 5–10 forints.

♦ *Gas station attendants:* Give the attendant 10–15 percent of the charge—the higher amount if he washes the windshield and checks the oil.

♦ People appreciate tips in American dollars. It's a good idea to bring a supply of singles with you.

Private Homes

♦ Many families live in apartments with little living space, so don't be offended if people you know don't invite you to stay with them. If you plan to visit friends or relatives, arrange to stay at a hotel if at all possible.

♦ If friends or relatives don't invite you to dinner, don't be surprised. Their homes might be too small even to invite you for a meal, so they might prefer to entertain you elsewhere.

♦ If you use the phone in a private home, offer to pay for each call (2 forints for a local call). If your hosts won't accept payment, give flowers at a later time.

♦ If you are invited to stay with someone, don't try to help in the kitchen. Hungarians prefer that guests relax, not work.

♦ Adapt to whatever water supply is available. Apartments have hot water only if they have either central heating or an individual gas boiler. Feel free to take a daily bath or shower if there's hot water; otherwise, you'll have to settle for a cold shower.

Gifts: If you're a dinner guest, bring a gift— it's considered rude to appear empty-handed. Bring Western liquor or wrapped flowers (other than chrysanthemums, which are for funerals).

♦ To give friends or relatives a real treat, take them to a restaurant in one of the large hotels, such as the Intercontinental or the Hilton.

♦ If you're going to stay with a family, consider bringing gifts from the U.S., such as cigarettes, liquor, perfume, clothing, dress fabric, permanent press sheets, or tablecloths.

Business

Hours

Businesses: 8:00 A.M. to 4:00 P.M., Monday through Friday, and 10:00 A.M. to 1:00 P.M. on Saturday. On Friday, people often only work half the day.

Government offices: 8:00 A.M. to 4:00 P.M., Monday through Friday, and 8:00 A.M. to noon on alternate Saturdays.

Banks: 9:00 A.M. to 1:00 P.M., Monday through Friday, but hours may vary.

Stores: 10:00 A.M. to 5:00 P.M., Monday through Friday, and 9:00 A.M. to 1:00 P.M. Saturday. Food shops are open 7:00 a.m. to 6:00 P.M., Monday through Friday, and supermarkets and department stores are open till 3:00 P.M. on Saturday. A handful of convenience food stores are open 24 hours.

Business Practices

♦ Hungary has the most improved business infrastructure among Eastern European countries. Business contacts with the West have increased since the autumn of 1989.

♦ To prepare yourself to do business in Hungary, contact the commercial attaché at your country's embassy in Budapest or, in the U.S., get in touch with the U.S. Department of Commerce—specifically the Eastern Europe Business Information Center (EEBIC)—and the Hungarian Embassy. Another contact is the Commercial Offices for the Republic of Hungary in the U.S., located in Chicago, New York, and Washington D.C. Also contact any associations with members who do business in Hungary. Pool your information, and set up meetings with contacts before you go to Hungary.

♦ Two of the best resources to establish contacts are the Hungarian Chamber of Commerce in Budapest and the InvestCenter, an agency of the Ministry of Foreign Trade, also located in Budapest. Don't look as though you haven't done any research—such as by asking, "Is Hungary a good place to do business?" Be prepared with serious, specific proposals.

♦ Every year Hungary has two large, important trade fairs called BNV. The spring fair features industrial goods (electronics, iron, and steel). The autumn fair is for consumer goods. Companies from all over the world participate. To get a booth you must begin preparations from 18 months to 2 years in advance. Contact the American Embassy in Budapest for information. All U.S. companies exhibit their products and services in one section of the fair.

♦ Be cautious about getting involved in a partnership arrangement. Since the fall of communism, Hungary has seen a lot of wheeling and dealing, with some Americans setting up partnerships with people they have known for only a week. People might try to pressure you, saying a certain deal won't be around for long, but don't jump into any deal. Assume you're in Hungary to do business over the long haul.

♦ Unless you are fluent in Hungarian, you can write business letters in English. Businesses expect to translate letters. You may have to wait longer for a response, however; some companies do not have enough translators to translate your letter immediately.

♦ Don't plan a business trip to Hungary during July or August or from mid-December to mid-January, the common vacation times. Check the dates for the big ski week in mid-January so you can avoid that period too.

♦ The roles of men and women are more strictly defined than in other countries. At a meeting you'll always be offered a drink. A woman will probably get the drink, but she doesn't regard the task as demeaning, and the men won't treat her as though she's performed an "inferior" task. The men will have some other task that they perform exclusively—the business equivalent of taking out the garbage.

♦ A Western businesswoman shouldn't encounter any serious problems in Hungary, though much depends on the nature of her business. She'll have an advantage in the travel and fashion industries, but the world of finance is somewhat less hospitable to women. If a woman and a man have equal backgrounds and experience, the man will stand a better chance.

♦ Staying at one of the large international hotels has advantages. First, you'll make a better impression on Hungarian businesspeople. Second, if you need secretarial service, the hotel will help you find it. (The business centers at hotels vary in quality, however. If you need more than minimal secretarial help, call the American Chamber of Commerce or the office of the commercial attaché at the U.S. Embassy.)

♦ Bring many business cards with you— twice as many as you think you'll need— and give one to everyone you meet during the course of your business dealings.

♦ Have your business cards printed in English on one side and Hungarian on the other. In Hungarian, surnames come first, so on one side your card will say "John Smith," and on the other, "Smith John."

♦ To make an excellent impression, have any brochures translated into Hungarian. Even if Hungarians know English, they find it much easier to read material in their own language.

♦ Consider hiring an interpreter if you do not speak Hungarian or German well enough to conduct business (German is widely spoken by educated Hungarians). Often, Hungarian businesses—even rural factories—are willing to provide interpreters.

♦ If you're staying in one of the large international hotels, ask for an interpreter there. You can also find one through IBUSZ, the national tourist agency.

♦ If you're dealing with a business or factory in an outlying area, you'll almost certainly need an interpreter.

♦ When you hire an interpreter, be sure to specify the type of business you'll be doing. You can find interpreters familiar with technical terms in a variety of businesses.

♦ Cultivate patience. Hungary still has a cumbersome bureaucracy and a long tradition of slowness, indecisiveness, and mulling over even simple decisions. There is no tradition of getting things done quickly, so phone, telex, and fax services operate at a slow pace.

Meetings and negotiations: Set up appointments at least one month—preferably two—in advance. Since the collapse of communism, Hungarian offices have been inundated with requests for appointments and don't have the staff to respond rapidly. After a month, follow up with a phone call or telex (few places have faxes).

♦ Don't expect to make appointments for Saturday or Sunday, though that might be possible in extreme circumstances—for example, if you'll only be in Hungary for one weekend. The Hungarian won't be happy but will probably agree to see you.

◆ It's acceptable to suggest business appointments from 8:00 A.M. to 3:30 or 4:00 P.M. Hungarians tend to be early risers so early appointments don't bother them.

◆ Don't be reluctant to interact with people at a lower rank than your own. Many of these employees have been around a long time and can provide much insight into the company. There might be a great deal of mutual respect between that person and top management. A favorable introduction from such a person might be a big plus.

◆ Different companies make decisions in different ways. Sometimes one person makes the decisions; sometimes, an entire department. Often, decisions take a long time. Because of their history, Hungarians are used to avoiding responsibility for decisions.

◆ Use a combination of patience and prodding. Don't let matters rest. Follow up with phone calls, reminding the Hungarians that you're still interested in the project. Give reassurances about the quality your company is offering, and gently prod them to a decision.

◆ Written contracts are common. They will be in English. Be sure both parties interpret the words the same way.

Entertainment: Business entertaining has decreased since the fall of communism. In the past, top bureaucrats had budgets for entertaining in lavish style. They wanted to ensure a lavish reception when they traveled in the West, and often prolonged negotiations so they could travel abroad frequently. Now that many companies are privately owned and have to foot the bill for entertaining, they are cutting back.

◆ If you want to discuss business over a meal, suggest lunch. Dinner should be a social occasion.

◆ A businesswoman will almost never be allowed to pay for a meal, even if she's suggested it. To pay is to cheapen herself. The Hungarians' attitude is that she their guest, even though she is there doing business.

◆ It's unusual to include spouses when entertaining or being entertained. A husband and wife from abroad may invite a Hungarian businessman's wife, but she might not come (she might not speak English).

◆ If your business dealings are successful, consider hosting a cocktail party for your Hungarian colleagues. Greet all the guests at the door, and be prepared to give a short speech (in English).

Gifts: Many Hungarians give business gifts. Bring American gifts with you rather than sending them after you get home—the Hungarian postal service is not reliable. If you think that the Hungarian with whom you'll be dealing has children, bring something from your area for the children—buttons or sweatshirts from the local sports team, T-shirts from the local university, or U.S. flags. The next time you call, you'll find it easy to get an appointment.

Holidays & Celebrations

Holidays: New Year's Day (January 1); Anniversary of the Hungarian Revolution and 1848 War of Independence (March 15); Easter Monday; Labor Day (May 1); Constitution Day (August 20); Founding of the Republic Day (October 23—the date on which both the 1956 Revo-

lution broke out and the Republic was announced in 1989); Christmas (December 25); and December 26.

♦ On Easter Monday, Hungarian girls and boys participate in a celebration based on an old fertility ritual. Men and boys go from house to house visiting unmarried women and spraying them with perfume. The men then give the women hand-painted eggs, and the women offer the men *schnapps*. People in the countryside sometimes follow an older tradition: the women put on five or six dresses, layered, then go outside, where the men dump buckets of water on them.

Transportation

Public Transport

Mass transit: The English pronunciation of "bus" means "fornication" in Hungarian! Pronounce the word "boos" or "ow-to-boos."

♦ Buses, trolleybuses, and streetcars run from 4:00 or 5:00 A.M. to 11:00 P.M. or midnight. The Metro (subway) runs from 4:30 A.M. to 11:30 P.M.

♦ Buy tickets for the bus, streetcar, or trolleybus at the Metro or at tobacconist shops and street stands. Buy in quantity, in case you end up at a streetcar stop far from a Metro; you can't buy tickets on streetcars. Yellow tickets are good on subways, streetcars, and trolleybuses. Blue tickets are for buses only. You can also buy daily,weekly, and monthly passes. For monthly passes you need a passport-size photo to use as an I.D.

♦ When you get on a streetcar or trolleybus, validate your ticket by putting it in a little

box affixed to a pole. Keep any ticket after you've validated it, in case an inspector gets on.

♦ Bus tickets within towns are different from and slightly more expensive than streetcar or trolleybus tickets.

♦ Express buses, marked with an *E* and numbered in red, stop only at main stops.

♦ For a long-distance bus trip, you can buy a ticket with a seat reservation up to 30 minutes before departure. After that, you can buy a ticket from the bus driver, but you might have to stand.

♦ In the countryside, bus service might be limited to only one run a day.

♦ To find the subway, look for a red *M* on a large white background. (There are three lines: red, yellow, and blue. On the printed subway map, the yellow comes out as orange.)

♦ Subway tickets cost 8 forints and are good for one hour. To validate your ticket, put it into the orange machine at the subway entrance.

♦ Express trains, which stop only at major centers, require seat reservations. International trains have sleeping cars and couchettes. You can buy tickets in advance at train stations, or sometimes you can buy them on the train.

♦ Most trains have buffets in the first- and second-class sections.

♦ Most Hungarians buy one-way train tickets. If you want a round-trip ticket, specify "return."

Taxis: Order a taxi by phone or go to a taxi stand, located outside hotels, railway stations, and theaters and at major intersections. You can also hail one on the street.

◆ For safety, buckle your seat belt in taxis.

◆ Taxis have different fares and meters, but some run faster than others. If you think the meter has been running very fast, don't tip.

◆ If a taxi driver (often, one bringing you in from the airport) tells you you can't pay him in forints but must pay in foreign currency, tell him you know it's not true. If he persists, ask him to take you to a police station.

Driving

◆ You do not need an International Driver's License to drive in Hungary.

◆ Consider carefully whether you really need or want to drive in Hungary. Penalties for accidents can be severe.

◆ Front-seat occupants must wear seat belts. Children must sit in the back seat.

◆ Unless otherwise posted, the speed limit in built-up areas is 60 kph, on main roads is 80 kph, on highways is 100 kph, and on motorways is 120 kph.

◆ Traffic police speak only Hungarian and might not be able to help you if you need directions.

◆ It's illegal to blow your horn in a built-up area, except to avoid an accident.

◆ Other driving advice: (1) Vehicles coming from the right have the right of way. (2) Streetcars *always* have the right of way. (3) On highways, repeatedly switching lanes is prohibited. (4) On both highways and secondary roads, it's illegal to reverse, make U-turns, or stop at islands.

◆ Don't have *anything* to drink if you're going to drive—even one drink is against the law. Police conduct spot checks constantly. If you've been drinking and are involved in an accident, you can be imprisoned for years. The minimum punishment for drunk driving is a huge fine.

Legal Matters & Safety

◆ Don't bring a hunting weapon unless you have permission to do so (obtainable at Hungarian embassies or consulates).

◆ When leaving Hungary, at any authorized travel office or bank, you can reexchange back to dollars up to 50 percent—but not more than $100 U.S.—of any money you had exchanged from dollars to forints. Be sure to keep your original exchange receipt because you will have to present it as proof that you exchanged U.S. dollars for forints.

◆ Westerners have little difficulty leaving the country. Customs officials might check for Hungarian currency or works of art, neither of which may be taken out of the country.

◆ Watch for "No Entry" *(Tilos a bemenet* or *Nem bejárat)* signs posted near military and border areas and don't go too close.

◆ If someone approaches you offering to buy any electronic gadget you have, don't do it. It's black market activity, not worth the risk of getting caught.

◆ Hungary has no legal drinking age or hours.

◆ Street crimes are increasing in Hungary's larger cities. Pickpockets are common in tourist sections. So be careful—don't carry all your credit cards or identification in one pocket or purse. Rental cars and cars with foreign license plates are prime targets for break-ins. Be sure to ask rental agencies if broken windows and the theft of articles are covered under the insurance you purchase.

◆ Walking in well-lit sections of town is relatively safe, as is using the Metro.

Key Phrases

English	Hungarian	Pronunciation
Good morning	Jó reggelt	yoh REG-gelt
Good day	Jó napot	yoh NAH-pot
Good evening	Jó estét	yoh ESH-teht
Good night	Jó ejszakát	yoh EY-so-kaht
Please	Kérem	KEH-rem
Thank you	Kôszônôm	KUR-sur-nurm
You're welcome	Nincs mit	ninch mit
Yes	Igen	I-gen
No	Nem	nem
Mr., Sir	úr (after last name)	oor
Mrs., Madam	né (after last name)	neh
Miss	kisasszony after last name	KISH-us-soin
Excuse me	Bocsánat	BOH-chah-nut
Good-bye	Viszontlátásra	VIS-ohnt-lah-tahsh-rah
I don't understand.	Nem értem.	nem EHR-tem
I don't speak Hungarian.	Nem tudok magyarul beszélni.	nem TOO-dok MA-jar-rule bess-ale-knee
Does anyone here speak English?	Beszél itt valaki angolul?	BESS-ehl eet VAH-lah-kee ONG-goh-lul

Ireland

Yes, most of the clichés about Ireland are true. It is green with a capital "G," the people love to talk, and many of them love—almost as much—to have a drink.

The Irish will make you feel completely at home within minutes—within seconds if your ancestors were Irish. You can be completely yourself, and the Irish will enjoy—or at least cheerfully tolerate—your eccentricities.

Don't worry about offending anyone in Ireland by using the wrong fork or forgetting to shake hands. The Irish have survived blows more severe than lapses in protocol. In fact, the ways to offend the Irish are few: unkindness, defending British behavior in Ireland over the centuries, and probably the worst lapse of taste—not buying your round in the pub.

Greetings

◆ Shake hands when you're introduced, every time you meet and leave people you don't know well, and when you meet a good friend you haven't seen for a long time.

◆ When shaking hands, men should wait for a woman to extend her hand first.

◆ At a large party, introduce yourself. At a small party, wait for your hosts to introduce you.

◆ Using first names after a short acquaintance is common, but stick to last names when you first meet someone and whenever the Irish address you by yours.

◆ People in the countryside almost never use the greeting "Good afternoon." Instead, shortly after noon they start saying "Good evening." "Good night" is also used as a greeting; it's not confined to departures.

Conversation

◆ Enjoy the legendary Irish eloquence by engaging the people you meet in conversation.

◆ Good topics of conversation: the beauty of the Irish countryside, Gaelic culture, Irish handicrafts, sports such as soccer and horse racing, or the weather (in Ireland you'll never run out of comments on the weather).

◆ Topics to avoid: Northern Ireland and the IRA, Ireland's relationship with the United Kingdom, religion, feminism, or the contrasts between Ireland and America.

◆ The Irish resent being stereotyped as cute little leprechauns or charmingly eccentric local characters.

◆ When the Irish describe someone as "plain," it's a compliment. They're indicating the person doesn't put on airs and is the salt of the earth.

Money

◆ The unit of currency is the Irish pound (abbreviated £), made up of 100 pence (abbreviated p).

◆ Coins come in denominations of 1, 2, 5, 10, 20, and 50p.

◆ Notes come in denominations of £1, 5, 10, 20, 50, and 100.

◆ British pounds are accepted only in large hotels and in shops frequented by tourists.

Telephones

◆ Public telephones have slots at the top for 10p, 20p, and 50p coins. Deposit 20p for a local call and 50p for a long-distance call within Ireland. Dial the number; the money will drop down when the phone is answered. When you hear a beep, deposit more money. If you don't want to fish for coins, deposit several coins before making your call. The phone will use them during your call and return any unused ones when you hang up.

◆ You can make international calls from any public phone or from the post office.

◆ Some Dublin phones accept phone cards, which you can buy in varying units at post offices and some small shops. These cards are particularly useful for calling abroad.

◆ The Emergency Number to summon police, the fire department, or an ambulance is **999.**

In Public

◆ The Irish are not very demonstrative and are uncomfortable with people who are.

◆ When shopping, don't hand over the money to pay for your purchase until the clerk has wrapped your merchandise.

◆ If you want to meet people, go to the lounge section of a pub.

◆ When you encounter a "queue" (line) at a bus stop, theater, or shop, take your place at the end. Never push ahead.

◆ Public bathrooms are available even in small towns. You'll also find them in train and bus stations.

◆ Some public toilets are labeled in Gaelic: *Fir* for men and *Mna* for women.

Dress

◆ Bring a raincoat; it's a necessity year-round.

◆ If you want to fit in, wear tailored clothes for casual wear—especially appropriate are dark tweeds and wools.

◆ Ireland is rarely warm enough for shorts, but when it is, wear them only at the beach—never in town.

◆ For business, men should wear suits and ties or tweedy sport jackets. Women should wear suits or wool blazers with wool skirts. Choose subdued colors.

◆ Dress for a dinner party is fairly casual, unless it's a business meal. Men don't need jackets and ties.

♦ If an invitation mentions formal dress, that means tuxedos for men and short cocktail dresses for women.

♦ Beaches have no bathhouses. It's perfectly acceptable to change on the beach while holding a towel around yourself.

Meals

Hours and Foods

Breakfast: 8:00 to 10:00 A.M. Expect a major meal with juice (usually canned) and/or cereal, followed by the "fry-up": eggs, grilled sausage (or sometimes fish on the coast), bacon, tomatoes, "black pudding" (blood pudding) cut up into small pieces and grilled, and brown bread and butter. Hot toast is served afterward with butter and marmalade; it's in poor taste to have marmalade with the "fry-up." For a beverage choose tea or coffee.

Lunch: 1:00 to 2:00 P.M. Midday meals might be hot dishes—such as steak-and-kidney pudding or boiled bacon and cabbage (the bacon is like roast pork that has been cured and boiled)—or cold meals such as ham or cheese salad (ham or cheese slices with lettuce and tomato). Salads come with one type of dressing—"salad cream," a thinner, tarter version of mayonnaise.

Tea: Sometime between 4:00 and 6:00 P.M. Some people have a light snack of tea and pastry, but others have a meal with substantial sandwiches and two or three different desserts.

Dinner: 5:00 to 8:00 P.M. The type of dinner depends on how heavy the midday meal was. If dinner is not the main meal of the day, a "tea" or "fry-up" (see Breakfast) might be served.

♦ A heavier dinner served at a dinner party might start with drinks such as vermouth, sherry, wine, whiskey, or brandy. The meal begins with a fish course or soup, followed by meat (usually a roast with two kinds of potatoes, such as mashed and roasted), and vegetables. Then comes cheese and crackers, dessert, coffee or tea, and port or spirits. Wine is often served with the meal.

Table Manners

♦ Try to be on time when invited to a meal, but the Irish—especially in the countryside—tend to be very late.

♦ Refusing a drink is a major insult. If you really don't care to drink, explain that you don't drink for health reasons.

♦ If you are offered a drink, raise the glass before you take a sip and say "Cheers."

♦ When you eat in a private home, your plate might be brought to you with food already on it. Even though you had no choice in the selection or portion sizes, try to eat everything on your plate.

♦ The small plate next to your dinner plate is not for bread, but for the peelings you're supposed to remove from boiled potatoes. Bread is seldom served with dinner.

♦ Smoking during the meal is acceptable.

♦ Don't eat and run. People tend to stay up late in Ireland, but look for signs that your hosts are getting tired.

Eating Out

♦ Irish restaurants—even gourmet restaurants—give you huge portions.

♦ When you order a sandwich, you will usually get only one paper-thin slice of meat or cheese on the bread.

♦ In rural areas, try hotel restaurants for complete menus and good food. Most serve dinner between 6:30 and 9:00 P.M. If you arrive later, food won't be available.

♦ If you want a late meal in Dublin, look for a Chinese restaurant. Many stay open until 11:00 P.M.

Pubs: For a reasonably priced lunch, go to a pub. Pub hours are 10:00 A.M. to 11:30 P.M., Monday through Saturday, and 12:30 to 2:00 P.M. and 4:00 to 10:00 P.M. on Sunday. Some pubs in major cities close between 2:00 and 3:30 P.M.

♦ Pubs have two sections: the bar and the lounge. Women traditionally frequent the lounge, though drinks are more expensive there.

♦ In small towns, women seldom go to pubs. Sometimes they sit in another area of the building, such as a TV room.

♦ Don't expect drinks to be served with ice. You'll get ice if you ask for it, but only one or two cubes.

♦ If you want to try the Irish "national" drink, order Guinness stout, which is served cool. If you've sampled Guinness in the U.S. and haven't like it, give it another try in Ireland. Many Irish won't drink the Guinness served in the U.S.

♦ If you want the equivalent of American beer, order lager served cold. Normally, Irish beer is served at room temperature.

♦ Women are expected to order only half-pints (10 ounces) of beer or stout. Some pubs won't even serve pints to women. A man who orders a half-pint, however, will have his virility questioned.

♦ Try these other pub drinks: whiskey (Irish whiskey) and scotch (Scotch whisky), both usually drunk neat; shandy (beer and lemonade); and gin and tonic.

♦ If you're a man with a group, buy a round of drinks. Women are not allowed to buy.

Specialties

♦ Foods to try in Ireland are colcannon (a mix of potato and cabbage); fish and chips; plaice (a good local fish); Galway oysters; grouse; "mixed coddle" (boiled bacon and sausages); pheasant; smoked and fresh salmon; steak-and-kidney pie; and trout.

♦ In Ireland "bacon" means pork fat for cooking. To get bacon to eat, ask for "rashers."

Hotels

♦ For inexpensive accommodations, stay at a Bed & Breakfast (B&B), usually rooms in someone's house. The price includes a large breakfast. Some B&Bs offer an optional "high tea" around 6:00 P.M. that might include a dish such as chicken and chips followed by cakes and tea.

♦ In a B&B, ask when it is convenient to take a bath. You might be sharing a bathroom with the family, so try to avoid using it when people are rushing to leave for work.

♦ At a small hotel, if you have the chance, buy the manager a drink and have a chat. Don't be pushy, but take advantage of such an opportunity if it arises. Managers can help make your stay especially pleasant.

♦ At a hotel, ask whether they provide a "baby-listening" connection between the main desk and your room. If so, you can go to the hotel restaurant without getting a babysitter; if your baby starts to cry, someone will come for you.

♦ In some hotels, hot water is shut off during the day and is not available until evening.

◆ Irish hotel rooms are cooler than American rooms, so plan your clothing accordingly.

Tipping

◆ *Restaurants:* A 10–15 percent service charge is usually added to the bill, and no extra tip is expected. If the service was  very good, you might want to leave something extra. In some restaurants, children work waiting tables, and you might want to give them extra change as you leave. Never tip in pubs.

◆ *Porters:* Tip 20–30p per bag.

◆ *Hotel maids:* Don't tip for short stays or for the usual services such as making beds. If you stay for more than a week, you might want to leave the equivalent of $1.00 a day.

◆ *Taxis:* Tip 50p for short-to-moderate distances (a fare of about £1); tip £1 for a ride of 20 minutes or so.

◆ *Cloakroom attendants:* Tip 20p.

Private Homes

◆ The Irish are used to people dropping in unannounced, but it's better to call ahead.

◆ Expect children to be involved in family functions.

◆ Members of the Irish clergy are often invited to family functions. Treat them with respect and deference.

◆ If you are a Catholic staying with a family, plan to attend Sunday Mass with them.

◆ If you stay in someone's home, dress modestly. Always dress for breakfast, and never walk around the house in a nightgown or pajamas.

◆ Taking a daily bath is fine, but be sure to ask your hosts when it would be convenient. Many Irish homes have no shower.

◆ Washcloths are rarely used. If you aren't given one, don't ask for one.

◆ If you make phone calls, whether local or international, insist on paying for every one. Place calls through the operator so you'll know the cost. Telephone rates are high, so the Irish don't use phones for long chats.

◆ Offer to help with daily chores such as setting the table and washing dishes.

Gifts: If you're invited to dinner, good gifts are a bottle of wine, flowers (especially if you know your host will have already chosen the dinner wine), a box of chocolates, or a selection of continental cheeses.

◆ If you're a houseguest, select a token gift, such as linen towels. Giving gifts, especially expensive gifts, is much less common in Ireland than in the U.S. Don't give expensive or ostentatious gifts.

◆ If someone gives you a gift, open it immediately.

◆ If you're invited to dinner in someone's home, don't be surprised if everyone is asked to get up and entertain with a song, music, a poem, or a dance. You can refuse, but your participation would be much appreciated.

Business

Hours

Businesses and government offices: 9:30 A.M to 5:30 P.M., Monday through Friday.

Banks: 10:00 A.M. to 12:30 P.M. and 1:30 to 3:00 P.M., Monday through Friday; on Thursday to 5:00 P.M.

Stores: 9:00 A.M. to 5:30 P.M., Monday through Saturday.

Business Practices

♦ To find business contacts in Ireland, contact the Industrial Development Authority (IDA) in New York.

♦ Although Gaelic is the official language of Ireland, don't make special arrangements for translations. It's spoken only in a section of western Ireland and is never used in business discussions.

♦ Avoid business trips to Ireland during the first week in May (when most businesspeople are busy with trade fairs), July and August (vacation times), or the Christmas and New Year period.

♦ Not many women hold high-level business positions in Ireland, but foreign businesswomen will be taken seriously.

♦ Fax machines are widely available.

Meetings and negotiations: Make business appointments in advance by letter, telephone, or fax.

♦ The Irish are not very time conscious and might not be punctual for an appointment. Someone who offers to meet you in five minutes will more likely turn up in half an hour.

♦ Business cards aren't commonly used, but bring them along so you can leave one with a secretary if the person you want to see is unavailable.

Entertainment: Business lunches are much more common than business dinners.

♦ There are no general rules about including spouses in business dinners. If you want to include the spouse of an Irish businessperson in a dinner party, mention that specifically in your invitation.

Gifts: Giving gifts is not commonly a part of business dealings.

Holidays & Celebrations

Holidays:
New Year's Day (January 1); St. Patrick's Day (March 17); Good Friday; Easter Monday; June

Bank Holiday (first Monday in June); August Bank Holiday (first Monday in August); Halloween; Christmas (December 25); and St. Stephen's Day (December 26).

♦ On St. Patrick's Day, the Irish go to church sporting sprigs of shamrock in their lapels. Dublin has parades, but all in all, the celebrations are lower key than those in the U.S.

Transportation

Public Transport

Mass transit:
Bus fares are based on the distance trav-

eled. A conductor will come to your seat for the fare. You don't need exact change.

♦ On double-decker buses, the upper deck is for smokers.

♦ If you want to travel around the countryside, try buses—the routes cover most parts of Ireland.

♦ Trains offer smoking and nonsmoking cars as well as storage bins for luggage at the rear of each car. People selling tea and snacks bring carts up and down the aisle.

♦ Consider getting one of the many travel passes. The Dublin Explorer gives unlimited access to bus and commuter rail service (except during rush hours) within 20 miles of Dublin for 4 consecutive days. Other passes come with 8- and 15-day options; some allow bus and rail travel in the Republic of Ireland, and others include Northern Ireland.

Taxis: Look for taxis at taxi stands and on the streets, or phone for one. The minimum charge is 50p.

Driving

♦ Like the British, the Irish drive on the left side of the road.

♦ Irish drivers tend to ignore the lines separating lanes and in the country often drive down the center of the road.

♦ All occupants of a car must wear seat belts or face a severe penalty.

♦ Children under 12 must sit in the back seat.

♦ Speed limits are 30–40 mph in towns and cities and 55 mph on open roads.

♦ All road signs are in both English and Gaelic and are sometimes painted on the roads themselves.

♦ Black and white signs give speeds in miles; green and white signs give speeds in kilometers.

♦ Don't drive too far to the left, because many roads have ditches running alongside them. Also hazardous are the hedges on either side of many roads; they are often high and obstruct the view.

♦ In the country, be prepared to stop suddenly for farm animals.

♦ If possible, avoid driving in cities during rush hours: 8:00 to 9:30 A.M. and 5:00 to 6:30 P.M.

♦ Don't drive after drinking even a pint or two of beer. Failing a Breathalyzer test can bring a fine of up to £500 or six months in jail.

♦ Always lock your car, put any valuables in the trunk, and park in supervised lots.

Legal Matters & Safety

♦ When you enter Ireland, don't try to bring in any pornography or books on the  government's censorship list (most fiction is allowed).

♦ The "Irish guards" is the common name for the Irish police. They might stop you for an identity check because of the problems in Northern Ireland.

♦ The legal drinking age is 18.

♦ Hitchhiking is not as common in Ireland as it used to be. If you do hitchhike, never use the phrase "get a ride"; it's obscene. Use instead the phrase "have a seat" or "have a lift."

♦ Women can travel alone in Ireland safely. Large cities have rough sections, but you can find out about them at your hotel.

◆ When walking in Dublin, don't take much money or your passport. Leave them in your hotel's safety deposit box.

◆ If you get sick, every small town has a district nurse and doctors on call. Medical service is excellent and relatively inexpensive.

Key Phrases

Below, we provide American words or terms and their Irish counterparts.

American/Irish

bacon/rashers

child/wain

country lane/boreen

a couple of drinks/jar

excellent/fairly

fried bread/dip

impertinence/guff

insulated/cut

a loud-voiced person/thundergub

a meal/a feed

raining gently/mizzlin

slow/dither

Italy

Visiting Italy can be a journey from legend to legend: the Forum in Rome, the Uffizi in Florence, the Piazza San Marco in Venice. Between legends, of course, you should make many stops for a nourishing bowl of pasta, a mellowing flask of wine, or a reviving cup of espresso.

The American image of Italy is composed partly of TV commercials in which large maternal figures urge their children to eat ever more pasta, and partly of gaudy Italian restaurants. You might be surprised at how much that image differs from reality, especially in northern Italy. The people there are as thin and chic as those in Paris; even small-town residents spend considerable money on their wardrobes. And their houses feature tasteful decors in subtle colors and materials.

If you arrive in Italy from one of the more frenetic American cities, you won't find much difference in the pace in Italy's industrial north. Southern Italians, however, have a much more relaxed approach to life. Join them in this and you'll come to appreciate the Italian phrase *"Dolce far niente"*—"It's sweet to do nothing."

Greetings

◆ Shake hands when greeting or leaving people, no matter how brief the encounter.

◆ Expect a great deal of physical contact in greetings. Friends often look as though they're kissing each other on both cheeks; actually, they touch their cheeks together without really kissing. Women friends accompany this gesture with a soft kissing sound, but men do not.

◆ If no one is making formal introductions, especially at parties, introduce yourself by stating your name and shaking hands.

◆ Don't use Italians' first names until they call you by yours.

◆ For any official registration—for example, hospitals, airline reservations, or universities—Italian women must use their premarriage family names.

Conversation

◆ Good topics of conversation: food, restaurants, sports such as soccer and bicycling, or family life. People will appreciate your showing an interest in such subjects as local art, food, or wine. You'll make an even better impression if you learn something about these subjects beforehand.

◆ Topics to avoid: Italian politics (unless an Italian brings the subject up) or World War II. Don't tell dirty jokes to anyone you don't know extremely well.

◆ Sentiments about sports teams run strong, so don't say anything negative about regional or national teams.

◆ Don't ask new acquaintances what they do for a living.

◆ If people don't ask you questions (for example, at a dinner party), that doesn't mean they're ignoring you. Try to join in the conversation yourself, and then people will respond. It's considered rude to keep asking questions of people one has just met.

Money

♦ The Italian unit of currency is the lira (plural lire, abbreviated L).

♦ Coins come in denominations of 10, 20, 50, 100, 200, and 500 lire.

♦ Notes come in denominations of 1,000, 2,000, 5,000, 10,000, 20,000, 50,000, and 100,000 lire. Notes are graduated in size (except the 2,000-lira note) and feature the portrait of a different important Italian figure on each denomination.

Telephones

♦ The Italian phone system does not work very well. It's often easier to place a call to another country than to another city within Italy.

♦ Some public phones still use tokens *(gettoni),* which you can buy in a cafe or a tobacconist shop, but these phones are disappearing.

♦ Most public telephones now accept coins. Though they accept 100-, 200-, or 500-lira coins, they have only one coin slot.

♦ For a local call, which costs 200 lire, deposit either one *gettone* or two 100-lira coins. Usually that gives you a three- to five-minute call, though in some places local

calls have no time limit. If there is a time limit, the call is cut off automatically when your time is up, and adding more *gettoni* won't help. Either call again or have the other person call you back at the pay phone.

♦ Many phones now also accept telephone cards (called *carta telefonica),* which you can buy at cafes, gas stations, or kiosks. The cards look like credit cards and come in amounts ranging from 1,000 to 10,000 lire. On the back you'll find a list of rates for various times of the day and days of the week.

♦ Phones that accept telephone cards are identified by a small orange box on the side of the telephone. Before you use the card, break off the perforated corner in the upper left. Inside the booth, insert the card in the box to the right of the phone; the amount shown in the window tells you how much money you've used. When the window shows zero, you've used up your card and must either end your call or insert another card.

♦ You can call overseas from a public phone by using your international telephone credit card, by using several 10,000-lira telephone cards, or by calling collect. You can also call from a telephone office (called SIP), where the operator will place the call for you. You must pay in cash. Don't call directly from your hotel or you'll probably pay an exorbitant surcharge.

♦ When you answer the phone, say "PRONto."

♦ The Emergency Number to summon police, the fire department, or an ambulance is **113.** People at that number speak foreign languages.

In Public

♦ Always stand when an older person enters the room. Italians are very respectful to elders.

♦ Participate in the *Passeggiata,* an evening ritual that occurs almost everywhere except in large, urban areas. Every evening, between 6:00 and 8:00 P.M., people dress up in good clothes and stroll through town. It's a good time to arrange to meet someone for coffee or an aperitif in a cafe. If you meet someone you know, stop, shake hands, chat a little, and shake hands again in parting. (Someone who knows many people might take two hours to go from one end of the street to the other.)

♦ Italians often walk arm-in-arm with members of the same sex.

♦ In larger towns and cities, you can bargain in English, but in smaller towns you'll have to use Italian. In markets, offer one-half to three-quarters of the asking price, and bargain from there. In a store, offering to pay in cash, rather than with a credit card, will often get you a discount, but be sure to ask. Shopkeepers who don't want to bargain or to offer a discount will just say "No" and won't be insulted by your attempt.

♦ If you wish to photograph people, ask first. They'll usually be pleased.

♦ Don't take photos of military installations or factories, or in museums that forbid photography. Look for signs showing a camera with an "X" across it.

♦ The only public toilets in most towns and cities are in hotels, restaurants, cafes, and train stations. Many are labeled *W.C.*; men's rooms might say *Signori* or *Uomini,* while women's rooms might say *Signore* or *Donne.* Public toilets on the street are labeled *Gabinetti Publici.*

♦ If you're driving in the country, you'll see grassy rest areas but no public toilets. Look for a restaurant or gas station instead.

♦ Most public toilets have no toilet paper, so bring tissues with you. (Some of the toilets don't have seats, either.)

Dress

♦ Even casual wear in Italy is elegant. You might feel uncomfortable if your clothes are the least bit scruffy.

♦ For casual dress, men may wear pants and casual shirts, and women may wear pants or skirts. Jeans are fine if they're not worn or dirty. Don't wear shorts in cities.

♦ For business, men should always wear suits and ties. Businesswomen should dress expensively—in chic, understated clothing—and never wear anything conspicuous or revealing.

♦ To an elegant restaurant, men should wear jackets and ties; women, skirts or very dressy pants. In other restaurants, pants, neatly pressed jeans, sweaters, and shirts are fine for both men and women.

♦ To the theater, men should wear dark suits and ties, and women should wear dresses and heels. For an opening, dress formally in tuxedos and long dresses. (The formal event of the year is December's opening of the La Scala Opera season in Milan.)

♦ When visiting churches, women traditionally cover their heads and arms. Shorts are not allowed in churches.

Meals

Hours and Foods

Breakfast *(la prima colazione):* 8:00

A.M. Breakfast is usually a light meal of bread and butter and *cappuccino* (half strong coffee and half hot, foamy milk) or *cioccolato caldo* (hot chocolate).

Lunch *(la colazione):* 1:00 P.M. The main meal of the day, lunch usually begins with a pasta dish. The main course is meat (often veal) with potatoes or vegetables. Bread is served throughout the meal and salad follows. Wine and water usually accompany the meal. Lunch ends with cheese and fruit, followed by espresso (strong, black coffee served in small cups), which is drunk rapidly, not lingered over.

◆ On Sundays or when people have company, lunch is often preceded by aperitifs such as vermouth, Campari, or Cynar (made from artichokes). An *antipasto* (appetizer) such as *prosciutto* (thin slices of salty ham) and melon, or chopped liver on bread triangles, is served before the pasta dish. The main course is followed by cheese, then pastries, then fruit to cleanse the palate. Espresso and a digestive (a bitter after-dinner liqueur such as Fernet Branca) follow.

Dinner *(la cena):* 8:00 P.M. Expect a light meal of soup, cold cuts, salad, and fruit. A dinner party will have the same courses described for the Sunday lunch.

Breaks: In offices, people take coffee breaks between 10:00 and 10:30 A.M.

Table Manners

◆ In northern Italy, be punctual when invited to a meal; in southern Italy, you can be 15 minutes to a half an hour late.

◆ The host and hostess sit on opposite sides of the middle of the table, with the most important male guest to the hostess's right, and the most important female guest to the host's right.

◆ The host or another man should pour the wine. Italians think it unbecoming for a woman to pour wine.

◆ If you don't want your host to keep refilling your wine glass, keep it almost full by taking tiny sips.

◆ However much you enjoy Italian wines, *don't* get drunk. The Italians view wine almost as a food, not as a vehicle for escape or relaxation, and find drunkenness extremely offensive.

◆ Before the meal, people often wish everyone a good appetite and an enjoyable meal by saying "bwon ah-pay-TEE-toe."

◆ Either the hostess will serve everyone, beginning with the most important female guest, or the food will be passed around the table on serving platters.

◆ You might see your hostess cutting steak, pizza, or chicken with scissors. Don't be surprised; they're especially for food.

◆ Don't begin eating until the hostess does.

◆ Your place setting might include a stack of three plates: a large one on the bottom for the main course, a deep dish for pasta, and a small plate on top for the antipasto.

◆ When you eat spaghetti or other types of pasta, don't cut it or twirl it around your fork with the aid of a spoon. Instead, take two or three strands at a time and twirl them around your fork, using the deep sides of the pasta plate as you would a spoon.

◆ If you're dining in a home, don't expect all the food to be piping hot. Because of the large number of courses, the main course—for example, roast meat—might be luke-warm.

◆ When cheese is served, use your knife (not your fingers) to pick up a piece and put it on bread or a cracker.

◆ Italians don't use bread plates. Instead, they place a few slices of bread or a roll on the table at each place setting.

◆ At a family meal in a home, feel free to sop up gravy with bread if you see others doing it, but don't do it in a restaurant or at a dinner party.

◆ To be polite, decline seconds when they are first offered. Your hostess will insist, at which time it's polite to accept. If you don't want seconds, tell her you really can't eat any more. In the unlikely event that you'd like seconds and no one offers them to you, ask politely. The hostess will feel compli-mented.

◆ When you finish eating, put your knife and fork parallel on the plate, with the fork tines down.

◆ Don't smoke between courses. It's consid-ered impolite because it spoils the taste of the food.

◆ If you invite people to dinner (or a night-club or movie), you don't need to invite couples or "fix up" a single man or woman. Italian women feel comfortable attending group functions alone. And if you're a single person invited to dinner, don't feel as though you need a date.

Eating Out

◆ Try eating in a variety of places:

• A *bar* or *caffè* is a cafe that caters to families. You can get pastries, croissants, doughnuts, coffee, soft drinks, aperitifs, or wine. If you

want an American-style bar, try a large hotel.

• An *espresso bar* serves small cups of very strong coffee. As the name suggests, espresso is gulped, not sipped. Stand at the bar, drink your coffee quickly, and leave.

• A *gelateria* is an ice cream parlor.

• A *pizzeria* is a pizza parlor.

• A *ristorante* is an elegant, expen-sive restaurant.

• A *rosticceria* offers prepared food to take out. Most serve a variety of salads and chicken, duck, quail, pigeon, and other small birds, coated with olive oil and fresh herbs and cooked on a spit over an open fire. You can put together a deli-cious, inexpensive picnic to enjoy in a park or in your hotel room.

• A *tavola calda* (literally "warm table") is a lunch bar where you eat standing, sitting on stools at a counter, or seated at a table.

• A *trattoria* is a medium-priced restaurant that serves simple meals.

◆ Wine is the most popular drink. Try these widely available wines: for reds, Chianti, Barolo, and Barbera; for whites, Verdicchio, Soave, and Frascati. The most popular brandy is *grappa*, made from grape skins.

◆ To make sure both the food and the price are agreeable, check the menu you'll find displayed outside the restaurant.

◆ On a menu, *pane e coperto* means that there is a bread and cover charge.

◆ If a menu has the word *etto* with the prices for meat or fish, it means that the price is per 100 grams (about four ounces). When ordering fish, you can ask the waiter to bring out the raw fish to see whether it is the size you want. When ordering steak, you can ask for small, medium, or large.

♦ In a *bar* or *caffè*, you'll pay less if you stand at a counter than if you sit at a table. When eating or drinking at a counter, you pay at the cash register first, then take your receipt to the counter and put it there with a tip of 50–100 lire, depending on what you're ordering. *Then* give your order to the barman. You might have difficulty getting served if you don't observe this custom.

♦ To attract a server's attention in a restaurant, raise your hand slightly and say "kah-meh-RYEH-ray" to a man, or "See-nyor-EE-nah" to a woman.

♦ If you're a single woman, you'll have no trouble dining alone in northern Italy. Don't look around a great deal, or men will stare and smile at you—but they'll seldom bother you at your table.

♦ In southern Italy, in contrast, people aren't used to seeing women dining alone. At any ordinary restaurant, men will invariably come to your table and try to pick you up. The best solution is to eat your evening meal in your hotel restaurant.

♦ Restaurant checks won't be brought to you until you ask for them by saying "Eel Kon-toe."

♦ If you suggest that someone have a meal with you, pay the whole bill. If people invite you, they'll pay. Try to return a lunch or dinner invitation within a few days, if possible.

♦ When you leave a restaurant, keep the receipt from the check with you. It's possible, though unlikely, that tax police will stop you outside and ask to see your receipt. Don't panic; they're just checking on the restaurant's tax compliance.

Specialties

♦ Try to experience the different cooking styles and specialties of Italy's various regions.

♦ In Bologna, try *mortadella* (similar to bologna with peppercorns); *prosciutto* (paper-thin slices of dried, salted ham); and *tortellini* (small, doughnut-shaped pasta filled with meat). Bologna also has many pork dishes.

♦ In Florence and Tuscany, sample *bisetecca alla Fiorentina* (steak from Chianiana cattle, charcoal-broiled with olive oil, salt, and pepper) and *fagioli all'ucceletto* (white beans with garlic, olive oil, sage, and tomato paste).

♦ In Genoa, order *gnocchi* (potato-flour dumplings) and *pesto* (a sauce made from crushed basil leaves, garlic, olive oil, Parmesan cheese, and pine nuts, served with pasta).

♦ In Milan and Lombardy, look for *osso buco* (veal shank in tomato sauce with onions, wine, and stock) and *polenta* (cornmeal of a porridgelike consistency).

♦ In Naples, taste *mozzarella in carrozza* (a deep-fried cheese sandwich) and pizza.

♦ In Rome, sample *abbacchio al forno* (roast suckling lamb) and *cannelloni* (tube-shaped pasta filled with meat or ricotta cheese and covered with a tomato sauce).

♦ In Sicily, try *caponata* (eggplant, tomatoes, green pepper, and olives, cooked in olive oil) and *cassata alla Siciliana* (layers of sponge cake alternating with cream, ricotta cheese, candied fruit, chocolate, and liqueur).

♦ In Venice and the Veneto, taste *fegato alla Veneziana* (thin slices of calves' liver sauteed with onions) and *risi e bisi* (rice and peas).

Hotels

♦ When you check in, leave your passport at the desk for a few hours so the clerk can fill out forms for the police.

♦ In pensions, watch out for energy-saving light switches in stairways (watch for them in older apartment buildings, too). When you press the switch, the lights go on—but only for one minute. You have to get to the switch on the next landing to get another minute's light. To save worry, carry along a pocket flashlight.

♦ Even four-star hotels don't have wash-cloths. Most four- and five-star hotels do, however, have hair dryers attached to the bathroom wall.

♦ Water taps are marked *C* for hot and *F* for cold.

♦ Whenever you go out, leave your key at the desk. The management will get upset if you don't.

♦ If you're a woman traveling alone, stay in first-class hotels. If you go to a hotel bar, men will undoubtedly try to pick you up; just ignore them.

Tipping

♦ *Restaurants:* A 10-percent service charge is included in restaurant checks, but leave 5 percent more if the service was very good.

♦ *Cafes and bars:* Tip 15 percent if you're at a table and the bill doesn't include a service charge. Leave 200 lire if you stand at a counter or bar and drink a cup of coffee. Tip 500 lire or more if you stand at a counter or bar and have something like cocktails, sandwiches, or pastries.

♦ *Porters:* Give 1,500 lire per bag.

♦ *Hotel maids:* Leave 1,000 lire per day.

♦ *Taxis:* Fares include a tip, but give an extra 5 percent anyway.

♦ *Ushers:* Tip 1,000 lire.

♦ *Cloakroom attendants:* Give 200–300 lire.

♦ *Washroom attendants:* Tip 100 lire.

♦ *Church attendants who show you around:* Tip 500–1,000 lire.

♦ *Gas station attendants:* Give 1,000 lire—more if they perform an extra service such as cleaning the windshield.

Private Homes

♦ You can drop in, but not between 2:00 and 4:00 P.M., when people may be resting.

♦ Italian children usually eat with the family, even when there are guests. Make sure to include them in your conversation.

♦ If you spend several days with a family, you'll be given a napkin ring with a cloth napkin to reuse. At the end of each meal, fold the napkin and replace it in the ring. (The ring designs are different so your hosts can identify individual napkins.) Napkins are usually changed every five days.

♦ Electricity is expensive, so turn off the lights whenever you leave a room.

◆ Before you take a bath, ask your hosts if it's convenient. Use as little water as possible.

Gifts: If you're invited to a meal, bring individual pastries, a box of chocolates, flowers, or two or three bottles of wine. If you bring flowers, get an odd number and don't choose chrysanthemums, which are associated with funerals. If you don't have time to buy a gift beforehand, send one the next day.

◆ If you stay with a family for several days, bring a gift with you or send a gift after you leave. Good choices are whiskey, cognac, California wines, cigars, or something typical of your region in the U.S., such as crafts or quilts. Never give a brooch, a handkerchief, or a set of knives, all of which are associated with sadness.

Business

Hours

Businesses: Business hours vary by region.

◆ In northern Italy, most businesses are open from 9:00 A.M. to 5:00 P.M., Monday through Friday, with a very short lunch break (longer for a business lunch).

◆ In southern Italy, businesses are open from 9:00 A.M. to 1:00 P.M., Monday through Friday, close for lunch until 4:00 P.M., then reopen until 7:00 P.M. or even 9:00 P.M.

◆ Many businesses used to open for a half day on Saturday; they no longer do. An Italian businessperson might agree to see you on Saturday for an extremely urgent matter, but that would be rare.

Government offices: 8:00 A.M. to 2:00 P.M.,

Monday through Friday, with some regional differences. To contact a senior bureaucrat in a ministry, call between 10:00 A.M. and 1:00 P.M.

Banks: 8:35 A.M. to 1:35 P.M. and 3:00 to 4:00 P.M., Monday through Friday.

Stores: 9:00 A.M. to 1:00 P.M. and 3:30 or 4:00 to 7:30 or 8:00 P.M., Monday through Saturday. In northern Italy, the lunch break is shorter and stores close earlier. In some towns, shops may close one day per week.

Business Practices

◆ If you don't have a contact in Italy, get in touch with either the commercial attaché at your embassy or the Italian Institute for Foreign Trade, which promotes Italian exports and has offices in many countries.

◆ Make initial contacts with Italian businesspeople by letter, fax (now widely used in Italy), or telex—*not* by telephone. Follow up later with a phone call.

◆ When you arrive in Italy and want to confirm arrangements, it's still best to use a fax. Phone calls might not be returned, since the Italian phone system does not work very well.

◆ Don't schedule business trips to Italy between Christmas Eve and January 6 (the Epiphany), or from the middle of July through August, when most Italians vacation.

◆ In northern Italy, the pace of business is brisk, but in southern Italy, poor organization and scarce resources mean that business is conducted more slowly.

◆ Little business is done at home on evenings or weekends, so don't ask on a Friday afternoon if something (such as a proposal) can be ready first thing Monday morning.

♦ Personal relationships are important to Italians—money is not their only drive in business—so take advantage of any social occasion where you might meet potential business contacts. Ask others about any person you're interested in. *Don't*, however, try to discuss business—or even give out business cards—in a social setting.

♦ You won't find Italian women at top levels in business. Foreign businesswomen, however, are taken seriously. Businesswomen accompanied by businessmen will have to make it clear that they are not secretaries and should dress carefully (see Dress).

♦ Unless you speak fluent Italian or your contacts speak English, you'll need a translator. Italy has many translating agencies. You can also find an interpreter through your hotel, consulate, or embassy.

Meetings and negotiations: Make appointments two to four weeks in advance.

♦ When you go to a meeting, shake hands with everyone in the room, then exchange business cards with anyone you haven't met before. The person at the head of the table will be the one directing the meeting, though not always the most senior.

♦ Italian businesspeople are very formal, so don't use first names. People rarely use first names with their bosses.

♦ To speed the negotiating process, have important documents and agreements translated into Italian.

♦ Don't show any urgency in negotiating or you'll weaken your bargaining position.

♦ Italians don't consider big, formal meetings an appropriate place to decide important business matters. Instead, the people at

those meetings will communicate later with top-level people. Major decisions are usually made behind the scenes.

♦ Most decisions are now made by consensus, unlike in the past, when the head of an Italian company had the power to make all final decisions.

Entertainment: Don't expect or issue an invitation to a business breakfast. It's not done in Italy.

♦ At a business meal in a restaurant, the group will probably be small, to ensure better service.

♦ Always permit the Italian to choose the restaurant—even when you issue the invitation.

♦ When you invite an Italian businessperson to a meal, ask which colleagues should be included.

♦ Don't expect to be invited to a meal in a home unless you are on intimate terms with an Italian businessperson.

♦ Feel free to bring your spouse to a business-related dinner, but not to a lunch. Don't, however, expect your Italian hosts to bring their spouses.

♦ *Don't* drink too much. Drunkenness is considered a character weakness.

♦ Even if you issued the invitation, there will usually be a fight over the check, and you'll have to *insist* to pay. A foreign businesswoman will find it almost impossible to pay for a business meal.

Gifts: Good business gifts are coffee-table books, liquor typical of your country (for example, American wines), top-quality pen sets, and cigarette lighters. Special foods are also appreciated—lobster or smoked salmon packed in dry ice for the trip would be very well received.

Holidays & Celebrations

Holidays:

New Year's Day (January 1); Epiphany (January 6); Easter Monday; Liberation Day (May 1); Assumption of the Virgin (August 15); All Saints' Day (November 1); Immaculate Conception (December 8); Christmas (December 25); and St. Stephen's Day (December 26).

◆ Italians celebrate the arrival of spring on *Pasquetta* (the Monday after Easter) with the first picnic of the year.

◆ *Ferragosto* (August 15) is also celebrated with picnics in the countryside or at seaside resorts. *Ferragosto* originated as a pagan fair in the days of the Emperor Augustus, probably as a thanksgiving for the harvest.

Transportation

Public Transport

Mass transit: In most cities, you pay one fixed rate on city buses, no matter how far you travel. (This flat rate might vary from city to city, however.) In some cities you must buy a ticket for either 500 lire (good for 70 minutes) or 1,000 lire (good for two hours). You can take several buses during this period. Buy tickets at tobacconist shops, bars, cafes, or kiosks.

◆ Board buses at the back and validate your ticket in the machine there. Keep your ticket; inspectors sometimes check them and you'll be fined if you don't have one.

◆ To ride streetcars, you must buy your ticket in advance at a kiosk or tobacconist shop, or at booths outside the stations where streetcar service begins. You can buy either one or two tickets, or a book of ten.

◆ When you enter the streetcar, put your ticket in the machine, which stamps it.

◆ In Rome and Milan, use the subways, which also have flat rates. The subway stations have coin-operated ticket machines; keep the ticket until you get off the subway, in case there is an inspection. The Milan subway has an extra charge for a suitcase.

◆ Italy has several types of trains:

•IC (Intercity) are express trains with both international and domestic routes. They have first-class (some air-conditioned) and second-class seating. You can reserve seats.

•EC (Eurocity) trains provide only international service; some offer food and drink.

•EXPR (Espresso) trains are often used for international service. Most have both classes, but a few only have second-class seating. Some have food and drink available.

•DIR (Diretto) trains are semiexpress trains, often with only second-class seats, that make many stops.

• LOCALE trains are the slow, local trains that go to rural areas and stop frequently. Most have no first class.

◆ You can reserve seats on some trains at Italian travel agencies or station booking offices. If someone is sitting in your seat when you board, ask the train master to find you another seat.

◆ Keep your ticket until you get off the train.

◆ Most international and long-distance trains have dining cars.

◆ You can get sleeping cars on international express trains and those between major Italian towns. First class offers a choice of single or double compartments; second class has three berths to a compartment. Some trains also have couchettes. Both second-class berths and couchettes are unisex and come with blankets and pillows.

◆ If you wish to accompany someone onto the platform of a large-city train station, you must purchase a platform ticket for a very small fee.

◆ If you are a woman traveling alone by train, don't go into a compartment in which there is a man alone.

◆ All long-distance trains have police officers on board. If you have any trouble, ask for them.

Taxis: To find a cab, go to a taxi stand. If you call instead, you must pay the distance the driver has to come to pick you up.

◆ Taxis charge an extra 500–1,000 lire at night.

Driving

◆ You don't need an International Driver's License; a U.S. license is sufficient.

◆ Seat belts are compulsory for drivers and front-seat passengers.

◆ Round signs mean that an activity is forbidden, square signs mean that it is allowed. Triangular signs warn drivers to be cautious.

◆ If you see a sign saying *Zona Pedale,* it means that the street is for pedestrians only—no cars allowed.

◆ Speed limits change constantly. Currently, the speed limit on roads outside of cities is 90 kph. In cities, the speed limit is 50 kph.

On toll highways, it is 110 kph for cars with engines smaller than 1,000 cc, and 130 kph for those with larger engines.

◆ Whenever you drive in the passing lane, keep your left blinker flashing.

◆ Streetcars have the right of way.

◆ Watch out for three-wheeled vehicles, scooters, bikes, and motorcycles, which are often driven erratically.

◆ Major highways have emergency telephones with one button to call for a tow truck and another to call for an ambulance. A light will come on when your message has been received.

◆ Most gas stations accept only cash.

◆ The police use machines to photograph your license plate, so speeding could get you a ticket—and a huge fine—months after the event.

◆ If you're stopped for a violation, either pay the fine immediately or ask for an injunction, which allows you to pay at the police station. You can contest the ticket, but it's usually cheaper and easier to pay immediately. Fines can be severe, ranging from $10 U.S. to $500 U.S., depending on the offense.

◆ Enforcement of drunk driving laws is getting stricter; the police sometimes administer Breathalyzer tests.

◆ Parking is a problem in cities: there are few parking spaces on the street and not many parking garages. Avoid towaway zones, which are indicated by signs showing a car in midair.

◆ When on the outskirts of towns, always park on the right side of the road.

Legal Matters & Safety

◆ Italy has no legal drinking age, and bars and restaurants can serve liquor 24 hours a day.

◆ If you need a police officer in a large city, seek out one who speaks English. In small towns, police seldom speak English but will try to find an interpreter.

◆ If you need a lawyer, ask for recommendations at the Chamber of Commerce or the American Consulate. Be sure to discuss the fee in advance; the Italian Bar Association does not accept cases on a contingent fee basis.

◆ Women should not walk alone late at night. The Milan and Rome subways are usually safe near the center of both cities, but to travel a long distance after 11:00 P.M., take a taxi.

◆ In large cities such as Rome, Naples, Milan, and Turin, be alert to avoid robberies. If you notice someone staring at your purse, necklace, or bracelet, try to melt into a crowd of people. Purse-snatching and pickpocketing have been on the rise. Bands of children carry a newspaper that they hold against the victim; some of the children distract the person, while others pick pockets under the cover of the newspaper. In Rome and Palermo, some motorcyclists have been known to ride close to the sidewalk, grab a purse, and take off.

◆ Keep your money and documents in a money belt, if possible. If you must carry a purse, carry it on the side facing away from the street, and in restaurants and cafes, keep it on your lap.

◆ Most thieves aren't interested in passports. If yours is stolen, check with your embassy or the police, because it might well turn up.

Key Phrases

English	Italian	Pronunciation
Good day	Buon giorno	bwon-JOR-no
Good evening	Buona sera	BWO-nah SAY-rah
Please	Per favore	payr fah-VO-ray
Thank you	Grazie	GRAT-see-ay
You're welcome	Prego	PRAY-go
Yes	Si	see
No	No	no
Mr., Sir	Signor	see-NYOR
Mrs., Madame	Signora	see-NYOR-ah
Miss	Signorina	see-nyor-EE-nah
Excuse me	Scusi	SCOO-zee
Good-bye	Arrivederci	ar-ree-vay-DEHR-chee
I don't understand.	Non capisco.	non ka-PEE-sko
I don't speak Italian.	Non parlo italiano.	non PAHR-lo ee-tahl-YA-no
Is there anyone here who speaks English?	C'è qualcuno qui che parla inglese?	chay kwal-KOO-no kwee kay PAHR-lah een-GLAY-say

The Netherlands

In the flat, canal-crossed country of the Netherlands, you'll find windmills and tulips, just as you expected. But you'll also find some of the world's greatest art and best Indonesian cuisine (the latter thanks to Dutch colonialism), and some of the most eccentric young people.

You'll also find that the Dutch speak superb English, which makes it extremely easy for travelers to explore everything the Netherlands has to offer and to get to know the Dutch people.

Greetings

◆ Always shake hands when greeting and leaving someone—even young children.

◆ Everyone stands up when exchanging greetings or departing.

◆ Close friends often kiss on both cheeks in greeting. Men, however, don't kiss other men.

◆ At a business or social gathering, if you're not formally introduced, introduce yourself to each person and shake hands. Just state your last name.

◆ When you're introduced to someone, repeat your name as you shake hands.

◆ If you don't introduce yourself before speaking, the Dutch will consider you too casual and might even be offended.

◆ Address a medical doctor as "Mr.," not as "Dr."

◆ Don't use first names until the Dutch do.

Conversation

◆ Good topics of conversation: Dutch politics; travel; vacations; or sports such as

soccer, cycling, and ice-skating.

◆ Topics to avoid: American politics (unless you're prepared to hear some strong views from the Dutch) or money and prices (the Dutch think Americans always discuss money).

◆ The Dutch are politically oriented, so be sure to read up on world politics before arriving in the Netherlands.

◆ Don't make jokes about the Royal Family. The Dutch are very fond of their royalty and resent such remarks. Many homes have pictures of the Queen; people would appreciate your acknowledging them.

◆ You may ask about someone's profession or family, but don't probe. The Dutch aren't as formal as the French or the Belgians, but they still value their privacy.

◆ Don't offer personal compliments until you know someone well.

◆ When you're talking to people, don't chew gum or keep your hands in your pockets.

◆ Feel free to strike up a conversation with another person in a cafe, even if you're a single woman.

Money

◆ The unit of currency is the gulden (plural gulden, abbreviated Fl), made up of 100 cents.

◆ Coins come in denominations of 5, 10, and 25 cents and 1, $2\frac{1}{2}$, 5, and 10 gulden. Be careful: the 5-gulden coin looks like the 5-cent coin. Both are the same size and copper-colored, but the 5-gulden coin is thicker.

◆ Notes come in denominations of 5, 10, 25, 50, 100, 250, and 1,000 gulden.

Telephones

◆ There are two types of public telephones: one for coins and one for telephone cards. Both types  have only one slot. If you aren't using a card, deposit either one or $2\frac{1}{2}$ gulden, depending on the phone. No matter whether you use coins or a card, a meter will tell you how much money you have left. Phones don't make change.

◆ Buy telephone cards, which are green and about the size of a credit card, at the post office. You can choose cards with varying numbers of units.

◆ To make international long-distance calls, go to the post office (P.T.T.).

◆ When you answer the phone, say your last name instead of "Hello."

◆ The Emergency Number for police, fire, or an ambulance is **0611.**

In Public

◆ Don't touch or be physically demonstrative with anyone except relatives or good friends. People occasionally touch  the shoulder of good friends when shaking hands.

◆ If you see friends at a distance, greet them by waving, not shouting.

◆ When you enter a shop or a train compartment, always say "Good morning" or "Good afternoon" to everyone present. Each person will probably reply.

◆ Shop clerks wait on only one person at a time and even escort each customer to the door. Never interrupt, no matter how great your hurry.

◆ When waiting to be served, notice which people are ahead of you. Speak up when it's your turn.

◆ When a man walks with a woman, he should walk on the part of the sidewalk nearest the street.

◆ Men should stand when a woman enters the room.

◆ Never issue an invitation you don't really mean ("I'll call you in a few days" or "I'll call you to come over to dinner next week.") The Dutch are very literal and will take you seriously.

◆ Look for public toilets in parks, railway stations, bus stations, recreation areas, department stores, and small separate buildings on city streets. Toilets are marked with signs saying *Toiletten* or *W.C.* Women's rooms say *Dames* and men's rooms, *Heren*.

Dress

◆ Don't go sightseeing in halter tops or shorts. Blue jeans are acceptable, however.

◆ For business, men should wear suits and women should wear suits or dresses.

◆ When dining in a Dutch home, men should wear suits and ties, and women should wear dresses or skirts and blouses. A man should never remove his jacket unless the host does. (He probably won't.)

◆ To an elegant restaurant, men should wear jackets and ties, and women should wear dresses or skirts. To other restaurants, pants and jeans are acceptable for both sexes, and men don't need jackets.

◆ For theater events, any level of dress is acceptable—except for openings, when men usually wear tuxedos, and women wear cocktail dresses.

◆ When visiting a church, women may wear pants.

Meals

Hours and Foods

Breakfast (het ont bijt): 7:30 A.M. Expect several kinds of breads and rolls, sliced meats and cheeses, sometimes hard-boiled eggs, and tea.

Lunch (de lunch): Noon in the country and 1:00 P.M. in cities. In rural areas lunch is the main meal (see Dinner). In cities, most people have open-faced sandwiches.

Dinner (het diner): 6:00 P.M.; slightly later for a dinner party. Dinner often starts with tomato or clear vegetable soup. The main course consists of meat (often braised beef) or broiled fish, boiled potatoes or rice, vegetables, and salad. The meal ends with fruit, ice cream, or pudding—caramel pudding and rice and fruit puddings are popular—and coffee.

◆ At dinner parties, women usually have a before-dinner sherry, while men usually drink *jenever* (gin flavored with juniper berries, served chilled and straight). Mixed drinks aren't common, but wine is popular. The meal is as described above, accompanied by wine. After dessert, coffee is usually served in demitasse cups in the living room. If you want your coffee black, be sure to tell the hosts before it's served. Most Dutch take their coffee with cream and sugar.

Breaks: At 10:00 A.M., many people break for coffee and cookies or small pastries, and at 4:00 P.M., they have tea and cookies.

Table Manners

◆ If you're invited to dinner in a home, be on time.

◆ Don't help yourself to hors d'oeuvres. The hosts will pass around the first few servings.

◆ If you're served a drink before dinner and haven't finished it when you're summoned to the table, leave it behind.

◆ In many homes the family offers a prayer before meals.

◆ The hostess might serve herself first— once a custom to prove the food wasn't poisoned. Don't start eating before she does.

◆ The usual beverages with a meal are wine and water. Most Dutch drink beer only with Indonesian or Chinese food.

◆ Before drinking any alcoholic beverage,

wait until everyone's drink has been poured. It's customary for everyone to raise glasses simultaneously and say "Proost."

◆ You won't receive a separate salad plate.

◆ All types of food are eaten with a knife and fork—including sandwiches, fruit, and sometimes even pieces of bread.

◆ Keep both wrists on the table.

◆ Try to eat everything on your plate.

◆ Your hostess will offer second helpings after everyone has finished the first.

◆ Don't expect bread to be served with the meal.

◆ If the hostess leaves the table and goes to the kitchen, the men should rise when she returns.

◆ Don't get up during a meal, even to go to the bathroom—it's considered rude.

◆ You may smoke between dinner courses, but ask first.

◆ To show you've finished your meal, place your utensils paralled on the plate; it doesn't matter in which direction.

◆ Leave after coffee is served, usually around 10:00 P.M. If coffee is served a second time, that's a clear signal to leave.

Eating Out

◆ Restaurants are expensive. Try the following alternatives:

• *Bars/Cafes* serve all kinds of alcohol. Some also offer open-faced sandwiches. One popular choice is an open-faced roast beef sandwich with an egg on top. If you sit at a table, you'll be served by a waiter.

• *Broodjeswinkels* are deli-like sandwich shops that offer open-faced sandwiches eaten with milk or buttermilk.

•Indonesian restaurants, though inexpensive and informal, offer an elaborate meal—the *rijsttafel* (rice table), which has plain steamed rice as a foundation for 15 to 50 different dishes. Put some rice on your plate and add a spoonful of each dish around it. Eat the meal with a fork and spoon.

• *Poffertjes* (which means pancakes) are restaurants that serve only that dish. The pancakes are small balls of fried dough, served with powdered sugar and a choice of topping, such as honey and rum or syrup.

•Snack bars all over the country serve soup, sandwiches, cakes, pastries, coffee, and soft drinks. Snack bars with an "A" license also have beer and wine.

•Street stalls sell herring, salted and served on toast, a favorite Dutch snack. If you buy a herring filet at a stall, hold it by its tail and take several large bites. The herring might be raw. Street stalls also sell smoked eels; the smaller ones are tastier.

• *Shwarma* are run by Arabs and serve many Middle Eastern dishes, including lamb cooked on a vertical spit and served with vegetables, in Arabic bread.

•Most major towns have many ethnic restaurants such as Chinese, Indian, Middle Eastern, or Argentinean.

◆ The Dutch eat early—usually at about 6:00 or 7:00 P.M. Most restaurants close by 9:00 or 10:00 P.M. In Amsterdam, many restaurants stay open until 11:00 P.M.

◆ Check prices before you enter. Dutch restaurants must post a menu in an outside window.

◆ Many restaurants (except ethnic restaurants) have a tourist menu, which offers three courses and costs about half of the regular menu. The price of the tourist menu is fixed annually throughout the country.

◆ Seat yourself at all restaurants except very elegant ones.

◆ Dutch restaurants serve excellent coffee. Each year, one of the Dutch newspapers rates the coffee in every restaurant and awards a major prize for the best.

◆ Someone entertaining several people at a restaurant usually chooses and orders for the whole party.

◆ When you eat with a group in a restaurant, pay your share unless you've been specifically invited as a guest. If someone does treat you to a meal, reciprocate as soon as possible.

◆ If you plan to pay by credit card, check in advance to make sure that the restaurant accepts them. A few don't.

Specialties

◆ Try these Dutch specialties: *erwtensoep* (a thick pea soup, often served with bread and smoked sausage or pig's knuckle, but seldom available in restaurants during the summer); *croquetje* (chicken and veal croquettes); *uitsmijter* (an open-faced sandwich topped with sliced meat, fried eggs, and sliced pickles); *hutspot* (a stew of beef, mashed vegetables, and herbs); *lamstongen met rozijnensaus* (lamb's tongue in a raisin and white wine sauce); and *flensjes* (small crepes, served for dessert).

◆ Also try these Indonesian specialties, typically served at a *rijsttafel*: *saté* (pork cooked on wooden skewers and served with peanut sauce); *kroepoek* (shrimp crackers); *bebottok* (meat steamed in coconut milk); *babi pangang* (pieces of roast suckling pig in a spicy sauce); *seroendeng* (fried coconuts and peanuts); and *sambals* (different kinds of very hot red and green pastes).

Hotels

◆ Even inexpensive hotels offer good service and comfort.

◆ English is spoken even in the smallest hotels.

Tipping

◆ *Restaurants:* Most restaurants include a service charge in the check, but leave a little change on the table if the service was very good. If a service charge isn't included, leave 15 percent.

◆ *Porters:* Tip 1–2 gulden, more if they perform a special service.

◆ *Hotel maids:* Leave 2 gulden per day.

◆ *Taxis:* For fares up to 20 gulden, give 1–2 gulden; over that amount, tip 10 percent of the fare.

◆ *Ushers:* Give 1–2 gulden.

◆ *Cloakroom attendants:* Tip 1–2 gulden.

◆ *Washroom attendants:* Leave 50 cents in a dish (25 cents in department stores).

Private Homes

◆ The Dutch take pride in their home furnishings. Offer compliments on them.

◆ Remember that birthdays are extremely important in the Netherlands. Families post a birthday calendar, noting all family members' birthdays, on the door of the downstairs bathroom. If you're staying with a family, check the calendar so you can offer birthday wishes.

◆ Before using the phone, always ask permission. If you need to make several calls, offer to pay. If your hosts refuse payment, give them a gift.

◆ If you stay with a family, you'll be expected for meals unless you indicate otherwise. It's also courteous to let your hosts know when you'll be out and at what time you'll return.

◆ Make your bed, tidy your room, and offer to help with the dishes.

◆ Bathe daily if you wish, but your Dutch hosts will be surprised if you wash and blow-dry your hair every day.

Gifts: If you're invited to dinner, bring flowers and unwrap them before you present them. If your host picks you up at your hotel, you may ask to stop at a florist on the way to the home. It's also courteous to send flowers or a plant the next day instead. If you know the family has children, bring them candy. Bring wine only to the home of close friends; many people pride themselves on their wine cellars and would be insulted.

◆ If you stay with a family, bring the newest paperback books and magazines, attractive paper napkins, typical American crafts (such as Native American jewelry), or T-shirts with sayings.

Business

Hours

Businesses and government offices: 8:30 A.M. to 5:30 P.M., Monday through Friday.

Banks: 9:00 A.M. to 4:00 P.M., Monday through Friday, plus 5:00 to 7:00 P.M. on Thursday.

Stores: 8:30 or 9:00 A.M. to 5:30 or 6:00 P.M. on weekdays. Some shops also open from 7:00 to 9:00 P.M. on Thursday or Friday nights. Shops are open 9:00 A.M. to 5:00 P.M. on Saturday. Some small shops close from 1:00 to 2:00 P.M. All shops must close for a half day each week; the day varies.

Business Practices

◆ Make contacts in the Netherlands through the Dutch Consulate in your area, the Dutch Embassy in the U.S., or the Dutch Chamber of Commerce *(Kamer van Koophandel)*.

◆ Don't plan business trips from June through August or around Christmas. Both are popular vacation periods.

◆ Use correct titles in business dealings, especially when writing business letters. Titles for professionals such as lawyers or engineers can be complex. Buy an executive-style calendar that lists the proper forms of address.

◆ Before you go to the Netherlands, do your homework. You'll need a thorough knowledge of the market, including your competition.

◆ Women have the same chance of success as men in the Netherlands.

◆ Most Dutch businesspeople speak English, so you probably won't need an interpreter.

◆ You don't need to translate your business cards.

◆ For individual clients, you don't have to have written materials translated. If your material will eventually be used in the consumer market, translations are useful but not necessary.

◆ Fax and telex services are available everywhere.

◆ Don't worry about encountering clannishness. The Dutch are open and friendly. Offices celebrate every small occasion, even the arrival of a new secretary, with cream cakes for everyone.

◆ The Dutch are highly organized and don't like anything to be impromptu or spontaneous. Avoid making spur-of-the-moment suggestions such as "Let's go out to dinner tonight."

◆ You won't make a better impression by staying in the most expensive hotels and eating in the best restaurants. The Dutch retain a bit of Calvinism and will see your high expenses as meaning a higher cost for your product.

Meetings and negotiations: Make appointments from abroad at least two weeks to one month in advance. Dutch businesspeople travel a great deal.

◆ Make business appointments for between 9:00 A.M. and 4:00 P.M., Monday through Friday.

◆ Be absolutely punctual.

◆ Men arriving for an appointment might be greeted by an attendant in a reception room

and offered a cigar. They should tip the attendant 1 gulden when they leave.

◆ You'll be offered a beverage: coffee in the morning, tea in the afternoon, and a cold drink in warm weather. If you are hosting a meeting, make sure you do the same.

◆ Exchange business cards at initial meetings and when you're introduced to new people at subsequent meetings.

◆ The Dutch are practical and down-to-earth. Your presentations should be factual and contain many figures. Use charts and visuals if they are necessary, but don't include them just to impress.

◆ If you say you'll do something—for example, putting something in the mail the next day—be sure to do it.

◆ Don't expect lengthy bargaining. Negotiations will probably proceed swiftly. Determine your price and stick to it.

◆ Decisions in larger companies are made by a consensus among many people. In smaller companies, one person at the top usually makes the decisions.

◆ Dutch time estimates for having something ready are reliable.

◆ Written contracts are the usual practice.

Entertainment: Dutch businesspeople like to entertain and be entertained. Business lunches are common, though business dinners are more popular for formal meetings.

◆ If your host doesn't specify whether spouses are included in the party, ask. American spouses are often invited to business functions.

◆ Entertain only people with whom you are negotiating.

◆ Businesspeople enjoy both French restaurants and typical Dutch restaurants, which have a pleasant ambience.

Holidays & Celebrations

Holidays:

New Year's Day (January 1); Good Friday; Easter Monday; the Queen's Birthday (April 30); Ascension Day (five weeks after Easter); Whit Monday (eight weeks after Easter); the Feast of St. Nicholas (December 5; most businesses are open until noon); Christmas (December 25); and December 26.

◆ On the evening before the Feast of Sinterklaas (Saint Nicholas), children leave their shoes by the fireplace with sugar lumps and carrots for Sinterklaas's horse. The next morning they receive a large gift as well as small treats in their shoes. Good friends leave gifts at the door and run away.

◆ On this day family members also give each other gifts, each with a humorous poem attached. For instance, a teenaged girl might get a poem teasing her about her boyfriend. Each person also receives her or his initial in chocolate. If you're included in a celebration, have a gift, with a funny poem, for each family member. Popular foods for this day are marzipan (almond paste) in different shapes, fondant, and *speculaas* (spiced ginger cookies), with hot chocolate or hot wine to drink.

Transportation

Public Transport

Mass transit: Buses, subways, and streetcars use the same tickets. Amsterdam has a subway between the city center and the airport. Rotterdam has a full subway system.

◆ Bus, subway, and streetcar tickets come in strips *(strippenkaarten)*. Fold down the appropriate number of strips, depending on your distance, and stamp them in a machine on the vehicle (bus, subway, or streetcar). The machine will stamp the ticket with a time 15 minutes ahead; you can change vehicles before that time. Although you can't use strip tickets on trains, you can purchase them at train stations, as well as at post offices, the central bus station, subway stations, bookstores, and some tobacconist shops.

◆ If you travel by streetcar, you must purchase your ticket in advance; if you travel by bus, you can buy them from the driver but they're more expensive.

◆ You can also purchase one-, two-, or three-day passes that provide unlimited travel on all forms of transportation in a city. You can buy the passes and get pamphlets explaining them at bus and train stations, drug stores, and tobacconist shops. Passes aren't stamped; you just show them when you board.

◆ For long-distance trips, consider buses, which have bathrooms and are heated in winter and air-conditioned in summer. You don't need to book in advance unless you're traveling to another country.

◆ Dutch train service is excellent. Employees speak English, and ticket sales are fully computerized. Trains are frequent and have both first- and second-class service. First class has comfortable chairs with foot rests and dining cars *(restauratie wagen)*. You'll also be comfortable in second class, where snacks, coffee, and tea are sold from carts.

Taxis: Either get a taxi at a taxi stand or

phone for one.

◆ All taxis use meters. The fares are higher between 1:00 and 6:00 A.M.

Driving

◆ You don't need an International Driver's License; a U.S. license is sufficient.

◆ The Netherlands has one of the best road systems in Europe.

◆ Seat belts are mandatory for all passengers, and children must sit in the back seat.

◆ Traffic from the right has the right of way, even if it is emerging from a tiny side street. Streetcars *always* have the right of way.

◆ The speed limit in built-up areas is 30 or 40 kph and on highways is 100 or 120 kph.

◆ Watch out for bicyclists, who can be very aggressive.

◆ Laws regarding drunk driving are strict. Police have the right to stop drivers and give Breathalyzer tests on the spot.

◆ If stopped for a traffic violation, foreigners usually have to pay fines right away.

Legal Matters & Safety

◆ If you stay longer than three months, you must register with the police. Failure to

do so can mean immediate deportation.

◆ Prostitution is legal in the Netherlands. Women should avoid Amsterdam's Red Light District, where many prostitutes sit in shop windows. It's in poor taste for women to go there and stare. Ask at your hotel which areas in Amsterdam are best bypassed.

◆ Shops that sell sex paraphernalia are legal and common, even in small towns.

◆ The legal drinking age is 16, and bars and restaurants can serve liquor 24 hours a day.

◆ Although it's legal to buy and smoke marijuana in the Netherlands, it's illegal to bring it into the country.

◆ Some coffeehouses offer different types of marijuana and hashish on a special menu. A "No drugs" sign appears in the window of coffeehouses that don't offer drugs and bars that don't want patrons using them.

◆ If you're a woman traveling alone, you can feel safe going to a restaurant or bar by yourself, but you shouldn't go out alone after 11:00 P.M. Use a taxi if you need to be out late, and watch your purse carefully, especially on buses and streetcars.

Key Phrases

English	Dutch	Pronunciation
Good morning	Goedemorgen	hoo-de-MOR-ghen
Good afternoon	Goedemiddag	hoo-de-MID-dahkh
Good evening	Goedenavond	hoo-dun-AH-vawnt
Please	Alstublieft	ahl-stew-BLEEFT
Thank you	Dank U	dahnk you
You're welcome	Geen dank	hain dunk
Yes	Ja	ya
No	Nee	nay
Mr., Sir	Mijnheer	muh-NAYR
Mrs., Madam	Mevrouw	muhv-ROW*
Miss	Juffrouw	yuf-ROW*
Excuse me	Pardon	Par-DAWN
Good-bye	Tot ziens	Tawt seens
I don't understand.	Ik begrijp het niet.	ik be-CHAYP** heht neet
I don't speak Dutch.	Ik spreek geen Nederlands.	Ik SPRAYK hain NAY-der-lunts
Does anyone here speak English?	Spreekt er hier iemand Engels?	SPRAYKT ehr EE-mahnd EEN-gehls?

*"ROW" is pronounced as in "cow."

**"CH" is pronounced like a gutteral "k," as in the Scottish word "loch," only softer.

Norway

Thanks to the discovery of North Sea oil, Norway has one of the highest standards of living in the world. It is also the northernmost country in Western Europe, with fully half the country above the Arctic Circle.

Norwegians take pride in being self-reliant people who can also put aside personal interests for the common good. Great efforts have been made to save the country's natural beauties for everyone to enjoy.

The Norwegian people work very hard for nine months of the year because the weather offers opportunities to do little else. But at the first promise of good weather, they rush off to enjoy their summer places and three months of summer sports.

Greetings

◆ Shake hands when you're introduced, greeting someone you know, or taking leave.

◆ Good friends of the younger generation, whatever their sex, hug one another in greeting. Members of the older generation shake hands, even with close friends.

◆ Norwegians often address men by just their last names—as in "Good morning, Hansen"; it's not considered rude.

◆ At a small party, wait for your hosts to introduce you. At a large party, introduce yourself.

◆ Rise when you're introduced.

◆ Use first names only with close friends.

Conversation

◆ Most Norwegians speak English, and some also know French and German.

◆ Good topics of conversation: your hosts' interests or hobbies; politics; participatory sports, such as sailing, hiking, or skiing; spectator sports, such as soccer; or what your hosts did on their last vacation.

◆ Topics to avoid: criticism of other peoples or customs, or personal life (avoid questions such as "What do you do?" or "Are you married?").

◆ Norwegians are typically reserved about themselves and sometimes feel that Americans are too casual and glib about private issues. It takes time to get to know people.

Money

◆ The unit of currency is the krone (plural kroner, abbreviated NKr or NOK), made up of 100 øre.

◆ Coins come in denominations of 5, 10, 25, and 50 øre and 1 and 5 kroner.

◆ Notes come in denominations of 10, 50, 100, 500, and 1,000 kroner.

Telephones

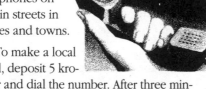

◆ Look for public phones on main streets in cities and towns.

◆ To make a local call, deposit 5 kroner and dial the number. After three minutes, you'll hear a beep that means you need to deposit more coins. Have extra coins handy so you can deposit the money quickly and avoid getting cut off.

◆ Norway has no telephone cards.

◆ You can dial directly to over 40 countries from Norwegian phones. You can also make long-distance calls at a *telegrafkontor* (telephone office).

◆ Ask for an English-speaking operator if you need assistance.

◆ Answer the phone by giving either your last name or your phone number.

◆ When you use a telephone directory, note that the letters Å, AE, and Ø are at the end of the alphabet.

◆ Emergency numbers are as follows:

Police	002
Fire	001
Ambulance	003

In Public

◆ Never speak in a loud voice.

◆ Avoid demonstrative gestures, such as slapping people on the back or putting your arm around their shoulders.

◆ If you like to gamble, look for slot machines in cafes and restaurant entrances. Most machines take 1-krone coins, and the proceeds go to charity.

◆ Feel free to take photographs; there are few restrictions. At village festivals, where people wear traditional dress, ask permission before you photograph individuals. They'll almost always be delighted to pose for you.

◆ You'll find public toilets on the street as well as in the usual places. They are marked *W.C.;* those for women are labeled *Damer* and those for men, *Herrer.*

◆ Before you use a stall in a public toilet, wait for an attendant to clean it. Pay a fee if one is posted; otherwise leave 1 krone.

Dress

◆ For casual occasions, feel free to wear clean, pressed blue jeans and T-shirts—but only if the fabric is not faded or torn. Wear shorts only in the countryside.

◆ Business dress is fairly casual. Men can wear sport jackets, but should always wear ties. Women may wear suits, dresses, or dress pants.

◆ If invited to dinner in a home, men should wear suits, and women should wear dresses, skirts and blouses, or dress pants.

◆ In better restaurants, men must wear jackets and ties. More casual attire is fine for smaller or neighborhood restaurants.

◆ For opera or ballet openings, dress fairly formally: dark suits for men and cocktail dresses for women. To a regular performance, men should wear jackets and ties, and women should wear dresses or skirts.

◆ If an invitation to a wedding or party specifies formal wear, men should wear tuxedos or tails, and women should wear short or long dresses.

◆ When Norwegian women enter someone's house in cold weather, they often remove brown woolen long underwear from beneath their skirts or dresses. Women visiting Norway during the winter might also want to wear long underwear.

Meals

Hours and Foods

Breakfast (frokost): 8:30 A.M. A typical breakfast includes cheeses, cold cuts, soft-boiled eggs, bread, and coffee or tea.

Lunch (lunsj): Around noon. This is a light meal of open-faced sandwiches (usually a thin piece of rye bread with artistically arranged meat, fish, and cheese toppings) and fruit.

Dinner (middag): 5:00 to 6:00 P.M. for a family meal; 7:00 P.M. for a dinner party (6:00 P.M. in the winter). A dinner party begins with an appetizer (usually a delicacy such as smoked or cured salmon, fjord shrimp, or a small meat salad) or soup, accompanied by white wine. At formal dinners, both appetizers and soup are served, the soup first.

◆ The main course is usually meat or fowl—roast beef, reindeer, goose, and pheasant are common—served with boiled potatoes and vegetables and sometimes a salad. Red wine accompanies this course.

◆ Dessert follows—often ice cream with liqueur, or fruit (cloudberries, strawberries, or fruit salad) with whipped cream. Typical dessert drinks are port and madeira. The meal ends with coffee and cognac or another liqueur.

◆ A city family will have its main meal in the evening. They will eat meatballs or fish-cakes with potatoes and a thick pea porridge or cooked cabbage with caraway and vinegar. The meal will be accompanied by lingonberries and paper thin flatbread. Dessert will be ice cream or—in the summer—fresh fruit. With the meal, people drink water or milk; on rare occasions there will be beer and wine. Coffee is served immediately after the meal.

◆ In the countryside, the main meal is at noon, and the evening meal is light: perhaps scrambled eggs, smoked salmon, cold cuts, pancakes, or leftovers from the noon meal. There will always be two or three kinds of homemade bread. About $1\frac{1}{2}$ to 2 hours after dinner, people will have coffee and cake.

Table Manners

◆ If you're invited to a meal, be punctual. If there is predinner cocktail time, it will be brief. In some homes, people go immediately to the table for the meal.

◆ If there are cocktails, you'll probably be offered sherry, scotch, or champagne rather than mixed drinks. Sometimes smoked meats or cheeses accompany the drinks. Take small amounts of cheese, using the slicer provided.

◆ The host and hostess sit at opposite ends of the table, with the male guest of honor to the hostess's left and the female guest of honor to the host's left.

◆ Dinners often last several hours, because of the many courses and much conversation.

◆ Food is passed around the table on platters, except at formal dinners. Take small portions at first, because it's considered rude not to finish everything on your plate. Your hosts will understand that the food might be strange to you, however, and won't be insulted if you don't finish a portion of a dish after tasting it.

◆ Don't start eating until your hosts do.

◆ Eat open-faced sandwiches with a knife and fork. Never pick them up with your hands.

◆ To show you're finished, cross your utensils in the middle of the plate.

◆ *Aquavit,* a liquor distilled from grain or potatoes and often flavored with caraway seed, is served on special occasions. Toast someone by looking at the person, sipping the *aquavit,* looking at the person again, and then putting your glass down. A beer chaser follows the *aquavit.*

◆ If you don't want to drink wine or beer, feel free to drink water. Bottled water, such as Perrier, is usually served.

◆ Before you light a cigarette, wait to see what the others at the table do. Norwegians commonly smoke between courses.

◆ At the end of the meal, thank the hosts. This doesn't signal the end of the evening, however—at a dinner party in a home, the meal might even be followed by dancing.

◆ If you attend a dinner in the summer, stay until 11:00 P.M. Since it stays light until midnight, your hosts might suggest an after-dinner walk, followed by a liqueur back at the house. In winter people go to bed earlier, so plan to leave by 10:00 P.M.

Eating Out

◆ Different eating places serve different kinds of food:

● A *bistro* offers a wide selection of open-faced sandwiches, beer, wine, and soft drinks.

● A *kafe* serves open-faced sandwiches, coffee, tea, and sometimes beer and wine. In some communities, *kafes* also serve hard liquor. (Note: some restaurants with *kafe* in their names serve full meals; don't confuse them with real *kafes.*)

● *Kaffestovas* are self-service cafeterias where you can get simple hot foods such as meatballs, fish cakes, and stews.

● *Konditori* are pastry shops offering simple open-faced sandwiches, pastries, and coffee. No liquor is served.

● Outdoor food stands sell snacks such as sausages, waffles, or hamburgers. Feel free to eat these snacks on the street.

◆ If you go into a *kafe* and there are no free tables, ask to share a table. Don't do that in a regular restaurant, however.

◆ You might see young people snapping their fingers to attract a waiter's attention, but it's considered rude. Instead, raise your hand and extend your index finger.

◆ At a restaurant or hotel smorgasbord, take only what you can eat. Norwegians are scandalized by wasting food. You can always return for second helpings.

◆ If you order a mixed drink (such as scotch and soda), you'll pay a separate charge for the soda water.

◆ You can't order wine or beer before 11:00 A.M. There are three types of beer: *Brigg,* which is low in alcohol; *Pils,* which is lager; and *Export,* which has the highest alcohol content.

◆ You can order drinks with hard liquor only between 3:00 and 11:45 P.M. Hard liquor is not sold at all on Sundays or holidays.

◆ Women are safe going alone to a bar or restaurant.

Specialties

◆ Fresh fish figures prominently on Norwegian menus. Sample these fish and seafood specialties: *gravlaks* (salmon cured with dill); *sild* (herring, prepared in many different ways); *kokt torsk* (poached cod); *reker* (fjord shrimp); *steke marinert makrell* (grilled, marinated mackerel); *fiskepudding* (fish pudding with bread crumbs and cream); and *torsk med eggesaus* (poached codfish steaks with egg sauce).

◆ Also try *fenalar* (cured, baked leg of mutton); *flatbrod* (crisp, thin rye bread); *himmelsk lapskaus* (fruit salad with nuts, served with rum and egg sauce); and *rabarbragrot* (rhubarb compote).

◆ Depending on your feelings about exotic foods, you might want to try—or avoid—*hval biff* (whale meat, which tastes like liver and has the consistency of steak); *gjetost* (a cheese that tastes more like sweet fudge); *sylte* (head cheesc, a fatty, gelatinous salami made from a calf's head).

Hotels

◆ When you check into a hotel, show your passport to the desk clerk. You don't need to leave it.

◆ When you go out, take your room key with you.

Tipping

◆ *Restaurants:* Both restaurants and hotels add 15 percent to the bill as a service charge. Leave an extra 5–10 kroner in a restaurant if the service was excellent.

◆ *Porters:* Give hotel porters and bellboys 2–5 kroner per bag. Airport porters have fixed rates.

◆ *Hotel maids:* Leave 2–5 kroner per day.

◆ *Taxis:* Round the fare up to the nearest 10 kroner.

◆ *Washroom attendants:* Look for signs posted in washrooms indicating the fee.

Private Homes

◆ If you visit someone in the countryside, arrive at 3:30 or 4:00 P.M. People usually have their main meal at noon, followed by a nap. Late afternoon is reserved for visitors.

◆ If you visit someone in the city, call ahead.

◆ If you visit people in the city, you'll be offered liquor or coffee. People in the countryside are more likely to serve coffee and pastries.

◆ If you make any phone calls from someone's home, offer to pay for them. Daytime local calls from a home cost about 10 cents a minute; after 5:00 P.M., they're free.

◆ If you stay with a Norwegian family, feel free to go out by yourself. Your hosts will be pleased to show you around but won't smother you by insisting on accompanying you everywhere.

♦ If you stay for several days, offer to help set or clear the table. Your offer will probably be declined unless other guests are coming for the evening. In general, Norwegians enjoy playing host and prefer to have guests relax and enjoy themselves.

♦ Feel free to bathe every day. Always ask whether it's convenient, however, in case the water must be heated.

Gifts: If you're invited for a cup of coffee, bring pastries or a box of chocolates.

♦ If you're invited to a meal, bring a bottle of wine, chocolates, pastries, or flowers. Liquor is a welcome gift, since it's very expensive. If you bring flowers, don't choose carnations, any white flowers such as lilies, or any kind of wreath (even at Christmas); they're all reserved for funerals.

♦ If you stay with a family, bring an example of an art or craft typical of your region, such as Native American jewelry or scrimshaw. Other good choices are an American antique, a bottle of American liquor, or frozen steaks or roast beef. Meat is expensive in Norway, so it's a much-appreciated gift.

Business

Hours

Businesses and government offices: 8:00 A.M. to 4:00 P.M., Monday through Friday.

Banks: Hours might vary in different communities, but most banks are open between 9:00 A.M. and 3:00 P.M., Monday through Fri-

day. Many banks stay open until 6:00 P.M. on Thursday. Banks close slightly earlier during June, July, and August.

Stores: 8:30 or 9:00 A.M. to 4:00 or 5:00 P.M., Monday through Friday; Saturday from 8:30 or 9:00 A.M. to 1:00 or 2:00 P.M.

Business Practices

♦ Arrange business contacts through the Norwegian Trade Council in New York.

♦ Avoid business trips to Norway in July and August, when many people vacation. In early September, many people take a week off to go hunting. Other vacation times are the two weeks before and the three weeks after Christmas, the week before and after Easter, and the days before and after June 21, the midsummer festival.

♦ You'll need several trips to Norway to conclude a business arrangement.

♦ You don't need to create an "image" by staying at the most expensive hotel. Middle-range hotels are fine.

♦ Business cards or proposals written in English will be fine.

♦ Norwegian businesspeople might come across as abrupt. Often it's because they don't know how to express subtleties in English.

♦ Women won't have trouble doing business in Norway, where they're respected in all areas of business.

♦ You'll find fax machines in post offices, hotels, and businesses.

Meetings and negotiations: Before you arrive in Norway, make appointments two or three weeks in advance. Once you're in the country, a week should be enough.

♦ Schedule appointments between either 10:00 A.M. and noon or 2:00 and 4:00 P.M.

Norway

Although the normal working day is either 8:00 A.M. to 4:00 P.M. or 9:00 A.M. to 5:00 P.M., people work later in the winter. In summer, people rarely stay later than 2:00 or 3:00 P.M. on Friday.

◆ Be punctual. If you're going to be even a little late, telephone to explain.

◆ Bone up on Norwegian culture and accomplishments to prepare for the initial conversation. Norwegians take pride in their history, and you'll be a step ahead if you know the king's name and something about such cultural figures as playwright Henrik Ibsen.

◆ When you meet with Norwegian businesspeople, don't bring up personal matters or try to be familiar. You might, however, find Norwegian businesspeople more relaxed than their Swedish counterparts. Casual conversation—even jokes—are more common at business meetings in Norway than in Sweden.

◆ Distribute copies of your materials only to those who make decisions. Note, however, that decisions in Norway are made at a much lower level than they are in the U.S.

◆ Use visuals in your presentation, if possible. Norwegians are impressed by them. In fact, Scandinavians in general like gadgets of all sorts.

◆ Once written agreements have been made, people tend to stick to them.

Entertainment: Norwegian businesspeople don't usually go to lunch; instead, they eat sandwiches at their desks. If you invite people to lunch, however, they'll usually accept the offer.

◆ A Norwegian businessperson might invite you home to a meal.

◆ Spouses aren't included at business meals in restaurants.

Gifts: Good business gifts are scotch, cigarettes (if you know someone smokes), or picture books from your area.

Holidays & Celebrations

Holidays: New Year's Day (January 1); Maundy Thursday (the Thursday before Easter); Good Friday;  Easter Monday; Labor Day (May 1); Constitution Day (May 17); Ascension Day (five weeks after Easter); Whit Monday (eight weeks after Easter); Christmas (December 25); and December 26.

◆ On Constitution Day, all the schoolchildren in the country parade in their home towns or city, waving Norwegian flags, while everyone else watches. The day is also a celebration of spring and the biggest celebration of the year.

Transportation

Public Transport

Mass transit: Within city limits, you pay one flat rate on  buses, trolleys, and subways. You might pay an extra charge if you go to a suburb.

◆ Discounted fares are available. In Oslo you can buy a card—valid for one, two, or three days—that allows unlimited travel on all public transportation within Oslo; gives half price on commuter trains, both to and from Oslo; and covers admission to museums.

♦ Another bargain is a 24-hour Tourist Ticket, which allows unlimited travel on local buses, subways, trolleys, suburban railways, and local ferries. It's sold at Narvesen kiosks (marked with a blue and white *N*), the Oslo Tourist Board, main subway stations, post offices, and ticket offices. When you first use the card, it's stamped with the date and time.

♦ When you get on a bus, pay the driver or conductor. You don't need exact change.

♦ Enter a trolley from the rear and then pay the driver or conductor.

♦ When you take the subway, put exact change in the machine at the station entrance. A stamped ticket will come out.

♦ Keep your bus and trolley tickets if you plan to transfer. Tickets are stamped with the time and are good for an hour.

♦ In Oslo, public transportation operates on the honor system. If you're checked and don't have a ticket, you'll pay an on-the-spot fine of about $13.00 U.S. If you're using a discount card, be sure to get it validated in the special machines on platforms and in trolleys.

♦ All trains traveling on main routes have both first and second classes with buffet or dining cars. Overnight trains have sleeping cars but not couchettes.

Taxis: Either reserve a taxi in advance or look for a taxi stand, indicated by a green box with a telephone in it.

♦ Taxis are in short supply during rush hours (around 8:30 A.M. and 4:00 P.M.)

Driving
♦ You do not need an International Driver's License to drive in Norway.

♦ Seat belts are compulsory for the driver and front-seat passengers.

♦ If the back seat has seat belts, passengers must wear them.

♦ The speed limit in built-up areas is 50 kph, outside built-up areas is 80 kph, and on motorways is 90 kph.

♦ If you're planning to drive outside Oslo, allow extra time; the roads are narrow and bumpy. (Also allow time for crossing the many fjords by ferry.)

♦ Low-beam headlights are required at all times from September 1 through April 30.

♦ If you're driving in the north or on mountain roads, stock up on gas whenever you can, because gas stations are scarce.

♦ Don't have even one drink if you plan to drive. Police often set up roadblocks to check for drunk drivers, and you can be fined, lose your license for a year, or spend three weeks in jail if you have even a little alcohol in your blood. No exceptions are made for foreigners.

♦ If you go to a party or restaurant where you will be drinking even a little, take a taxi home. Norwegians regard the taxi fare as part of the expense of an evening out.

♦ Speeding carries the same penalties as drunk driving.

♦ In cities, park at meters, which are free after 5:00 P.M.

Legal Matters & Safety

♦ If you plan to stay in Norway longer than three months, be sure to request permission from the passport police.

♦ Liquor is sold by the bottle only in government-owned liquor stores, which are open from 10:00 A.M. to 5:00 P.M., Monday through Friday, and from 10:00 A.M. until noon or 1:00 P.M. on Saturday. Lines are long. Outside Oslo, some towns do not even have liquor stores.

◆ The legal drinking age is 20.

◆ Women are usually safe walking alone at night. As always, however, consider the neighborhood first and be cautious.

Key Phrases

English	Norwegian	Pronunciation
Good morning	God morgen	goo MAW-ern
Good day	God dag	goo dahg
Good evening	God kveld	goo kvehl
Please	Vaer så snill	VAHR so SNIL
Thank you	Takk	tahk
You're welcome	Vaer så god	VAHR so GOO
Yes	Ja	yah
No	Nei	nay
Mr., Sir	Herr	har
Mrs., Madam	Fru	froo
Miss	Frøken	FROO-ken
Excuse me	Om forlatelse	ohm fah-LAHT-el-seh
Good-bye	Adjø	ahd-YER
I don't understand.	Jeg forstår ikke.	yay for-SHTOHR IK-keh
I don't speak Norwegian.	Jeg snakker ikke norsk.	yay SNO-kehr IK-keh norsk
Is there anyone who speaks English?	Finnes der noen somkar engelsk?	Finz dehr NO-en SOHM-kehn EN-gelsk

Poland

If you travel to Poland, you'll probably be surprised by how much the Poles know about the U.S. and how interested they are in American life. Many Poles have relatives in the U.S. who keep in touch through letters and visits.

You'll also be impressed by the post-World War II restoration of such old cities as Warsaw, Gdansk, and Cracow (though the pollution might lessen your enjoyment of their beauties) and by people's warmth and hospitality.

Greetings

◆ Shake hands when you're introduced, when you greet someone you know, and when you leave. A man should wait for a woman to extend her hand first.

◆ A Polish man often kisses a woman's hand when they're introduced, when he greets her at subsequent meetings, and when he leaves. American men should simply shake Polish women's hands.

◆ When close friends or relatives meet, they embrace and kiss on one cheek, then on the other, then again on the first.

◆ At a party, expect your hosts to introduce you, but if there's a large crowd, introduce yourself.

◆ Married couples have slightly different last names. The woman takes her husband's surname but changes the last letter to "a." (For example, Mr. Mayevski's wife would be Mrs. Mayevska).

◆ Don't use first names until the Polish do. Using first names is a sign of true friendship and is considered so important that friends celebrate the occasion by drinking together in a little ritual called (just as it is in Germany) *bruderschaft*. If you are invited to share this ritual drink, intertwine right arms, drinks in hand, and say "BROO-tehr-shahft."

Conversation

◆ Good topics of conversation: American daily life, the state where you live, places you vacation, your family, or Poland and its cultural history.

◆ Poles are curious about life in America. Many have relatives in the U.S. and will want to talk about them.

◆ A topic to avoid: religion.

◆ Poles might ask how much money you make per hour—another example of their curiosity about American life. They don't mean to be offensive. Explain that although Americans make more money than Poles, the cost of living is higher in the U.S.

Money

◆ The unit of currency is the zloty (abbreviated Zl), made up of 100 groszy

◆ Coins come in denominations of 1, 2, 5, 10, and 20 zlotys.

◆ Notes come in denominations of 50, 100, 200, 500, 1,000, 2,000, 5,000, 10,000, 20,000, 30,000, 100,000, 200,000, 500,000 and 1 million zlotys.

Telephones

◆ There are no telephone cards.

◆ Look for public phones in hotels, restaurants, cafes, and phone booths. Some phones accept 20-zloty coins, some phones only accept tokens. The tokens cost 500 zlotys.

◆ Tokens can be purchased at kiosks, hotels, and restaurants.

◆ To make a local call, deposit a 20-zloty coin. Dial *very slowly* to make sure your call gets through. When your money runs out, you'll hear a tone. Deposit more money to continue the call.

◆ Making long-distance calls can be time-consuming; try to call from the post office.

◆ It's much easier to receive calls from the U.S. *to* Poland than to call the U.S. *from* Poland. You might find lines out of the country busy, and you might have to wait for hours for your call to go through. For faster connections to the U.S., call after midnight (in Poland).

◆ Answer the phone by saying "hah-LO."

◆ Emergency numbers in Warsaw are as follows (other areas have different numbers):

Police	997
Fire	998
Ambulance	999

In Public

◆ Talk quietly in public. Poles speak more softly than Americans do.

◆ Never chew gum while you are talking to someone.

◆ Polish men have rather traditional views of female behavior and tend to be most helpful to women who avoid directness or abruptness in social or business encounters.

◆ Never, ever toss any garbage away. Poles don't litter and are shocked by anyone who does.

◆ Don't walk on the grass unless you see others doing so, or you might get a ticket.

◆ If you're lost, look puzzled and invariably someone will offer to help you. People will be willing to find you a map or even take you home for a cup of tea and a rest.

◆ A woman who asks a man for directions might be seen as flirting. It's better to ask a Polish woman or a police officer.

◆ Bargain only in open markets, never in state-run stores. Offer one-half the asking price and negotiate from there.

◆ Be discreet about taking pictures. Never photograph soldiers, military installations, or industrial plants.

◆ When a Polish man flicks his finger against his neck, that means you're invited to join him for a drink of vodka.

◆ You'll find public toilets in hotels and restaurants. A triangle identifies the men's room and an *O* denotes the women's room.

Dress

♦ For casual dress, men and women can wear jeans or other pants. For dressier occasions, jeans with dressy shirts or blouses are fine.

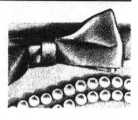

♦ For business, men should wear suits and ties, and women should wear dresses.

♦ When dining in someone's home, men should wear jackets and ties, and women should wear dresses, skirts, or dressy pants (designer jeans are fine) and blouses.

♦ When dining in expensive restaurants, men should wear suits, and women should wear dresses.

♦ Theater events, including openings, don't require formal dress. Men wear dark suits, and women wear dresses.

♦ If an invitation specifies formal wear (such as for a New Year's Eve party), men should wear tuxedos, and women should wear long dresses.

♦ When visiting a church, women may wear pants but should avoid short skirts or low-cut dresses.

Meals

Hours and Foods

Breakfast *(snia-danie):* 7:00 to 8:00 A.M. Usually the meal consists of rolls, butter, jam, and tea.

Lunch *(obiad):* 3:00 to 4:00 P.M. Poles don't take a lunch break at work; instead, they eat this main meal of the day right after they get home. They begin with a beef, tomato, or fruit soup, then have a meat course with vegetables or a salad. Beer or vodka accompanies the meal. Next comes stewed fruit or pastry and, finally, tea with lemon and sugar.

♦ If you're invited to a meal, it will probably be on Sunday at around 1:00 or 2:00 P.M., because most Polish women work Monday through Saturday. The meal will be much like that described above, with the addition of appetizers such as steak tartar (raw hamburger) or smoked eel, served with vodka. The main course might be veal cutlet with seasonal vegetables, or a dish such as stuffed cabbage rolls. Beer, vodka, or wine accompany the meal.

Dinner *(kolacja):* 8:00 to 9:00 P.M. Usually a lighter meal, supper consists of a sandwich, pastry, and tea.

Breaks: At 10:00 A.M., people stop work to eat a sandwich.

Table Manners

♦ Be no more than 15 minutes late if invited to a meal.

♦ Many apartments are small, so meals are served at a table in the living room.

♦ The guest of honor is seated at the head of the table.

♦ Toasting is a major feature of many meals. The host will probably toast you with vodka. Return the toast later in the meal by saying "nah zdrah-vyeh" ("To your health").

♦ Unless you're a prodigious drinker, don't try to match the Poles shot for shot when they drink vodka. The vodka can be very strong, and they're used to drinking it neat and in one gulp. Either ask for only a little in your glass or simply say you've had enough.

♦ Serve yourself from the platters of food passed around the table, unless you receive a plate with food already on it.

♦ If serving yourself, take small helpings because you will be offered second and third helpings, and not accepting them implies you didn't like the food.

♦ Don't start eating until everyone has been served.

♦ If soup is served, you will be given a spoon unless it's a clear soup served in a bowl with two handles. Then drink from the bowl.

♦ When people insist that you take seconds, refuse politely twice and then, if you care to, accept on the third offer. When you're full, leave a little food on your plate, or put your fork and knife horizontally on the plate with the tines facing left, or your hosts will refill it.

♦ Coffee is in extremely short supply, so unless it's served, don't ask for it. It's usually served only after formal dinners.

♦ If you want to smoke between courses, it's polite to ask the hostess.

♦ Don't leave a dinner party early or your hosts will be insulted. Poles love to stay up and talk into the wee hours of the morning, even if they have to get up early the following day. Don't expect your hosts to offer clues such as yawning or telling you they must get up early.

♦ Thank people for their kindness to you by taking them to dinner at a restaurant. Many Poles enjoy eating out but have few opportunities to do so.

Eating Out

♦ Look for the following kinds of eating places:

   • A *mleczny* is a milk bar where you can get a fast meal and eat either standing or seated at a counter. You can choose ice cream, yogurt, drinks made with yogurt, fruit drinks with milk, or *pierogi* (vegetable-filled turnovers). Alcoholic drinks are not available.

   • *Karczma* are old, restored taverns and inns with regional folk decorations. They serve typical Polish specialties and alcoholic beverages.

   • A *kawiarnia* is a cafe that serves wine, soda, coffee, pastries, and cheeses.

   • *Restauracja* are restaurants, which are rated from A (the best) to D. Look for the rating in the restaurant window before you go in. Also check the menu, which you'll see posted in a window.

♦ American-style bars don't exist. The closest approximations are in cafes and hotels.

♦ You'll find the best food in first-class hotels.

♦ Most restaurants close by 10:30 P.M.

♦ Service is slow in most restaurants. If you're in a hurry, go to a *mleczny* (milk bar).

♦ If you speak English in a restaurant, you'll be served more promptly and receive special attention.

♦ Restaurants don't always have everything that's listed on the menu. Before you order, ask the waiter what's available.

♦ Each restaurant in Poland has one meatless day a week because of erratic meat supplies.

♦ Wines are imported and extremely expensive, so don't order until you know the price and the quantity. Prices are usually by the glass. When you order, specify carefully the quantity you want.

♦ If you are a woman traveling alone, choose one of the more expensive restaurants or you might find men joining you uninvited. If that does happen, move to another table or leave.

♦ Pay the waiter at the table.

♦ If the food or service is unsatisfactory, look for the "complaint book," where you can write down what displeased you. Complaining won't ensure immediate action, however.

Specialties

♦ Grains, potatoes, and cabbage are mainstays of the Polish diet. Some specialties are *barszcz* (beet soup with vegetables and sour cream); *golabki* (stuffed cabbage rolls); *karp po zydowsku* (steamed slices of carp on root vegetables, served hot or cold in its own aspic); *bigos* (a hunter's stew of pork, ham, sausages, beef or game, onions, mushrooms, and cabbage or sauerkraut); *kaczka* (wild duck with apples); *zajac* (hare in sour cream); *sarnina* (roast venison); *kielbasa* (sausage); *kolduny* (beef turnovers); *kulebiak* (mushrooms and cabbage in pastry); *zrazy zawijane* (steak rolled up with mushrooms and served with rice); and *bryndza* (sheep's milk cheese with chives).

♦ Depending on your tastes, you might want to try—or avoid—two appetizers: *tartar* (raw hamburger with onions, pickles, and anchovies) and *wegorz* (smoked eel, considered a delicacy).

Hotels

♦ Book your hotel room at least two months in advance, because good hotel space is in short supply. If you arrive without a reservation, your chances of finding an acceptable room are slim.

♦ Even in four-star hotels, don't expect the usual amenities. You might find only one small bar of soap. A few hotels have refrigerators, but they're usually empty.

♦ If you arrive in Poland without a hotel reservation, consider renting a room in a private home. Most cities have bureaus, called *Biuro Kwaterunkowe*, where you can arrange such a rental. People are hospitable and will probably treat you more as a guest than a paying patron. Meals might be included—a real plus, since home cooking is usually much better than restaurant food.

♦ Some hotels keep your passport for a few days, and others don't. If your hotel does, they'll give it to you if you need it to change money. Ask at the desk whether you should return it when you're done.

♦ Whenever you go out, leave your key at the desk. Hotel room keys are enormous and awkward to carry.

♦ If you need extra towels or other supplies for your room, ask the floor attendant at your hotel. If you use this person's services frequently, give a small gift when you leave.

Tipping

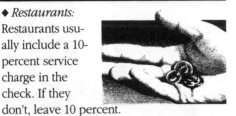

◆ *Restaurants:* Restaurants usually include a 10-percent service charge in the check. If they don't, leave 10 percent.

◆ *Porters:* Tip 200–500 zlotys per bag.

◆ *Hotel maids:* Though 200–500 zlotys per day is an acceptable tip, maids prefer a gift—soap, tea, coffee, lipstick, or pantyhose.

◆ *Taxis:* Give drivers 5–10 percent of the fare.

◆ *Washroom attendants:* Look for signs that tell you how much to pay the attendant, who supplies toilet paper and towels.

Private Homes

◆ Poles are always eager to welcome foreign guests, partly because it lets them travel vicariously.

◆ Plan to visit people on Sunday, the customary day for company.

◆ Before you visit, call or write to find out whether it's convenient. Never drop in unexpectedly; your hosts will want to serve you something to eat and will be embarrassed if they don't have anything.

◆ Eat only lightly before you visit to leave room for the wine, tea, and pastries you'll be offered. People are insistent that guests eat.

◆ If you're visiting relatives during your stay, expect to receive many gifts, such as home-made preserves and hand-knit items.

◆ If you're staying in a private home, register yourself with the local police. Hotels do this for guests.

◆ Don't be surprised if friends or relatives actually move out and stay with friends to give you the entire apartment while you visit.

◆ If you are a guest for several days, offer to help clear the table and do the dishes. Your offer probably won't be accepted. Polish kitchens are tiny, and your hosts will tend to pamper you, but offering to help is a nice gesture.

◆ Don't feel you must include your hosts in every activity. They'll suggest places to see and ways to get there, but feel free to go off by yourself if you wish.

◆ Before you take a bath, always ask whether it's convenient. Unless the apartment is relatively new and has constant hot water, your hosts will need time to heat the water.

Gifts: If you're invited to a meal, bring flowers, candy, liquor, or wine. Flowers are the best choice because they are expensive. Give an odd number of flowers (but not chrysanthemums, which are reserved for funerals).

◆ If you stay with a family, give a gift of food, such as fruit. Poles appreciate receiving food because it's expensive.

◆ Other good gifts are chocolates, canned hams, cognac, coffee, tea, or perfume.

◆ Good presents from the U.S. are coffee, cigarettes, American whiskey, records, pocket calculators (either solar or with batteries included), American canned hams, or ballpoint pens. For close friends, bring blue jeans, pantyhose, tights, and men's or women's corduroy pants. Women enjoy imported soaps and perfume.

◆ Paper has become expensive in Poland, so stationery or typing paper can also make a welcome gift for someone who uses it. For good measure, add some correction fluid.

Business

Hours

Businesses and government offices: 8:00 A.M. to 3:00 P.M., or 9:00 A.M. to 2:00 P.M., Monday through Friday; 8:00 A.M. to 1:30 P.M. on Saturday.

Banks: 8:00 or 9:00 A.M. until noon or 2:00 P.M., Monday through Saturday.

Stores: 9:00 or 11:00 A.M. to 7:00 P.M., Monday through Saturday.

Business Practices

◆ To find the name of the right person to contact at a Polish firm, write the Commercial Section of the American Embassy in Warsaw, the trade association for your product or service, or the Eastern Europe Business Information Center, Room 7412, U.S. Department of Commerce, Washington, DC 20230. Phone: (202) 377-2645.

◆ English is the second language for business; French and German are next.

◆ To make the best impression, have your correspondence translated into Polish. It's acceptable, however, to write business letters in English; most Polish businesspeople either understand English or can have the letters translated.

◆ Be sure to bring business cards. Although translation isn't essential, you'll make a bet-

ter impression if they're in English on one side and Polish on the other.

◆ Staying in the best hotel won't particularly impress people.

◆ Top hotels have fax machines and copying machines, but you might want to bring copies with you, since the copiers are slow and of poor quality.

◆ Your host organization will provide an interpreter. If you wish to bring your own, ask your hotel or the U.S. Embassy for a recommendation.

◆ Feel free to bring written materials in English.

◆ Businesswomen should take care not to appear brash or pushy. Polish men, who regard them first as women and second as businesswomen, will probably be flirtatious—and perhaps cautious. But although they might treat women condescendingly, they might also be more accommodating than they would be with men.

◆ In Warsaw, look for an English-language newspaper called *Warsaw Voice,* which is written for a business audience.

Meetings and negotiations: From abroad, make appointments at least one month in advance. Follow up with reminders, even after the appointment has been confirmed.

◆ Try to arrange appointments between 10:00 A.M. and 2:00 P.M. Remember that people usually work from 8:00 A.M. to 3:00 P.M. without a lunch break. Then they go home and have a big meal about 3:30 P.M. People often take a "second breakfast" break around 10:00 A.M., when they might go out or eat at their desks.

◆ Be punctual. Poles will be as well.

◆ Keep your presentation simple. Don't worry about elaborate graphics. Most people still work with manual typewriters, so they're not used to elaborate displays.

◆ Polish businesspeople aren't clannish or closed to outsiders. They're eager to attract Western business. In fact, they're so anxious to bring negotiations to a positive outcome that they might promise to do something much more quickly than they actually can. Allow for that factor in estimating times. The sheer volume of requests since the Revolution has swamped offices and made it impossible to meet deadlines.

◆ If you're doing business with any state-run organization, be patient and don't expect quick decisions. Negotiations might take weeks or months (and several trips to Poland). To some extent, the speed with which business will be conducted will depend on how much the Poles want what you are offering.

◆ It is important to have a written contract. To obtain a lawyer, consult an English-language newspaper that lists lawyers, fax services, and other business services. These newspapers are available in every major city. Or consult the Commercial Section of the Polish Embassy in the U.S.

◆ Decisions are made by a few top people, but you might meet with people at various levels before you reach the director.

Entertainment: A Polish businessperson might suggest a lunch date for 4:00 or 5:00 P.M.

◆ If you entertain Polish businesspeople, take them to the restaurant of an international hotel. Invite only department heads or those whose status is equal to your own.

◆ Don't include spouses in a business invitation unless you've been a guest in the family home. If the dinner is simply a social occasion, you can include spouses—people

do enjoy getting dressed up and going out.

◆ If you're a businesswoman and want to entertain Polish businessmen, use your hotel restaurant. If the headwaiter speaks English, tell him you want the meal charged to your room. An alternative is to excuse yourself during the meal and speak to the headwaiter about payment then.

◆ If you don't want to drink a lot at a business meal, leave some in your glass. A glass is refilled as soon as it's empty.

Gifts: See the Gifts section on page 182.

Holidays & Celebrations

Holidays:
New Year's
Day (January 1);
Easter and Easter
Monday; National Day (May 3);
Assumption of the
Virgin (August 15); All Saints' Day (November 1); National Day of Independence (November 11); and Christmas (December 25 and 26).

◆ If you're invited to a party on New Year's Eve, bring flowers, candy, or wine, and especially gifts for children. This is Poland's most important holiday.

Transportation

**Public
Transport**
Mass transit:
Buy bus and
streetcar tickets
at kiosks. Stamp
your ticket in the machine as you board. If you plan to travel frequently by bus and streetcar, buy extra tickets, since the kiosks

are sometimes closed. In an emergency, you can ask someone boarding a bus to sell you a ticket. Keep the ticket handy in case an inspector asks for it, or you'll have to pay a fine.

◆ Train fares, even for first class, are very reasonable, but trains tend to be late, and many don't have dining cars or smoking sections. Some train stations attract groups of pickpockets. The Warsaw Central Station is very dangerous.

◆ First class on trains is cleaner and has more comfortable seats and fewer people per compartment. There is usually one attendant per car.

Taxis: To get a taxi, line up at a taxi stand, where you might have a long wait. Let the elderly or sick go immediately to the head of the line.

◆ Taxis are inexpensive, but the price doubles after 11:00 P.M.

◆ Prices on taxi meters are out of date. Ask at your hotel what the fare should be.

Driving

◆ You'll need an International Driver's License to drive in Poland. Carry it and your passport whenever you're driving.

◆ Seat belts are mandatory for all occupants of a car.

◆ The speed limit on open roads is 90 kph and in built-up areas is 50 kph.

◆ Horn blowing is prohibited in built-up areas.

◆ Although many cities have recently paved roads, they're poorly lit, making night driving difficult.

◆ Be careful driving in rural areas at night. There are many drunk drivers (despite strict drunk-driving laws) and unlit carts.

◆ Speeding and most other traffic violations result in a fine of 50,000 zlotys or more, payable on the spot. If the police believe you didn't understand the traffic signs, you might just receive a warning.

◆ Don't have even one drink if you plan to drive. When Poles go out for an evening, the driver abstains from liquor completely. If you're caught drinking and driving—even if you've only had one beer all evening—your license might be revoked.

Legal Matters & Safety

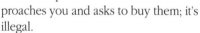

◆ The legal drinking age is 18.

◆ Don't sell your clothes if someone approaches you and asks to buy them; it's illegal.

◆ Crime has increased in recent years. (The police, who once had great power, are now demoralized and universally hated.) Be especially careful in train stations and on trains.

◆ Women traveling alone should take taxis after dark.

Key Phrases

English	Polish	Pronunciation
Good day	Dzień dobry	dzhen DO-bree
Good evening	Dobry wieczór	DO-bree VYEH-choor
Please	Proszę	PRO-sheh
Thank you	Dziękuję	dzhen-KOO-jeh
You're welcome	Proszę bardzo	PRO-sheh BARD-zo
Yes	Tak	tahk
No	Nie	nyeh
Mr., Sir	Pan	pahn
Mrs., Madam	Pani	PAH-nee
Miss	Panna	PAH-nah
Excuse me	Przepraszam	pshe-PRA-sham
Good-bye	Do widzenia	do-vee-DZHEN-ya
I don't understand.	Nie rozumiem.	nyeh ro-ZOO-myehm
I don't speak Polish.	Ja nie mówię po polsku.	ya nyeh MOOV-yeh po POL-skoo
Does anyone here speak English?	Czy ktoś mówi po angielsku?	chih KTOSH MOO-vee po ahn-ghee-EL-skoo

Portugal

Most visitors find Portugal a wonderful surprise, because they have no fixed image of the country beforehand. There's no equivalent of the Arc de Triomphe or the Tower of London planted in our minds before we go, so the beautiful countryside and colorful fishing villages are quite unexpected.

Cultivate patience before you visit Portugal. Things don't get done overnight. It once took one of the authors a week of daily visits to a travel agent just to get a ticket from Oporto to Paris. On the plus side, the agent never billed for the ticket!

Greetings

♦ When you are introduced to someone, shake hands. If you are meeting a group of people, shake hands with each person in the group.

♦ Close friends don't shake hands. Instead, men embrace and slap one another on the back, and women kiss on both cheeks.

♦ Men should rise when being introduced; women need not.

♦ Use first names only with close friends.

Money

♦ The unit of currency is the escudo (abbreviated $), made up of 100 centavos.

♦ Coins come in denominations of 50 centavos and 1, $2\frac{1}{2}$, 5, 10, 20, 25, 50, and 100 escudos. The new 1-, 5-, and 10-escudo coins, which are yellow, can be confused with older coins. Check carefully.

♦ Notes come in denominations of 100, 500, 1,000, and 5,000 escudos.

Conversation

♦ Good topics of conversation: the beauty of Portugal, vacations, wines, hobbies, your and your acquaintance's families, or sports such as soccer.

♦ Topics to avoid: money issues, such as salaries and the cost of living, or personal questions about someone's job.

Telephones

♦ Look for public telephones on main streets, generally close to buildings. Many cafes also have public telephones. You can make both local and long-distance calls from telephone centers, called TLPs. TLPs are usually found at train stations and look like trailers.

♦ Many public phones take $2\frac{1}{2}$-, 5-, and 25-escudo coins. A three-minute local call costs 10 escudos. Put the coins in a slot at the top of the box and, once the connection is made, the coins will drop. You must add more coins when a warning tone sounds and a light over the dial goes on.

◆ If you phone from a cafe, pay the waiter at the end of the call.

◆ A newer *credifone,* which has instructions in English, accepts telephone cards. You can buy the cards, which look like blue credit cards, for various amounts of time at post offices and TLPs.

◆ Make long-distance calls from the post office or TLP.

◆ When you answer the phone, either give your name or say "ish-TAH" in a questioning voice.

◆ The Emergency Number to summon police, the fire department, or an ambulance is **115.**

In Public

◆ The Portuguese are reserved with gestures, so don't be demonstrative.

◆ To wave to someone, extend your arm, palm up, and wave your fingers toward you and away from you. To beckon someone, extend your hand, palm down, and wave your fingers or whole hand.

◆ Feel free to bargain in markets where local crafts are sold, but don't bargain in shops or food markets.

◆ Defer to older people both in public and in private. Always wait until they finish speaking before saying anything.

◆ When with an older person, walk on the curb side of street.

◆ Don't eat anything but ice cream cones in the street.

◆ Going to the cinema is a social occasion in Portugal. People dress up and socialize in the foyer before the film and during the two intermissions. You must buy movie tickets in advance, just as you would theater tickets in the U.S.

◆ Don't photograph military installations. Many places have signs showing a camera with a "**X**" through it, indicating that photography is forbidden. (Often the purpose is to promote slide sales, not to guard national security.)

◆ Look for public toilets in cafes, restaurants, train stations, and public gardens and at historical sites and some highway rest stops. You won't find any in gas stations.

◆ Most public toilets are marked *WC,* with *S* on the door for women and *H* on the door for men.

Dress

◆ The Portuguese tend to dress quite elegantly at all times, so dress more formally than you would in America, even for casual occasions.

◆ For business, men should wear suits and ties, even when it's very hot. (If Portuguese businessmen remove their jackets, however, you may do the same.) Women should wear dresses and heels.

◆ If you're invited to dinner, in a home or restaurant, men should wear suits and ties, and women should wear dresses.

◆ For the theater or cinema, men should

wear jackets and ties, and women should wear dresses or skirts and blouses.

◆ A theater opening calls for formal wear: tuxedos for men, and dark, short dresses for women.

Meals

Hours and Foods

Breakfast (o pequeno almoço): 7:30 to 8:00 A.M. A typical breakfast features bread, butter and jam, and coffee mixed with hot milk.

Lunch (o almoço): Noon to 2:00 P.M. Lunch usually begins with soup, followed by fish or meat with rice or potatoes and a vegetable. Salad accompanies the main course and is often served on the same plate. Wine and bread are served with the meal (cornbread in the north and wheat bread in the south). The meal ends with fruit, dessert (something sweet or cheese and crackers), and coffee.

Dinner (o jantar): 7:30 to 8:00 P.M. This is a large meal with the same courses as lunch. At a dinner party, a fish course might be added before the main course. The most common before-dinner drinks are dry white port or scotch for men and Cinzano for women. Wine is served with the meal, but in summer people sometimes drink beer. After dinner, *aguardente,* a strong local brandy, might be served with the coffee.

Breaks: If you're invited to someone's home at 4:00 P.M., you'll be served a variety of appetizers, such as codfish cakes and Portuguese sausages baked in bread. Otherwise, people commonly have pastry and tea or espresso at 5:00 P.M.

Table Manners

◆ Try to be on time when invited to a meal, but the Portugese may be late.

◆ If dishes are passed around the table family-style, help yourself first, because you're the guest, and then pass them to older people at the table.

◆ Take very small first portions, because you'll be pressed to take seconds and you're expected to eat everything on your plate.

◆ Don't start eating any course until everyone has been served.

◆ At a formal dinner, the host will say a few words to the guests before the meat course begins.

◆ Never eat with your hands. Use a knife and fork even for fruit.

◆ Never put your elbows on the table.

◆ Don't use bread to soak up gravy.

◆ Leave your napkin on the table; don't put it in your lap. (If you do, people will keep asking whether you need a napkin.)

◆ To show you've finished, place the knife and fork on your plate pointing away from you, with the fork tines up.

◆ Before you leave the table, be sure to fold your napkin.

◆ Smoking is customary after a meal but not between courses. Ask permission from your hosts.

◆ If you're invited to dinner, feel free to stay until 11:00 or even 11:30 P.M. Most people don't go to bed before 11:30 P.M. or midnight.

Eating Out

◆ Look for the following types of eating places:

• A *cafe* offers coffee, drinks, small

snacks, sandwiches, and croissants with ham.

● A *cervejaria* has a pub-like atmosphere and features beer, snacks (usually seafood such as clams and shrimps), and small steaks cooked in heavy olive oil.

● A *pastelaria* serves pastries, small snacks, coffee, tea, wine, and local brandy.

● A *restaurante* serves full meals. At the entrance, look for a sign indicating whether a restaurant is first, second, or third class. Few first-class restaurants have a menu posted in the window.

◆ Portuguese restaurants don't have set, fixed-price menus; you order a la carte.

◆ When you enter a first-class restaurant, wait for a maitre d' to seat you. In other restaurants, seat yourself.

◆ In an inexpensive restaurant, it's acceptable for two people to share one dish. Portions are huge.

◆ Children of any age are welcome in restaurants. Those up to eight years old are charged half price, and very young children can share your food.

◆ To signal the waiter that you want to place your order or receive your check, raise your hand.

Specialties

◆ A popular food in Portugal is *bacalhau* (salt-dried codfish). The Portuguese call it *"o fiel amigo"* ("the faithful friend") because they have over 300 ways to cook it. It is frequently baked with tomatoes, olives, garlic, and potatoes.

◆ Other Portuguese specialties are *bolinhos de bacalhau* (codfish cakes with parsley,

coriander, and mint); *caldo verde* (a popular soup made with mashed potatoes, kale, and slices of sausage); *presunto* (air-cured mountain ham); *porco com amêijoas à alentejana* (pork marinated with clams, onions, pimentos, tomatoes, coriander, and lemon juice); *lombo de porco com pimentos vermelhas doces* (marinated pork loin with sweet red peppers); *amêijoas na cataplana* (clams cooked in a special metal container and prepared with onions, hot pepper, garlic, paprika, sausage, tomatoes, parsley, and ham); and *escabeche* (fish pickled with carrots, onions, and bay leaves).

◆ For dessert, try *flan* (caramel custard) and *figos recheados* (dried figs stuffed with chocolate and almonds, served with port).

Hotels

◆ In larger towns, top-rated hotels (Portugal's hotels are rated from one to five stars) will be up to international stan-

dards, but in small towns and rural areas even the better hotels may not be.

◆ Ask to see your room before you register, especially in a very new hotel. Some travelers have registered in a modern lobby only to find that important features of their room (e.g., the plumbing) were not functioning.

◆ You must leave your passport at the desk when you register.

◆ Your hot-water faucet will have a red dot and the cold-water faucet a blue one.

Tipping

◆ *Restaurants:* A service charge is included, but leave an additional 5 percent in a moderately priced restaurant and 10 percent in a deluxe restaurant.

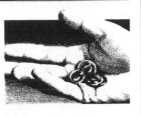

◆ *Porters:* Give 100 escudos for each bag.

◆ *Hotel maids:* Leave 300 escudos for a stay of less than a week. For longer stays, leave 500 escudos.

◆ *Taxis:* Tip 20 percent for short trips, 15 percent for longer trips.

◆ *Ushers:* Give 25 or, if they give you a program, 100 escudos.

◆ *Cloakroom attendants:* Tip 25 escudos; 50 escudos at a deluxe restaurant.

◆ *Washroom attendants:* Tip 25 escudos.

◆ *Gas station attendants:* Give 25 escudos.

Private Homes

◆ Don't give yourself a house tour by wandering through rooms and don't follow your hosts into the kitchen unless they specifically invite you there.

◆ If you must make a phone call from a private home, ask permission first and be sure to pay for it. For a local call, you can look up the price in the telephone directory; for a long-distance call, ask the operator in advance how much the call will cost.

◆ If you stay with a family for a few days, offer to help in the kitchen. Usually your hosts will refuse. To the Portuguese, hospitality means that they entertain while guests enjoy themselves.

◆ People who have entertained other American houseguests will understand if you want a daily bath, but others might not. Always ask your hosts whether a bath is convenient, because they might have to heat the water in advance.

Gifts: If you're invited to dinner, don't feel obligated to bring a gift. Instead, reciprocate by taking your hosts to a restaurant.

◆ If you feel more comfortable bringing a gift, expensive chocolates are the best choice. Flowers are the next-best choice; just don't bring inexpensive flowers or chrysanthemums, which are reserved for funerals. Never bring wine—it's relatively inexpensive, and most people have good wine cellars.

◆ If you stay with a family, consider bringing a gift from the U.S., such as American handicrafts, Native American jewelry, or books about the U.S.

Business

Hours

Businesses: Usually 9:00 A.M. to noon and 2:00 to 6:00 P.M., Monday through Friday.

Some, however, do business from 8:30 A.M. to noon and 1:30 to 6:00 P.M., Monday through Friday.

Government offices: 9:00 A.M. to noon and 2:00 to 5:00 P.M., Monday through Friday.

Banks: 8:30 A.M. to 2:45 P.M., Monday through Friday.

Stores: 9:00 A.M. to 1:00 P.M. and 3:00 to 7:00

P.M., Monday through Friday; 9:00 A.M. to 1:00 P.M. on Saturday. In Lisbon, many shopping centers are open until midnight.

Business Practices

◆ Make business contacts before you go to Portugal. Good sources of contacts are the Commercial Section of the Portuguese Embassy in your country or the Portuguese Consulate in your area. Other sources are the Chamber of Commerce and the Industrial Association in Portugal.

◆ You'll need to make several trips to accomplish your goal. Negotiations might proceed slowly, but once they are completed, the job will be well done.

◆ Before you go to Portugal, study your competition. You'll be quizzed about competitors and what they offer.

◆ Don't plan a business trip between mid-July and mid-September, when many Portuguese vacation.

◆ Before you go, check your tentative itinerary with the Portuguese Tourist Office to be sure you aren't planning your visit during a community's holiday, when businesses close.

◆ Women trying to set up their own businesses in Portugal will face many obstacles, but women coming from abroad to do business won't encounter discrimination. Portuguese respect professional women such as doctors, lawyers, and engineers.

◆ Bring business cards. Don't worry about having them translated.

◆ Staying at a luxury hotel won't impress the Portuguese; they're more interested in your competence and knowledge.

◆ If you're doing business with a small company, hire an interpreter, because the company might not have any English speakers.

Find an interpreter through the American Language Institute in Lisbon, the Yellow Pages, or the company with which you'll be doing business.

◆ Quick photocopying services are hard to find. Allow at least half a day to have copies made. (Portuguese businesspeople are cost-conscious, however, and don't expect reams of paper and copies.)

◆ Most businesspeople have an office fax number and will let you use it to send and receive overseas messages.

◆ Government agencies have tighter budgets than privately owned businesses do. Their expense accounts for entertainment will be less.

Meetings and negotiations: If you're using a fax or telex, make appointments one week in advance. If you're sending a letter, write three to four weeks ahead and have the letter translated into Portuguese.

◆ If you're meeting with the managing director of a company, don't suggest an appointment before 10:00 A.M.

◆ Portuguese businesspeople keep their business and private lives completely separate. Saturday and Sunday are reserved for family, not business.

◆ Keep a relaxed attitude about time. Try to be punctual, but people will be tolerant if you're late. Expect the Portuguese to be 15 to 30 minutes late.

◆ Exchange business cards at the beginning of the meeting, when introductions take place.

◆ When you are offered a drink (usually coffee, a soft drink, or an alcoholic drink), be sure to accept something.

◆ Use visuals and charts only if they are very important to your proposal. Many offices lack adequate facilities to display them—few offices have overhead or slide projectors, and Portuguese VCRs are incompatible with those in the U.S.

♦ Decisions are made by a few individuals at the top of the company or agency.

♦ Contracts are more difficult to secure than they are in the U.S., but participation in the European Community (EC) is making them more prevalent. Contracts in English are fine, since most Portuguese businesspeople read English.

♦ Portuguese businesspeople are extremely helpful, but they're also unreliable in meeting deadlines. Doing business in the EC is beginning to remedy that situation.

Entertainment: Plan to do business at lunch rather than dinner. Dinner with business colleagues is a social occasion. Spouses, both foreign and Portuguese, are included only at dinners.

♦ If you entertain, invite superiors in the company or agency if they are involved in making decisions.

♦ Ask people you invite to a meal which restaurant they would prefer. The Portuguese are more impressed by the quality of the food than by the restaurant's expense.

Gifts: Once you have established contact with Portuguese businesspeople, ask them what gift they would like from the U.S. Many people like to receive technical books, which are difficult to obtain, or computer programs.

Holidays & Celebrations

Holidays:
New Year's
Day (January 1);
Shrove Tuesday
(the day before
Ash Wednesday);
Good Friday; Liberty Day (April 25); Labor Day (May 1); National Day (June 10); Feast of St. Anthony (June 13; Lisbon only); Feast of St. John (June 24; Oporto only); Assumption Day (August 15); Proclamation of the Republic (October 5); All Saints' Day (November 1); Independence Day (December 1); Feast of the Immaculate Conception (December 8); Christmas Eve (December 24); and Christmas (December 25).

♦ In Lisbon, join in the celebrations on the Feast of St. Anthony, the city's patron saint. Parades take place on the evening of June 12, and businesses and stores close on June 13. There are folk dance competitions, and some areas of the city are closed off for dancing in the streets. If you are invited to someone's home, bring flowers.

Transportation

Public Transport
Mass transit:
In Lisbon, the
Metro (subway)
is identified by
a large sign with an *M* on it. The fare is 35 escudos, however far you travel. There are pickpockets, so watch your purse or wallet.

♦ Lisbon bus and streetcar fares are determined by zone. You must have a ticket when you get on; cash is not accepted. Validate the ticket in the machine as you board.

♦ In Lisbon, you can buy passes for seven days of unlimited travel on buses, streetcars subways, and ferries. They're sold at orange-and-white kiosks throughout the city.

♦ Buy train tickets before you board, or you'll have to pay extra.

♦ Trains between Lisbon, Oporto, and Faro offer both first and second class, and have air-conditioned cars with bar and restaurant service.

Taxis: Either hail a taxi on the street or go to one of the taxi stands you'll find scattered throughout cities.

♦ Taxis have meters, but ask at your hotel what the fare to your destination should be. Beyond city limits, drivers can turn off the meter and calculate the fare by mileage.

♦ Large bags might cost you a 50-percent surcharge.

♦ By law, passengers must enter and exit a taxi on the sidewalk side, not the street side.

Driving

♦ You must have an International Driver's License to drive in Portugal.

♦ All occupants of a car are required to wear seat belts.

♦ Don't drive in Lisbon. The Portuguese, who are usually kindness personified, become maniacs behind the wheel.

♦ If you want to drive in the countryside, do it on weekdays, when there are fewer Portuguese on the road. Be cautious, because roads are poor, and the Portuguese tend to tailgate at high speeds.

♦ Avoid driving in mountainous regions, because people don't use their horns or stay in their lanes when going around sharp curves.

♦ The speed limit on highways is 120 kph; on other open roads, 90 kph; and in built-up areas, 50–60 kph, depending on traffic density.

♦ If a police officer stops you for a traffic violation, pay the ticket later. If you believe you did nothing wrong, explain your actions to the officer and you might avoid the citation.

♦ Laws against drinking and driving exist.

♦ Parking is a chaotic free-for-all. Cars park almost anywhere, often on sidewalks. In downtown city areas, however, parking regulations are more strictly enforced. If your car is towed, go to the police station.

Legal Matters & Safety

♦ Drinking hours are unrestricted, and there is no legal drinking age. Liquor and wine are sold in supermarkets and pastry shops.

♦ As a pedestrian, be aware that drivers pay no attention to crosswalks. *Always* watch for traffic when crossing streets.

♦ Women can go safely to a cafe alone, but not to a bar or nightclub, or they might receive unwelcome attention.

♦ To be safe, women should take taxis after 8:00 or 9:00 P.M., when there are few people on the streets.

Key Phrases

English	Portuguese	Pronunciation
Good day	Bom dia	bawng DEE-a
Good afternoon	Boa tarde	BO-a TAR-deh
Good evening	Boa noite	BO-a NOY-tuh
Please	Por favor	por fa-VOR
Thank you (said by man)	Obrigado	o-bree-GAH-doo
Thank you (said by woman)	Obrigada	o-bree-GAH-dah
You're welcome	De nada	day NAH-dah
Yes	Sim	seeng
No	Não	NAH-oo
Mr., Sir	Senhor	sayn-YOR
Mrs., Madame	Senhora	sayn-YOR-a
Miss	Menina	ma-NEE-nah
Excuse me	Con licença	con lee-SEN-sa
Good-bye	Adeus	a-DAY-oosh
I don't understand.	Eu não compreendo.	ay-oo NAH-oo com-pree-ENG-du
I don't speak Portuguese.	Eu não falo português.	ay-oo NAH-oo FAH-loo por-too-GAYSH
Does anyone here speak English?	Há alguén aqui que fale inglês?	ah AHL-goyng a-KEE kay FAHL een-GLAYSH

Romania

If you were to fly from Paris directly to Bucharest, you might suffer a brief attack of déjà vu. With its wide boulevards and parks, Bucharest has often been called the Paris of Eastern Europe.

As a Western visitor to Romania, you'll be the object of great curiosity. Travel abroad by Romanians has been extremely restricted, and people are eager to know what American life is like. They might be familiar with the United States' less attractive aspects, which have been stressed in the local press. But they'll also be eager to know how you live: Do you have a car? What kind? How much do you earn? As a guest in the country, you must walk a fine line between boasting about the United States' luxuries and defending its record on unemployment and rights for minorities and women.

Greetings

♦ Shake hands when you're introduced and each time you meet or leave someone, no matter how often you may meet that person in a day.

♦ Men should rise when they're introduced to someone. Women need not.

♦ Romanian men often kiss women's hands lightly when they're introduced. American men should simply shake Romanian women's hands.

♦ Good friends are openly affectionate. Women greet each other by kissing on both cheeks, and male friends may kiss on the cheek if they haven't seen each other for a long time.

♦ At a party, wait for your hosts to introduce you to each person there.

♦ Because you're a foreigner, Romanians will probably treat you formally. Don't use first names unless they do.

Conversation

♦ In Bucharest, French is more widely spoken than English among people over 55. Younger people speak English and Russian. In Transylvania, many people speak Hungarian and German.

♦ Good topics of conversation: sports, travel, politics, or international subjects such as films, music, fashion, and books.

♦ Topics to avoid: controversial subjects or any negative aspects of Romania, such as waiting lines for food and the AIDS babies.

♦ When you first meet people, you can ask questions about their families, jobs, or money.

Money

♦ The unit of currency is the leu (plural lei, abbreviated L), made up of 100 bani.

◆ Coins come in denominations of 25 bani and 1, 3, 5, 10, and 50 lei.

◆ Notes come in denominations of 10, 25, 50, 100, 500, and 1,000 lei.

◆ If someone offers to exchange money at a favorable rate, don't do it. The practice is illegal, and the person might be an undercover police officer.

Telephones

◆ Look for public phones on streets and in hotels, candy stores, cafes, and restaurants.

◆ To make a local call, deposit 1 leu. You'll hear a signal when your three minutes are up. Insert more money to continue your call.

◆ To make long-distance calls within Romania, start by depositing 3 lei. A light comes on when you need to deposit more money. Long-distance calls can be placed from any public phone.

◆ To make a long-distance call outside Romania from a public phone, go to the post office, where you pay when the call is finished. Calls to North America take a long time because there are few lines.

◆ Romania has no telephone cards.

◆ Answer the phone by saying "ah-LOH."

◆ Emergency Numbers are as follows:

Police	051
Fire	081
Ambulance	061

In Public

◆ Shops sometime charge Westerners higher prices than Romanians.

◆ Most stores have long lines and short-tempered salesclerks. Be patient.

◆ Don't photograph industrial plants or military installations. In fact, before taking any picture, check carefully for a sign showing a camera with an "X" through it (the international symbol for "No Photography Permitted"). In Romania, violating this ban is a serious offense.

◆ If someone approaches you on the street and asks to buy your clothes, don't do it! It might be an undercover agent.

◆ Look for public toilets in cafes, restaurants, and hotels. The men's room is labeled *Bărbaţi;* the women's room, *Femei.*

◆ In public toilets, you must pay for toilet paper and tip the attendant. Carry tissues and small bars of soap with you, because many toilets have no soap, towels, or toilet paper.

Dress

◆ Romanian men and women wear jeans everywhere.

◆ For business, men should wear dark suits, white shirts, ties, and well-polished shoes. Younger men can wear lighter-colored suits and striped or colored shirts. In hot weather, short-sleeved shirts without jackets are acceptable. Women should wear suits and heels.

♦ For dinner in a restaurant or in someone's home, dress up: suits for men and dresses for women. In better restaurants, men must wear ties.

♦ Formal wear (tuxedos for men, long skirts for women) is never worn.

♦ To the theater, older men should wear jackets and ties, and older women should wear dresses or skirts. Younger men need not wear jackets and ties, and younger women may wear pants, a dress, or a skirt.

♦ To theater openings, men should wear dark suits, and women should wear a dress or a skirt.

♦ Shorts are fine at the beach, but don't wear them in cities.

♦ When visiting a Greek Orthodox church, women should wear skirts and have their shoulders covered, though they need not cover their heads.

Meals

Hours and Foods

Breakfast (micul dejun): 6:00 A.M. for factory workers; about 7:00 A.M. for others. Most Romanians eat bread, butter, marmalade, and tea or milk.

Lunch (dejun): Noon. A family meal begins with soup, often vegetable or vegetable beef, or an appetizer such as eggplant salad. The main course might be fish, stew, or stuffed cabbage. Bread, wine, and water usually accompany the meal. Dessert consists of fruit or preserves.

♦ A more formal meal begins with plum or pear brandy and appetizers such as feta cheese cubes, olives, and small meatballs.

The main course is often grilled pork or beef served with salad. Dessert might be fruit, coffee cake, strudel, or chocolate cake. Turkish coffee and cognac are served after dessert.

Dinner (masa de seara): 7:00 to 7:30 P.M. This is usually a fairly light meal consisting of leftovers, noodle or dumpling dishes, or cheese and rolls. Yogurt and tea follow. A dinner party is similar to a formal noon meal.

Breaks: A morning coffee break is common.

Table Manners

♦ Be punctual when invited to a meal.

♦ If you're a dinner guest, you'll sit at the end of the table opposite your host, so everyone can hear the conversation.

♦ Toasts are common at both formal and informal meals. Touch glasses several times during the meal and say "noh-ROC" ("Good luck") or "sah-LOOT" (To your health").

♦ Keep your napkin on the table, not in your lap.

♦ When your plate is brought to you, sample everything on it. Don't distress your hosts by implying that you dislike a particular food.

♦ Salad is served with the meal. Put it on your regular plate.

♦ After dinner in a home, plan to leave about 10:00 P.M. If the host puts the cork back into the wine bottle, that's a signal for guests to go.

Eating Out

♦ Try the following alternatives to regular restaurants:

  • A *bar* sells alcoholic drinks, pastries, tea, coffee, and cigarettes.

  • A *braserie* serves coffee, alcoholic

drinks, pastries, and pretzels. Some also have grills.

• Both standard restaurants and many outdoor restaurants serve complete meals.

◆ Most restaurants are open from 7:00 A.M. to 10:00 P.M. Try to eat dinner early, because by 9:00 P.M. many restaurants run out of food. If you offer $3 to $5 U.S., however, food might magically appear.

◆ Many restaurants—especially those outside Bucharest—serve only one selection per day: meat, potatoes, vegetables or rice, and bread.

◆ Seat yourself in all but the most expensive restaurants (those with menus and napkins). You may join people at a table with an unoccupied seat.

Specialties

◆ Look for these special Romanian foods: *mititei* (grilled, spiced, skinless sausages served as appetizers); *sarmale* (cabbage leaves stuffed with pork balls); *mămăgliă* (corn mush, usually served as a side dish); *ghiveci* (a variety of vegetables, cooked in olive oil and served cold); *pîrjoale* (highly spiced meat patties); *nisetru la gratar* (grilled Black Sea sturgeon); and *scrumbii la gratar* (grilled herring).

◆ For dessert, try *baclava* (layers of thin pastry filled with nuts and cinnamon and drenched in a honey syrup); *cataif cu frisca* (a pastry soaked in syrup and served with whipped cream); and *placinta cu brinza* (sweet cheese pie).

Hotels

◆ You must pay for your hotel room in hard currency.

◆ When you check in, expect the clerk to keep your passport overnight so everything can be copied onto forms for the police.

◆ The hotel staff can give you good advice on restaurants and tourist attractions.

◆ If you break anything in your room, be sure to pay for it. If you don't, the maid must pay.

◆ Don't take any towels or ashtrays as souvenirs. Before you pay your bill, someone will check to see whether anything is missing, and you might be asked to open your suitcase in the lobby.

Tipping

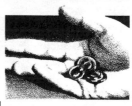

◆ *Restaurants:* A 12-percent service charge is included in the bill. If you want to tip waiters for exceptionally good service, hand it to them directly instead of leaving it on the table.

◆ *Porters:* Give 30–50 lei per bag.

◆ *Hotel maids:* Leave 105 lei per week.

◆ *Taxis:* Tip 10 percent of the fare.

◆ *Washroom attendants:* Tip 5 lei.

◆ Though tipping in foreign currency is illegal, people do appreciate receiving hard currency.

Romania

◆ To improve service, offer American cigarettes. Giving a pack to a hotel clerk, for example, might get you an otherwise unavailable room.

Private Homes

◆ Call before you visit a private home; only close friends drop in— normally around 3:00 P.M. and after 8:00 P.M.

◆ If you call from a phone in a private home, offer to pay. If your hosts won't accept money, buy them a gift before you leave the country.

◆ Your hosts might offer to buy your clothes. You can either sell them or give them as gifts.

◆ If you stay in a private home, offer to help in the kitchen. Your hosts will be pleased by the offer, though they'll probably refuse.

◆ If you really want to help, offer to shop and pay for some of the food. To buy food, Romanians must wait in long lines with lots of pushing and shoving. If both husband and wife work outside the home, they must line up after work and would be very grateful if you undertook this chore.

◆ Check with your hosts about taking baths. In some homes, water can be heated for daily baths, but many apartments have hot water only twice a week.

Gifts: If you are invited to a meal, bring wrapped flowers (make sure it's an odd number; roses or carnations are good choices), chocolates, or wine.

◆ If you stay with a family, give jeans, perfume, cosmetics, or coffee beans, which are in short supply. Good gifts from abroad are watches and calculators for men; perfumes, cosmetics, and pantyhose for women; and toys for children.

Business

Hours

Businesses and government offices: 8:00 A.M. to 4:00 P.M., Monday through Friday, and 8:00 A.M. to 12:30 P.M. on Saturday.

Banks: 9:00 A.M. to noon and 1:00 to 3:00 P.M., Monday through Friday, and 8:00 A.M. to noon on Saturday.

Stores: 8:00 A.M. to noon (or 9:00 A.M. to 1:00 P.M.) and 4:00 to 8:00 P.M., Monday through Saturday. Some are also open from 8:00 A.M. to noon on Sunday.

Business Practices

◆ To find business contacts in Romania, call the Romanian Economic Agency in New York at (212) 682-9120.

◆ Write any letters to Romanian businesses in English, so the recipients will pay special attention to them.

◆ Once you've established a successful relationship with a company, you can expect to do business for a long time.

◆ Romanians treat women respectfully, but for the most part, business is a man's world.

◆ Foreign businesswomen should act in a professional, forthright manner, should not be flirtatious, and should dress conservatively.

◆ Bring a large supply of business cards printed in both English and Romanian, with your title on them.

◆ At a business meeting, you'll usually find at least one person who speaks English.

◆ Find an interpreter through the National Tourist Office. If you're dealing with government officials, they'll have interpreters available.

◆ To make a good impression, stay at one of the country's prestigious hotels.

◆ Some companies have fax machines, but message transmission is very slow because of poor telephone connections.

Meetings and negotiations: From abroad, make appointments several months in advance. Reconfirm your appointment several times, especially when dealing with government officials.

◆ Be punctual, even though the Romanians will keep you waiting.

◆ Business decisions will be made by a group that might include people you've never met.

◆ Cultivate patience. Romanians operated for years with no profit motive—they earned the same no matter whether they made 50 sales or 500—and changing that psychology will take a long time. The country's bureacracy also slows down decision making.

Entertainment: Business lunches and dinners are major events that include five or six courses and last several hours. The most popular restaurants for business entertaining are those in the best hotels (which accept only hard currency) or in former palaces.

◆ Business dinners don't begin until 8:00 or 9:00 P.M., because people work long hours.

Gifts: To celebrate the signing of a contract or the Christmas holiday, give gifts such as

lighters or pens with your company's name on them. Don't give expensive gifts.

Holidays & Special Occasions

Holidays:
New Year's (January 1 and 2); Easter (celebrated according to the Orthodox calendar); Labor

Day (May 1 and 2); Romanian National Day (December 1); and Christmas (December 25 and 26).

◆ As we go to press, Labor Day is still being celebrated. It's not certain whether that two-day celebration will continue. If you need to know, check with the Romanian Embassy.

Transportation

Public Transport
Mass transit:
Bus fares depend on the distance trav-

eled. When you board, tell the conductor where you want to go.

◆ Long-distance buses have reserved seats, but you can buy your ticket no earlier than the day before you travel. For shorter distances, you can buy a ticket for standing room.

◆ Board streetcars at the rear door and pay the conductor on your right. Keep your ticket; inspectors sometimes check them. Exit via the front door.

◆ Trains are of three types: rapid, *accelerat,* and personal. Rapid and *accelerat* trains cost a bit more but are well worth it: a $3\frac{1}{2}$

hour ride on a rapid train might take 12 hours on a personal train.

♦ First-class train compartments have six seats; second-class compartments have eight. The first class seats are larger and more comfortable. Both classes are available on all three types of trains. Sleeping cars *(wagon-lits)* are available for long trips.

♦ Trains making trips of three hours or more have a restaurant car; those making shorter trips have no snacks or food.

♦ Buy train tickets at the station, but no more than ten days in advance. For travel within Romania, foreigners can use hard currency to buy train tickets at the ONT (tourist bureau) or the CFR Agency, which is a ticket agency for planes and trains (every city has one).

Taxis: Look for taxis on the street and at taxi stands, which you'll find near large restaurants, theaters, and train and bus stations. You can also phone for a taxi.

Driving

♦ You won't need an International Driver's License to drive in Romania.

♦ Seat belts are not compulsory.

♦ The speed limit in built-up areas is 60 kph; on all other roads it's between 80 and 90 kph.

♦ You must carry a red-reflector warning triangle to use in case of breakdown.

♦ Keep your passport handy in case you encounter a roadblock, where police stop people for security checks.

♦ If you're stopped for a traffic violation, you'll pay an on-the-spot fine.

♦ Drinking and driving is absolutely prohibited. The police administer on-the-spot fines.

Legal Matters & Safety

♦ Until the leadership stabilizes, be prepared for confusion among officials and frequent changes in regulations.

♦ Customs officials will ask why you're visiting Romania. "Sightseeing" or "business" are the usual answers.

♦ *Never* argue with the police.

♦ The legal drinking age is 18 but is not strictly enforced. Recently the government has been trying to restrict the sale of liquor before noon, but without much success.

♦ Women walking alone after dark are quite safe. Few people have cars, so the streets are crowded with pedestrians. Also, the police patrol constantly.

♦ Minor crimes, however, have been on the rise. Watch your wallet and purse. A small sum of money to a Westerner might be a month's salary to a Romanian.

Key Phrases

English	Romanian	Pronunciation
Good morning	Bună dimineaţa	BOO-na dee-mee-NAH-tsah
Good day	Bună ziua	BOO-na zee-wah
Good evening	Bună seara	BOO-na SEH-rah
Please	Vă rog	vah ROG
Thank you	Mulţumesc	muhl-tzoo-MESC
You're welcome	Cu plăcere	koo plah-CHAY-ray
Yes	Da	dah
No	Nu	noo
Mr., Sir	Domnule	DOM-noo-lay
Mrs., Madam	Doamna	DO-ahm-nah
Miss	Domnisoara	dom-mee-SHWAH-rah
Excuse me	Scuzaţi-mă	scoo-ZA-tsee-mah
Good-bye	La revedere	lah ray-vay-DAY-ray
I don't understand.	Nu înţeleg.	noo int-zeh-LEG
I don't speak Romanian.	Nu vorbesc româneşte.	NOO vor-BESC ro-mahn-ESH-teh
Does anyone here speak English?	Vorbeşte cineva aici engleza?	vor-BESH-teh SHEE-nay-vah AICH en-GLAY-zah

The Russian Republic

To Winston Churchill, the former Soviet Union was "a riddle wrapped in a mystery inside of an enigma." The last several years bear out his observation. Russia has led the world on a roller coaster ride—from dictatorship to glasnost to coup to (perhaps) democracy.

The mystery and romance of Russia, and the amazing strength of the Russian people, have long mesmerized the world. During the siege of Stalingrad in World War II, the Russians provided an almost incredible example of fortitude. Not coincidentally, Russia produced two of the great romances set in the midst of war and revolution: Leo Tolstoy's *War and Peace* and Boris Pasternak's *Doctor Zhivago*.

Whatever the future of Russia, the country's character will probably not change. It's many layers are similar to one of the country's best known symbols, the *matrioshka* doll: open one doll and there's another inside, and inside that another, and so on....

Please note that the advice on the Russian government and bureaucracy—and attempts to deal with either, whether as a traveler or as a businessperson—is accurate as we go to press. As we have all learned since 1989, however, governments, leaders, laws, and regulations can change with breathtaking rapidity.

Greetings

♦ Shake hands—with your gloves off—when you're introduced. When shaking a woman's hand, don't use a firm grip; Russian women shake hands limply. A man should wait for a woman to extend her hand first, and a younger woman should wait for an older woman.

♦ Good friends of either sex kiss when they meet.

♦ Russians commonly use three names: the first name, the patronymic (their father's first name), and their last name. A typical man's name might be Anton Pavlovich ("son of Pavel") Chekov; a woman's might be Anna Pavlovna ("daughter of Pavel") Chekova. To be formal—appropriate when you first meet someone—use the first name and patronymic (Anton Pavlovich). Don't use first names alone until the Russians do.

♦ Russians call foreign men *Gospodin* plus the last name, call foreign women *Gozpozha* plus the last name, and sometimes call one another *Tovarisch* ("comrade"). Foreigners should avoid using *Tovarisch*.

Conversation

♦ Good topics for conversation: politics; mutual interests such as literature, art, concerts, and films, including Western films; or current events in the Russian Republic.

♦ The Russian people, unable to voice political views for decades, are now eager to share theirs and hear yours. New acquaintances might want to tell you all about the difficulties of contemporary Russian life; listen sympathetically, but don't add complaints of your own.

◆ Topics to avoid: personal problems or family difficulties.

◆ St. Petersburg (formerly Leningrad) and Moscow have a long-standing rivalry. Don't effusively praise one city to people from the other.

◆ Russians will ask you what you think of the Russian Republic and, since they generally think of the West as Paradise, they'll be surprised if you say you like their country. Tell them specifically what you like and why; a vague, general compliment sounds patronizing.

◆ You'll be asked countless questions about life in the West—including about your salary. If you answer frankly, be sure to explain the costs of medical insurance, rent, a university education, and other expenses.

Money

◆ The unit of currency is the ruble (abbreviated Rub), made up of 100 kopecks.

◆ Coins come in denominations of 1, 2, 3, 5, 10, 15, 20, and 50 kopecks and 1 ruble.

◆ Notes come in denominations of 1, 3, 5, 10, 25, 50, and 100 rubles.

◆ Avoid 25-, 50-, and 100-ruble notes. People rarely have that much change.

◆ Never change money on the street. It's illegal, and you'd probably be cheated— given worthless Yugoslavian dinars or blank paper hidden in a stack of rubles.

◆ The ruble is almost worthless; however,

you can buy almost anything with either hard currency or luxuries such as coffee, tea, soap, jeans, condoms, watches, batteries, T-shirts, Nikes, Marlboro cigarettes, cosmetics, or cassettes. Carry lots of small bills in hard currency for tipping, buying things on the street, or "bribery."

◆ *Beriozka* stores, which have the widest selection of goods and are open only to foreigners, require hard currency. Even many museums sell books and souvenirs only for hard currency.

Telephones

◆ Look for public telephones on streets and in hotels and restaurants. For a local call, deposit a 2-kopeck coin (or a 10-kopeck coin or two 1-kopeck coins) and talk for as long as you want.

◆ Two types of telephones are available: the *telefon-automat* (marked ТЕЛЕФОН-АВТОМАТ) and the *taksofon* (marked ТАКСОФОН). On a *taksofon,* 2 kopecks gives you a three-minute call, after which you'll be cut off; you must deposit two more kopecks and redial. On a *telefon-automat,* you can talk as long as you want for 2 kopecks.

◆ Post offices in most towns and cities have telephone sections. Large cities have separate telephone offices as well.

◆ To place a call from any telephone office, order and pay for the call a day ahead, specifying how long you want to talk. At the appointed time, someone will summon you in Russian, announcing the city or country and which booth to use. If you get no answer, you'll get a refund.

◆ If you're calling a hotel guest from outside the hotel, you can't leave a message; you must keep calling. You can also phone from room to room in a hotel.

◆ To call abroad from your hotel, book and pay for the call at the Telephone Desk at least three hours—or even a day—ahead. A call booked for 10:00 will come through between 10:00 and 11:00—in your hotel room, if you wish. The minimum call is three minutes. Estimate the time you need carefully; if you run over, you might get cut off, but you won't get a refund for any unused time. If no one answers your call, bring your receipt to the Telephone Desk for a refund.

◆ Although you can't call overseas from your room, you can make local and some long-distance calls. If you want to call long-distance within Russia, ask at the hotel's main desk whether the city has an automatic connection. If it does, ask for the area code, and call from your room; the charge will appear on your hotel bill. If the city doesn't have an automatic connection, the hotel operator must place the call for you.

◆ In some hotels you must pay for long-distance calls in hard currency, and the cost is about $10 U.S. per minute. In others you can pay in rubles and the cost is about $1 U.S. per minute. You can call long-distance from the Telephone Office (which charges the lower ruble rate), but you might have to wait for hours, so you're usually better off calling from your hotel.

◆ Emergency telephone numbers are as follows:

Police	02
Fire	01
Medical Aid	03

In Public

◆ Among all classes of Russians you'll encounter superstitious traditions and gestures, including the following:

• If you whistle indoors, all your money will fly out the window.

• Lighting a cigarette from a candle is very bad luck; you must set things right by spitting three times over your left shoulder. (The devil sits on the left shoulder and an angel on the right.)

• It's bad luck to spill salt on the table. You must throw the salt over your left shoulder.

◆ Physical contact in public is limited, though young girls do walk arm-in-arm. In private, friends embrace warmly.

◆ Close women friends often sit side by side and hug or touch each other on the hand or arm. (Russians feel less need for spatial distance than most Americans do; there's no real Russian word that means "privacy").

◆ Russian people stand very close when conversing—sometimes only a few inches apart. You might feel uncomfortable with this closeness, but don't back away or Russians will think you're rejecting them.

◆ Don't whistle in public. It's rude.

◆ If a woman narrows her eyes, she is showing apprehension or discouraging a flirtation.

◆ Don't put your thumb between your index finger and your middle finger—it's an obscene gesture.

♦ People jostle constantly in streets and shops, regarding it as necessary rather than rude.

♦ When you sit, don't show the soles of your feet or shoes. It's rude.

♦ To protect the beautiful parquet floors in many museums and palaces, visitors must get slippers from a bin at the entrance and wear them over their shoes. Be careful on smooth marble staircases!

♦ Russian churches have no pews; people stand for services. If you visit a church, don't talk or put your hands inside your pockets.

♦ When you buy anything in a local store, choose the item, go to the cashier and pay for it, and then take your receipt back to the counter to pick the item up. If you don't know how much to pay, have the salesperson write down the amount and hand that to the cashier.

♦ At most shops, people wait in long lines and then push and shove to see what's behind the counter. (Many items—records, books, food, bakery goods—are kept behind the counter; clothing is on racks.) The saleswomen aren't obliged to sell anything, so they tend to ignore customers. Say "DYEY-voosh-ka" ("Miss") to attract their attention.

♦ Beriozka shops (which are very expensive and take only hard currency), mark prices in rubles. The ruble was devalued in 1989, so to find the approximate cost in dollars, double the stated price in rubles. To buy souvenirs for a mere fraction of the Beriozka shop price, try local stores, markets, or kiosks.

♦ Try bargaining in open-air markets, but not in stores, where all prices are fixed. In markets, watch for inflated prices; as soon as vendors see that you're foreign, they'll expect more money.

♦ Russia has an important—though illegal—barter economy. Soviets barter constantly with one another. As a foreigner, you'll be approached by waiters in hotel restaurants and young boys and young men on the street eager to barter Russian goods for American dollars or goods. Engaging in such bartering is risky, however—although everyone does it, you could be arrested. Be careful.

♦ Don't photograph harbors, bridges, tunnels, power stations, airports, train stations, or border areas, or take photographs from airplanes or trains.

♦ Before you photograph people, always ask their permission.

♦ Public baths have separate sections for men and women. You pay a small entrance fee, then go to a communal changing room (don't bring valuables with you, because you can't lock them up). Clean yourself either in a shower or at a long bench with hot and cold faucets and buckets. From there you go to the steam room, where you'll sweat profusely. After that, you can jump into a pool of cold water. People go back and forth between the steam room and the pool; they also scrub each other and hit each other with birch branches to stimulate circulation. Massages are also available, but you must make an appointment in advance.

♦ Look for public toilets (marked ТУАЛЕТ, or M for men and Ж for women) in Metro (subway) stations and on some streets. Most have no toilet seats, just a bowl, and some have just a hole in the floor. They have no toilet paper, so bring your own.

♦ In cities, try to use the public toilets in hotels, which have toilet seats and paper.

Dress

◆ During spring and summer, Russian buildings are unheated and can be quite chilly. From October through May, how-

ever, they are kept very warm, and removable layers of clothing are essential.

◆ For sightseeing, men may wear a shirt and pants. Women may wear pants and a shirt, a skirt and blouse, or a dress. Shorts are acceptable only at beach resorts.

◆ For business, men should wear a suit with a white shirt, subdued tie, and black shoes and shouldn't remove the jacket unless the Russians suggest it. Women should wear a suit or a dress.

◆ For dinner in a home, men should wear pants with a shirt and sweater, and women should wear a dress, or a skirt or pants with a blouse or sweater.

◆ For a theater or restaurant meal, men should wear a jacket and tie, and women should wear a dress, skirt, or dressy pants.

◆ For the theater and theater openings, men should wear a suit, and women should wear a dress.

◆ When you enter a theater, museum, or restaurant, leave your coat and any large bags at a *garderobe*. (Wearing or carrying your coat inside is rude.) There's no fee or tip.

◆ To visit a church, women should wear a hat or scarf, a long-sleeved top, and a skirt.

◆ Some resorts near the Black Sea and a few on the Baltic Sea have special beaches for nude sunbathing. Men and women swim and sunbathe separately.

Meals

Hours and Foods

◆ The Russian Republic has serious food shortages, so meals and bever-

ages vary according to what's available.

Breakfast *(zahvtrahk):* 8:00 A.M. Typical foods are bread, butter, cheese, sausage, and eggs (boiled or fried) or *kasha* (hot cereal) with tea or coffee.

Lunch *(ahbyed):* Noon to 1:00 P.M. The meal usually begins with appetizers—perhaps smoked fish, beet salad, sardines, or fish with a carrot-and-onion sauce—followed by a soup such as *borsch* (beet soup), chicken broth, *shchi* (cabbage soup), or *pokhlyobka* (mushroom and barley soup). Next comes beef, fish, or chicken (considered a luxury) with potatoes, rice, or noodles. Dessert might be *kompot* (stewed, dried fruits). Tea or coffee follow the meal.

Dinner *(oozhin):* 6:00 to 8:00 P.M. A light meal, dinner might consist of one of the following: cheese or kielbasa sandwiches, pasta, canned fish with either potato or beet salad, smoked fish, or sausages. Generally, no beverage is served with the meal; tea is served afterward.

◆ All meals include bread; a meal without it is considered incomplete. Wasting bread is considered sinful, so don't take a piece unless you're sure you're going to eat it.

◆ Coffee or tea is served after lunch or dinner with dessert—cake, chocolates, and cookies. Liqueurs might be served with dessert. People often continue drinking vodka and/or wine after dessert; if so, they sometimes keep eating bread or other food, supposedly to prevent intoxication.

◆ Tea is a favorite beverage, often drunk from a glass rather than a cup. Russians seldom put milk in tea, but they sometimes add lemon or a spoonful of jam, or sip the tea through a sugar lump placed in the mouth.

Table Manners

◆ It's polite to arrive on time for a meal.

◆ When you arrive, you'll go straight to the table. Cocktail hours are rare.

◆ Most Soviet apartments have only two rooms: a kitchen and an all-purpose dining-living-bedroom. Dinner guests usually sit close together and spend the whole evening at the table, although a space might be cleared for dancing after the meal.

◆ Each table setting will include a small hors d'oeuvres plate, a large plate for the main course, a shotglass (for vodka), a glass for juice or mineral water, and a glass for wine (usually sweet).

◆ After everyone sits down, hors d'oeuvres (*zakuski*) and bread (rye or—considered more elegant—white) will be served.

◆ The host will begin the meal by proposing a toast, with everyone drinking a shot of vodka in one gulp. Toasts continue throughout and after the meal. (Be sure to eat something after each toast or you'll quickly get intoxicated.) Never drink before the first toast.

◆ You might be asked to propose a toast during the meal. You'll impress people by giving a little speech in Russian; you can write it out phonetically and read it.

◆ If you don't want to drink vodka, say you have to drive or you have a medical problem that prevents you from drinking it.

◆ Before people begin eating, they say "pree-YAHT-nah-vah ah-pay-TEE-tah,"
which means "good appetite."

◆ Serve yourself from platters that are passed around.

◆ Don't start eating until your hostess does.

◆ Both homes and restaurants serve some foods—such as mushrooms, rice, or potatoes in sauce—in small covered pots that keep the foods warm.

◆ Eat slowly, because as soon as you empty your plate, your hosts will refill it. They'll keep urging you to eat unless you state firmly that you are completely full.

◆ Many Russians smoke during the meal as well as between courses.

◆ To show you've finished, set your knife and fork horizontally on your plate.

◆ Russians consider it impolite to eat and run; even informal dinners often last several hours. Stay for about an hour after coffee or tea is served.

Eating Out

◆ The lack of restaurants means you'll eat most meals in hotels, which tend to have few choices and poor-quality food. Other restaurants are scarce, and getting in requires either making reservations several days ahead or bribery.

◆ Consider bringing an assortment of snacks (such as raisins, peanut butter, and crackers) to eat as meals or during long bus or train rides.

◆ You'll see the following types of eating places:

  • Cafeterias, called *stolovaya,* usually have very bad food.

  • Kebab bars or *shashlichnaya* are open-air barbecue stands that sell skewered meat with bread and ketchup.

• *Pelmeni* bars, called *pyelmennaya,* serve meat-filled dumplings, boiled and served in a bouillon sauce.

• Sausage bars or *sostsochnaya,* offer tough-skinned sausages filled with cereal.

• *Bliny* bars, called *blinnaya,* serve heavy pancakes with margarine and plum jam or smoked fish.

• At an ice cream parlor or *cafe morozhenoye* you can sit and eat ice cream; other street-corner stands and kiosks *(morozhenoye)* also sell ice cream.

• A *bulotchnaya* sells bread.

• A *konditerskaya* offers cookies and pastries.

♦ Restaurants require advance reservations (at least 24 hours, even for a hotel restaurant), made through Intourist at your hotel. Only bribery can get you into a restaurant without a reservation—and even then, you might be turned away or have to stand in line for hours.

♦ Russia has no cafes where you can sit and have a snack and drink while sightseeing. You can carry snacks and drinks purchased from the *Beriozka* shop at your hotel, or use the cafes and bars at Intourist hotels, paying in hard currency.

♦ Many vending machines sell water. Water with syrup (such as lemon or apricot), requires a 3-kopeck coin; plain water costs 1 kopeck. One sanitation problem is the machines' drinking glasses, which everybody uses; the only water available for washing them is cold. In addition, the glasses are often stolen.

♦ Most restaurants open from noon to 3:00 P.M. and 6:00 to 11:00 P.M.

♦ Some restaurants accept only hard currency.

♦ Many restaurants ban smoking, but most restaurants in Intourist hotels allow it.

♦ Drink service is usually quick, but food service is slow.

♦ If you dine with Russians in a restaurant, expect the dinner to take up the entire evening.

♦ Women should never pay or offer to pay—either for themselves or for the whole group—if there is a man in the group. Russian women seldom dine in restaurants, even in groups, without a man.

Specialties

♦ Look for the following appetizers: herring, either pickled or in a mustard or sour cream sauce; smoked salmon; liver pâté; eggplant salad; mushroom salad; marinated mushrooms; *salat olivier* (chicken, potatoes, carrots, and peas in a dilled sour-cream sauce); vinaigrette of beets; garlic cheese spread; *piroshki* (meat- or vegetable-filled turnovers); *ikra* (caviar of many types, including beluga, sevruga, and fresh or saltwater salmon); and *bliny* (buckwheat pancakes served with pickled herring, caviar, or sliced smoked sturgeon, butter, and sour cream).

♦ Favorite Russian soups are *borsch* (beets and cabbage in beef stock); *ukha* (a clear fish soup); *pokhlyobka* (pot luck).

♦ For salads, try *agurtsi so smetanoi* (cucumber and sour cream salad with dill).

♦ Russian main courses include *beef stroganov* (sauteed beef with mushrooms and onions in a sour cream sauce); *satsivi* (chicken with a sauce of pounded walnuts, garlic, and red and black pepper); *tziply-onok tabaka* (pressed, fried chicken with

Tkemali sauce, made from sour plums, garlic, coriander, and lemon juice); *kotlety po-kyivski* (chicken Kiev); *shashlyk* (shish kebab); *kotlety* (deep-fried meat patties); and *bitki* (fried beef patties with caraway seeds and beets).

◆ Common desserts in homes are *kisel* (a thick or thin pudding made from fresh fruit) or cakes.

◆ Russian beverages include *kefir* (a kind of buttermilk, considered a good hangover remedy); *kvass* (a yeasty, nonalcoholic beer sold at stands for a few kopecks); and mineral water.

Hotels

◆ When you check into a hotel, your passport and visa will be held for 24 hours.

◆ You'll be given a card showing the hotel's name and your room number. Keep it; it's your identification for changing money or going to other foreigners-only hotels, and you can also show it to people if you need directions back to the hotel. Some hotels have female attendants on each floor who'll take your card and give you your room key. When you go out, leave the key with the attendant, and she'll return your card.

◆ Bribery is a way of life; if you need something (such as extra towels or hot water for coffee or tea), give the floor attendant soap, tea bags, or pens.

◆ Hotels have no room service. You might want to bring instant beverages to have in your hotel room. Either carry along an immersion heater (with converter) or bring a mug or Styrofoam cups and ask the floor attendant for boiling water.

◆ Hotel maids make beds daily but sometimes change linen only once a week. If you'd like the sheets changed more often, try bribing the maid with soap, tea, coffee, or cigarettes.

◆ Hotels provide very small towels and no face cloths. If you want a large, fluffy towel, bring one from home and then leave it for the maid as a tip.

◆ Hotels rarely offer amenities such as shampoo or stationery. Some furnish refrigerators; if there isn't one and you need something refrigerated, ask the floor attendant.

◆ Hot-water faucets are marked with a red dot; cold-water faucets, with a blue dot.

◆ Bathroom outlets can accommodate only electric razors. You must plug your hairdryer into a bedroom outlet, which might be far from a mirror (bring your own mirror if that's inconvenient). You'll need a converter unless you have a convertible dryer.

◆ Laundry service takes two full days, so allow plenty of time—especially if you're leaving. The maids actually do the laundry and prefer to be paid in American cigarettes, soap, or cosmetics rather than in rubles.

◆ Hotels have hard-currency bars that serve alcoholic drinks, snacks, Italian espresso, and soft drinks. In many large hotels, you can buy vodka and Western beer with hard currency.

◆ Intourist hotels have service bureaus where you can check schedules and buy tickets for theaters, concerts, and special events. Some have bus service to performances, for a fee.

♦ Russian citizens sometimes have difficulty getting into Intourist hotels. (The intent is to keep black marketers from bothering the guests.) If you are expecting Soviet guests, either have them call your room or wait for them outside. Just show your hotel card and your guests will be admitted.

Tipping

♦ Because of the tremendous short-ages, Russians appreciate receiving consumer goods as tips— soap, Marlboro

cigarettes, tea, coffee, disposable razors, ball-point pens, hairspray, and pantyhose are popular.

♦ *Restaurants:* Leave odd change.

♦ *Porters:* Give cigarettes.

♦ *Hotel maids:* Give any of the items listed above.

♦ *Taxi drivers:* If they use a meter, tip $1 U.S. or give a pack of Marlboro cigarettes.

♦ *Intourist guides:* These guides are not supposed to take tips, but give them good loose tea, coffee, cosmetics, pantyhose, cologne, or English-language detective novels.

Private Homes

♦ Feel free to drop in unan-nounced. Many people have no phone, so it's dif-ficult to call in advance.

♦ Before you enter, remove the shoes or boots you've worn outdoors. Either bring another pair with you or wear slippers pro-vided by your hosts.

♦ If you stay with a family, be prepared for cramped living quarters and no privacy. (Russians like to have overnight guests despite the space constraints.) The living-room couch will probably be a family mem-ber's bed.

♦ If you stay for a few days, you'll be over-whelmed by kindness and hospitality. Food will be abundant, despite the difficulty of obtaining it, and the best way to show your appreciation is to eat heartily.

♦ Most women work all day and must spend several additional hours shopping for food. You can either bring food items from abroad or buy them at a foreigners-only *Beriozka* store. Don't offer to do the shop-ping yourself unless you speak Russian well, know where to find specific items, and know whether your hosts have barter arrangments with any merchants. If you don't mind sharing long waits and crowded public transportation, offer to meet your hostess after work to help carry packages.

♦ Most couples work, but they'll be happy to show you around as time permits.

♦ If the family offers to help you change money on the black market, decline politely. The offer in itself is no cause for alarm—many Russians participate in the black market as a matter of survival. If they pressure you, say you've already exchanged enough money or don't think it's worth the risk. In most cases the family is just trying to help by offering you a secure route to cheap rubles, but continued pressure sug-gests they are interested in you primarily as a black-market business resource.

◆ If you offer to help with chores, your hosts will probably decline. If other guests are coming, you might be permitted to help with small chores such as setting the table; there's seldom room in the kitchen for more than one person.

◆ Be careful of people's pride. If, for example, you want to give someone some of your clothes, be tactful and make an excuse ("I have so many souvenirs, there's no room in my suitcase").

◆ Don't effusively admire any object in a Russian home or the family might feel obliged to give it to you.

◆ Take a bath every day, if you wish. Most Russians don't bathe daily but understand if guests do. Water is inexpensive, and most apartments have hot water. In rural areas, however, few single-family houses have hot water, and some have no running water.

◆ In May or June hot water is turned off by district, supposedly so the pipes can be cleaned. You'll have to heat water for washing on the stove.

Gifts: Russians who want to offer guests a nice meal usually must barter or spend hours in lines. Show your appreciation by bringing a nice gift—liquor from abroad or from airport duty-free shops or a hard-currency store, cosmetics, Marlboro cigarettes (even nonsmokers can use them for barter), candy, or an uneven number of flowers. People probably won't open gifts in front of you, and their thanks, though sincere, will be subdued.

◆ If you stay with a family, bring gifts from abroad: good choices are soap, tea (bags or loose), cigarettes, cigarette lighters, perfume, eye make-up, or jeans. For children, bring chewing gum, puzzles, pop-music cassettes, clothing, or toys.

◆ Don't give a pregnant woman a baby gift; wait until after the baby is born.

Business

Hours

Businesses and government offices: Usually 9:00 A.M. to 6:00 P.M., with a lunch break from 1:00 to 2:00 P.M.

Banks: 9:00 A.M. to 5:00 P.M., Monday through Friday, with a lunch break from 1:00 to 2:00 P.M. or 2:00 to 3:00 P.M.

Stores: Usually 8:00 or 9:00 A.M. to 8:00 or 9:00 P.M., Monday through Saturday. Most food stores close for lunch between 1:00 and 2:00 P.M., and many are open on Sunday. Small department stores close from 2:00 to 3:00 P.M. Any store might sometimes close for the day for inventory, cleaning, technical problems, or no reason at all.

Business Practices

◆ You'll need a network of contacts to succeed in business in the Russian Republic. To find contacts from the U.S., contact the U.S.-U.S.S.R. Trade and Economic Council in New York. In England, contact the Department of Trade in London. Another source is your embassy's Commercial Department in Moscow; the embassy's commercial attaché can help set up appointments.

◆ The recent, sweeping changes throughout the Russian Republic and the former Soviet Union have had a profound effect on business. Russian businesspeople are developing a more entrepreneurial approach; in the past they were more formal, inward-looking, and suspicious of private initiative.

◆ Decentralization of the trade structure has

caused complications, with the various republics striving for economic autonomy.

◆ Decisions are now made at many more levels. Both central and local agencies claim decision-making power.

◆ The greatest problem for foreign businesspeople is Russia's lack of a business culture. Many Russians are bewildered by such mundane concepts as cost, pricing, and profit and are unaware of—and shocked by—world prices.

◆ In the past, most Russian businesspeople disliked risks. Because they use the government's money, they face persecution for unsuccessful ventures. Now that's changing.

◆ Doing business in Russia will be frustrating. Dealing with government officials (who can deliver only in their areas of direct responsibility) requires considerable patience. In addition, you'll face the prospect of rude secretaries and telephone operators, unwillingness or inability to answer questions, and telexes going unanswered for weeks. Making last-minute changes can be impossible.

◆ In the past, all Russian workers, even if unmotivated or unproductive, were guaranteed full employment. Firing a worker was almost impossible. Trade unions have governed all work situations, and the pace has been much slower than in Western Europe or North America. Now this is all beginning to change.

◆ Another frustration is the lack of telephone switchboards. Each official has a direct line that is never answered by co-workers and seldom by secretaries, and it has a number the official rarely gives out.

◆ Before dealing with a cooperative (a group of people who start a semiprivate, nongovernment enterprise such as a restaurant, club, kiosk, hair salon, laundry, or farm) ask friends, acquaintances, or new business associations about their reputation.

◆ Business travelers can obtain a visa in just a few days, provided they have a letter or telex from a Russian firm or ministry stating that they'll be doing business in the country.

◆ Send the same people from your company on each business trip to the Russian Republic—even though the Russian team might change constantly. Building good personal relationships is important, as is seeing business contacts regularly.

◆ Mail to Russia from abroad takes several weeks to arrive. To shorten that time, address the envelope in Russian, with the country and city on the top line (plus the district index number), the street and number on the second line, and the addressee's name on the third line.

◆ Don't plan business trips to Russia during the latter half of July, all of August, or early September, the most popular vacation times. Also avoid the time from April 30 to May 10, which encompasses the May Day celebrations.

◆ Bring your own translator, preferably one from your home country.

◆ Russian women in top-level positions are rare. Foreign businesswomen, however, will be regarded as equal to men, as long as they are competent.

◆ To show respect, have all correspondence and advertising material written in Russian.

◆ Bring business cards printed in English on one side and Russian (in the Cyrillic alphabet) on the other. Ask any Russians who don't have business cards to write down their names on paper.

◆ Photocopying facilities are rare (most Russians still use carbon paper), so bring any copies you'll need.

◆ Fax machines are rare even in major cities, and you must reserve them in advance. Outside of major cities they are nonexistent.

◆ If you want to leave behind samples or a video (some machines will make tapes for use on European VCRs), you'll need a letter of explanation from your sponsor. Often, the sponsor will meet you at customs to help you through.

Meetings and negotiations: Make appointments from abroad at least six weeks in advance—preferably by telex or fax, because letters take a week to two months to reach the Russian Republic. Follow up your initial message with a telephone call several weeks later.

◆ Arranging meetings is a slow process, so don't aim for impromptu meetings. Let the Russians determine the time and place, and don't expect confirmation until the last minute.

◆ Even if your time is short, don't try to do business after hours. Russians reserve weekends for their families. In addition, contacting a Russian official after hours or at home will make you both look as though you're trying to fix a deal.

◆ Russians prefer to have several people attend meetings in case there are misunderstandings later.

◆ At a meeting, the two sides sit facing each other, with senior negotiators in the middle. Most Russian offices are open-plan and crowded, and have special rooms reserved for meetings. Be punctual, because the rooms are used frequently by different groups. Meetings usually last an hour but might end abruptly if someone else has reserved the room.

◆ Meetings may begin with several minutes of conversation about general topics such as the weather, holidays, and nonpolitical current events.

◆ After the initial introduction, hand out a profile of your company with its results (for a diversified company, show the results in relevant areas), written in Russian.

◆ During your first meeting verify the bona fides of the people you're dealing with (except ministry officials). Feel free to ask whether people are registered to do business with a foreign company; if they are, they should bring letters of intent stating that fact.

◆ Even after you identify the key contacts for your project, a host of other people might appear and want to participate. Include them as well, even if you have to start over.

◆ Include on your "team" someone who understands Russian and can take notes during each meeting. Make the notes very specific and summarize them at the end of the day, asking "Does everyone agree?" This precaution ensures that people remember accurately what was said.

◆ Russians are heavy smokers, and smoking during meetings is common. Even so, it's polite to ask before you light up.

◆ The Russians will tell you they're negotiating with your competitor; you must demonstrate the benefits of doing business with your company.

◆ Be specific about your product. Russians are interested in details.

◆ Be careful with materials (such as slides or promotional materials) for which you have exclusive rights or a copyright. Many Russians don't accept the concept of exclusive rights and might reproduce material without permission or compensation.

◆ Negotiations can be lengthy, sometimes because even straightforward information—such as the cost of an item—isn't available.

◆ When negotiating, don't move on to a second topic until discussion of the first topic is completed.

◆ Be firm, but polite—*not* aggressive.

◆ If the Russians won't give a price, you might be able to speed negotiations by saying "I'm willing to pay X amount." Determining price is an art rather than a hard business decision.

◆ Business decisions are often made by people at the top. Some agreements may need to be signed by someone in the relevant ministry.

◆ Time estimates will be unreliable unless your money, equipment, or technology are considered very important, in which case everything will be ready on time.

◆ Written contracts can be difficult to obtain, depending on how much the Soviets want what you're offering. Be polite but insistent. Once the contract is signed, it's set in stone.

◆ Be sure to have one copy of the contract in English and another in Russian.

◆ Treat Russian workers (if, for example, you visit a factory) politely. If you must criticize, be as tactful as possible.

Entertainment: Let the Soviets initiate business entertaining. Generally, you'll be taken to a restaurant (rarely a home because apartments are so small) after business hours. Dinners are more common than lunches. If you're dealing with a government ministry or state committee, you might be taken to the theater or ballet rather than to dinner. Senior trade and government offi-cials seldom socialize with foreign business contacts in the evening except for official functions.

◆ Business dinners begin about 6:00 P.M. and last for two hours. First a Russian will make a speech discussing peace, cooperation, and understanding. Then someone from your firm should give a short speech, stressing the same themes. The guests then sit down and are served.

◆ At many formal banquets there are no chairs; people move around freely and talk.

◆ At business dinners, red wine, white wine, vodka, and fruit juices are often served.

◆ Often, several organizations are involved in a contract with a foreign company. It's useful to host a reception and bring all the essential people together—but not until you have been entertained by the Russians.

◆ As a foreign businessperson, you should host a dinner at the conclusion of a deal or the end of a symposium. The best location is the restaurant or a special room in your hotel. (Station one member of your group at the hotel entrance to ensure that your Russian guests can get in.) Another option is to ask Soviet businesspeople to arrange a restaurant dinner, making it clear that you are paying.

◆ When entertaining, include only the people with whom you are negotiating.

◆ If you host a dinner, have a bar with Western liquor and vodka.

◆ Spouses aren't included in business lunches or dinners (partly because of the large quantities of vodka often consumed).

Gifts: Russians appreciate—indeed expect—business gifts, especially at New Year's. Don't, however, give expensive gifts (more than $25 U.S. in value) or they'll look like bribery. Good choices include calculators, good-quality pens, pocket knives, key rings, ties, or, at the end or beginning of the year, diaries or calendars.

Holidays & Celebrations

Holidays:
New Year's
Day (January 1);
International
Women's Day
(March 8); May
Day (May 1 and 2); Victory Day, the anniversary of Nazi Germany's defeat (May 9); Constitution Day (October 7).

◆ Constitution Day may not be celebrated anymore. People are waiting for October 7 to see what will happen.

Transportation

**Public
Transport**
Mass transit:
You'll find Met-
ros (subways)
in Moscow and
St. Petersburg (formerly Leningrad). Metros open at 6:00 A.M. and run until 1:00 A.M.; you can transfer until 12:30 A.M. Trains come at least once a minute.

◆ On the Metros, station signs are in Cyrillic and are difficult to see from the trains. Try counting the number of stops (using the maps in the stations before you get on) and writing down the name of your stop in Cyrillic so you can check with fellow passengers.

◆ The Metro fare is 15 kopecks. The stations have coin-changing machines and cashiers (КАCCA) who can change bills. You put a 15-kopeck coin or three 5-kopeck coins in a slot and literally jump on a rapidly moving escalator. Keep to the right, and jump off at the end.

◆ For buses, streetcars, or trolleys get tickets in advance at a kiosk or from a driver. The cost is 15 kopecks to travel any distance. You validate the ticket, on the honor system, in a machine when you enter. If you're too rushed to buy a ticket before you get on, you might be able to buy one from other passengers, who carry books of ten.

◆ You don't have to buy train tickets through Intourist, but you'll probably find it easier (avoiding problems with lines, schedule changes, and language problems) to do so.

◆ Overnight trains offer "soft class" (two people to a compartment) and "hard class" (four people to a compartment). Sleeping compartments are not segregated, so you might find travelers of the opposite sex sharing your compartment. You can store your luggage in overhead compartments or under the bed. A third section has bunk beds without compartments.

◆ Every car has an attendant who will knock on your compartment door to wake you twenty minutes before your stop—and if you're lucky, to serve you a glass of tea.

◆ Long-distance trains have restaurant cars. Otherwise, you can buy cookies, sandwiches, and tea from the train attendants.

◆ Trains are better than planes for winter trips under eight hours, since the weather often causes long flight delays.

◆ To fly to other republics you must pay in hard currency.

◆ Any form of transportation is available—

for a price. Travelers have successfully hired even ambulances for routine travel.

♦ Smoking is forbidden on all domestic flights and in Metro stations.

Taxis: Taxis usually wait for fares in front of hotels. You can also book one through your hotel's floor attendant.

♦ Taxis on the street seldom stop, but you can often convince one to do so by holding out a pack of Marlboro cigarettes.

♦ If a taxi driver does not want to take you somewhere, offer him a pack of cigarettes (especially Marlboro); that may cover the cost of the ride, or the driver may accept the cigarettes as a tip and also charge you for the ride.

♦ Taxis have meters, but drivers often refuse to turn them on because they want more money. Ask at your hotel what the fare should be, and negotiate before you get in. Few drivers speak English, so write down numbers when you negotiate. Many drivers only accept hard currency.

Driving

♦ Russia has many unfamiliar rules and regulations for driving, as well as road signs in Cyrillic letters, so consider hiring a car and driver.

♦ A car's front-seat occupants must wear seat belts.

♦ On highways, the speed limit is 90 kph; in towns and populated areas, it's 60 kph.

♦ To drive through the Russian Republic, you must have a prearranged, fixed itinerary before you enter the country. It's extremely difficult to change your itinerary once you're in the country, partly because of the shortage of hotel space. Don't change your itinerary without approval or you might be stopped by the State Automobile Police

(S.A.P.) for not passing certain checkpoints at certain times. If you wish to make changes, check with Intourist at your hotel; if your changes are approved, you'll get a document to show the S.A.P., and the S.A.P. stations will be contacted.

♦ Carry two sets of maps: one in the Roman alphabet for your own use; and one in Cyrillic to show when you need directions.

♦ License plates are color-coded, so the police know who is driving each car—a diplomat, for example, or a renter.

♦ Cars, not pedestrians, have the right-of-way.

♦ Streetcars and trolleys have priority. If a streetcar or trolley stops and its doors open, cars must not pass it.

♦ In large cities, left turns are prohibited at most intersections. You must go beyond the street you want, then make a U-turn by a blue sign with a curved white arrow.

♦ On rural roads, watch out for cows and other animals crossing the road.

♦ Gas stations are rare—sometimes 100 or 250 kilometers apart. Most take vouchers, called *talon,* sold at Intourist offices or hotels. Some gas stations accept rubles but often have no gas.

♦ Whenever you leave your car, put the windshield wipers in the glove compartment so they won't be stolen. Spare parts are scarce.

♦ Don't drink and drive. It's a criminal offense.

♦ At night, use only your parking lights, not your headlights. Never use your headlights in cities. Use high beams on highways between towns, but when you reach a village, switch to parking lights.

Legal Matters & Safety

♦ Don't bring more than one Bible (for personal use) into the country.

♦ Pornography is illegal, and some customs officials have very broad definitions of pornography.

♦ When you go through passport control upon arrival, you'll stand in front of the passport official for several minutes. He'll look at you, stare into your eyes, look back at your passport, look over your head at a mirror, look back at you, and so on. Don't be alarmed; it's normal procedure.

♦ The Russians take narcotics *very* seriously. If you are caught importing or accepting drugs, you'll be put in a Russian jail. The American Embassy has no recourse.

♦ In cities, Russians must show their passports in shops. If they're not from that city, they might not be allowed to buy anything.

♦ In recent years crime has increased by 50 percent. Robberies often occur in airports and near hotels, where tourists congregate. Don't go out alone late at night; if you do, wear a money belt.

♦ People will ask you to trade things. Officially, this trading is discouraged because it might be illegal to take the items (such as military regalia) out of the country. If someone gives you rubles for an item, you might not be able to spend all the rubles, and you can't take them out of the country.

♦ To cross large avenues, use the underground passageways. If you don't and are caught jaywalking, the fine is 10 rubles, payable on the spot.

♦ To extend your stay in a specific city or add a city to your itinerary, make arrangements with Intourist at your hotel.

♦ When you leave the Russian Republic, take your luggage to an X-ray machine before you check it. You can't take out antiques, caviar, military uniforms, or books published in the Soviet Union before 1975 (unless you have permission and pay 100 percent duty).

♦ Bring along any medication you use; even aspirin is unavailable. You might want to bring disposable needles and syringes in case of an emergency, since they aren't available in Russia—but bring copies of an explanatory letter from your physician (translated into Russian), or customs officials might think you're importing drug paraphernalia.

♦ Product shortages are severe, so bring extras of anything you need, such as contact lens solution, razor blades, or eyeglasses.

♦ Bring an adequate supply of contraceptives. Russian-made condoms are scarce and of poor quality.

♦ Sanitary napkins and tampons are unavailable (Russian women use cotton), so bring an adequate supply.

♦ If you're in frail health, don't go to the Russian Republic, which lacks antibiotics, adequate anesthetics, and disposable hypodermic needles.

♦ In St. Petersburg (formerly Leningrad), don't drink—or even brush your teeth with—tap water or eat unpeeled fruits or vegetables, or you'll risk a parasitic disease called giardia. Giardia has an incubation period of two weeks and causes severe diarrhea; there is a medication to cure it. Bottled Russian mineral water tastes terrible, so buy the expensive Finnish bottled water in the *Beriozka* store in your hotel.

Key Phrases

Below we give each word in English and its pronunication—but not its spelling—in Russian. Since the Russian language uses the Cyrillic alphabet, a Russian wouldn't recognize the word printed in the Roman alphabet (and you probably wouldn't recognize it printed in the Cyrillic alphabet).

English	Pronunciation of Russian
Good morning	DO-brah-yeh OO-trah
Good day	DO-bree dyen
Good evening	DO-bree VYEH-cher
Please	pah-JAHL-stah
Thank you	spah-SEE-bah
You're welcome	pah-JAHL-stah
Yes	dah
No	nyet
Mr., Mrs., Miss	(Use first name and patronymic.)
Excuse me	cez-vee-NEE-tyeh
Good-bye	dah svee-DAHN-yah
I don't understand.	yah nyeh pah-nee-MAH-you
I don't speak Russian.	ya nyeh gah-vahr-YOU pah ROOS-kee
Is there anyone who speaks English?	KTOE nee-bood gah-vah-REET pah ahn-GLEE-skee

Spain

Spain is a synonym for romance: castles, the Man of La Mancha, the flamenco. Even bullfighting—which some visitors consider barbaric but which the Spanish regard as art—is romantic. From this romance emerges the image of the proud Spanish hero. To this day, a Spanish male's overriding concern is with honor.

When dealing with Spaniards, either socially or in business, never forget their pride in their individuality. And never offend Spaniards' honor by causing embarrassment—you'd be attacking something sacred.

Greetings

♦ Shake hands when you're introduced and when meeting or leaving someone.

♦ Spanish people are openly affectionate. Male friends embrace when they meet, and women embrace and kiss each other on the cheek. If you are meeting an old friend or a relative, do the same.

♦ A Spanish "last" name consists of the surname followed by the mother's family name. In correspondence, use both names (for example, Mr. Garcia Lopez), but in conversation, use only the surname (Mr. Garcia).

♦ Use family names—not first names—until you become well acquainted.

♦ People who are older or of higher rank might call you by your first name, but you should still address them as Mr., Mrs., or Miss plus the last name.

Conversation

♦ Good topics of conversation: politics (but don't make political comparisons between Spain and the U.S.), American lifestyles, or sports—especially soccer.

♦ Topics to avoid: religion, the Spanish Civil War, or the Franco regime.

♦ Don't ask new acquaintances about their family, job, interests, or hobbies.

♦ Never make negative comments about bullfighting.

♦ People will interrupt you frequently. They're not being rude—just animated.

Money

♦ The unit of currency is the peseta (abbreviated Pta).

♦ Coins come in denominations of 1, 5, 25, 50, 100, 200, and 500 pesetas.

♦ Notes come in denominations of 200, 500, 1,000, 2,000, 5,000, and 10,000 pesetas.

Telephones

◆ You'll find gray public telephones in booths on city streets, at train stations, and at

airports. They have slots for 5-, 25-, 50-, and 100-peseta coins. (A short local call costs at least 10 pesetas.)

◆ To make a call, place several coins in the groove at the top of the phone, lift the receiver, and dial the number. Coins will fall into the phone as needed. Newer phones have electronic displays that tell you how much time you have left for the money you deposited.

◆ Spain has no telephone cards.

◆ If you can't find a public phone, ask to use one in a restaurant or bar. Most bartenders will let you make a local call. Pay at the end of the call.

◆ For long-distance calls within Europe, use a public telephone.

◆ To call overseas, go to the *telefónica*, or telephone exchange. Every town has one. In large cities, they're open from 9:00 A.M. to 9:00 P.M.; in smaller communities, from 9:00 A.M. to 2:00 P.M. Don't call abroad from your hotel room or you'll probably pay a large surcharge—even for a collect call.

◆ When answering the phone, say "DEE-gah-may."

◆ The Emergency Number to summon police, the fire department, or an ambulance is **091.**

In Public

◆ The American "okay" sign, with thumb and index finger forming a circle, is a vulgar gesture in Spain.

◆ Never swear. Many people are religious, and swearing offends them. Swearing in front of women is especially offensive.

◆ When you enter a shop, office, or reception area, say "Good day" (see Key Phrases).

◆ Spaniards are rarely punctual for social occasions or business appointments. Arriving 15 to 30 minutes late is common and acceptable. The only event for which punctuality is required is a bullfight.

◆ If you ask directions, the Spanish might be so eager to help that they'll give you wrong information rather than admit they don't know. Avoid yes-or-no questions, such as "Is the train station over there?" (To please you, a Spaniard may say "Yes," whether it is or not.) Instead, ask "Where is the train station?"

◆ If several people start scrambling madly for a phone booth or taxi, just smile and step aside. When they realize you're a tourist, they'll usually let you go first.

◆ If you enjoy gambling, look for casinos, slot machines in bars, and booths on the street where you can buy lottery tickets.

◆ Spanish men often call out expressions of admiration as women pass on the street. If the women don't react or acknowledge them, the men won't bother them.

◆ If a woman returns a Spanish man's gaze, he'll think she's interested in him.

◆ Don't photograph military areas or policemen in uniform. Many museums request that you leave your camera at the door.

◆ Before you photograph a person close up, ask permission.

◆ You'll find public toilets in hotels, restaurants, cafes, bars, museums, and department stores (where they're usually on the top floor). The doors are marked *Señoras* for women and *Caballeros* for men.

◆ Men and women often use the same public toilets, especially in small towns. A unisex toilet will usually be marked *W.C.*

Dress

◆ Spaniards dress elegantly, even for casual occasions. Don't wear scruffy or worn clothing if you want to fit in.

◆ For business, dress well to give an impression of accomplishment. Men should wear jackets and ties, even in warm weather, and choose subdued colors and black shoes. It's customary to keep jackets buttoned except when sitting. Women should wear dresses or blouses and skirts, never pantsuits.

◆ When invited to dinner, men should wear jackets with ties and black shoes. Women should wear dresses or skirts and blouses.

◆ To elegant restaurants, men should wear a jacket and tie, and women should wear a dress or dressy pants. At other restaurants, men don't need to wear a jacket and tie.

◆ If an invitation specifies formal wear, men should wear tuxedos, and women should wear long dresses. Usually formal dress is reserved for charity balls and official dinners.

◆ To theaters and theater openings, men should wear dark suits, and women should wear cocktail dresses.

◆ When visiting churches, women may wear pants but should avoid sundresses and other clothes that expose the shoulders. Women needn't wear hats or other head coverings. No one should wear shorts.

◆ Wear shorts only at the beach or in resort areas.

Meals

Hours and Foods

Breakfast (*desayuno*): 7:00 to 8:00 A.M. The meal consists of

rolls, butter, marmalade, and either coffee with hot milk or cocoa. In a restaurant, waiters will pour half a cup of coffee, then add hot milk until you tell them to stop.

Lunch (*almuerzo*): 2:00 to 3:00 P.M. The main meal of the day, lunch usually starts with soup, followed by salad and a main course of fish or meat with vegetables. Wine and water usually accompany the meal. Lunch ends with fruit, pastries, and coffee, usually served in a small cup.

Dinner (*cena*): 9:00 to 10:00 P.M. A typical family dinner is light—perhaps a potato omelet or cold cuts, cheese, and bread. A social dinner is often preceded by a stop at a *tapas* bar (see Eating Out). Before-dinner drinks include *jerz* (sherry), whiskey, gin and tonic, and *vermut* (vermouth) served with ice or sparkling water. (The Spanish also mix many kinds of liquor with cola; scotch and cola is common.)

◆ The meal at a dinner party usually

includes a soup or appetizer, followed by meat or fish, vegetables, and salad. Bread and wine are served throughout the meal. Fruit is a common dessert, but ice cream or cakes are often served at social occasions. Coffee and cognac or other liqueurs end the meal.

Breaks: About 10:30 A.M., people go to cafes for coffee and a sandwich or pastry.

Table Manners

◆ If you're invited to dinner in a home, be 15 to 30 minutes late. If you arrive on time, your hosts might not be ready.

◆ The guest of honor sits to the host's right; the hostess sits at the end of the table opposite the host.

◆ Each place setting has two stacked plates—the top one for the first course, the bottom one for the main course—a wine glass, and a water glass. Dessert utensils, including a fruit knife and fork, are above the plate.

◆ If you don't want wine, ask for juice or a soft drink. There is no social pressure to drink. Plain or bottled water is usually served with meals.

◆ Bread-and-butter plates aren't used. Instead, put bread either on a coaster next to your plate or on the table. Butter is served with bread only at breakfast.

◆ Food is served in various ways. Sometimes it's passed around the table on platters; sometimes the hosts serve or offer the serving honor to a guest. If a family has a maid, she usually serves.

◆ If you aren't hungry, be honest and you won't be pressed to eat. Spaniards don't like to see food wasted, so it's better to decline food than to leave it on your plate.

◆ Smoking during the meal is acceptable.

◆ To show you've finished, lay your fork and knife side by side on the plate. Leaving them on opposite sides of the plate implies that you either weren't satisfied or haven't finished.

◆ Leave about midnight, unless conversation is lively and everyone is obviously having a good time. Spaniards tend to stay up late.

Eating Out

◆ Unique to Spain are *tapas* bars, which offer a wide variety of appetizers and drinks.

●Spaniards usually precede dinner in a restaurant by visiting a few *tapas* bars at about 7:00 P.M., but some people start about 8:00 P.M. and make their meal of the *tapas*.

●Some popular *tapas* are shrimps, octopus, marinated mushrooms, potato omelets, snails in hot sauce, small squid, and red peppers with oil. The least expensive *tapas* are olives and potato chips.

●Customary drinks with *tapas* are sherry, beer, and wine.

●Most *tapas* bars have some tables, but people usually eat standing at the bar. Most portions are big enough for two and come with two forks. Bread is often served with *tapas*.

◆ Spain has a wide variety of eating places:

●An *asador* is a restaurant that features steak, roast suckling pig, roast lamb, and fish.

●A *bar* serves *tapas*, alcoholic drinks, soft drinks, coffee, and tea.

● *Cafés* serve *tapas*, sandwiches, some hot meals such as fried eggs or hamburgers, alcoholic drinks, and coffee.

• *Marisquerías* are restaurants that serve only seafood.

• A *merendero* is a seaside fish restaurant; you can usually eat outside.

• A *mesón* serves many varieties of *tapas* and wine. Most have a decor more pleasing than that of a bar.

• *Pastelerías* offer pastries, sandwiches, tea, coffee, and soft drinks.

• *Tabernas* are the oldest type of restaurant. Most are family businesses that offer home-style cooking with a standard menu and a few daily specials.

◆ Women alone shouldn't go to a bar or a *mesón*.

◆ Spanish restaurants don't serve breakfast. Instead, you must eat at your hotel or a cafe. Few restaurants open before 1:00 P.M. for lunch; 2:00 or 3:00 P.M. is the norm. In the evening, restaurants open about 8:30 P.M. and close sometime between midnight and 2:00 A.M. The usual time for dining is 9:30 or 10:00 P.M.

◆ If you're concerned about cost, check the prices before you take a table. Restaurants must prominently display a price list both outside and inside.

◆ Menus in better restaurants are in Spanish, French, and English.

◆ To summon a waiter, hold up an index finger and make eye contact.

◆ If you want meat cooked rare, be emphatic. Most restaurants overcook steak by American standards.

◆ Restaurant food is rarely hot or even warm. If you want a hot meal, tell the waiter specifically.

◆ Waiters won't bring you a check until you ask. If you're in a rush, ask for the check when your food is served.

◆ Some restaurants give you the ceramic jug in which your wine is served, but don't take one without asking. Ceramic shops sell similar jugs.

Specialties

◆ Try these Spanish treats: *churros* (deep-fried crullers served for breakfast); *gazpacho* (a cold soup of tomatoes, cucumbers, peppers, onions, garlic, olive oil, and vinegar); *sopa de ajo* (garlic soup with garlic cloves, olive oil, egg, and bread); *cocido madrileño* (a meal of soup followed by garbanzo beans and meat—ham, chicken, beef, and salt pork—with three kinds of sauces, carrots, leeks, and cabbage); *paella* (rice with saffron, clams, mussels, squid, chorizo sausage, chicken, pork, ham, and olive oil); *empanadas* (meat-filled turnovers); *tortilla de patata* (a potato-and-onion omelet); and *zarzuela de mariscos* (Catalonian shellfish stew flavored with herbs and saffron).

◆ For dessert try *flan* (caramel custard) and *turrón* (candy made of almonds, egg white, and honey).

◆ *Anguilas* (eels sauteed in olive oil and garlic) are served on the plate with the eyes sticking out. Spaniards consider them an expensive delicacy.

◆ *Morcilla* is fried blood sausage, and *calamares en su tinta* is squid prepared in its own ink.

Hotels

♦ Top-rated hotels have all the conveniences and amenities, while less expensive hotels often lack air-conditioning and can be oppressive in the summer.

♦ When you register, be ready to show your passport. The desk clerk might need it to fill out forms but will give it back within a few hours.

♦ Hot-water faucets are marked *C;* cold-water faucets, *F.*

♦ When you go out, leave your key at the desk.

♦ If you have a complaint, go to the manager. If your bed wasn't made properly, for example, talk to the manager, not the maid. Hotels and restaurants have official complaint forms that government inspectors check monthly. If you're not satisfied, fill one out and you might get a refund later.

Tipping

♦ *Restaurants:* If the tip isn't included in the bill, leave 15 percent. For exceptional service, leave another 5 percent on the table. Waiters also greatly appreciate compliments.

♦ *Porters:* Tip hotel porters 50 pesetas per bag. Airport porters charge a fixed rate of 60 or 90 pesetas per bag.

♦ *Hotel maids:* Tip 500 pesetas per week.

♦ *Taxis:* If drivers use a meter, give 10 per-cent; if they don't, don't tip.

♦ *Ushers:* Give 10 pesetas.

♦ *Washroom attendants:* Tip 5 pesetas.

♦ *Gas station attendants:* Give 50 pesetas if they provide an extra service such as washing your windshield.

Private Homes

♦ Before visiting, call ahead to make sure it's convenient. Visiting times are usually 4:00 to 6:00 P.M.

♦ Many people have a *siesta* or nap after the noon meal, so don't call or plan to visit at that time.

♦ If you are invited to someone's home, consider it a great compliment. Spaniards don't invite foreigners into their homes until they know them well. They are more likely to entertain them in a restaurant.

♦ When you visit a home, stay at least two hours or you'll be considered rude. If you're invited to a meal, stay for a few hours afterward.

♦ The Spanish are formal about invitations and don't extend them on the spur of the moment.

♦ Children are regarded as very special members of the family. No matter whether you're visiting or staying with a family, be sure to pay attention to the children.

♦ In traditional Spanish homes, the children don't eat with the adults. In most families, however, children and adults eat together.

♦ If you make a phone call from a home, offer to pay. There's a charge for each call.

♦ If you stay with a Spanish family, your

hosts will expect to spend all day with you. If you'd like some time by yourself, be diplomatic; if possible, offer to meet the family for dinner.

◆ Don't snack in the home. Spaniards eat meals at set times and don't snack the way Americans do. Never go to the refrigerator and help yourself.

◆ Water is heated by electricity, which is expensive. Ask when it's convenient for you to bathe and don't use a lot of water.

◆ If the family has servants, let them handle chores such as clearing the table. If the family has no hired help, offer to clear the table and do the dishes—though your hosts will probably refuse.

Gifts: If you're invited to dinner, send or bring flowers (but not dahlias or chrysanthemums, which are associated with funerals). Don't choose any food gifts except pastries, cakes, or chocolates.

◆ If you're a houseguest, consider bringing gifts from the U.S. Good choices are blue jeans, pocket calculators, small electric appliances that use or adapt to 220-volt current, American crafts such as quilts, whistling teakettles, or American towels (which are much thicker than those in Spain).

◆ If you've been out for the day, bring the children candy or a small toy.

◆ If you're given a gift, open it immediately.

Business

Hours

Businesses and government offices: 9:00 A.M. to 1:30 P.M. and 4:00 to 7:00 P.M.,

Monday through Friday, and 9:00 A.M. to 1:30 P.M. on Saturday. Some businesses are closed all day Saturday.

Banks: 9:00 A.M. to 2:00 or 3:00 P.M., Monday through Friday, and 9:00 A.M. to 1:00 P.M. on Saturday. During the summer, banks close at 1:30 P.M., Monday through Friday, and at 12:30 P.M. on Saturday.

Stores: 9:30 A.M. to 1:30 P.M. and 4:00 to 8:00 P.M., Monday through Friday; 9:30 A.M. to 2:00 P.M. on Saturday.

◆ Almost everything—from businesses and government offices to schools—closes from 1:00 to 4:00 P.M. for the *siesta*.

◆ Department stores, however, are generally open from 10:00 A.M. to 8:00 P.M., Monday through Saturday, without a break.

◆ Most businesspeople get to work between 9:00 and 10:00 a.m., leave for a long lunch at 2:00 p.m., return at 4:00 or 5:00 P.M., and stay until 8:00 or 9:00 P.M.

Business Practices

◆ When planning a business trip, check with the Spanish Tourist Office to make sure the celebration of a Spanish city's patron saint's day won't interfere with your work schedule.

◆ Develop Spanish contacts who can help you cultivate relationships with businesspeople or government officials. Spaniards value personal influence, and accomplishing anything on your own is difficult.

◆ Find contacts through the Commercial Section of the Spanish Embassy or the local Spanish Consulate, or through the Spanish-U.S. Chamber of Commerce in New York.

◆ You'll need at least one trip to Spain to make a deal. The Spanish like to negotiate in person. They assume that if they establish a relationship with you, you'll feel obliged to give them a good price and a high-quality product.

♦ If you correspond with Spanish firms, write in English in a formal style. An English letter translated into Spanish might not appear sufficiently formal and flowery and might offend the recipient.

♦ Keep your correspondence formal—even though you might develop informal personal relationships after your first meeting.

♦ Avoid business trips to Spain from mid-July through the end of August, when most people vacation.

♦ Most large firms conduct business in both English and Spanish, so you won't need a translator.

♦ Bring business cards in Spanish on one side and English on the other. Spanish business cards have the two names used in all correspondence—the surname and the mother's family name.

♦ Spain is a class-conscious society. Don't get too friendly with low-status employees or you might diminish your counterpart's respect for you.

♦ If you're a foreign businessman dealing with a female Spanish counterpart, don't be overly familiar or condescending.

♦ In general, Spanish women adhere strictly to traditional roles. A very few women have executive positions—usually in the service sector.

♦ Foreign businesswomen should act in a professional manner, dress elegantly but conservatively, and not in any way be flirtatious. They will then be taken seriously.

♦ Fax machines are common and are available in large hotels.

Meetings and negotiations: Make appointments from the U.S. by telex, fax, or telephone ten days to two weeks ahead. If you use international mail, allow three weeks to a month.

♦ Suggest business appointments between 10:00 A.M. and 12:30 P.M. Most businesspeople take care of appointments in the morning and do paperwork in the afternoon.

♦ Be punctual, but expect your Spanish counterparts to be 15 to 30 minutes late. Don't complain about the wait.

♦ When you arrive for a meeting, you'll be taken to a private office, private conference room, or meeting room. The office's size and furnishings will tell you the person's upper- or middle-management status.

♦ At the first meeting you'll be evaluated as a person and asked questions about your background, education, and interests. Only then can serious discussions begin. Spaniards dislike the impersonal efficiency often associated with Americans, and value knowing businesspeople as individuals.

♦ If you speak a little Spanish, you'll make a good impression by using it during the opening conversation. Begin by praising and showing an interest in Spain and the local area.

♦ Have any documents, pamphlets, or brochures you plan to use in your presentation translated into Spanish.

♦ When you make your presentation, be direct and clear. Spanish businesspeople might not risk appearing uninformed by asking for clarification.

♦ Focus on tangibles in your presentation. Bring samples.

♦ If a Spanish businessperson moves from behind the desk to a separate meeting area, that's a favorable sign. Remaining behind the desk is placing distance between the two of you.

♦ Many Spanish businesses are made up of family members who value family and friends over material acquisitions. You might find yourself dealing with someone who seems unqualified or unprepared, but don't say anything—the person might be a family member, and you'll offend their honor, which to Spaniards takes precedence over organization and efficiency. Imposing a decision in direct language is also considered humiliating.

♦ You might encounter frequent disruptions over personal matters that to you seem trivial—but in Spain, personal matters take priority over business matters.

♦ The top manager makes the final decision; middle managers conduct the negotiations and transmit the information on which the decision is based.

♦ Progress toward making a deal will be slow but steady. The Spanish enjoy bargaining and are good at it. In your initial price, leave room for negotiating.

♦ At the end of your initial meeting, try to obtain a specific date for another meeting.

Entertainment: At a business lunch (usually scheduled for 2:00 or 2:30 P.M.), expect drinks before and wine with the meal. Lunch is supposed to be a leisurely meal, personal and relaxed, so don't rush through it.

♦ After the second or third meeting, it's appropriate to invite your Spanish counterparts to lunch. Make sure you request that the bill be given to you, or your guests will grab it. You may also invite people for a drink after work.

♦ You'll be invited to business lunches and dinners. If several people entertain you, reciprocate by inviting them all out to a meal together.

♦ If you're invited to dinner, don't discuss business; it's purely a social occasion. If you want to invite your Spanish counterpart to dinner, wait until you've established good rapport.

♦ Spouses don't go to business dinners unless specifically invited.

♦ If you're invited to someone's home in the evening, expect drinks but not dinner. After the drinks, your hosts will take you to a restaurant. Many executives like to entertain in restaurants because they live in apartments too small for comfortable entertaining.

♦ *Never* get drunk. Spaniards consider drunkenness totally unacceptable.

♦ If you're a woman, you'll find it difficult to pay for a Spanish businessman's meal. Try to speak to the maitre d' or waiter in advance and leave cash or a credit card. If that isn't possible, leave the table discreetly at the end of the meal and pay then. If you're entertaining frequently, use the same restaurant so the staff will come to know your strategy.

Gifts: Good business gifts are American wine or high-quality gifts typical of your region, such as those you find in museum shops—photographic books of your region, paperweights, and carved wooden duck decoys.

Holidays & Celebrations

Holidays:
New Year's Day (January 1); Epiphany (January 6); St. Joseph's Day (March 19);

Maundy Thursday; Good Friday; Labor Day

(May 1); Corpus Christi (eight weeks after Easter); St. James Day (July 25); Assumption Day (August 15); Columbus Day (October 12); Immaculate Conception (December 8); and Christmas (December 25).

♦ The Spanish exchange gifts (less elaborate than those in the U.S.) on January 6, rather than on Christmas. On the evening of the fifth, children put their shoes out on the balcony, and the next morning they find small gifts in them. If you're staying with a family at that time, buy a small gift for each child.

♦ New Year's Eve is a time for family celebrations. At midnight, people drink champagne and eat one grape for every stroke of the clock.

♦ Each city celebrates its patron saint's day. The festivities can be fascinating.

♦ If a holiday falls on a Tuesday or Thursday, it's customary to take a long weekend.

Transportation

Public Transport

Mass transit:
To save money, buy passes for buses, sub-

ways, and commuter trains at the station instead of on the vehicle.

♦ You'll find subways only in Madrid, Barcelona, and Valencia. They run from 6:00 A.M. to 1:00 A.M. and are always crowded—and in the summer, uncomfortably hot.

♦ Subways have a single fare, no matter how far you travel. Save money by buying round-trip or season tickets, both available at ticket offices in all subway stations. Keep your ticket until you get off.

♦ When you take a bus, pay when you board and keep your ticket stub until you get off.

♦ The only intercity buses for which you'll need reservations are luxury long-distance buses.

♦ Buses with different destinations depart from different places, so ask the local tourist office for your departure point.

♦ Trains are of three types: a *Tranvía* is a slow train; a *Talgo* is a fast, comfortable intercity train; and a *Rápido* is an express train with sleeping accommodations.

♦ Trains seldom have refreshment service. Bring your own food and drink.

Taxis: Regular taxis have "TAXI" painted on the outside and have meters on the inside. Hail a taxi on the street or order one from your hotel.

♦ Some cities have taxis called *gran turismos,* which have no meters. They are more spacious and luxurious than regular taxis, but also more expensive. You might have to take one if you're pressed for time, but always negotiate the fare in advance.

Driving

♦ An International Driver's License is recommended but not required.

♦ Drivers and front-seat passengers must wear seat belts outside city limits.

♦ Children must ride in the rear seat.

♦ The speed limit on a highway is 120 kph, in cities is 60 kph, and on all other roads is 90 kph, unless posted otherwise.

♦ Blowing your horn is not permitted in cities.

♦ Parking is limited in the central areas of some Spanish cities. Kiosks and tobacconist shops sell tickets that show how long you've paid to park. Place the ticket inside the windshield.

◆ Red and white stripes on the curb signify a no-parking zone.

◆ On highways, red and yellow striped poles indicate emergency phones, which have instructions in English. You press one button for an ambulance and another for a tow truck. A light goes on when the message is received.

◆ If you're stopped for a traffic violation, be polite. Don't argue or get excited, and *don't* try to bribe the police officer.

◆ Get a personal bail bond when you get your green card for insurance or you rent a car. If you have an accident and don't have one, you might end up in prison for a long time.

◆ Spanish roads are classified by letter: *A* is for motorways; *H* is for main roads; and *C* is for small roads.

◆ If you're going to drive in rural areas, bring cash to pay for gas. Few gas stations accept credit cards.

◆ Never leave anything in your car—even maps or books. Burglaries are frequent, so lock everything in your trunk.

◆ Spain's drunk-driving laws are less strict than those elsewhere in Europe; nevertheless, if you drink and are involved in an accident, you'll be heavily fined.

◆ If you're involved in an accident in which Spanish people are injured —whether or not you've been drinking—you'll face heavy fines or imprisonment.

Legal Matters & Safety

◆ Spain has no legal drinking age and no restrictions on when you can buy drinks in bars or restaurants.

◆ Thieves frequent restaurants. Working alone or in pairs, they often spill food on tourists and then pick their pockets or purses while helping them clean up.

◆ Women going out alone after dark anywhere in Spain should take a taxi or a bus. The subway stations in Madrid and Barcelona have long, dark corridors that might be dangerous.

Key Phrases

English	Spanish	Pronunciation
Good day	Buenos días	BWAY-nos DEE-ahs
Good afternoon	Buenas tardes	BWAY-nahs TAR-des
Good evening	Buenas noches	BWAY-nahs NO-chase
Please	Por favor	POR fah-vor
Thank you	Gracias	GRAH-see-ahs
You're welcome	De nada	day NAH-dah
Yes	Sí	see
No	No	no
Mr., Sir	Señor	sen-YOHR
Mrs., Madam	Señora	sen-YOHR-ah
Miss	Señorita	sen-yohr-EE-tah
Excuse me	Perdóneme	pehr-DOH-nay-may
Good-bye	Adiós	ah-DYOS
I don't understand.	No entiendo.	no en-TYEN-doe
I don't speak Spanish.	No hablo español.	no AH-blo es-pahn-YOL
Is there anyone here who speaks English?	¿Hay alguien aquí que hable inglés?	aye AHL-gyehn ah-kee kay AH-blay een-GLAYS

Sweden

Sweden might be best known for giving the world two Bergmans: the beautiful Ingrid; and Ingmar, the brilliant director whose films have explored the darker side of humanity, always a Swedish concern.

Swedish people tend to be reserved but friendly. Oddly, you might find that they're more comfortable talking to foreigners than to each other. Swedes are at their most charming—warmer and more open—during holiday celebrations. They're devoted to their strong holiday traditions, some of which go back centuries. They're also at their best when involved in sports. A friend who lived in Sweden for 14 years said, "When you see Swedes swimming or skiing or lifting their faces to the sun, they have an almost pagan joy in nature."

Greetings

◆ Always shake hands when greeting or leaving people—especially older people.

◆ Good friends kiss on one cheek when they meet.

◆ Use first names only with friends.

◆ Upper-class Swedes traditionally refer to each other in the third person rather than as "you" (they'd say "How is Mrs. Olson today?" instead of "How are you?"). This custom is changing, but if you want to be very correct when talking to an older person, do the same.

◆ If you enter a roomful of people and there is no one to introduce you, shake each person's hand and give your name.

◆ When you meet people who have had you to their house for dinner, say "tahk fur seest" ("Thanks for last time") right away.

Conversation

◆ If Swedes seem abrupt or overly serious when you first meet them, don't be put off. Despite their fluency in English, they might find subtleties of expression difficult.

◆ When you speak to people, look them directly in the eye.

◆ Good topics of conversation: Sweden's economy and high standard of living; sports, especially soccer and hockey; the city you're staying in; how Swedes spend their summers (or whatever season you are there); or opera, ballet, theater, and concerts.

◆ Swedes are proud of their culture and history. They are extremely pleased—not to mention astonished—if foreigners know something about the country's background.

◆ Younger people like to discuss music—especially reggae, blues, and jazz.

◆ Topics to avoid: personal matters such as family problems, income, or how much something costs.

◆ Don't compliment someone you've just

met or you'll be regarded as insincere.

◆ Use the word "like" instead of "love," as the Swedes most often do when showing enthusiasm for something (e.g., "I liked the movie last night"). Swedes consider Americans' use of "love" excessive.

Money

◆ The unit of currency is the krona (plural kronor, abbreviated SEK), made up of 100 öre.

◆ Coins come in denominations of 10 and 50 öre and 1 and 5 kronor.

◆ Notes come in denominations of 10, 50, 100, 500, 1,000, and 10,000 kronor.

Telephones

◆ You can find public telephones on the main streets of cities and towns.

◆ Public telephones are of different types: some simply cut you off when the money runs out; others let you deposit more money when a tone sounds; still others have a display screen that tells you how much more to deposit.

◆ A local call costs 2 kronor.

◆ Sweden has no telephone cards; you must use coins.

◆ You can use a credit card for international calls from hotels, airports, and some museums. The surcharge will appear on your credit card bill. You can also make interna-

tional calls from telephone offices, which you'll find in main train stations.

◆ Most operators speak English, but if you reach one who does not, ask for the language assistance operator.

◆ When you use a telephone directory, note that the letters Å, Ä, and Ö are at the end of the alphabet.

◆ Swedes answer the phone by giving their phone number or their last name.

◆ The Emergency Number to summon police, the fire department, or an ambulance is **90000.**

In Public

◆ When men pass an acquaintance on the street, they should lift their hats.

◆ If you see someone you know at a distance, nod your head or raise your hand.

◆ Don't embrace, touch, or put your arm around anyone except a close friend.

◆ Wait patiently in lines for trains, buses, and theaters.

◆ Women can talk to men in bars of large hotels without danger of hassles. Most Swedish women like to be courted—often a lengthy process—not picked up. Going to a discotheque, however, is regarded as asking to be picked up.

◆ Public toilets are located in cafes, restaurants, and hotels. Men's rooms are marked *Män*, women's rooms are marked *Krinnor*.

Dress

◆ Swedes are fashion-conscious and wear up-to-date, elegant clothes even for casual occasions. The only setting in  which they dress informally is at summer homes in the country.

◆ For business, men should wear suits and ties, and women should wear dresses or suits.

◆ Dress up for dinner unless you're invited to a picnic.

◆ If an invitation specifies formal wear, men should wear tuxedos; women, cocktail dresses.

◆ To the theater, opera, and ballet, men should wear a jacket and tie, and women should wear a dress or skirt.

◆ For theater openings, dress has become less formal. Men should wear a dark suit, and women should wear a dress or dressy pants.

◆ Don't wear shorts in the city.

◆ The traditional Swedish costumes so popular on travel posters are worn only in Lapland and at festival times.

◆ At the beach, many women go topless and small children go nude. People change into their bathing suits on the beach, sometimes using a towel as a shield.

Meals

Hours and Foods
Breakfast
(frukost): 7:00 or 8:00 A.M., except in country summer  homes, where breakfast is served after everyone is up (about 10:00 A.M.). You'll be served coffee or tea, cheese, rolls, and honey and assorted jams.

Lunch *(lunch):* Noon to 1:00 P.M. This meal might consist of either a hot dish or open-faced sandwiches (pieces of bread with artistically arranged toppings). Mineral water, fruit juice, wine, or beer accompany the meal. Coffee follows dessert.

Dinner *(middag):* 6:00 P.M., or 7:00 P.M. for a formal dinner, which has four courses. The first course might be shrimp, smoked salmon, caviar canapés, marinated herring, or fruit soup. The second course is meat or fish, potatoes (usually boiled), and a vegetable. A salad course follows, then a dessert such as ice cream and fruit, or crepes and fruit.

◆ With hors d'oeuvres people drink *aquavit* (a liquor distilled from grain or potatoes and often flavored with caraway seed). *Aquavit* is served very cold, in small glasses. All Swedish women sip *aquavit.* Most men do also, though some drink it in one gulp, which foreign men shouldn't do because of its potency: three glasses will get you drunk. Most people switch to wine or beer when the meal begins.

◆ Wine accompanies a formal dinner; beer might be served at a less formal meal. After dessert, coffee might be served with brandy or cognac; it is never served with the meal and is usually taken in the living room.

Breaks: Swedes break for coffee around 10:00 or 11:00 A.M. and around 3:00 P.M.

Table Manners

◆ Swedes are more likely than most Europeans to invite new acquaintances to dinner, but the Swedes will be very formal.

◆ If you're invited to dinner, be *precisely* on time.

◆ Predinner cocktail hours are rare. If offered, before-dinner drinks are usually vodka, scotch, vermouth, or wine.

◆ If you don't care for alcohol, you won't be pressed to drink or have your preference questioned.

◆ At a formal dinner party, don't drink until the host makes a short speech and offers the first toast. During the hors d'oeuvres, he'll toast with *aquavit*.

◆ Husbands and wives don't sit together at dinner. The male guest of honor sits to the left of the hostess, the female to the right of the host. A man traditionally caters to the woman seated to his right for the evening— serving her wine, making sure she has enought food, and engaging her in conversation.

◆ Swedes think Americans eat rudely, by shoveling food into their mouths. Cut only as much food as you're about to put in your mouth.

◆ At a formal meal, use a butter knife for butter, not your dinner knife.

◆ To be polite, have at least a taste of everything.

◆ The *smörgasbord* is a unique Swedish meal that many Americans regard as an all-you-can-eat buffet, a haven for gluttons. To Swedes, however, it's an opportunity to sample many different types of breads, cheeses, and meats.

◆ At a *smörgasbord,* begin by sampling herring, eaten with boiled potatoes and sour cream. Then get a clean plate and try the other fish dishes. Get another clean plate and sample the cold meats and salads, then another clean plate for the hot meat dishes.

◆ During the meal, people toast with wine. To toast someone, look into the person's eyes and say "skole." Bow your head slightly and take a sip. Before you put the glass back on the table, meet the person's eyes again and nod. This is also the way to toast with *aquavit* with the hors d'oeuvres course.

◆ If there are fewer than six people at the table, each guest should toast the hostess by saying "Thank you" (see Key Phrases). If there are more people, don't toast her; she must drink when toasted and would have to drink a great deal.

◆ When the meal ends, the male guest of honor thanks the hostess on behalf of all the guests, beginning by tapping his knife on a glass.

◆ At a dinner party, be prepared to sing a song—either a drinking song or a song befitting your country, such as your national anthem.

◆ After dinner, leave no later than 11:00 P.M. in the winter and 1:00 A.M. in the summer.

◆ On the day after a dinner party, call and thank your hosts for the meal, send flowers and a note, or do both.

Eating Out

◆ Sweden has a variety of eating places:

• *Cafes* serve sandwiches, hot and cold lunches, and wine.

• *Cafeterias* are self-service, but the food is cooked to order.

• *Källare* are medium-priced restaurants.

- *Konditori* are good bets for sandwiches, pastries, and coffee.

◆ Liquor is expensive in restaurants, so many people have a drink at home before going out to eat.

◆ Liquor is not served before noon in bars and restaurants.

◆ If you want ice water, ask for it; it's not usually served.

◆ To get a waiter's attention, say "Sir" or "Miss" quietly in English.

◆ Excessive noise or drunkenness can get you thrown out of a restaurant.

Specialties

◆ Sweden is famous for its open-faced sandwiches and *smörgasbords*. Other specialties are *gravlax* (salmon cured with dill); *Janssons frestelse* (a casserole of sprouts, potatoes, cream, and onions); *lütfisk* (dried codfish treated with lye, soaked, boiled, and served at Christmas with cream sauce, boiled potatoes, and peas); reindeer meat; and cloudberries.

◆ In late August, people in northern Sweden enjoy *surströmming* (sour, specially treated herring eaten with thin bread, potatoes, and strong cheese).

◆ In winter, the traditional Thursday meal is *ärter med fläsk* (pea soup and a platter of small, thin pancakes served with lingonberry jam).

◆ A traditional dessert is *ostkaka* (a cake made with cheese, cream, and cinnamon, served with lingonberries).

◆ At Christmastime, Swedes serve *glögg*, an alcoholic drink similar to apple cider, with raisins or walnuts.

Hotels

◆ Accommodations are inspected and rated by the Swedish government.

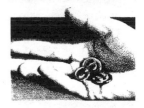

◆ Hotel room rates are lower between mid-June and August and, in many city hotels, on weekends all year.

◆ Stockholm, Goteborg, and Malmö offer special city packages that include accommodations and breakfast.

Tipping

◆ *Restaurants:* A service charge of 13 percent is included in the bill, but waiters expect an additional 10–15 percent.

◆ *Porters:* Give hotel doormen and porters 3 kronor.

◆ *Hotel maids:* Usually don't tip, but for exceptional service, give 6 kronor per day.

◆ *Taxis:* Tip drivers 10–15 percent.

Private Homes

◆ In cities, people don't drop in on one another unless they are close friends. However, when they are at summer homes in the country, people are more informal and do drop in.

♦ Be punctual when invited to a home.

♦ Don't be surprised to be invited for a mid-week party. People entertain as much during the week as on weekends.

♦ If you're invited to a Swedish home for the evening, don't assume that dinner's included unless that's specified.

♦ If you are staying with a family, offer to help with household chores such as setting the table and washing the dishes.

Gifts: If you're invited to a meal, bring unwrapped flowers or a bottle of wine or liquor (which is greatly appreciated because it's so expensive). You may also bring candy, but no other kind of food.

♦ If you stay with a family, bring books, records, or cassettes from the U.S. If you visit a family you know well, bring blue jeans. Don't bring crystal or other products for which Sweden is famous.

Business

Hours

Businesses and government offices: 8:00 A.M. to 4:00 P.M., or 9:00 A.M. to 5:00 P.M., Monday through Friday.

Banks: 9:00 A.M. to 4:00 P.M., Monday through Friday, and 9:00 A.M. to noon on Saturday. Electronic banking is available 24 hours a day.

Stores: 9:30 A.M. to 5:00 or 6:00 P.M., Monday through Saturday. In cities, each neighborhood has one night when shops stay open until 8:00 P.M. In Stockholm, some large supermarkets and stores are open evenings and Sundays.

Business Practices

♦ Like other Scandinavians, Swedes are open to international influences. They are knowledgeable about international politics and business.

♦ You don't need letters of introduction to do business with Swedish firms. However, if you wish to make business contacts before you go, get in touch with the Swedish Trade Council in Chicago.

♦ If you're proposing a major deal, you'll need to make several trips to Sweden.

♦ In Sweden, business has become increasingly fast-paced since the mid-1980s—partly because Swedes find bargaining embarrassing, so they move negotiations along quickly.

♦ Don't plan business trips to Sweden in June, July, or August or from February 20th through March 1, popular vacation times. Swedes take at least five weeks of vacation a year.

♦ Written materials in English—including business cards—are fine.

♦ Staying at the best hotels won't enhance your image. A good middle-range hotel is fine.

♦ Women will have no problem doing business in Sweden. There are many women in high business positions.

♦ Fax machines are widely available in businesses, hotels, and post offices.

Meetings and negotiations: Make appointments from abroad two or three weeks in advance.

♦ People often work later in the winter. In the summer, they rarely stay past 2:00 or 3:00 P.M. on Friday afternoons.

♦ Schedule an appointment for whenever

people will see you—there are no preferred times.

◆ Be punctual. So will the Swedes.

◆ Prepare for your initial meeting by reading about Sweden's culture and accomplishments. It's helpful to know such details as the king's name.

◆ Give business cards to everyone with whom you're negotiating.

◆ To impress the Swedes, use visuals in your presentation. Like other Scandinavians, Swedes like gadgets of all sorts.

◆ When you speak to a group, keep gestures to a minimum. Don't talk with your hands.

◆ Don't come across as boasting or exaggerating.

◆ Have all the details of your project at your fingertips.

◆ Distribute copies of your materials only to decision makers.

◆ Avoid physical contact, such as patting someone on the back.

◆ Decisions are made at a lower level than they are in the U.S.

◆ Once you have an agreement, a contract will follow. Swedes are good about sticking to agreements.

Entertainment: Swedes usually take about an hour for lunch and eat at their desks. Only top executives dine out regularly.

◆ If you would like to entertain businesspeople, ask the staff at your hotel to suggest a restaurant, ask your guests to suggest one, or suggest some restaurants to your guests and ask them to choose.

◆ If you invite Swedes to lunch or dinner, include only the people with whom you're negotiating.

◆ If a lunch or dinner will be entirely social, invite spouses—both foreign and Swedish. Don't include spouses if there will be business discussions.

◆ A businesswoman will have no problem treating Swedish businessmen to a meal.

Gifts: Bring American liquor or wine. Other popular gifts are traditional Native American crafts and contemporary American crafts, such as pottery and wood carvings; or coffee table books on the American West and on Native American cultures.

◆ If you're going to meet someone's wife, bring guest hand towels with unusual designs or pancake mix and maple syrup.

Holidays & Celebrations

Holidays:
New Year's Day (January 1); Epiphany (January 6); Good Friday; Holy Saturday; Easter Monday;
Labor Day (May 1); Ascension Day (five weeks after Easter); Whit Monday (eight weeks after Easter Monday); Midsummer weekend (the weekend preceding June 24); and Christmas Eve and Day (December 24 and 25).

◆ At Midsummer (June 21), the usually reserved Swedes celebrate exuberantly. People build maypoles in their yards, and children make wreaths of flowers. The night is filled with dancing, singing, and feasting on shrimp, beer, and wine.

◆ Whit Sunday (or Pentecost) is traditionally a day for picnics. It's also a popular day for Lutheran confirmations and weddings.

◆ During the summer, life is more hectic

than it is in the winter, and there are constant festivals and celebrations.

Transportation

Public Transport

Mass transit: On buses and subways, you pay according

to the number of zones you plan to travel through.

◆ The Stockholm subway can be unpleasant at night. Because of the harsh drunk-driving laws, many drinkers take the subway.

◆ In Stockholm, Goteborg, and Malmö you can get tourist-discount tickets—valid for one, two, three, or four days—that include free travel on public transportation, sightseeing tours at a discounted rate, and reduced admission fees to museums. Buy them at major bus or subway stations.

◆ Trains are comfortable, reliable, and clean, with good express services linking major cities. Most trains have first and second class as well as dining cars or self-service buffet cars. Overnight trains have sleeping cars and couchettes.

◆ Be *sure* to observe the "No Smoking" signs on trains.

Taxis: Hail taxis on the street or call for them. Taxi stations are found throughout cities, so taxis are readily available.

Driving

◆ Seat belts are mandatory for all occupants of a car.

◆ The speed limit in built-up areas is 50 kph, outside built-up areas is 70–90 kph, and on motorways is 90 kph.

◆ *Don't* drink and drive. The penalties are severe, and even foreigners can have their licenses revoked for a year. Some groups have a designated driver who abstains for the evening.

◆ Always drive with your headlights on, day and night.

◆ Incorrectly parked cars will be towed.

Legal Matters & Safety

◆ Women can walk alone at night or eat alone in a restaurant without being bothered.

Swedish men won't approach women without encouragement—except if women go alone to restaurants that feature dancing.

◆ Swedish police officers are polite and helpful. In Stockholm, most of them speak English.

◆ The drinking age is 18 in restaurants and for purchasing beer in shops. To buy other alcoholic beverages, you must be 20.

Key Phrases

English	Swedish	Pronunciation
Good morning	God morgon	gude MOHR-gohn
Good afternoon	God middag	gude MID-dahg
Good evening	God afton	gude AHF-tohn
Please	Var vänlig	vahr VEHN-leeg
Thank you	Tack så mycket	tahk soh MICK-et
You're welcome	Varsågod	VAR-so-gude
Yes	Ja	yah
No	Nej	nay
Mr., Sir	Herr	hair
Mrs., Madam	Fru	frew
Miss	Fröken	FROEHK-ken
Excuse me	Ursåkta mig	OO-er-SECT-uh may
Good-bye	Adjö	ahd-YEU
I don't understand.	Jag förstår inte.	YAH for-STOHR IN-teh
I don't speak Swedish.	Jag talar inte Svenska.	YAH tah-lahr EEN-teh SVEHN-skah
Does anyone here speak English?	Finns det någon som talar engelska här?	Finns date NO-gon som TAH-lahr EN-gels-skah HARE

Switzerland

A trip to Switzerland is a real three-for-the-price-of-one excursion: visiting its three different regions is like visiting France, Germany, and Italy—all in one country.

Switzerland is justly famous for its beautiful mountain scenery. It should be equally famous for its cleanliness: even in the cheapest hotels, everything is spotless.

The Swiss are also honest. One traveler left a cafe where she'd eaten lunch and realized about half an hour later that she'd left her brand new $300 camera on a chair there. She went back, and when he saw her worried face, a young man picked the camera out of the drawer and said, "Your camera, madame?"

Greetings

♦ Men should always rise when they're introduced. Women should rise only when introduced to an older person or a guest of honor. Men, women, and children should all shake hands when they're introduced.

♦ When you meet an aquaintance on the street, stop and shake hands. It's also customary to shake hands when you leave someone.

♦ At a party, wait for the hosts to introduce you. If the party is large or your hosts are busy, introduce yourself.

♦ In the French part of the country, women friends embrace and kiss twice on each cheek. In the Italian region, women friends embrace but don't kiss.

♦ In both the French and Italian regions, male friends who haven't seen each other for a long time sometimes embrace.

♦ People in the German region tend to be more reserved. Only women embrace or kiss, and then only if they've been apart for a long time.

♦ Do not use first names until your Swiss acquaintance does.

Conversation

♦ English is widely understood and spoken in all three regions of Switzerland.

♦ Swiss people aren't very open with people they've just met. They take a long time to establish friendships, but when they do, they're loyal for life.

♦ Good topics of conversation: international politics; participatory sports such as sailing, hiking, and skiing; spectator sports such as soccer and bicycle racing; what you like about Switzerland; or your travels in general.

♦ Topics to avoid: someone's age, family, personal life, or profession.

♦ Don't discuss money or salaries. It's considered rude.

♦ Serious political discussions are common even at parties. The Swiss are well informed about world affairs and express their opinions strongly, and some might sound anti-

American. Don't take such discussions personally; the Swiss find them an enjoyable pastime.

♦ Military service is a touchy topic. People are passionate in their views, and discussions about it can lead to major arguments.

Money

♦ The unit of currency is the franc (abbreviated SFr), made up of 100 centimes (called rappen in the German region).

♦ Coins come in denominations of 5, 10, 20, and 50 centimes and 1, 2, and 5 francs.

♦ Notes come in denominations of 10, 20, 50, 100, 500, and 1,000 francs.

Telephones

♦ You can find public telephones on main streets in towns and cities.

♦ To make a local call from a public phone, deposit 40 centimes and dial. You'll get four to five minutes, after which you'll hear a tone; deposit more money if you wish to continue. If you don't have a 40-centime coin, deposit a larger amount and you'll get change when you hang up.

♦ If you plan to use public telephones frequently, buy a telephone card, sold at kiosks and post offices.

♦ To call long distance, either call from a post office, airport, or railroad station and pay when you finish, or call from a public phone and deposit the money as you talk.

♦ People answer the phone in the French region by saying "Ah-LO"; in the Italian section by saying "PRON-toe"; and in the German section by stating their name.

♦ The Emergency Number to summon police, the fire department, or an ambulance is **117.**

In Public

♦ If you see an acquaintance on the other side of the street, simply call out a greeting without stopping to chat.

♦ Sit up straight in public. The Swiss (particularly older Swiss) consider sloppy posture rude.

♦ To get to your seat at a play or a concert, face the people in your row, with your back toward the stage.

♦ Be on time for all social and business engagements. The Swiss are extremely punctual and find tardiness offensive.

♦ Help elderly people getting on or off a bus or carrying heavy bags. Stand and give your seats to the elderly as well.

♦ Some pushing and shoving occurs in lines for buses, ski lifts, and cinemas. To get a place, you might have to do likewise.

♦ Don't toss litter on the street, or you might be severely rebuked.

♦ When you enter a shop, say "Hello" to the clerk.

♦ Don't try to bargain in any Swiss store or market.

♦ Public toilets are found in all train stations

(even in little villages), cafes, and restaurants. Generally, *W.C.* is the symbol for toilets.

Dress

♦ Shorts and jeans are fine for casual wear in rural areas. Don't wear shorts in cities.

♦ For business, men should wear suits and ties, and women should wear dresses, suits, or elegant pants.

♦ For dinner in someone's home or at an elegant restaurant, men should wear trousers, shirts, and sweaters, and women should wear skirts or elegant pants.

♦ For meals at regular restaurants, men should wear pants and shirts, and women should wear pants or skirts.

♦ To theaters, men should wear a jacket and tie, and women should wear a dress or skirt.

♦ Wear formal clothes—tuxedos for men and long dresses for women—to balls, theater openings, formal weddings, or any occasion for which an invitation specifies formal wear.

Meals

Hours and Foods

♦ Names for meals and the types of foods served at them vary by region; see the chapters on France, Italy, and Germany for more detail.

Breakfast: 7:00 A.M. Families have a sit-down meal of cheese, bread, butter, jam, and coffee with milk.

Lunch: Noon. Usually the main meal of the day, lunch begins with soup, followed by a main course of meat, vegetables, potatoes, and green salad. Typical beverages are mineral water and wine or beer. Fruit is the usual dessert except on Sunday, when cake, pastries, or pudding are served.

Dinner: 6:00 to 7:00 P.M. This is a light meal consisting of soup followed by either salad and eggs or bread with cheese, ham, or salami.

♦ At a dinner party, the meal usually starts about 7:00 or 8:00 P.M. with before-dinner drinks such as wine, beer, Campari, Cynar (made from artichokes), *blanc-cassis* (white wine with a blackberry liqueur), or *Pastis* (anise liqueur). The meal might begin with soup followed by the main course: meat (a pot roast, a pork roast, roasted or stewed venison, or veal), vegetables, potatoes or rice, and a green salad. The meal ends with fruit and cheese, and/or cake or pudding. Espresso follows, along with after-dinner drinks such as *grappa* (brandy made from grape skins), cognac, *Kirsch* (cherry liqueur), and *Pflumwasser* (plum brandy).

Breaks: The Swiss break for coffee around 10:00 A.M.

Table Manners

♦ Be punctual when you're invited to dinner—it's important.

♦ If you're invited to a dinner party, consider it a compliment. The Swiss are very private and seldom open their homes to strangers.

♦ If you're invited to cocktails or dinner, expect the party to be small. Most houses and apartments have limited space.

♦ If you're the guest of honor, sit in the middle along the side (not at the head) of the table.

♦ Don't drink wine until the host proposes a toast. Then look the host in the eye and say "To your health" in the language of the region (French: "SAHN-tay"; Italian: "sah-LOO-tay"; German: "prosht"). Clink glasses with everyone at the table.

♦ Help yourself to food passed around the table on platters. If you know you won't like something, take a small portion anyway, to be polite.

♦ If you want seconds, cross your fork over your knife, with the fork pointed diagonally to the left and the knife to the right. Your hosts will offer seconds and feel complimented if you accept.

♦ If your hosts offer seconds and you don't want any, decline politely. You won't be pressed to eat more, as you would be in some countries.

♦ Break bread and rolls with your hands instead of cutting them with a knife.

♦ If your hosts serve fondue, you'll see a chafing dish holding the fondue in the center of the table. Take the long fork beside your plate and spear a cube of bread. Dip the bread into the fondue and twist the fork to break the cheese strand as you pull the bread out. Tradition says that if the bread slips off the fork and into the fondue, you must buy a bottle of white wine for the group.

♦ To show that you've finished eating, place the knife and fork horizontally across the plate, both pointing to the right.

♦ Don't smoke between courses.

♦ Don't discuss diets or weight control when dining in a Swiss home.

♦ After a dinner party, leave about mid-night. If there are other guests, take your cue from them but don't stay much later than that.

Eating Out

♦ Names for the following types of eating places are given in French, then Italian, then German.

• A *bar* (the same in all three languages) has tables and a counter and offers sandwiches and alcoholic drinks.

• A *café/caffè/Café* serves sandwiches, croissants, coffee, soft drinks, and one daily special. Typical specials might be bratwurst and potato salad, or stew with potatoes.

• A *pâtisserie/pasticceria/Bäckerei* serves coffee, tea, soft drinks, and pastries, but no alcoholic beverages.

• A *restaurant/locanda/Wursthaus* is a more rustic, usually small restaurant. Most offer hearty meals of typical Swiss dishes and drinks, at very reasonable prices.

♦ In the cities, most restaurants are German, French, or Italian. Chinese restaurants, considered exotic, are also expensive.

♦ Check available dishes and prices by looking for menus posted outside. All but the fanciest restaurants display menus.

♦ In all but the finest restaurants, seat yourself. When in doubt, ask a waiter whether you should choose your own table.

♦ If a small restaurant or cafe has no free tables, feel free to join strangers at a table with available space. Strangers dining at the same table seldom strike up a conversation, so if you feel uncomfortable eating in silence, bring a book or magazine with you.

♦ Before-dinner cocktails are rarely ordered.

Specialties

◆ Specialties throughout Switzerland are *fondue* (cheese, usually Emmentaler or Gruyère, melted with white wine, garlic, flour, and *Kirsch,* cherry liqueur) and *raclette* (cheese grilled until it melts and gets crispy, served with cocktail onions and small boiled potatoes).

◆ All cafes and luncheon counters offer *Birchermuesli,* a breakfast dish made from oat flakes, yogurt, berries, and fruits of the season. It's considered highly nutritious.

◆ In French Switzerland, try *croûtes aux morilles* (mushrooms served on toast); *choucroute garnie* (sauerkraut with ham, sausages, and boiled potatoes); and *friture de perchettes* (fried fillets of lake perch).

◆ In Italian Switzerland, try *busecca* (vegetable and tripe soup); *lumache* (snails served with walnut paste); *zampone* and *coppa* (sausages); *risotto con funghi* (rice with mushrooms); and *ravioli al pomodoro* (ravioli with tomato sauce).

◆ In German Switzerland, try *Leberspiessli* (calves' liver and bacon); *Geschnetzeltes* (minced veal in a thick cream sauce); *Bündnerfleisch* (paper-thin slices of dried beef, served with grated pepper as an appetizer); *Bernerplatte* (sauerkraut with smoked pork chops or bacon, or with sausages and boiled potatoes); and *Rösti* (grated parboiled potatoes fried in butter).

◆ Another German Swiss specialty is *St. Galler Bratwurst,* a white veal sausage. Considered the ultimate in sausage-making art, these sausages are never eaten with mustard or other condiments, though some restaurants saute them with onions. They're also sold at outdoor grills and stands on the street. The standard accompaniment is a crisp brown roll, or *Büürli.*

Hotels

◆ When you check in, show your passport but don't leave it at the desk.

◆ When you go out, keep your room key with you instead of leaving it at the front desk.

◆ In better hotels, your room might come equipped with a refrigerator stocked with champagne, white wine, and soft drinks. Check off each drink you use on the slip attached to the refrigerator. The maid will check the list when you leave, and you'll pay when you check out.

Tipping

◆ *Restaurants:* The bill includes a service charge. Round up to the nearest franc and leave extra for exceptional service.

◆ *Porters:* Give 1 franc per bag.

◆ *Hotel maids:* Usually don't tip, but for exceptional service, give 1 franc per day.

◆ *Taxis:* Taxi fares include a service charge. Round up to the nearest franc.

◆ *Gas station attendants:* Tip 2 francs.

Private Homes

◆ Before you visit, call to ask whether it's convenient. Never drop in.

◆ No special times

or days are set aside for visiting people.

◆ If you're a houseguest, be exceptionally neat and tidy. Make your bed when you get up and don't leave clothes on the bed or on chairs.

◆ Offer to help with washing the dishes, setting the table, and cooking. Your hosts will probably refuse.

◆ If you're staying with a family, replace your napkin after each meal in the napkin ring provided. Napkins are reused for several meals.

◆ Many Swiss bathrooms have energy-saving water heaters that heat up overnight. Ask your hosts when would be a good time to shower.

Gifts: If you're invited to dinner, bring chocolates or flowers (but not red roses or carnations, which signify romantic love, or chrysanthemums or white asters, reserved for funerals). You don't need a huge bouquet; three flowers or a flowering branch are sufficient. If you give candy, make sure it's the best quality. If you have no time to shop in advance, send flowers the next day.

◆ If you're a houseguest, bring gifts from the U.S., such as bath towels, records, whiskey, or handmade crafts from your home region. Give chocolates to the children in the family. Don't give huge gifts; they're considered vulgar and ostentatious.

Business

Hours

Businesses and government offices: 8:00 A.M. to noon and 2:00 P.M. to 6:00 P.M., Monday through Friday.

Banks: 8:30 A.M. to 4:30 P.M., Monday through Friday.

Stores: 8:00 A.M. to 12:15 P.M. and 1:30 to 6:30 P.M., Monday through Friday, and 9:00 A.M. to 4:00 P.M. on Saturday. In larger cities, some shops don't close for lunch.

Business Practices

◆ Get information on business contacts from the Swiss Office for Trade and Promotion in Zurich, which can provide publications covering thousands of manufacturers and suppliers of services. The agency also furnishes information on joint ventures, Swiss manufacturing and service organizations, and fairs and exhibitions.

◆ When you write to a Swiss company, address the letter to an individual, but address the envelope to the company. An envelope addressed to an individual won't be opened if the person is away, sometimes causing a long delay.

◆ Don't plan business trips to Switzerland during July and August, the traditional vacation months.

◆ Women who are knowledgeable in their field can do business successfully in Switzerland. Swiss women generally are not found in high-level business positions.

◆ Language is usually no barrier in business dealings, since English is the language of business in Switzerland.

◆ Bring business cards in English. The Swiss respect age, so if your company is old, add the year of its founding to your card. The Swiss also respect titles and degrees, so consider putting your academic degrees and corporate title on your card. Titles in English are more impressive.

◆ Fax machines are available everywhere.

Meetings and negotiations: Suggest appointments in the morning, anytime after 9:00 A.M.

♦ From abroad, telephone, telex, or fax requests for appointments at least a week ahead. If you make the contact by letter, allow at least two to two-and-a-half weeks. If you're already in Europe, call for an appointment three or four days in advance.

♦ Be *sure* to be on time. In some parts of Switzerland, you'll be "docked" any amount of time you're late: if you're 20 minutes late for an appointment scheduled for an hour, you'll forfeit an additional 20 minutes— leaving you with only a 20-minute meeting!

♦ Hand your business card to the receptionist, even if you've arranged the appointment in advance. Also give a card to the person with whom you're meeting.

♦ In the German region, people will come right to the point, without any initial small talk. In the French and Italian regions, people will probably take a slower, more casual approach, including some opening small talk about your trip, where you are staying, and similar subjects. However, people won't be interested in cultivating personal relationships until negotiations are completed.

♦ Swiss businesspeople are conservative and proceed toward decisions very deliberately. Be patient and avoid high-pressure sales approaches.

♦ You needn't have the materials for your presentation translated.

♦ Keep your presentation brief, to the point, and error-free. Errors create a bad impression.

♦ When you prepare for your meeting, study your competition, because you'll be quizzed on the subject.

♦ When you make your calculations, find out whether duties will be levied on your product through the European Community.

♦ Once a decision has been made, the Swiss are extremely reliable.

Entertainment: Business lunches are more common than business dinners. Dinners among businesspeople are social occasions.

♦ If you're invited to lunch, you might be taken to the company cafeteria.

♦ You're more likely to be entertained in a restaurant than invited to someone's home.

♦ If you invite people to lunch, include only those with whom you are negotiating. You might also want to include the boss's secretary, who'll be pleased—and might give you some inside tips.

♦ When you entertain, let your Swiss guests choose the restaurant.

♦ Include spouses in dinner invitations.

Gifts: Give a good bottle of whiskey or cognac; food from your area, such as lobsters, maple syrup, or Florida oranges; Maglites (flashlights that come in different sizes and last for years); or photographic books from your region.

Holidays & Celebrations

Holidays:
New Year's Day (January 1); January 2; Good Friday; Easter Monday; Ascension Day (five  weeks after Easter); Whit Monday (eight weeks after Easter); Independence Day (August 1), Christmas (December 25); and December 26.

♦ On Independence Day, you'll see fires everywhere. People bring kindling to the highest place in their neighborhoods and, at night, light huge bonfires. Children carry candle lanterns. People have picnics that usually include cooking sausages. If you're staying with someone, offer to help build the fire or do the cooking.

Transportation

Public Transport

Mass transit: Bus and street-car stops have automatic

ticket-dispensing machines with instructions in English. They take exact change.

♦ Keep the ticket to present to any inspector who boards the vehicle.

♦ Switzerland has no subways.

♦ Trains are frequent and precisely on time. A traveler with only two minutes to make a connection can rest assured the connection will be made, perhaps with time to spare.

♦ On intercity trains, the upcoming station is announced over the public-address system in French, German, and Italian.

♦ Trains have dining cars that serve excellent meals and between-meal beverages.

♦ If you're staying in Switzerland for an extended period, buy a *Halbtax Abonnement* from the SBB (railroad), which lets you buy all SBB tickets for half price. The Swiss railway also runs the lake steamers and the yellow postal buses that go over mountain passes and up to the highest villages, so your half-price pass can take you just about anywhere.

♦ If you have large suitcases, ship them by

railway for a modest fee. They'll be waiting for you at your destination.

♦ To rent a bicycle, go to any SBB station. When you finish with the bicycle, return it to any station.

♦ If you're flying Swissair, check your luggage at any SBB station.

Taxis: Either phone for a taxi or look for a taxi stand near railroad stations, bus stations, airports, and major places of business.

Driving

♦ Seat belts are mandatory for all occupants of a car.

♦ Children under 12 must sit in the back seat.

♦ The speed limit in built-up areas is 50 kph, outside built-up areas is 80 kph, and on motorways is 120 kph.

♦ Always obey the rules of the road, even when you see Swiss drivers traveling very fast. If you switch lanes quickly without signaling, or violate other rules, nearby drivers might get upset.

♦ Right-of-way rules are as follows:

• At an intersection, vehicles coming from the right have the right of way.

• When main highways and secondary roads intersect, traffic on the main highway has priority.

• On mountain roads, ascending vehicles have priority over those descending.

• Pedestrians have the right of way at street crossings.

• Streetcars have the right of way everywhere.

♦ Winter driving in the mountains requires caution. Always check weather conditions in advance and make sure your car is adequately equipped.

◆ While driving through tunnels, make sure your low beams are on.

◆ Respect Swiss police officers, and don't argue with them if you're stopped for a traffic violation. Most violations require paying an on-the-spot fine, usually about 100 francs.

◆ *Don't* drink and drive. If you're caught, you could go to prison.

Legal Matters & Safety

◆ Switzerland has no minimum drinking age; teenagers can have wine and beer anywhere. Young people are so accustomed to having both beverages with meals  at home that they usually prefer soft drinks when they go out.

◆ Switzerland isn't quite as safe as it used to be, primarily because of the availability of drugs. The most common crime is purse snatching. Ask your hotel staff or your hosts which areas are unsafe.

◆ In cities, women should take taxis after dark.

Key Phrases

See Germany, France, and Italy.

Turkey

What will surprise you most about Turkey is that it *won't* surprise you—at least, not at first. In large cities, people look and dress like Western Europeans, and the street signs are written in familiar Roman letters.

Your first suprise might come when you hear the amplified voice of the *muezzin* calling people to prayer. You'll hear the *muezzin* five times a day, and religious Muslims will respond each time.

Muslim countries have a strong tradition of hospitality, and Turkey is no exception. Americans often issue insincere invitations ("Do drop in when you're in the neighborhood" or "We must have lunch some time"), but Turks don't. Their warmth and offers of hospitality are always sincere.

In small villages, visitors are so rare that people you've just met might offer to house and feed you. Feel free to accept; it's a wonderful way to experience a rich new culture.

Greetings

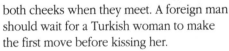

♦ Shake hands when you're introduced, using a firm handshake.

♦ Good friends of either sex kiss on both cheeks when they meet. A foreign man should wait for a Turkish woman to make the first move before kissing her.

♦ Show respect to elders by rising to greet them when they enter a room.

♦ If you enter a room in which there is a group, greet and shake hands with each person, beginning with elders, and shake hands again when you leave.

Conversation

♦ The second most common languages in Turkey—especially for business—are English and French. However, not everyone will speak these languages.

♦ Good topics of conversation: families, professions, personal hobbies and interests, or noncontroversial international affairs.

♦ Topics to avoid: communism, the conflict with Greece over Cyprus, or the Armenian and Kurdish situations.

♦ When you discuss any aspect of Turkish politics, don't take sides.

♦ Don't make any negative comments about Kemal Atatürk, Turkey's first president.

♦ Never argue with elders or speak to them in a loud voice.

♦ If Turks raise their chins, shut their eyes, and tilt their heads back, they're saying "No."

Money

♦ The unit of currency is the lira (plural lira, abbreviated TL), made up of 100 kurus (though inflation has made the kurus obsolete).

♦ Coins come in denominations of 50 and 100 lira but are practically worthless.

♦ Notes come in denominations of 100, 500, 1,000, 5,000, 10,000, and 20,000 lira.

♦ American dollars and German Deutschmarks are accepted everywhere.

♦ Turkey has no black market for currency.

♦ Don't plan to use credit cards except in Istanbul and Ankara, where they are accepted by major hotels and some restaurants and shops.

Telephones

♦ Public telephones are of several types. The most common are yellow push-button phones that take either tokens (jetons) or telephone cards (telekarts), but not both (the older ones accept only medium-sized tokens). Black, red, or gray wall phones take only tokens: on the black phones you insert the token after the other party answers; on the red and gray phones you insert it before you dial and, if you don't get through, the token is returned.

♦ Buy tokens and telephone cards at post offices or from kiosks or children near banks of public phones. Tokens come in three types: small (for local calls); medium (for long-distance calls within Turkey); and large (for calls outside the country).

♦ Most phones that accept telephone cards are in areas frequented by tourists. Insert the card in a slot. A display at the upper left tells you how many units are left on your card, before and after your call. A local call takes one unit; a long-distance call within Turkey takes four to five units; and an international call takes many units.

♦ Make long-distance calls from newer phones.

♦ International calls from a post office take several hours to go through. If you need to get through more quickly, you can call from your hotel room, but you'll pay much more.

♦ When you use a telephone directory, note that the Turkish undotted letter I comes immediately before the dotted letter i.

♦ When you answer the phone, say "ah-LO."

♦ The emergency number to summon police, the fire department, or an ambulance is **011.**

In Public

♦ Don't kiss, hold hands, or otherwise show affection with a member of the opposite sex in public.

♦ If a man wants to speak to a Turkish woman, he must be formally introduced. Few Turkish women will go out on dates unless accompanied by a sister or a friend.

♦ Women seldom go out alone in Turkey. The best way for a woman to avoid unwelcome attention is to go with a friend.

♦ If the national anthem is played (such as before a soccer game or during holiday activities), stand quietly without moving or chewing gum. People will be offended if you don't stand up.

♦ Don't cross your arms while facing someone; it's considered rude.

♦ When you speak with someone, don't put your hands in your pockets. It's a sign of disrespect.

♦ When you sit, keep both feet flat on the ground. Crossing your legs or showing the soles of your shoes or feet is discourteous.

♦ To summon someone, wave your hand up and down, not from side to side.

♦ If Turks shake their heads from side to side, they're signaling "I don't understand," not "No."

♦ Don't visit mosques at prayer time (dawn, noon, midafternoon, dusk, and evening) or on Friday, the holy day.

♦ To enter some historic mosques, you must buy a ticket.

♦ Before you enter a mosque, remove your shoes and pay the attendant 500 lira for the use of slippers.

♦ Don't walk in front of anyone praying in a mosque.

♦ Bargain when you shop, especially in bazaars and markets, but don't grossly underbid. Start by offering half the posted price and negotiate from there. If you're interested in a large item, be prepared to take coffee or tea with the shopkeeper. If you leave without making your purchase, the shopkeeper might run after you and agree to your price.

♦ Before you photograph anyone in smaller towns or villages, ask permission. The Muslim religion forbids reproducing the human image.

♦ Ask permission before taking pictures in a mosque. You might be allowed to photograph the building but not the people.

♦ Don't photograph military installations.

♦ Look for public toilets near mosques and in shopping areas, restaurants, hotels, and train stations. Unisex toilets are marked *W.C.* or *OO.* Women's rooms are marked *Kadin;* men's rooms, *Erkek.*

♦ You must pay 200 Turkish lira to use the toilet and to get toilet paper. Pay an additional 200 Turkish lira for a moist, perfumed towel.

♦ Most hotels and many restaurants and train stations have Western-style toilets; some other places have squat-type toilets. Bring toilet paper or tissues with you; some bathrooms have none.

♦ If you stay somewhere that has no bath— or if you'd just like to try something different—visit a public bath *(hamam).* There are separate baths for men and women.

♦ Most public baths have a large, central bathing area with marble steps, but more modern facilities have private tubs. You'll get a towel when you pay your fee. If there's a central bathing area, soap yourself at the stone sink, use the flat cup to pour water over yourself, then go soak in the water. If you pay extra, someone will wash and dry you.

Dress

♦ Because Turkey is a Muslim country, women are expected to dress modestly. Avoid short skirts or low-cut blouses.

♦ For casual dress, men should wear shirts and pants, and women should wear pants or skirts. Wear shorts only at resorts.

♦ For business, men should wear conservative suits; in hot weather, omitting the jacket or tie is acceptable. Women should wear suits and heels.

♦ The balls held at New Year's and the Turkish National Holiday (October 29) require formal dress (dark suits for men and long dresses for women).

♦ When visiting a mosque, women should cover their heads and wear long sleeves and pants or skirts. All visitors should remove their shoes (see In Public).

♦ At beach resorts, you'll see some foreign women going topless, which the Turks find offensive.

Meals

Hours and Foods

Breakfast (kahvalti): 7:30 or 8:00 A.M. Typical foods are hard-boiled eggs, olives, feta cheese, bread, rose-water, eggplant or fig marmalade, and tea. (Coffee is served before breakfast.)

Lunch (öğle yemeği): Noon. Lunch consists of soup, salad, a vegetable dish, and bread.

Dinner (aksam yemeği): 7:00 P.M. Before dinner appetizers are served, usually with *raki* (an anise liqueur), wine, or beer. The meal includes soup, a course of beans and meat, salad, yogurt, fruit, dessert, and coffee. Bread is available throughout the meal. With dinner, people usually drink water, cola, ginger-ale, or—unless they are very religious—beer or wine. Turkish beer has a higher alcohol content than does American beer.

♦ To be safe, always order meat well done (*piskin,* pronounced peesh-KEEN). Don't eat or drink any unrefrigerated milk products. Instead of tap water, drink bottled spring water, available everywhere. Outside large cities drink only bottled water.

Breaks: In Turkey, people break frequently for coffee.

Table Manners

♦ If you're invited to dinner, be punctual. If you go to a large gathering, such as a cocktail party, being a few minutes late is fine.

♦ Religious families never drink or serve alcohol.

♦ When you sit down to eat, your host will say "booy-ROON," which means, "Here, I am extending this to you."

♦ The hostess will either serve or ask someone else at the table to serve. As a guest you'll be served first, followed by the elderly and children.

♦ Your hosts will press you to eat a great deal and will be offended if you don't.

♦ Many people smoke between courses, but ask permission and take your cue from others at the table.

♦ If you're offered a toothpick after dessert, use it at the table, covering your mouth with your hand.

◆ If you're offered Turkish coffee after dinner, specify whether you want it sweet, medium, or without sugar. Don't drink the last few drops in your cup or you'll get a mouthful of muddy grounds.

◆ After the meal, tell your hostess "Zee-yah-deh OLE-soon," which means "Thank you for the energy you've spent."

◆ Don't get up from the table until everyone has finished.

Eating Out

◆ Look for the following eating places:

• *Kahve hane* offer coffee, tea, and *ayran* (a drink made from yogurt, water, and salt). They are frequented mostly by men, who go to listen to the radio, talk, and play backgammon. Turkish women go to coffee-houses only in large cities, and a woman who goes into one alone might be harassed.

• A *kebabci* serves different kinds of grilled *kebabs*.

• A *meyhane* is a local drinking place that serves only liquor.

• *Pasta hane* are pastry shops that offer coffee, tea, and pastries. Feel free to sit and chat for as long as you want.

• A *restoran* or *lokanta* is a full-service restaurant.

◆ The only bars are in deluxe hotels.

◆ Turkey has excellent fish restaurants, especially along the coast. Ask the price before you order. The waiter will ask whether you would like your fish broiled, fried, or baked.

◆ Service in Turkish restaurants is extremely fast. Servers might seem to be rushing you, but they're just being professional.

◆ If you don't understand the menu in a restaurant, either go to the kitchen to choose your meal or see whether the counter has a display of selections.

◆ Because Turkey is a Muslim country, you won't be able to order pork.

◆ Feel free to order and eat appetizers and then decide whether you want to order anything else. All restaurants, except those in international hotels, accept this practice.

◆ If you suggest dining out with someone, pay the entire check, ignoring any disagreement. If you're invited to a meal, you won't be allowed to pay anything, either. The concept of "Dutch treat" is unknown.

Specialties

◆ Sample these special Turkish foods: *börek* (cheese- or meat-filled pastries); *patlıcan salatası* (eggplant salad made from roasted, pureed eggplant mixed with yogurt and lemon); *imam bayıldı* (eggplant stuffed with tomatoes and onions and baked in oil); *bulgur pilav* (parched cracked wheat [bulger] cooked in a tomato stock); *cacık* (yogurt with grated cucumber, garlic, and olive oil); and *midya dolması* (steamed mussels stuffed with rice and pine nuts, served cold).

◆ Turkey offers many different kinds of grilled kebabs: *döner* (lamb cooked on a vertical spit); *köfte* (long, spicy hamburger patties cooked on a spit); and *şiş kebab* (lamb and vegetables cooked on a skewer).

Hotels

◆ Make your hotel reservations as soon as you decide to go to Turkey. Most major cities have four- and five-star hotels, but rooms are often booked far ahead.

◆ Ask whether the room price includes breakfast.

◆ Most hotels below first class lack shutters and shades, so you might be disturbed by noise, sunlight, and sign lights. If you'll be staying in such a hotel, consider bringing an eye mask and earplugs.

◆ Before you register, inspect your assigned room. If you don't like it, look at several until you find one you like. Avoid rooms facing the street, which are noisier, and make sure the lights, door locks, shower, and toilet all work.

◆ If you think the price is too high, try bargaining with the clerk. Don't bargain, however, in large hotels.

◆ Usually, only first-class hotels offer room service. Other hotels might be able to get food for you from a nearby restaurant.

Tipping

◆ *Restaurants:* If the bill doesn't include a tip, leave 15 percent. If it does, leave an additional 5 percent on the table or hand it to the waiter. (The service charge goes to the owner or maitre d'.)

◆ *Porters:* Give hotel porters 3–4 percent of your room rate.

◆ *Hotel maids:* Tip 2,000–4,000 lira per day.

◆ *Taxis:* Don't tip unless the driver performs a special service. If you wish, round up the fare (but not in a *dolmuş,* or shared taxi).

◆ *Ushers:* Tip 25 percent of the ticket price.

◆ *Cloakroom attendants:* Give 500 lira.

◆ *Bath attendants:* Figure 30 percent of the total cost, and divide it among the various attendants, who line up as you leave.

Private Homes

◆ You might be invited to stay with someone for a few days—even someone you meet casually on a train. Turks regard Americans with warmth and curiosity. If you want to refuse an invitation, say you've arranged to stay with someone else or will be leaving the country.

◆ If you want to visit people, call first and ask whether they'll be in. The customary visiting time is about 9:00 P.M.

◆ Your host might offer you cologne to refresh yourself. Pour the cologne into your hands and rub it on your face and hands.

◆ If you stay in a home, offer to help with the cleaning and dishes. If you're staying for only a few days, your hosts will probably refuse. If you're staying a week or more, insist on sharing the chores.

◆ Before you bathe, ask whether it's convenient. The water might need to be heated.

◆ Don't make long-distance calls from private homes. Your hosts will think it inhospitable to accept payment, and they'll be stuck with the bill. Local calls are fine.

Gifts: If you're invited to dinner, bring flowers (roses or carnations), candy, or pastries. If you know the family serves liquor, you may also bring wine. Glassware items, such as water goblets or a vase, make good gifts for special occasions.

♦ If the family has children, bring them chocolates or small toys.

♦ If you stay with a family, bring cosmetics or perfume for women and Cross pens or neckties for men. Top-quality chocolates are also appreciated. If your hosts read English, bring books in English.

♦ When you give a gift, the recipient won't open it in front of you because that would rudely direct attention toward the gift and away from you.

Business

Hours

Businesses, government offices, and banks: 9:00 A.M. to noon and 2:00 to 5:00 P.M., Monday through Friday. Executives usually get to work between 9:30 and 10:00 A.M. and lunch from noon to about 2:30 P.M.

Stores: 9:00 A.M. to 1:00 P.M. and 2:30 to 7:00 P.M., Monday through Friday; 9:00 A.M. to noon and 1:30 to 8:00 P.M. on Saturday.

Business Practices

♦ You'll need a contact in Turkey. Personal referrals are best, but if you don't have one, contact the Commercial Section of your country's embassy in Turkey.

♦ Don't plan a business trip to Turkey for June, July, or August, the most popular

vacation months. Also avoid the period of *Ramazan,* the dates of which change each year; for upcoming dates, check with the Turkish Tourist Office, Embassy, or Consulate.

♦ Write business letters in English, Turkey's second language. Companies dealing with foreign firms will have someone available who understands English.

♦ Learn a few words of Turkish. Most Turkish businesspeople speak English, but they'll be surprised and pleased at your effort. You can also conduct business in French or German.

♦ Foreign businesswomen will have no trouble being accepted. However, in Turkey there are few women in high-level positions.

♦ Bring business cards—to make the best impression, written in Turkish on one side.

♦ Stay in a top hotel to create a good image.

♦ Photocopying facilities are widely available, and most businesses and post offices have telexes and fax machines. Many hotels also have fax machines.

Meetings and negotiations: Suggest business appointments between 9:00 A.M. and noon and 2:00 and 5:00 P.M.

♦ Be punctual, but don't expect the Turks to be on time.

♦ When you arrive, give your business card to the receptionist, the person with whom you're meeting, and anyone else to whom you're introduced.

♦ You'll be offered tea when you first come to an office; be sure to accept.

♦ The business portion of the meeting will be preceded by small talk. You might be asked about your background, education, and work. Turkish men will be pleased if you ask about their sons.

♦ When you talk to businesspeople, look directly into their eyes and be sincere. Turks dislike phoniness.

♦ Know the details about your competitors; you'll be quizzed about their products and services.

♦ Written contracts are common.

♦ Decisions are usually made by one person at the top. Give copies of any proposals or documents to that person, who will distribute them to others.

♦ Cultivate patience. In Turkey, time estimates for having things ready are unreliable.

♦ If you visit a factory, shake hands with the workers when you arrive and again when you leave.

Entertainment: For business, lunches are more popular then dinners.

♦ Turkish businesspeople will probably invite you to dinner at restaurants, not at their homes.

♦ If you entertain, ask your guest to choose a restaurant. Turks prefer good food to a glitzy atmosphere.

♦ In your invitation, include only people with whom you're negotiating. If you've met their spouses, include them in any dinner invitations.

♦ When entertaining Turkish businesspeople, don't drink alcohol unless you know they do.

Gifts: If you know that someone drinks, bring a good bottle of whiskey or liqueur. Another good gift is a Cross pen.

Holidays & Celebrations

Holidays:
New Year's Day (January 1); National Sovereignty and Children's Day (April 23); Spring Day (May 1); Youth and Sports Day (May 19); Victory Day (August 30); and the Turkish National Holiday (October 28 and 29).

♦ People usually take off the afternoon preceding a public holiday. Some offices and stores close.

♦ Youth Day (May 19) is a major national holiday. When Mustafa Kemal Pasha (known as Atatürk) led Turkey to liberation and became its first president, he stressed the importance of the nation's young people. Holiday celebrations include sports events, radio broadcasts, and student speeches on radio and television and at ceremonies in school courtyards and stadiums.

♦ An important Muslim holiday is *Kurban Bayrami* (Feast of the Sacrifice), a four-day feast scheduled ten days earlier every year. Depending on their wealth, people sacrifice a sheep, goat, cow, or camel, keeping one-third of the meat and giving the rest to the poor. (This tradition derives from the story of Abraham and Isaac.)

♦ The holiest time in the Muslim year is *Ramazan,* which lasts for 30 days. The date is based on a 13-month lunar calendar and changes every year; get specific dates from the Turkish Consulate or Embassy. During *Ramazan,* people spend time during the day praying and reading the Koran in mosques and do not eat, drink, or smoke from dawn to dusk (which times are signaled by a cannon).

◆ Fasting during *Ramazan* is no longer universal, but to be considerate, don't eat, drink, or smoke in front of people between dawn and dusk. If you're staying with a family that observes the fast, either fast with them or eat in your room, unless they tell you otherwise. Some families insist that foreigners eat and might prepare food especially for them. Buy food for your own use at food stores, which remain open during the day. Some restaurants remain open at lunchtime in major cities—especially those in tourist areas and hotels—but not in small towns, where the owners would be stoned if they remained open.

◆ The end of *Ramazan* is celebrated with a three-day festival called *Seker Bayramı*. People visit relatives, then neighbors, then friends. You'll be served coffee, tea, and sweets.

Transportation

Public Transport

Mass transit:
Cities have bus and trolley service. On main

routes, vehicles come every two to five minutes until 11:00 P.M. or midnight.

◆ To ride buses within cities, buy tickets at the kiosks of major bus terminals or transfer points. If you end up on a bus without a ticket, someone will probably offer you one.

◆ If you take an intercity bus, buy your ticket in advance, if possible. Different companies have different schedules, so check with several ticket offices at the central bus terminals.

◆ On intercity buses, all seats are reserved.

Seats in the middle are the least bumpy, but you might want to sit near the front if you don't like cigarette smoke.

◆ On some buses only the driver's window opens. Even if other windows do open, however, the Turks—who dislike drafts—might keep them closed, even in the hottest weather.

◆ Intercity buses stop about every one-and-a-half hours to let passengers use bathrooms and buy snacks.

◆ Keep your bus ticket until you reach your final destination. Some companies have shuttle buses to take you into a city at no extra charge.

◆ Trains are a less expensive alternative to buses.

◆ Train schedules list the names of stations, not cities.

◆ You can reserve a sleeping compartment or a couchette. Reservations are easy to make and computerized, so booking a few days ahead is usually sufficient—though you might book earlier for a weekend train.

Taxis: Taxis are marked with a black-and-yellow checked band.

◆ Taxis have meters, but sometimes the driver must be reminded to turn it on.

◆ Shared cabs *(dolmuş)* ply specified routes, usually main bus routes. They're difficult to spot, especially at night. Some have a solid yellow band around them, others have no band, and still others are minibuses.

◆ A *dolmuş* will stop anywhere along the route. You don't need to talk to your fellow passengers or tip the driver. Women are expected to choose a side seat, never one between two men.

Driving

♦ To avoid bureaucratic hassles, carry an International Driver's License when you drive.

♦ Allow extra time for driving anywhere. Major traffic jams are frequent.

♦ Seat belts are compulsory for all occupants of a car.

♦ Watch carefully for bikes and carts, which sometimes go against the traffic so their drivers can see better. In the countryside, watch out for sheep and other animals crossing the road.

♦ Right of way is determined not by rules, but by who gets there first.

♦ Try to avoid driving at night. It's hazardous because many cars have badly adjusted headlights, or none at all.

♦ Parking is chaotic. Park where you can—even on the sidewalk.

♦ Foreigners involved in accidents often have to pay a great deal. Insurance coverage involves many conditions and delays—one reason why some foreign companies don't allow their businesspeople to drive in Turkey. If you can't afford the insurance, hire a car and chauffeur.

♦ There are severe penalties for drunk driving if you are involved in an accident.

Legal Matters & Safety

♦ Removing antiquities from the country without authorization carries severe penalties.

♦ Don't try to bring weapons or ammunition into or out of the country.

♦ Stay well away from drugs, unless you fancy life in a Turkish prison. If you're with someone who is carrying drugs—even if you know nothing about them—you can be arrested. Don't enter Turkey in the car or van of anyone you don't know and trust.

♦ Keep receipts from currency exchanges; you'll need them to change Turkish money into another currency when you leave.

♦ Watch out for pickpockets. In one common ploy, a group of women and children begin a fight, trapping a tourist in the middle. Then someone picks the victim's pocket.

♦ Turkish women almost never travel alone, so if you're a woman on your own, be especially careful outside major tourist areas. Don't accept invitations from men, but do make friends with women and with families.

♦ Women can go to restaurants alone during the day and until early evening (8:00 P.M); either dine early or plan to eat in a major hotel and take a taxi home.

♦ Even a group of two or three women is not safe walking at night. Any form of transportation is better than walking, but taxis are best.

♦ Drink bottled water instead of tap water, especially outside large cities.

♦ Avoid milk products and dishes containing milk that have not been properly refrigerated.

Key Phrases

English	Turkish	Pronunciation
Good morning	Günaydin	gewn-AHY-din
Good day	Iyi günler	Ee-yeh GEWN-lehr
Good evening	Iyi akşamlar	EE-yeh AHK-shahm-lahr
Please	Lütfen	LEWT-fen
Thank you	Teşekkür	teh-sheh-KEWR
You're welcome	Hoş geldiniz	hosh GEHL-din-iz
Yes	Evet	EH-vet
No	Hayır	hire
Mr., Sir	Bay	Buy
Mrs., Madam, Miss	Bayan	Buy-YAHN
Excuse me	Affedersiniz	Ah-feh-DEHR-sin-iz
Good-bye (said by one who's leaving)	Allah ısmarladık	Ah-LAHS-mahr-lah-dik
Good-bye (said by one who's staying)	Güle Güle	gew-LEH gew-LEH
I don't understand.	Anlamıyorum.	AN-lah-mee-yo-room
I don't speak Turkish.	Turkçe bilmem.	TURK-jeh BEEL-mem
Is there anyone who speaks English?	Ingilizçe bilen varmı?	een-geel-eez-JEH bee-LEN VAHR-meh

Yugoslavia

Since the Roman emperor Diocletian built his palace at Split, the Adriatic coast has been a magnet for travelers from all around the world.

Yugoslavia, with several republics, four languages, three religions (Catholic, Orthodox, and Muslim), and two alphabets, is a country of great diversity.

Though after World War II Yugoslavia, under the leadership of Marshal Tito, was a communist country, it broke away early from Soviet dominance. Among the freedoms Yugoslavs have enjoyed—and of which they have taken full advantage—is travel abroad. You'll find the people have first-hand, up-to-date knowledge of both Western Europe and the United States.

Note: The information in this chapter is accurate as we go to press. However, the armed conflicts among Serbs, Croats, and Slovenians may lead to dramatic changes in the boundaries, government, and customs of the country.

Greetings

♦ Shake hands when you greet someone but not when you leave (unless you're going on a long trip or ending a business meeting).

♦ A man should wait for a woman to extend her hand first.

♦ Friends embrace and kiss on the cheek when they meet.

♦ If you go to a large party, speak to each person as you're introduced. As a foreigner, you'll be the center of attention.

♦ Don't use first names until the Yugoslavs do—which will probably be quickly.

Conversation

♦ In most city and resort hotels and restaurants, people speak English. German is widely understood along the coast, and Italian is spoken in Istria and in other parts of the Adriatic coast.

♦ Good topics of conversation: life in America, your family and home town (you might want to bring a few photos), or shopping in the U.S.—what's available and how much it costs.

♦ Yugoslavs might ask personal questions such as "Are you married?" "What kind of work do you do?" or "How much money do you make?" soon after you meet. Feel free to do the same.

♦ Even if you avoid discussing political issues when you first meet someone, the topic will come up eventually. When it does, don't try to impose your views; instead, present them in a modest, nonargumentative way. Because of the country's different regions and religions, political perspectives vary.

Money

◆ The unit of currency is the dinar (abbreviated Din).

◆ Coins come in denominations of 1, 2, and 5 dinars.

◆ Notes come in denominations of 5, 10, 50, 100, 500, and 1,000 dinars.

◆ Some newer coins are of different sizes and colors than the older coins, but both types have the same value.

◆ Never exchange currency on the street, or with an individual who suggests doing so. You could be arrested for dealing in the black market.

Telephones

◆ Public telephones are scarce, and many don't work. Even those that do work require dialing many times to get through. Once you get through, the sound is usually poor. Public phones often have long lines be-cause not all people have their own phones.

◆ Buy tokens (žetoni) at post offices, kiosks, and tobacconist shops. Tokens come in three sizes: "A" for local calls, "B" for longer distances, and "C" for international calls.

◆ In Slovenia, public telephones take tokens different from those used elsewhere.

◆ Hotels will let you use the phones in their lobbies, but at an extra charge. For a local call, you can also ask to use the phone in a cafe.

◆ To make international long-distance calls, go to a town's central post office.

◆ Yugoslavs answer the telephone by saying "HAH-lo."

◆ Emergency Numbers are as follows:

Police	92
Fire	95
Ambulance	94

In Public

◆ Try bargaining at private outdoor stands that sell merchandise and produce, but never at government-owned stores.

◆ Join the Yugoslavs in korzo (an evening promenade) between 5:00 and 8:00 P.M. People of all ages stroll up and down each town's main street, gossiping and meeting friends. They often visit bars or pastry shops for a snack before returning home for supper.

◆ If you visit a mosque, leave your shoes outside.

◆ If you go to one of the gambling casinos restricted to foreigners, bring your passport.

◆ If you're a women traveling alone, you'll receive comments and passes from men. Don't feel threatened; such behavior is considered common and expected. Just ignore the men and go on with what you were doing.

◆ Never photograph military or naval installations, or your camera might be confiscated. Before you take any picture, look for a sign showing a camera with an "X" over it, which means that photography is forbidden.

◆ Before you photograph museums or church interiors, ask permission.

◆ Don't photograph people in villages or anyone in uniform (soldiers or police) without asking permission.

◆ Ask permission before photographing Muslims; reproducing the human image is against their religion.

◆ Public toilets are scarce. Try train stations, hotels, restaurants, and large department stores. Toilets are labeled *W.C.;* those for men are labeled *Muški;* those for women, *Ženski.*

◆ Public toilets generally are not very clean.

◆ Bring your own tissues for drying your hands and for use if there is no toilet paper.

Dress

◆ Wear shorts only at a lake or at the seaside.

◆ In the country-side, everyone wears jeans for walking or visiting.

◆ In towns, people wear dressier clothing even for casual occasions. Women usually wear skirts or dresses.

◆ For business, men should wear suits and ties. In hot weather, wait for other men to remove their jackets and ties before you remove yours. Yugoslav businesswomen wear very dressy clothes and heavy makeup.

◆ For formal dress occasions, such as official receptions and weddings, men should wear dark suits and ties, and women should wear dresses.

◆ For visiting churches and monasteries,

men should wear long trousers, and women should wear skirts and avoid sleeveless shirts or dresses.

◆ At beaches, many Yugoslavian men and women go nude, or women go topless. The sign *FKK* indicates a nude beach.

Meals

Hours and Foods

Breakfast (doručak): 8:00 A.M. In cities, many people just have coffee and later buy *burek* (cheese pies made with phyllo dough and served with yogurt) at small bakeries. In the countryside, people often eat bread, cheese, eggs, and warm milk with coffee. As a guest, you might be offered a shot of *rakia,* a homemade fruit brandy.

Lunch (ručak): 2:00 p.m. Often the main meal of the day, lunch might feature soup, meat with salad, potatoes, beans or rice, and a vegetable. In the south, the main course is usually a meatless mixture of vegetables and potatoes. Wine or beer is served with the meal. Dessert and Turkish coffee (if it's available) follow.

◆ If lunch is a formal meal, it begins with *lozovaca* (grape brandy), *šljivovica* (plum brandy), or sherry. Cheese, thinly sliced *pršuta* (dried, salted ham), or nuts are often served before the soup course. Salad follows, then the meat course. A typical dish might be hamburger kabobs or steak with French fries and peas. Dessert might be homemade cookies or cream cakes, followed by Turkish coffee and brandy or *fer net* (a digestive after-dinner drink with a somewhat bitter taste).

Dinner *(večera):* 9:00 P.M. Dinner might be another substantial meal, similar to lunch, perhaps featuring stewed cabbage with meat (fish on the coast).

♦ In a traditional home, you'll be offered a spoonful of preserves and a glass of water before the meal. Then you'll be offered *šljivovica,* then your meal. In a more modern home, you will be offered only *šljivovica* and then the meal.

Table Manners

♦ Don't worry if you're about 15 minutes late for dinner. It's acceptable.

♦ If you don't want alcoholic beverages, give a polite explanation when you refuse. Even if there's a carafe of water on the table, people will think it's odd if you drink only water with a meal.

♦ Wait for the hostess to seat you.

♦ Smoking between courses is acceptable.

♦ Serve yourself from platters of food as they're passed around the table. As the guest, you'll be given the platters first.

♦ To show that you've finished eating, set your knife and fork parallel on the plate.

♦ Dinner parties have a great deal of food, including several desserts, and last a long time. You'll be pressed to eat a lot, so taste everything but take small initial portions.

♦ Stay about one to one-and-a-half hours after the meal. Your host and hostess will never give signals that it's time to leave.

Eating Out

♦ Look for these alternatives to formal restaurants:

• *Kafić* are cafes that serve coffee, sandwiches, and hard liquor. Service is usually slow, so if you're pressed for time, pay when you're served.

"Toast" on a cafe menu means grilled ham or cheese sandwiches.

• A *kafana* offers beer, wine, grilled meats, and sometimes salads.

• A *čevabdžinica* serves only grilled meat, not full meals.

• *Express* are fast-food restaurants, many of them cafeteria-style. Most have counters for eating; some also have tables.

• A *poslastičarnica* (in the south) or *slasticarna* (in the north) serves pastries and ice cream by the scoop. Only the very best shops offer coffee or tea; most have lemonade or sometimes *boza,* a thick, cold, semifermented grain drink that people either love or hate. Fill up on the pastries; the usual order is two per person.

• A *pivnica* is a beer cellar, but wine and other drinks are also served.

• A *restoran* is a regular restaurant; a *riblji restoran* is a fish restaurant.

♦ Some items on a restaurant menu might not be available. Ask the server about available choices and local specialties.

♦ To summon the waiter, raise your hand, make eye contact, and say "KEHL-nehr."

♦ If you want to treat people to a meal, tell them first or you won't be permitted to pay.

♦ If you go to a restaurant with a group, one person pays the check. It's understood that the next time the group goes out, someone else will pay.

♦ When you get a restaurant bill, check it for accuracy.

♦ If you are a woman and want to go to a cafe alone, bring along something to do—

postcards to write or a book to read—to show you're not there to be picked up. To avoid harassment, don't make eye contact with men.

Specialties

♦ Each of Yugoslavia's regions has a distinctive character and special foods:

♦ In Serbia, try *sarma* (grape or cabbage leaves stuffed with meat and rice), *gibanica* (an appetizer made from phyllo pastry, cream cheese, and eggs) and *kajmak* (a cream cheese).

♦ In Croatia, look for *knedla od zemicke* (sliced steamed dumplings served with butter and sour cream) and *paški sir* (sheep's milk cheese).

♦ In Slovenia (where no meal is complete without soup), taste *vipavska čorba* (a thick soup of sauerkraut, pork, potatoes, and beans, served with sour cream) and *potica* (layered coffee cake with nuts).

♦ In Bosnia-Herzegovina (which has a Turkish way of life), try *bosanske cufte* (baked meatballs topped with an egg-and-yogurt custard) and *lokum* (Turkish delight, a jelly candy rolled in powdered sugar).

♦ In Montenegro, sample lamb, corn pudding, yogurt, and *pršuta* (dried ham).

♦ In Macedonia (where food tends to be very spicy), try yogurt, feta cheese, and *tarana* (a rice-like pasta used in soups and casseroles).

♦ In most regions, hamburgers *(pljeskavica)* are made from pork, not beef. Pork is the primary meat in all but Muslim regions, where the preferred meat is lamb. Beef tends to be of poor quality.

♦ Unless you thrive on exotic foods, don't order *beli bubrezi* (pigs' testicles that marinated for several days in wine, vinegar,

and onions and then grilled).

♦ In Bosnia, Serbia, and Macedonia, coffee is Turkish style. Don't drink all the coffee or you will end up with thick, muddy grounds in your mouth. In Croatia and Slovenia, espresso or cappucino is served.

Hotels

♦ Hotels are classified "A" to "D." "A" are luxury accommodations; "C" and "D" hotels might have shared bathrooms and infrequent hot water. Prices are strictly controlled and must be displayed in rooms. City hotels are more expensive than rural hotels of the same category.

♦ When you check in, the hotel will keep your passport overnight.

♦ Most room rates include breakfast—a roll, cheese, coffee, tea, and sometimes a boiled egg—which you can get as early as 5:30 or 6:00 A.M.

♦ Hotel food tends to be poorer in quality and much more expensive than food in local restaurants.

♦ Hotel maids usually begin work at about 6:00 A.M. If you don't want to be disturbed that early, put the "Do Not Disturb" sign on your door.

♦ Many rooms have no plugs for the sink and bathtub, so bring some with you.

♦ Some lower-class hotels turn the hot water off every afternoon.

♦ When you go out, leave your key at the desk.

♦ To save money and meet Yugoslavian

people, rent a room in a private home. People at bus and train stations will offer to rent you rooms, but to be safe go to the Tourist Office, where rooms are classified in categories. If you do rent from someone at a station, be sure to bargain over the price and don't commit yourself until you've seen the room. (You can check your luggage at the train station while you go to look at the room.)

♦ The Tourist Office can also arrange apartment rentals, advantageous if you're traveling in a group.

Tipping

♦ *Restaurants:* At most restaurants the check includes a 10-percent service charge, but give the waiter an extra 5 percent.

♦ *Porters:* Tip 10 dinars per bag.

♦ *Hotel maids:* Leave the equivalent of $5.00 U.S. for a week's stay. Don't tip for a shorter stay.

♦ *Taxis:* Give 10 percent or less of the fare.

♦ *Cloakroom attendants:* Tip 3 dinars.

Private Homes

♦ Don't visit or telephone between 3:00 P.M. and 5:00 P.M., when people rest. The best times to phone are between 10:00 A.M. and 1:00 P.M. and 5:00 and 8:00 P.M. Good friends can drop in. Others should call ahead.

♦ If you're invited to a home, being up to 30 minutes late is fine.

♦ If you must drop in on someone between 3:00 and 5:00 P.M., you might find the men in undershirts and the women in bathrobes. Don't be embarrassed; traditionally, people nap in the afternoon, and many don't dress in street clothes afterward.

♦ Your hosts might serve you preserved fruit in a thick sugar syrup, along with a glass of water or wine. Eat a spoonful of the fruit and then sip the beverage. When you're finished, you'll be offered Turkish coffee and a liqueur (often plum brandy); to avoid offense, accept either or both. If you drink brandy, your host will keep refilling your glass unless you leave some in it.

♦ If you call on several people in a single afternoon, eat a small amount at each stop. You'll offend your hosts if you don't accept something.

♦ If you use the phone in someone's home, ask permission first and offer to pay for your calls.

♦ If you stay with a family, say "Good morning" and "Good night" to each person (see Key Phrases).

♦ Offer to help with small chores but don't insist if your offer is refused. Even women who work outside the home take pride in doing all the housework and cooking themselves. Keep your hostess company in the kitchen while she's working, but don't expect to be allowed to help.

♦ Feel free to bathe daily, but consider washing your hair less often; Yugoslavs consider such frequent washing unnecessary and even harmful.

Gifts: If you're invited to dinner, bring wine or an odd number of flowers (but not thirteen). Good gifts from outside the country are whiskey (expensive in Yugoslavia) or foreign liqueurs such as Grand Marnier or Chartreuse.

♦ If you stay with a family, bring gifts from the U.S., such as American cigarettes, shirts, sunglasses, perfume, or blue jeans for teenagers.

Business

Hours

Businesses and government offices: 7:00 A.M. to 2:00 P.M., Monday through Saturday.

Banks: 7:00 A.M. to 7:00 P.M., Monday through Friday, and 7:00 A.M. to 1:00 P.M. on Saturday. Hours might vary locally.

Stores: In the summer, 7:00 or 7:30 A.M. to noon and 5:00 to 8:00 P.M., Monday through Saturday; in the winter, 8:00 A.M. to 1:00 P.M. and 4:00 to 8:00 P.M. Hours vary, however.

Business Practices

♦ To find business contacts in Yugoslavia, get in touch with the following organizations:

- Chamber of the Economy, 767 3rd Ave., 24th Floor, New York, NY 10017. Phone: (212) 355-7117.

- U. S.–Yugoslav Economic Council, 1901 North Fort Myer Drive, Suite 303, Arlington, VA 22209. Phone: (703) 527-0280.

♦ Long-term investments in Yugoslavia are difficult, because laws change frequently as officials are replaced.

♦ Try not to plan a business trip to Yugoslavia for July or August, the most common vacation months.

♦ Ask the Yugoslav National Tourist Office about the many local holidays when businesses close.

♦ Yugoslavs like Americans, so expect a very cordial reception.

♦ Many Yugoslavian women have positions in business, but there are not many in managerial positions. Foreign businesswomen will encounter no problems, but will have more success if they appear feminine and not aggressive.

♦ Yugoslav firms can provide an interpreter if one is needed, but if you'd like your own, try to get a personal recommendation. You can find an interpreter through the Translation Agency, but since the agency gives jobs arbitrarily, you might not get the best person. If you need someone with a special vocabulary, make that clear.

♦ Bring business cards. English is fine for cards and for any other materials.

♦ Photocopying services are widely available in cities, less so in rural areas.

♦ Almost all companies have telexes, but fax machines are still rare.

Meetings and negotiations: If you make appointments by letter, telephone, telex, or fax from the U.S., be sure to confirm them when you arrive in Yugoslavia. Make appointments 3 to 4 weeks in advance.

♦ Be punctual for any business meeting, although Yugoslavs may not be.

♦ Shake hands with each person present when you arrive and when you depart.

♦ You'll be offered juice, coffee, and brandy. To be polite, accept at least one.

♦ Even though Yugoslavian businesspeople are blunt and direct, don't give direct orders about how you want things done. Instead, explain carefully why your proposed course of action is advisable.

◆ Decisions are made by a few people at the top—sometimes only one person. Underlings have no say.

◆ Deadlines are often missed, so allow plenty of leeway in setting delivery times. If you really need something done, keep checking.

◆ Contracts are not regarded as iron-clad agreements. Even after you sign, keep checking to make sure the details are being observed.

Entertainment: Business dinners are more popular than business lunches.

◆ If you are entertaining, ask local residents for restaurant suggestions. Don't choose hotel restaurants, most of which serve poor quality food.

◆ Include both foreign and Yugoslav spouses in business entertaining.

◆ Don't be surprised to be invited to a business colleague's home for a meal.

Gifts: Give business associates something with your company name on it, whiskey, or high-quality liqueurs.

Holidays & Celebrations

Holidays: New Year's (January 1 and 2); Christmas (January 7); Labor Day (May 1 and 2); and Republic Day (November 29 and 30).

◆ Almost half the population is Eastern Orthodox and celebrates religious holidays in accordance with the Orthodox calendar. Christmas and Easter usually come later than they do on a Western calendar.

◆ Many Muslims in Yugoslavia observe *Ramadan,* a 30-day holy period during which they fast and refrain from smoking between sunrise and sunset. If you visit during this time (the dates follow the Arab calendar and change every year), don't smoke or eat in front of Muslim people. Many restaurants in Muslim regions close until after sundown.

Transportation

Public Transport

Mass transit: Most cities have efficient, inexpensive bus, streetcar, and trolleybus service. Many people use them, so avoid the rush hours from 7:00 to 8:00 A.M. and 3:00 to 4:00 P.M.

◆ City buses, streetcars, and trolleybuses have flat fares. Buy tickets either from the driver or in strips of six from a kiosk. Punch them in a machine when you enter the vehicle. Keep your ticket in case an inspector asks to see it.

◆ Intercity buses provide comfortable, frequent service and are a good option for rural travel, since not all towns have train stations. Although only international buses have bathrooms, other intercity buses make frequent rest stops.

◆ Reserve intercity bus seats at the station. For holiday periods, book well in advance; at other times, a few days should suffice.

◆ On trains, first-class compartments are roomy and comfortable and seat six people; second-class compartments seat eight.

◆ Some trains have dining cars, but the food

is poor and very expensive. Bring your own food and buy drinks (beer, coffee, or mineral water) on the train.

♦ For long-distance train trips, you can get a second-class couchette or a first-class sleeping compartment for two. If the ticket agent says no couchettes are available, try polite bribery and you might get one.

♦ Thieves frequent trains, particularly international trains, so watch your belongings. Sleep with your valuables under your pillow.

Taxis: Hail taxis on the street, or go to taxi stands, which are often found near bus stops or train stations. Negotiate the fare in advance unless the taxi has a meter.

Driving

♦ A U.S. driver's license is acceptable, but it's a good idea to have an International Driver's License in case of an accident.

♦ Think twice about driving in Yugoslavia, which has Europe's highest traffic-fatality rate.

♦ The driver and front seat passengers must wear seat belts.

♦ Children under 12 must sit in the back seat.

♦ Speed limits are 120 kph on highways, 60 or 80 kph in towns, and 100 kph on other roads.

♦ The country has two official alphabets: the Latin and the Cyrillic. Major signs are always in the Latin alphabet, but try to learn the Cyrillic alphabet to read street names in cities such as Belgrade.

♦ If you plan to drive around the country, try to bring road maps with you; they're difficult to obtain in Yugoslavia.

♦ Drive cautiously. Many Yugoslavs drive recklessly, including passing on hills.

♦ If you'll be driving in provincial cities or towns between 5:00 and 8:00 P.M., try to find out in advance where the *korzo* (evening promenade) is held, since that street usually closes to traffic during those hours.

♦ If you're driving along the Adriatic coast during or after a rain, be careful. Heavy traffic and oil and gasoline on the roads make them treacherous.

♦ If you're stopped for a traffic violation, you may have to pay a fine on the spot.

♦ Penalties for drunken driving are severe: a steep fine and/or imprisonment.

Legal Matters & Safety

♦ Although most customs officials are lenient with tourists, make sure that any merchandise you bring in is for your personal use, other than an occasional small gift.

♦ Walking after dark is safe in most areas. Find out from your hotel which areas are unsafe.

♦ If you are a woman, don't smile or make eye contact with any man who verbally harasses you. If you visit friends, they'll probably escort you back to your hotel after dark.

Key Phrases

If you need to ask "Does anyone speak English?" say it *in English*. Saying it in Serbo-Croatian somehow sounds arrogant to Yugoslavs.

English	Serbo-Croatian	Pronunciation
Good morning	Dobro jurto	DO-bro yootro
Good day	Dobar dan	DO-bahr dahn
Good evening	Dobro veče	DO-bro VAY-chay
Please	Molim	MO-leem
Thank you	Hvala	CHVAH-lah*
You're welcome	Molim	MO-leem
Yes	Da	dah
No	Ne	neh
Mr., Sir	Gospodine	gos-PO-dee-nay
Mrs., Madame	Gospodjo	GO-spod-yo
Miss	Gospodjice (on the Adriatic coast, Signorina)	Gos-PO-jee-tsay
Good-bye	Zbogom	ZBO-gom
Excuse me	Izvinite	Eez-VEE-nee-tay
I don't understand.	Ne razumem.	neh rah-ZOO-mehm
I don't speak Serbo-Croatian.	Ne grovorim srpsko-hrvatski.	neh GOV-o-reem SERP-sko-HER-vaht-ski

*"CH" is pronounced like a gutteral "k," as in the Scottish word "loch."

ABOUT THE AUTHORS

Nancy L. Braganti taught French for 14 years in England, Israel, and the United States. In addition to French, she speaks Spanish, Italian, and some Hebrew, and is currently learning Russian.

Elizabeth Devine is a professor of English at Salem State College in Massachusetts, where among other subjects she teaches travel writing. She has written travel articles for many publications, including *Travel/Holiday*, *TV Guide*, and *The New York Times*.

Best European Travel Tips

9th Edition

by John Whitman

2001 tips for saving money, time, and trouble in Europe. A "how to" guide to European travel that's the best-selling book of its kind.

Order #5070

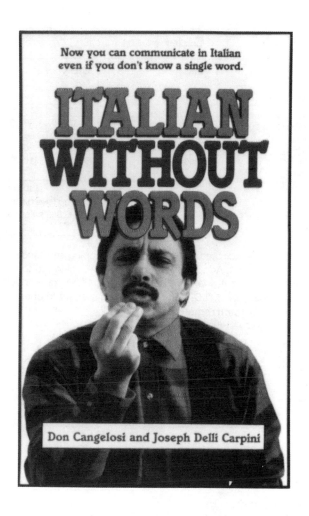

Now you can communicate in Italian even if you don't know a single word.

ITALIAN WITHOUT WORDS

Don Cangelosi and Joseph Delli Carpini

Italian Without Words

by Don Cangelosi and Joseph Delli Carpini

Now you can visit Italy and order a meal, make a date, curse like a trooper, or make intimidating threats without knowing a single word of Italian. This ingenious Italian "phrase book" contains the most common gestures and body language, so you can speak like an Italian without spending a fortune at Berlitz. It must be seen to be believed!

Order #5100

Order Form

Qty.	Title	Author	Order No.	Unit Cost	Total
	Best European Travel Tips	Whitman, J.	5070	$8.00	
	Dear Boss	Werther, W., Jr.	6080	$14.95	
	Euro. Customs & Manners	Braganti/Devine	5080	$8.00	
	Italian Without Words	Cangelosi/Carpini	5100	$4.95	
	Sand Castles Step-by-Step	Wierenga/McDonald	2300	$6.95	
	Shopping for a Better Environment	Tasaday, L.	6150	$10.00	
				Subtotal	
				Shipping and Handling (see below)	
				MN residents add 6.5% sales tax	
				Total	

YES! please send me the books indicated above. Add $1.50 shipping and handling for the first book and 50¢ for each additional book. Add $2.00 to total for books shipped to Canada. Overseas postage will be billed. Allow up to 4 weeks for delivery. Send check or money order payable to Meadowbrook Press. No cash or C.O.D.'s, please. Prices subject to change without notice. **Quantity discounts available upon request.**

Send book(s) to:

Name_____ Phone_____

Address _____

City _____ State _____ Zip_____

Payment via:

☐ Check or money order payable to Meadowbrook Press.
(No cash or C.O.D. please.) Amount enclosed $_____

☐ Visa (for orders over $10.00 only).

☐ MasterCard (for orders over $10.00 only).   Account # _____

Signature _____ Exp. Date _____

A **FREE** Meadowbrook Press catalog is available upon request.
You can also phone us for orders of $10.00 or more at 1-800-338-2232.

Mail to: Meadowbrook, Inc.
18318 Minnetonka Boulevard
Deephaven, MN 55391

(612) 473-5400   Toll-Free 1-800-338-2232   Fax (612) 475-0736